EMILY DICKINSON
THE CRITICAL REVOLUTION

EMILY DICKINSON

The Critical Revolution

by
Klaus Lubbers

Ann Arbor
The University of Michigan Press

For Gisela

PERMISSIONS

The author gratefully acknowledges the cooperation of authors and publishers in granting permission to reprint the selections named below:

Amherst College for passages from letters in the Dickinson collection; for lines from Willard Wattles' "The Bench," *The Amherst Graduates' Quarterly*, VI (May 1917).

The Atlantic Monthly for passages from Martha Hale Shackford's "The Poetry of Emily Dickinson," *The Atlantic Monthly*, CXI (January 1913).

Melville Cane and *Saturday Review* for lines from "Dickinsons and Todds," *The Saturday Review of Literature*, XXVIII (June 9, 1945). Copyright Saturday Review, Inc. 1945.

Harper and Row, Publishers, Inc. for passages from Millicent Todd Bingham's *Ancestors' Brocades: The Literary Debut of Emily Dickinson* (New York: Harper and Row, 1945).

Harvard University Press and the Trustees of Amherst College for lines from *The Poems of Emily Dickinson*, ed. Thomas H. Johnson (Cambridge, Mass.: The Belknap Press of Harvard University Press, Copyright 1951, 1955 by The President and Fellows of Harvard College); for passages from *The Letters of Emily Dickinson*, ed. Thomas H. Johnson (Cambridge, Mass.: The Belknap Press of Harvard University Press, Copyright 1958 by The President and Fellows of Harvard College).

Holt, Rinehart and Winston, Inc. for lines from "Letters to Dead Imagists," from *Complete Poems* by Carl Sandburg. Copyright 1916 by Holt, Rinehart and Winston, Inc. Copyright 1944 by Carl Sandburg. Reprinted by permission of Holt, Rinehart and Winston, Inc.

Houghton Mifflin Company for passages from Martha Dickinson Bianchi's *The Life and Letters of Emily Dickinson* (Boston: Houghton Mifflin Company, 1924); for passages from S. Foster Damon's

Amy Lowell: A Chronicle (Boston: Houghton Mifflin Company, 1935); for lines from Amy Lowell's *A Critical Fable* (Boston: Houghton Mifflin Company, 1922); for lines from Amy Lowell's *What's o' Clock* (Boston: Houghton Mifflin Company, 1925).

Alfred A. Knopf, for lines from Genevieve Taggard's *The Life and Mind of Emily Dickinson* (New York: Alfred A. Knopf, 1930); for lines from Robert Hillyer's *A Letter to Robert Frost and Others* (New York: Alfred A. Knopf, 1937).

Little, Brown and Company for lines from *The Complete Poems of Emily Dickinson*, ed. Thomas H. Johnson. Copyright 1929, © 1957 by Mary L. Hampson.

Louisiana State University Press for passages from R. P. Blackmur's "Emily Dickinson: Notes on Prejudice and Fact," *The Southern Review*, III (Fall 1937).

The Macmillan Company for passages from Granville Hicks's *The Great Tradition*. Copyright 1933, by The Macmillan Company.

The Sewanee Review for passages from Fred Lewis Pattee's "Gentian, Not Rose: The Real Emily Dickinson," *The Sewanee Review*, XLV (Spring 1936).

PREFACE

This investigation is first and foremost an account of the judgments passed on Emily Dickinson, the poet and the person, by her American and British readers in the course of a century. It is also intended as a minor contribution to such concerns as the revaluation of nineteenth-century American poetry by the twentieth, the development of modern American literary criticism and history, and the British reception of American literature.

Since the first critical reactions of Emily Dickinson's private readers can be traced back to the spring of 1862, 1962 seemed a fitting terminal year. Important work has been done since then, but to bring the chapter of Dickinson research up-to-date, while adding an informative survey of recent scholarship, would have failed to add substantially to the aim of a study chiefly historical in perspective. The geographical limitation was set after it had become apparent that American and British Dickinson criticism, though largely antithetic, forms a natural unity while European, South American, and Asian criticism, since its late inception, has adopted American views, shown little originality, and caused no reverberations in the United States.

In the first and second parts my method of presentation is strictly chronological, because I believed that significant results could only be achieved by closely retracing Emily Dickinson's posthumous reputation. In explaining why certain critics at certain times came to certain conclusions about her poetry, I had to resort primarily to contemporary sources since histories of American criticisms are sadly incomplete and, consequently, largely unsuitable for the illustration of critical tendencies. In the third part, for reasons discussed at the beginning of chapter IX, this chronological approach is abandoned in favor of rapid diachronic surveys.

Even after more than a generation of studies in the fame of authors, there is still much resistance in academic quarters to the idea of taking the verdicts of the past seriously. This may in large measure be due to the fact that this species of collective criticism developed simultaneously with the emergence of a militant organistic formalism which neglects literary history. Yet this opposition may also in part have been engendered by the frequent restriction of such enterprises to a mere assemblage of opinions, an enumeration of pros and cons, believers and doubters. "All these judgments cannot be true," a renowned Dickinson scholar, George Whicher, concluded in 1930 when compiling the first extensive Dickinson bibliography, "read *en masse,* they cancel each other out, leaving vacuity." True enough—if one conceives of past valuations and rankings in terms of a game or literary stock exchange. Though detailed historical research supplements and corrects the results of literary histories, the view of perspective criticism, most clearly stated by René Wellek, has also gained ground as a way out of the sham dilemma of the reconstructionist versus the antihistorical fallacies. The "total meaning" of a work of art, according to a well-known formulation, is "the result of a process of accretion, i.e., the history of its criticism by its many readers in many ages." Two years before this truth was stated, Henry W. Wells, in his *Introduction to Emily Dickinson,* had gained much the same insight: "To record what thousands of readers have experienced becomes realistic and significant, while to insist too narrowly upon one's own interpretation appears less original and creative than arrogant and egotistical."

K. L.

Mainz
August 1967

ACKNOWLEDGMENTS

In the preparation of this book I have incurred many obligations. My chief debt is to Professor Hans Galinsky of the University of Mainz, whose keen interest in American literature awakened my own. He drew my attention to the subject and counseled me as the manuscript developed.

I wish to express my grateful appreciation to the German Association of American Studies for a research grant which enabled me, while still working in Germany, to begin my search for sources on a large scale. I owe a debt of deep gratitude to the American Council of Learned Societies for an international fellowship in American Studies which enabled me to complete the research and write this book during thirteen untroubled months in New England. Without access to American libraries and collections it would have been impossible to complete the work with adequate documentation.

To Professor Hans-Joachim Lang, Mr. Jay Leyda, Professor Carl Dolmetsch, and Professor Hugh W. Hetherington I am indebted for helpful information. For their kind assistance in gathering source material, my special thanks are due Professor Martha E. Passe as well as the members of the staffs of Mainz University Library, Boston Public Library, Harvard College Library, Yale University Library, the Library of Congress, and particularly to the staff of Amherst College's Frost Library. I am grateful to Professor Newton F. McKeon for permission to inspect and quote from material in the Dickinson collection at Amherst College, and to Messrs. Charles R. Green and William F. Merrill for allowing me to profit from the rich harvest of Dickinsoniana gathered by the former in a quiet room in Amherst's Jones Library. It was there that I found Russell St. Clair Smith's painstaking Dickinson bibliography which was of such help that I wish I had discovered it years earlier. Also, I am grateful to Professor Donald O. White for reading the entire manuscript and to my friend of long standing, Professor Franklin D. Case, for his kind advice and encouragement.

Finally, I have to thank Mr. Graydon Ekdahl who kindly helped me with the translation of my German manuscript from chapter III on. One last debt, the greatest of all, is acknowledged in the dedication.

CONTENTS

The Poets light but Lamps—
Themselves—go out—
The Wicks they stimulate—
If vital Light

Inhere as do the Suns—
Each Age a Lens
Disseminating their
Circumference—

Part One

DISCOVERY

(1862-97)

I

PRIVATE READERS (1862-86)

If fame belonged to me, I could not escape her—if she did not, the longest day would pass me on the chase—and the approbation of my Dog, would forsake me—then—My Barefoot-Rank is better—[1]

EMILY DICKINSON'S SERIOUS LITERARY EFFORTS can be traced to the middle of her century. Her first poem appears in a letter late in the winter of 1850 (I, 91). On March 27, 1853, she wrote to her brother Austin, who had sent her a psalm of his own composition: "Now Brother Pegasus, I'll tell you what it is—I've been in the habit *myself* of writing some few things, and it rather appears to me that you're getting away my patent, so you'd better be somewhat careful, or I'll call the police!" (I, 235). In 1858 she began assembling her verses into packets. In the summer of 1861 she exchanged notes with her sister-in-law Susan Gilbert Dickinson over "Safe in their alabaster chambers." A year later, when she reached the height of her creative powers, she turned for advice to Thomas Wentworth Higginson. The turn to an outsider leads to the conjecture that she considered herself a poet who needed competent criticism and public recognition and, furthermore, that she hoped to have her verses published.

Her letter to Higginson and the ensuing correspondence took place during a period unfavorable to new talents. Critics unanimously admired a small group of established poets, deplored the worthlessness of lyrics of the day, and at the same time shut their ears to new voices. The poetic canon had become rigid: the New Englanders, Lowell and Holmes, Longfellow and Emerson, together with Bryant, were highly esteemed. The second series

3

of Lowell's *Biglow Papers* as well as Bayard Taylor's *The Picture of St. John* met with general critical approval, though Melville's volume of Civil War poetry was coolly received in 1866. Whitman's work, if mentioned at all, was a matter for dispute. Literary creations characteristic of the 1860's and 1870's were translations such as Longfellow's Dante, Bryant's Homer, Taylor's *Faust,* and narrative poems like Howells' *Mowers* and Lowell's *Fitz Adam's Story* or were sentimental "soap bubble" poetry[2] on traditional subjects with overly smooth rhymes, slack rhythm, and hackneyed imagery, which filled half pages in magazines and lapsed more and more to the status of a merely tolerated stopgap. When the generation of great Brahmins gradually fell silent and gave way to writers of occasional verse, increasingly written by women, public interest shifted to the novel—a change to which the sobering experience of the war may have contributed. "The characteristic fault of modern poetry," a noted reviewer, David Wasson, observed in 1867, "[is] its general *want of significance.*"[3] Even ten years later the situation had not improved. "In looking around at the publications of the younger American poets I am struck with the circumstance that none of them even *attempt* anything great," Lanier wrote to Taylor. "The morbid fear of doing something wrong or unpolished appears to have influenced their choice of subjects. Hence the endless multiplication of those feeble magazine-lyrics which we all know."[4]

Little is known about Emily Dickinson's critical reception up to 1886. Her seven poems published anonymously during the long span between 1852 and 1878 did not create a stir. Only a private, if large, circle of friends and acquaintances was able to form a fairly exact conception of her art. The poet sent a total of nearly six hundred verses to approximately forty correspondents, among them Helen Hunt Jackson, Mabel Loomis Todd, her posthumous editor, and Thomas Niles, editor of Roberts Brothers of Boston. Most were entrusted to four recipients: "Sister Sue" next door received 276 poems, Higginson 102; Samuel and Mary Bowles 37, the Hollands 35.[5] Because Lavinia, after her sister's death, destroyed nearly all of the letters addressed to Emily, the reactions of even these private readers can be reconstructed only with difficulty. The loss of letters written by Benjamin Franklin Newton, Henry Vaughan Emmons, and Catharine Scott Turner is particularly regrettable since their criticism, counsel, and encouragement must have meant a good

deal to Emily Dickinson in her decision to devote her life to her
art. Newton (1821-53), a law student in her father's office, was
her "tutor" until his early death; he was followed but not replaced by Emmons (1832-1912), "a beautiful, new, friend" (I,
183), who graduated from Amherst College in 1854, and, after
1859, by Mrs. Turner (1831-1917), Sue's friend, who paid several visits to Amherst.[6]

Susan Gilbert Dickinson valued Emily's poetry, as shown
by the great number of poems she received. As an amateur critic,
however, she appears to have been consulted only two times.

In the summer of 1861 Emily sent her the 1859 version of
her "alabaster" poem. Since Sue was obviously displeased with
the second stanza, Emily promptly followed it with a new version,
adding: "Perhaps this verse would please you better." Again her
sister-in-law objected: "I am not suited dear Emily with the second verse—It is remarkable as the chain lightening that blinds
us hot nights in the Southern sky but it does not go with the
ghostly shimmer of the first verse as well as the other one—It
just occurs to me that the first verse is complete in itself it needs
no other, and can't be coupled—Strange things always go alone."
What Sue thought of a third attempt, sent to her shortly after-
ward, we do not know. Emily, who had sought help and advice
from her, apparently let the matter rest there (II, 379-80).

Sue again expressed her opinion in an unsigned obituary
entitled "Miss Dickinson of Amherst," which appeared on the
editorial page of *The Springfield Republican* of May 18, 1886.
Impressed as she was by the deceased's work, she could vent her
admiration only metaphorically: "A damascus blade gleaming
and glancing in the sun was her wit. Her swift poetic rapture
was like the long glistening note of a bird one hears in the June
woods at high noon, but can never see. Like a magician she
caught the shadowy apparitions of her brain and tossed them in
startling picturesqueness to her friends, who charmed with their
simplicity and homeliness as well as profundity, fretted that she
had so easily made palpable the tantalizing fancies forever eluding
their bungling, fettered grasp."

Higginson's judgment of her writing mattered most to the
poet—"Your opinion gives me a serious feeling," she told him on
June 9, 1866, "I would like to be what you deem me" (II, 453).
His evaluation, which was to determine the fate of her work
during her lifetime, is typical of the attitude of a conservative
critic of his day and informative with respect to his later edi-

torial activity.[7] His advisory role cannot be deduced exclusively from his correspondence with Emily Dickinson without distortion of the truth. It is easy, and to some extent justified, to make the Colonel the scapegoat of poor contemporary taste in literature. This has been done over and over since the 1920's. And yet, one should not quite ignore his plea for culture at a time when few literati were committed to patriotic idealism. Like Stedman conservative in his aesthetic creed, he applied to modern writing the literary standards of the Greek, whom he held to be still unequaled.[8] Proficiency in Greek and Latin he considered indispensable, "for they remain still synonymous with accurate linguistic training, and with the study of *form* in literature" (p. 31). Instead of turning his back on an America still provincial in its spiritual attainments—"here art is still an alien" (p. 34)— he worked for more libraries, universities, and art galleries as a prerequisite for the growth of a truly "Athenian culture" in which American art and letters might flourish. "The true, great want is of an atmosphere in intellectual aims. An artist can afford to be poor, but not to be companionless" (p. 33).

This same kindly atmosphere of encouragement radiated from his "Letter to a Young Contributor," which he had written at James T. Fields's suggestion as a condensed public reply to a flood of private requests and petitions of young literary aspirants. It is worth glancing at the practical advice given in this essay since Higginson's critical principles are not expressed elsewhere with the same clarity. Applied to Emily Dickinson, they help to explain his understanding of her verse. The most important of his stylistic rules are:

Unwearied patience:
> Such being the majesty of the art you seek to practice, you can at least take time and deliberation before dishonoring it.

Liveliness:
> Charge your style with life, and the public will not ask for conundrums.

Lucidity:
> Labor, therefore, not in thought alone, but in utterance; clothe and reclothe your grand conception twenty times, until you find some phrase that with its grandeur shall be lucid also.
> Study each phrase so carefully that the most ingenious critic cannot alter it without spoiling the whole passage for everybody but himself.

Terseness:

> Be noble in the affluence and the economy of your diction; spare no wealth that you can put in, and tolerate no superfluity that can be struck out.

Avoidance of premature mannerisms:

> Have faith enough in your own individuality to keep it resolutely down for a year or two.

His stylistic ideal advocates a mode of writing "which unites the smoothness of the eighteenth century with the vital vigor of the seventeenth, so that Sir Thomas Browne and Andrew Marvell seem quite as near to us as Pope or Addison."[9]

While part of his advice—such as painstaking work and economy of expression—seemed merely to praise what Emily Dickinson herself most strove for, she must have felt concerned about some of his demands. Were not her verses enigmatic, likely to puzzle and perplex? Did they not occasionally lack clarity? Was she not retreating into an eccentric individualism both in life and work? Had not the editorial changes recently made in "The May-Wine" and "The Sleeping" shown that her language did not, after all, possess irresistible force? Unfortunately, of the correspondence initiated in 1862 and intermittently kept up until within a few days of her death, all but three of Higginson's letters are lost. The early ones, in particular, coming as they did from one qualified to judge, must have been of decisive importance to the recipient. In view of the situation, Higginson's opinions must be inferred chiefly from their refractions in Emily Dickinson's letters.

The poet's first letter takes up the cardinal point of the *Atlantic* essay: "Are you too deeply occupied to say if my verse is alive?" (II, 403). She seems acutely aware of a lack of distance from her own work and of the necessity of an objective consultant. Her second letter which asks: "Could you tell me how to grow . . . ?" implies a critical comment by Higginson on the four poems enclosed in the first letter ("Safe in their alabaster chambers," "The nearest dream recedes unrealized," "We play at paste," and "I'll tell you how the sun rose"). In this second letter she thanks the Colonel for the "surgery" (II, 404). Small wonder that the surgery consisted in objections to the form of the poems submitted. This becomes evident by a sentence alluding to a passage in the essay: "While my thought is undressed—I can make the distinction, but when I put them in the gown—they look alike, and numb" (II, 404). Higginson's second letter

7

brought "Balm," although it dissuaded her from publishing and found her verses "spasmodic" and "uncontrolled";[10] his third gave advice which caused the receiver to answer rather helplessly: "You are true, about the 'perfection'" (II, 418). Emily Dickinson used the surgeon-patient metaphor and played the part of disciple for decades. Over and over again she assured him of her obedience, admitted her mistakes, hoped for perfection, asked stubbornly for patience and instruction. As late as 1877 she quoted a sentence from Higginson's essay. However, as early as August 1862, she qualified her docility: "I shall observe your precept—though I dont understand it, always" (II, 415). In this conflict of different, indeed, incompatible views of poetry, the preceptor appears to have made greater efforts to understand his pupil's peculiarities than she made to heed his advice. His criticism of her "waywardness" drew new and more difficult poems accompanied by the question: "Are these more orderly? I thank you for the Truth" (II, 414). There is no getting around the suspicion that Puck soon began to trifle with Bottom—a suspicion strengthened by Higginson's later reminiscences.[11] A letter of May 11, 1869, affords direct insight into some thoughts of Higginson which were induced by the accumulated treasure of poetry in his possession:

> Sometimes I take out your letters & verses, dear friend, and when I feel their strange power, it is not strange that I find it hard to write & that long months pass. I have the greatest desire to see you, always feeling that perhaps if I could once take you by the hand I might be something to you; but till then you only enshroud yourself in this fiery mist & I cannot reach you, but only rejoice in the rare sparkles of light. . . . I should like to hear from you very often, but feel always timid lest what I *write* should be badly aimed & miss that fine edge of thought which you bear. . . . It isolates one anywhere to think beyond a certain point or have such luminous flashes as come to you— (II, 461)

It is difficult to form a clear idea of the development of this singular friendship. The letter passage shows the critic assuming the modest role of a reader more appreciative than intelligent yet striving for deeper understanding. Also Higginson's lecture, "Two Unknown Poetesses," which he gave at the Boston Woman's Club in November 1875, speaks for his high esteem of her work.[12] Most of Emily Dickinson's biographers have deplored that her search for a qualified judge of good writing ended with Higginson. They have intimated reproachfully that he literally did not understand her poems, that he prevented her from publishing, that she would have received more sympathy from Lowell or Emerson. The reproaches could more justly be turned against Holland and Niles who took such liberties with five of her poems that their bungling interference may well have set her implacably against the idea of making a public appearance.

Higginson drew as near Emily Dickinson as he could. If he wrote his sisters of his "eccentric" (II, 518) and "partially cracked" (II, 570) poetess, it was because he was quite aware of the strange and singular character of her life and work. He repeatedly urged her to come to Boston to attend monthly meetings of the Radical Club at Mrs. Sargent's—a great distinction, for it was here that the pick of advanced thinkers met— and, after her consistent refusals, pointed out to her such literary models as Joaquin Miller (II, 492) and Helen Hunt (II, 520). Through such efforts one senses the well-meant intention of luring her out of her self-imposed isolation. He had good reasons to believe that the poems, in the form in which he had received them, would never find public favor. It is quite a different matter that they always reminded him of "skeleton leaves, so pretty, but *too delicate*—not strong enough to publish."[13] An admirer of Emerson, Higginson was fascinated by her poetry's intensity and wealth of ideas. But how could it have permanence without the gift of form?

It was while staying with Higginson in the same Newport boardinghouse that Helen Hunt Jackson first saw some of Emily Dickinson's poems.[14] The letter she wrote from Colorado Springs to her childhood friend on March 20, 1876, is full of enthusiasm: "I have a little manuscript volume with a few of your verses in it—and I read them very often—You are a great poet—and it is a wrong to the day you live in, that you will not sing aloud. When you are what men call dead, you will be sorry you were so stingy" (II, 545). Her invitation to contribute to a projected anonymous anthology, *A Masque of Poets*—"I want to see some of your verses in print" (II, 563)—her visit to the Dickinson home on October 10, 1876, and her repeated requests for more poems testify to the sincerity of her approval. Her attempts to understand the art of her friend led her farther than Higginson: "This morning I have read over again the last verses you sent me: I find them more clear than I thought they were. Part of the dimness must have been in me" (II, 565). Whenever something remained nebulous, she simply asked the author for an explanation. Thus when reading the lines

Who fleeing from the Spring
The Spring avenging fling
To Dooms of Balm—

which Emily Dickinson had sent her on the occasion of her second marriage, she wanted to know prosaically: "I do wish I knew just what 'dooms' you meant though!" (II, 544). A year before her death, surprised at the great number of her friend's poems, she asked Emily's permission to be her literary executrix: "It is a cruel wrong to your 'day & generation' that you will not give them light. . . . I do not think we have a right to withhold from the world a word or a thought any more than a *deed,* which might help a single soul" (III, 841-42).

Just as Mrs. Jackson heard of Emily Dickinson through Higginson, Thomas Niles heard of her through Mrs. Jackson, the author of *Ramona.*[15] In a trickle of correspondence that passed between him and the poet in 1879, 1882, and 1883, Niles showed himself mildly infected by Helen Jackson's enthusiasm. Twice he offered to publish a selection of her lyrics (III, 726, 769). When she failed to respond, his interest cooled, and the matter ended there.

Like Higginson, Mabel Loomis Todd felt strongly attracted to, and strangely affected by, Emily Dickinson's work.[16] When she came to live in Amherst in 1881, the poet for her, as for most of the townspeople, was at first a myth. Before long, through Susan Dickinson's intervention, a peculiar friendship developed during which Emily Dickinson remained invisible behind doors left ajar. The young professor's wife sang and painted for the recluse poet and received flowers and verses in return. Her opinions of Emily Dickinson are recorded in two brief journal entries of February 8, and September 15, 1882:

> . . . went in the afternoon to Mrs. Dickinson's. She read me some strange poems by Emily Dickinson. They are full of power.
> His sister Emily is called in Amherst "the myth." She has not been out of her house for fifteen years. One inevitably thinks of Miss Haversham in speaking of her. She writes the

strangest poems, & very remarkable ones. She is in many respects a genius.[17]

The editorial changes made in the seven poems that saw print during Emily Dickinson's lifetime reflect Higginson's mixed display of censure and approval. Like Mrs. Jackson and Niles, Samuel Bowles of *The Springfield Republican* and his associate editor Holland also repeatedly requested verses for insertion in their paper. Yet none remained unaltered in its printed form.[18] The changes were presumably made by Holland, who had charge of the *Republican's* cultural department. The most incisive recastings occur in "I taste a liquor never brewed" which appeared as "The May-Wine" on May 4, 1861. The poem rhymed except for the opening stanza. In order to achieve a rhyme with "pearl" in the second line, the excellent Doctor recast lines three and four, changing

> *Not all the Frankfort Berries*
> *Yield such an Alcohol!*

to read

> *Not Frankfort berries yield the sense*
> *Such a delirious whirl*

—thus also regularizing the alternating four-and-three-beat meter. In the last line of the poem, he replaced the unusual metaphor of the tippler "leaning" against the sun by one less startling. As originally written, the line reads:

> *[To see the little Tippler]*
> *Leaning against the—Sun—*

As printed, it reads:

> *[To see the little tippler]*
> *Come staggering toward the sun.*

Holland, incidentally, was not to remain alone in his misgivings: later the poem proved a stumbling block for two severe old-school critics, Andrew Lang and Thomas Bailey Aldrich.

In "Safe in their alabaster chambers," which was carried in the issue of March 1, 1862, Holland improved the syntax by converting a singular into a plural form. His tampering with the punctuation of still another poem caused Emily Dickinson to warn Higginson: "Lest you meet my Snake and suppose I deceive it was robbed of me—defeated too of the third line by the punctuation. The third and fourth were one—" (II, 450). The poem that suffered most under the corrector's blue pencil was "Success," whose appearance, in the last volume of Roberts Brothers' No Name Series, was due to Helen Jackson's insistent coaxing of a reluctant consent. Niles smoothed off the rhythm and altered three words.[19]

In spite of Holland's and Niles's sympathies for Emily Dickinson's uncurbed art, they, as editors, were careful not to let her overstep those boundaries of poetic decorum which were laid down by the leading Boston reviews and still religiously observed by the poets and critics of the 1890's. Accordingly, they considered it necessary to improve careless rhyme, metrical and syntactic irregularities, and idiosyncrasies of language and style. Publication simply meant compliance with a set of stodgy rules. In her inability to fight her way through to such an inadmissible compromise, Emily Dickinson differed from Sidney Lanier who, on March 15, 1874, sent his wife a new poem, "My Two Springs," and added the revealing comment: "Of course, since I have written it to print, I cannot make it such as *I* desire, in artistic design: for the *forms* of today require a certain trim smugness and clean-shaven propriety in the face and dress of a poem, and I must win a hearing by conforming to these tyrannies,—with a view of overturning them in the future."[20]

Fragmentary as is our knowledge of what Emily Dickinson's first readers thought of her work, it shows that her verses were valued and remembered, copied and recommended. The Boston Reverend John Chadwick who, as he confided to Higginson in 1890, had had the "Sabbath" poem in his head "for more than 20 years, ever since it came out in the *Round Table*" (*AB*, p. 73), seems far from isolated. The taste of these early readers is still rather indiscriminate; their responses show surprise, spontaneous approval, indeed, enthusiasm—but also bewilderment. The power of her poetry attracted general notice, but only Helen Jackson described this power in plain words. In Sue Dickinson's and Higginson's figurative language, a certain helplessness and insecurity of judgment is reflected. Both employed metaphors of light and lightning to define the poet as a magician of thought; yet both, along with Mrs. Todd, used "strange" to suggest the quaint and peculiar. While language, meter, and rhyme were apt to shock and offend, thought and exactness of observation excited admiration. "How did that girl ever know that a boggy field wasn't good for corn?" Samuel Bowles is reported to have exclaimed when he came across the lines

> *He likes a Boggy Acre*
> *A Floor too cool for Corn—*

in "The Snake."[21]

To bring her work before the public must have appeared a delicate undertaking to such seasoned men of letters as Higginson and Holland, who thought the poems "too ethereal for publication."[22] Then again it is worth noting as a significant curiosity that "Success," when it made its première behind the mask of anonymity in 1878, was attributed by more than one critic to Emerson.[23]

The artist herself profited less from her readers than she may have hoped, although, doubtless, their interest supported her on the road taken. The certitude that she wrote as necessity dictated was her warranty of "truth"—genuineness—and this was her only concern, even if at times it drove her to despair. "My Business is Circumference," she wrote Higginson at the beginning of their friendship, "An ignorance, not of Custom, but if caught with the Dawn—or the Sunset see me—Myself the only Kangaroo among the Beauty, Sir, if you please, it afflicts me, and I thought that instruction would take it away" (II, 412). As instruction soon proved unprofitable, as the disciple would not comply with custom, the conventions of poesy, she had no alternative but to renounce fame and play out her part as grotesque outsider, banking meanwhile on Posterity.

II

THE "AUCTION" (1886-91)

In all my reading I have not found a more interesting book
of verse; one with so many beauties almost buried in so many
blemishes. The good things in it are like incomparable crystals
set in ugly fragments of worthless stone.[1]

On November 12, 1890, almost four and a half years after Emily
Dickinson's death, the first volume of her selected poems was
put on the market. Before the reviewers set pen to paper, a
division of manuscripts had taken place which was to have
disastrous consequences for the poet's posthumous fame up to
1955. The two accounts of what occurred behind the Amherst
scenes are biased, for both Millicent Todd Bingham and Martha
Dickinson Bianchi defend their mothers. In either case the black
sheep is Lavinia. A few facts are essential for an understanding
of the history of publication. Lavinia, as joint heiress of her
sister's estate, with Austin, discovered Emily's manuscripts
shortly after the poet's death and turned to her sister-in-law
Susan for help. Sue sent several poems to Boston and New York
magazines with requests for publication but met with polite
resistance. Discouraged by her failure, she returned the papers,
which thereupon got into Mrs. Todd's hands. The final breach
between the Todds and the Dickinsons in 1896 resulted in an
unfortunate dual publication process which was carried on by
Mrs. Todd with the aid of Higginson. This was continued, after
1932, by her daughter Millicent on the one hand and, on the
other, from 1914 on by Susan's daughter Martha in collaboration
with the dilettante Alfred Leete Hampson.

Susan Dickinson's attitude toward Emily Dickinson the
person and the poet consisted in simultaneous affection and an-

tipathy. In *Emily Dickinson Face to Face*, Martha Dickinson Bianchi, her daughter, wrote quite impartially: "Sue's young certainty of Emily's genius never wavered. She felt Emily was endowed beyond the rest of them—she *believed* Emily was inherently great, and she was jealous for her—and set her above rivalry, by turns. It was her test of lesser friends to read to them some of Emily's poems and watch the effect."[2] She concealed, however, that while trying to benefit from the hoarded treasure of 276 poems, her mother flinched from the dedication required to make the manuscripts acceptable from a printer's point of view and, even more, instinctively shrank from the idea of seeing her next-door sister-in-law famous. What hopes she held for her own family becomes evident in her later efforts to make Martha a poetic star in her own right. After the publication of *Poems* (1890), she reacted with hurt pride and alleged, not very convincingly, that she had planned an edition herself (*AB*, pp. 86-87).

The steps taken to prepare the Dickinson papers for the press can be traced here and there with the help of *Ancestors' Brocades*, which gives information about the editorial work during the decade following 1886. Of this material, the verdicts of Thomas Niles and his reader Arlo Bates are of interest. In the light of Thomas H. Johnson's variorum edition, the numerous alterations made with an eye to the reading public can be checked. To examine these is all the more important since up to 1955 Dickinson readers and scholars were entirely dependent on the polished texts printed from 1890 on. Also, Higginson's preface to *Poems by Emily Dickinson* and his introductory essay in *The Christian Union* are of great significance. Reader's report, textual changes, and introduction were three functions of the mediator's post between the artist and what she called the auction of man's mind, "that deliberate and almost brutal transition from the mystery of creation into the light of the public marketplace."[3]

Mabel Loomis Todd, the academically trained, artistically and literarily active wife of Amherst's professor of astronomy, spent more than two years on the difficult task of deciphering and copying the nearly thousand poems entrusted to her and of choosing between suggested authorial changes. Her decisions regarding variants were, as a rule, made intelligently. She recognized that many variants had merely been a strategy typical of the poet to encircle her meaning synonymously. In transcribing the difficult handwriting into lines and stanzas she proceeded competently. Later scholars have paid her high tribute.

In addition to that, however, Mrs. Todd's creative activity included typographical, stylistic, and prosodic improvement of the poems. Although she was quite right in assuming that such improvements would make Emily Dickinson's work more acceptable to the literary world of 1890, she rendered the poet no permanent service. The extent and nature of what Mrs. Todd's daughter halfheartedly defended as "creative editing" (*AB*, pp. 36-46) have never been systematically examined. An investigation of her editorial practices leads to the unexpected result that no fewer than 49 of the 116 poems included in the first series were textually manipulated (not counting alterations of spelling, capitalization, punctuation, faulty line and stanza divisions, mistakes corrected in reprints as well as readings not adopted in the text but put on the short list by the poet). This examination is not meant as a summary rejection of Mrs. Todd's work but rather as a contribution to the editorial problem of 1890: "Just how much shock, of form or of content, could the reader absorb?" (*AB*, p. 46).

Twenty-two changes aimed at correcting usage. Of these, nine concerned the substitution of "is," "are," and "was" for third person "be"; six, the replacement of Emily Dickinson's idiosyncratic subjunctive (which is perhaps best understood as "a continuing or universal present indicative"[4]) by the indicative; six, various grammatical and syntactic improvements;[5] one, a false verbal form.[6]

In seventeen cases words or phrases were replaced by others which distorted the meaning of the sentence. The underlying intention is not always evident; in most cases, simplicity of thought or imagery is aimed at. Here are four characteristic examples. In the line "So We must meet apart," the offending oxymoron was avoided by changing it to read "So we must keep apart." Another line read: "So unsuspected Violets / Within the meadows go—." How can violets "go"? the editor must have asked herself before altering it to "Within the fields lie low." In a third poem, the seasons "played" around the knees of Grandfather Mountain sitting in his "tremendous chair"; in *Poems* (1890), they "pray" instead. The best-known example of this category is the change from "As if the Checks were given" to "As if the chart were given," with the resultant transformation of the implied image of a train ride into that of a sea voyage.[7]

The most striking alterations are those made to achieve a

rhyme. Here, the editor recast entire lines. Only a few instances can be indicated in passing. In one poem Mrs. Todd did not recognize the existing intricate rhyme scheme and destroyed it by superimposing a second one. In another poem she achieved only an eye rhyme ("sown" and "town"); in a third, only a partial rhyme ("played" and "grain"). In a fourth, she avoided identical rhyme. Two lines of "A little road not made of man" show how, at a single stroke, she made several improvements. The second stanza reads:

> *If Town it have—beyond itself—*
> *'Tis that—I cannot say—*
> *I only know—no Curricle that rumbled there*
> *Bear me—*

As printed, the final lines read:

> *I only sigh,—no vehicle*
> *Bears me along that way.*

Here, "way" rhymes with "say"; second, the metric pattern of alternating four-beat and three-beat lines, which Emily Dickinson had varied to a sequence of a six-beat and a one-beat line, is normalized. Third, Mrs. Todd availed herself of variants and replaced "know" by more pathetic "sigh," "curricle" by more common "vehicle"; finally, the subjunctive disappeared.[8]

In comparison with these three predominating types of alterations, six further groups are fairly unimportant: the substitution of eight synonyms; the omission of a stanza in six poems, among them the metrically irregular fourth stanza of the well-known poem "Because I could not stop for death"; the mistaking of two versions for two stanzas of a poem in two cases; two changes in tense which destroyed the time structure of the respective poems; finally, one rhythmic regulation and the merging of two poems into one.

The poems had for the most part been edited in this fashion when Mrs. Todd, in November 1889, went to Cambridge to show Higginson a selection of two hundred fair copies. The Colonel, who had declined to collaborate in 1886 on account of overwork, now used his influence on behalf of the planned volume, though he was preparing for publication a book of his own sonnets and a revision of his translation of Epictetus. He suggested few further changes. His comment on the last line of

"The grass so little has to do" ("I wish I were a Hay") may be cited as an example: " 'It cannot go in so,' he exclaimed, 'everybody would say that *hay* is a collective noun requiring the definite article. Nobody would call it *a* hay!' " (*AB*, p. 58). Though less inclined than Mrs. Todd to make textual changes, as a practical-minded author he insisted on assigning titles to sixty-two of the poems, many of them inappropriate or stilted, such as the Latin titles "Astra Castra," "Resurgam," "Numen Lumen," or too stylish as "Rouge et Noir" and "Rouge Gagne." Still, he struck exactly a right note, for reviewers were later to invent titles even for some poems that had gone without them because, according to prevailing taste, a poem without a title was considered somehow defective. It was also at Higginson's suggestion that the lyrics were divided into the four groups "Life," "Love," "Nature," and "Time and Immortality."

Higginson's response to the two hundred poems prepared by Mrs. Todd was enthusiastic: "I can't tell you how much I am enjoying the poems," he wrote her on November 25, 1889. "There are many new to me which take my breath away & which also have *form* beyond most of those I have seen before. That one descriptive of the shipwreck for instance!" (*AB*, pp. 34-35). When the volume had come fresh from the press, he was equally delighted: "I am *astounded* in looking through. How could we ever have doubted about them" (*AB*, p. 72). In addition to these private testimonies of mingled enthusiasm and approval, there are two public ones: his essay in *The Christian Union*, intended to pave the way for the work of his former protégée by anticipating and obviating possible objections, and the preface which he wrote in August 1890, as official coeditor. Both essay and preface, conciliatory in attitude yet positive in tone, were frequently quoted and criticized by reviewers and remained influential well into the next century. Some of Higginson's formulations became household words of Dickinson criticism.

"An Open Portfolio" is a sincere reflection about poetic work that fascinated the Colonel and, at the same time, a model of ingenious argumentation. Objections were disposed of by quotations from respected writers while Emily Dickinson's obscure name was skillfully associated with the names of famous poets.

Private poetry, the critics might argue, must needs show defects, for the secluded poet is primarily concerned with the chronicling of his feelings without paying much thought to execution. In reply to this, Higginson adduces Emerson's argument that the poetry of the portfolio possesses the greatest charm, since it has the advantage of perfect freedom and candor and compensates for lack of form by richness of thought. Ruskin has emphasized that "No beauty of execution can outweigh one grain or fragment of thought." The private poet contents himself with a single fortunate stroke and closes the portfolio without filing and polishing later. After all, Emily Dickinson's lyrics show that even Celia Thaxter and Jean Ingelow, who both lived by the seaside, "never drew a sea picture in stronger lines than this secluded woman in her inland village." With what greater power was she able to depict the mightier storms and shipwrecks of the soul! Higginson praises the terseness and "superb concentration" of her language, the range of her moods from tenderness to iron strength, and a sixth sense in her nature poetry reminiscent of her fellow townswoman Helen Hunt. His final judgment appeared slightly changed in the preface:

"An Open Portfolio"	"Preface"
Her verses are in most cases like poetry plucked up by the roots; we have them with earth, stones, and dew adhering, and must accept them as they are. Wayward and unconventional in the last degree; defiant of form, measure, rhyme, and even grammar; yet she had an exacting standard of her own, and would wait many days for a word that satisfied.	In many ways these verses will seem to the reader like poetry torn up by the roots, with rain and dew and earth still clinging to them, giving a freshness and a fragrance not otherwise to be conveyed. . . . Though curiously indifferent to all conventional rules, [she] had yet a rigorous literary standard of her own, and often altered a word many times to suit an ear which had its own tenacious fastidiousness.

The preface, taking up the same thoughts in a similar though more concentrated form and a different arrangement, added some personal impressions—such as those received during his two Amherst visits ("I saw her but twice face to face, and brought away the impression of something as unique and remote as Undine or Thekla"). The comparison with Blake was altered in such a way that many critics interposed at this point:

"An Open Portfolio" (after the quotation of "I died for beauty")	"Preface"
The conception is weird enough for William Blake, and one can no more criticise a faulty rhyme here and there than a defect of drawing in one of Blake's pictures.	It is believed that the thoughtful reader will find in these pages a quality more suggestive of the poetry of William Blake than of anything to be elsewhere found,—flashes of wholly original and profound insight into nature and life.[9]

The sheaf of poems met with a cool reception from the publishers. Higginson tried his luck with Houghton Mifflin, for he was one of their readers, but was turned away on the grounds that the poems were much too "queer" (*AB*, p. 51 n. 3). Also Niles of Roberts Brothers, called on by Professor Todd, was reluctant to publish and suggested a hectograph edition of five hundred instead (*AB*, p. 52). Urged on by the Todds, and perhaps remembering that Helen Hunt, who ranked high in his esteem, had once commended Emily Dickinson to him, he announced himself willing to pass the verses to his reader whose verdict he returned to Higginson with the disappointing note: "It has always seemed to me that it would be unwise to perpetuate Miss Dickinson's poems. They are quite as remarkable for defects as for beauties & are generally devoid of true poetical qualities. If, however, Miss [Lavinia] Dickinson will pay for the plates . . ." (*AB*, p. 53). Arlo Bates's estimate[10] is the first considered opinion of a neutral critic based on a sizable portion of Emily Dickinson's work that has been preserved:

> There is hardly one of these poems which does not bear marks of unusual and remarkable talent; there is hardly one of them which is not marked by an extraordinary crudity of workmanship. The author was a person of power which came very near to that indefinable quality which we call genius. She never learned her art, and constantly one is impelled to wonder and to pity at the same time. Had she published, and been forced by ambition and perhaps by need into learning the technical part of her art, she would have stood at the head of American singers. As it is she has put upon paper what reminded her of a mood or an emotion, and in nine cases out of ten she has not got enough down to

convey the intelligence of her mood to any but the most sympathetic and poetical. There are some poems in the book, however, that are so royally good, and so many that to the poetical will be immensely suggestive, that it seems a pity not to have at least a small edition. (*AB,* p. 52)

He proposed as absolutely necessary a more rigorous selection and further alterations. His own choice cut the number of poems in half, leaving out such lyrics as "I died for beauty," "Safe in their alabaster chambers," and "How many times these low feet staggered." Mrs. Todd silently put back these three and others he had discarded. In view of his lukewarm opinion of Emily Dickinson's work, Bates estimated the sale of the book rather optimistically: "I think the force of the volume . . . would carry it farther than most volumes of verse go nowadays. Its faults are colossal, but it has the real stuff in no stinted qualities. . . . The religious poems are the weakest and least original, but their very conventions make them the best for the closing section as they are put. I do not think the volume would make a tremendous stir. I do think it would be a distinct success of esteem" (*AB,* p. 53). Harsh as it appeared, Bates's criticism did not fall short of the editors' expectations. Higginson thought it "excellent" (*AB,* p. 54), even though he disapproved of Bates's selection.

William Crary Brownell's little-known intercession on Emily Dickinson's behalf in these years is worth mentioning. In November 1887, Brownell, a friend of Austin Dickinson's, wrote to the editor of the newly founded *Scribner's Magazine,* Edward Burlingame: "Doubtless ere this you have heard from Mrs. [Austin] Dickinson. . . . To my newspaper trained sense the notion of a broadside of Miss D's things—3 or 4 pages say—such as could, I feel confident, be selected from the many she wrote, & printed not as a literary discovery . . . but merely as literature—which *I* think many of them are—seems a rather good notion." The only result of this letter as well as of Susan Dickinson's repeated requests was the inclusion of "Renunciation" in the August issue of 1890. Had Burlingame thought more favorably of Emily Dickinson's talents, a selection of her verse might conceivably have been published by the New York firm. When the volume appeared on Roberts Brothers' list, Brownell informed Charles Scribner: "Burlingame told me Roberts Brothers were to bring out a collection of Miss Dickinson's poetry—a scheme I should have liked for us rather."[11]

With the acceptance of the manuscript by Roberts Brothers, the poems had gained entry into a small but first-rate publishing house. Noted for the quality of its books, it was considered one of the best in the United States during the last third of the century thanks to Niles's editorial foresight and fastidiousness. In Boston, it was second only to the larger Houghton Mifflin. The book, with a layout designed for the holiday market, was a tastefully bound sextodecimo volume in a pasteboard box with gilt top and Emily's favorite flower, the Indian pipe, stamped in silver on the cover. The first edition of 500 copies, 480 of which were for sale, was exhausted within four weeks. Reprints became necessary in rapid succession.[12] In its selections, the first series of poems was the most successful of any Dickinson anthology before 1960. Many of its poems, with time, have proved to be of lasting value. Thematically, the editors had made few concessions to their readers. Exceptions—such as the holding over of the difficult eight-line portrait of a hummingbird for the second series—are rare.

Poems by Emily Dickinson, the outsider among the new books of the fall season, threw the press into commotion. The disconcerted majority of reviewers confined themselves to reporting and quoting, taking shelter behind Higginson's preface or the catchwords of their more courageous tribesmen. The notices in magazines and the prominent dailies, discussed hereinafter, dealt, as a rule, more exhaustively with the unusual newcomer. In many of them, intellect and feeling spoke with equal force, which explains the broad spectrum of responses ranging from sheer enthusiasm through approval and dislike to parody and sarcasm. The newspaper debate was stimulated and widened by a twofold missionary activity carried on by staunch advocates of the poet such as Howells and John White Chadwick and Higginson and Mrs. Todd. At the invitation of women's clubs, the latter gave several talks in the vicinity of Amherst and Boston. Among those present at Higginson's first reading from unpublished Dickinson letters on March 22, 1891, were Horace Scudder, editor of *The Atlantic Monthly*, Niles, Howells, Sam Longfellow, the poet's brother, and Edward Channing, the historian.

The great number and variety of the book notices, their prevailing brevity and general lack of coherent argumentation invite a systematic investigation comprising difficulties of understanding, aesthetic evaluation, comparisons, attempts at classification, biographical speculations, and British reactions.

Initial difficulties of understanding were countered by frequent endeavors to define the novel attributes of Emily Dickinson's poetry. Reviewers resorted to a host of adjectives which lingered on after they had become stale through repetition. Among these, "original," "startling," and the previously recorded "strange" stand out. The epithets tried to express the qualities of singularity ("striking," "remarkable," "curious," "uncommon"), intensity ("compelling," "close-packed," "terse," "powerful," "'suggestiferous,'"), oddness ("weird," "eery"), obscurity ("enigmatical," "orphic," "Delphic"), and roughness ("erratic," "tough," "rugged," "fragmentary"). Higginson's phrase "indifferent to all conventional rules" was passed on as "scornful disregard of poetic technique"; his formulation "flashes of wholly original and profound insight" reappeared as "profound in thought," "fine insight into life," "almost startling divination," "flashes that combine into vision."

Two critics found themselves unable to judge the poems objectively on account of their posthumous publication and their private character:

> The fact that the author herself does not present them to the public disarms the criticism that otherwise would object to them as obscure.

> We should resent them hotly, no doubt, were any liberty of cavilling ours. But none is possible; it is much as if, without her will or knowledge, we were reading, over the recluse woman's shoulder, the most intimate thoughts of her strong, ardent, melancholy soul as they flashed nakedly into life at the point of her pen in all the freedom of solitude save for her own parental eyes.[13]

While a few were disarmed, many were baffled by certain poems which presented difficulties even to readers as perceptive as Chadwick. Accordingly, characterizations were often helpless, hazily sensing that the new lyrics were different from, or more than, conventional poetry:

> The poems . . . stand as far apart from ordinary verse as do the flowers of the Monotropa—by a more than happy thought chosen to decorate the cover—from ordinary woodland blossoms.

> Compared with the better-known verses of the day, or even with most of those which have borne the test applied by generations of English-speaking readers, these posthumous

poems are like strange orchids among a mass of gay, sweet-smelling, highly cultivated, but not rare or unfamiliar flowers.

Emily Dickinson's poems are something more than the herbarium of flowers which the literary botanist may study simply to classify or label.[14]

Robert Bridges defined the flowers directly but vaguely as "poetry of importance," "intensely ethical," "philosophy in verse," and "most unreal as to the externals but deeply true in essentials."[15]

The idea that Emily Dickinson's "wild blossoms" were to be classed with the "field flowers of poesy"[16] bears some resemblance to the impression of primitiveness and barbarity left on the reviewers of the *New York Tribune* and *The Providence Journal* as well as on Maurice Thompson and Arlo Bates:

This woman certainly had genius;—but it was an uncurbed vine, whose roots sometimes touched sunless and unprofitable regions of thought and study.

There are carelessnesses and barbarities that are intolerably discordant in the high society in which they are found.

Something primitive and rude set over against the subtlest refinement of culture makes Miss Dickinson's verses still more forcibly remind us of the haphazard arrangement of natural mines.

There is a certain rude and half barbaric naivete in many of the poems. They show the insight of the civilized adult combined with the simplicity of the savage child. There is a barbaric flavor often discernible, as if this gentle poet had the blood of some gentle and simple Indian ancestress in her veins still in an unadulterated current.[17]

As was to be expected, the greatest feud broke out about the problem of artistic form. By opposing thought to syllables, grammar, and beauty of execution (in his quotation from Ruskin), Higginson had touched an allergic spot in the aesthetic theory of the 1890's, which equated form with correctness of meter, rhyme, and language. According to the well-meaning Colonel, the substance of a poem seemed separable from its form. Thus, with the possible alternative between thought and execution, he installed a critical two-way faucet. One could either side with Higginson or else attach greater weight to form, execution, expression. Bates, in his review in the *Boston Courier*, clearly realized the inevitable decision: "It is necessary to lay aside all fondness for technical perfection, and to give one's self up to the spirit, but this being done, the lover of the poetical will find the book a rare delight."

A group of critics felt the lack of form, as they understood it, to be so serious that they rejected the poems:

> These verses are largely fragmentary: they bespeak an unregulated fancy.

> Her verse has almost no vocal quality, as if she never sang it, or even said it, to herself. Yet in the rare cases where it has not this pathetic dumbness, there is heard a sweet note that is pitifully lost in jangling harshness or in silence.

> They seem to me so good that the finish ought to have been better. The rhyme should have been abandoned wholly or it should have been perfect—likewise the metre. . . . I admit the fascination of the defect, but I cannot make it out to be equal to the beautiful grace of genius.[18]

Maurice Thompson, in *America*, complained that the poet had "murdered art" in her ineptitude. Bates (in the *Boston Courier*) and the reviewer of *The Overland Monthly*, because of the intellectual content of Emily Dickinson's work, deplored the lack of "technical skill":

> Had Miss Dickinson possessed the aptitude and the will to learn technical skill, she would have enriched the language with lyrics which would have endured to the end of time, it might well be. . . . The book gives us keen delight, but it is delight mingled with regret equally keen for what it fails to be.

> One lays down the book with a feeling of perplexity that is akin to exasperation, that being so good they should not be better. They have true poetic quality in them no doubt, but as a whole they are too crude and fragmentary to admit of unqualified endorsement.

The comments of readers who had yielded to the force of Emily Dickinson's contemplative lyrics were registered a few notches higher on the critical scale. The first of these was Louise Moulton, in a highly emotional review. No book, she wrote, had equally carried her away since she had come to Boston (which was as far back as 1855). "And yet, if one were to judge the book by the theories of poetic art, one would hardly call most of its contents poems at all. Madder rhymes one has seldom seen— scornful disregard of poetic technique could hardly go farther —and yet there is about the book a fascination, a power, a vision that enthralls you, and draws you back to it again and again. Not to have published it would have been a serious loss to the world, and of how few volumes, alas, could this be said in these days when of making many books there is no end."[19] *The Springfield Republican, The Nation,* and *The Catholic World* made similar decisions.[20] Even the skeptical Thompson confessed in *America:* "Here is song that has a classic suggestiveness, as of a strange fortunate deposit wherein precious jewels, gold and crystals water-clear, are jumbled with worthless clay and fragments of coarse rock. . . . The poet's sight is perfect." For Chadwick, the book was ample evidence that "the adjunct of rhyme is not so necessary to the pleasure of verse as many have believed."[21] *The Nation* admitted that the terseness of "I died for beauty" so grasps the ear that the defect in rhyme is hardly noticed. Nathan Haskell Dole found the reckless rhyming balanced by "a quite remarkable sensitiveness to music."[22] William Hayes Ward, editor of *The Independent* and a leading Assyriologist, made light of the matter in a letter to Mrs. Todd: "She had a real genius, and it is extraordinary that with her sense of poetic thought and her sense of metre too, she had absolutely no sense of rhyme. . . . With her, rhyme was very much like the definition of comparative philology, that science in which the vowels count for nothing and the consonants for very little" (*AB,* p. 113).

The separate consideration of form and content reached an extreme in "Suggestions from the Poems of Emily Dickinson," an essay written by a young Amherst student. Entirely dispensing with the aesthetic problem, he treated the poems as versified philosophy, discovering the keystone of their power in their "intensely thought-provoking" character. They are skillfully suggestive without pretending to be explanatory and leave freedom for the reader's imagination.[23]

The texts cited so far are representative of the great majority. Common to all of them is a narrow and perfectionist standard of valuation: narrow, because it is limited to a few means of poetic expression (rhyme, rhythm, meter, melody); perfectionist, because it demands a smoothness of presentation peculiar to the fin de siècle, a glossy finish petrified in a cluster of metaphors in the reviewers' ABC. Anything deviating from such a poetics could not but fall short of the ideal.

Few readers were ready to put aside preconceived expectations and to try to do justice to the form of the new lyrics. A transitional opinion, expressing the occasional weariness in the face of the traditional jingling of gilt-edged verses, is voiced in a sentence quoted by *The Amherst Record* from the conservative *Critic:* "The rough diamonds in the collection have a value beyond that of many polished gems of poetry." Although it was but a step from such a consideration to the idea that Emily Dickinson might possibly have practiced her own *ars poetica,* only Thompson (in *America*), *The Catholic World,* and Samuel J. Barrows took it. Thompson acquired a taste for the charm of surprise caused by the sudden cessation of rhyme: "In a certain way these unaccountable discords serve to accentuate the beautiful snatches of melody with which they are so often associated. . . . A large part of the fascination of verse like this is generated by the friction of disappointment on delight." Barrows, the long-time editor of the Boston Unitarian weekly, meant to get at the root of the problem of form. He first elaborated the metaphor of the Aeolian harp, which had been introduced by *The Nation* (cf. n. 20):

> She was more like an Aeolian harp through which the wind swept over a delicately attuned nature, sometimes awakening the minor, sometimes the major chord, and now and then striking a dissonant note which only seemed to give more richness and piquancy to the harmony. Her poetry was never made of sustained notes or flowing strains. It was made of little gusts of song, snatches of melody, broken chords, and arpeggios.
>
> In music there are certain chords whose effect on the ear depends wholly on the way in which they are approached. If approached in one way, they are singularly hard and unmusical: approached in another, they take their place in the flow of melody, and we are conscious of no discord. So the effect upon the ear and the mind of one of Miss Dickinson's poems depends very much upon the way in which it is approached.
>
> Such poems cannot be tried by the rules of the school or any conventional canons. Yet they may remind us that the laws of literature and poetic art are not conventional and pe-

dantic like those of the old Mastersingers. . . . For daily companionship we may prefer ordinary people of familiar habit and average ability; but now and then what refreshment to come into contact with a soul of original insight, of rare and marked individuality.

Giving up the prevalent notion that Emily Dickinson's poetry is formless or fragmentary, he argues from the possible and justifiable musical *concordia discors* for the existence, side by side with smooth harmony, of a harsh, discordant harmony which, no doubt, displeases the ear but still produces a full chord.

Howells alone was fully convinced of Emily Dickinson's autonomous form: "Few of the poems in the book are long, but none of the short, quick impulses of intense feeling or poignant thought can be called fragments. They are each a compassed whole, a sharply finished point, and there is evidence, circumstantial and direct, that the author spared no pains in the perfect expression of her ideals." As an example he quoted

> *Presentiment is that long shadow on the lawn*
> *Indicative that suns go down;*
> *The notice to the startled grass*
> *That darkness is about to pass*

—a boldly chosen piece of evidence considering that the first line does not fit the metric and rhythmic pattern (though both stress and hypermeter could not better emphasize the meaning), that the first rhyme is suspended and the metaphor in the third line unusual. As elsewhere in his review, Howells probed deeper than most critics. His long familiarity with the New England character may have stood him in good stead. The following three sentences are harbingers of a change in aesthetic views which were not to find the approval of the majority until much later: "Occasionally, the outside of the poem, so to speak, is left so rough, so rude, that the art seems to have faltered. But there is apparent to reflection the fact that the artist meant just this harsh exterior to remain, and that no grace of smoothness could have imparted her intention as it does. It is the soul of an abrupt, exalted New England woman that speaks in such brokenness."[24]

Andrew Lang was not the only opponent dissatisfied with Howells' defense. It probably also challenged the anonymous critic who, in the March 1891 issue of *Scribner's*, took Emily Dickinson's work as a pretext to pick up the thread of the "time-honored" discussion of form and substance. A sensitive reader of her poetry, he declared, cannot but vaccilate between alternatives. While contemporaries are inclined to give preference to substance, the verdict of posterity is governed by formal criteria. "In other words, is there not an element of universality about perfection of form which significance of thought does not possess; or, at any rate, is not perfection more nearly attainable in form than it is in substance?" Artistic perfection consists in the existence of "rhyme and rhythm, cadence, purity, flawlessness, melody"; the lack of one or more of these six attributes is tantamount to formlessness and, hence, is "the antithesis of art": "Formlessness . . . not merely offends by perversely ignoring the conventionally established though rationally evolved and soundly based rules of the game it purports to play, but in announcing thus, boldly, its independence of any aesthetic, any sensuous, interest, it puts a severe strain on the quality of its own substance." Despite his adherence to "convention-steeped" principles, the reviewer hesitatingly admits that, alongside of old forms, new ones might conceivably exist: "If, as in Miss Dickinson's case, there be occasionally a subtle, but essential order in what, superficially, seems chaotic, it may legitimately be maintained that to lay any stress on this is merely to argue against conventionality and not at all in favor of amorphousness. It is simply to assert the elasticity of orchestration and to emphasize its range—to exalt the value of new forms over the old." Higginson's preface and Walt Whitman's apologists assert the existence of such new forms without, however, proving it.[25]

The style of Emily Dickinson's poems was even more difficult to cope with than their form. Yet while the form constituted a fundamental challenge to traditional poetry (to the increase of which not a few Dickinson critics of the 1890's were themselves prolific contributors) and thus presented a problem that could not well be ignored, language and imagery could be passed over in silence. The reviews show that, in spite of frequent intuitive sympathy to the experimenter with words, critical terminology broke down. Lilian Whiting found herself "pursuing almost a new language";[26] Chadwick admired, but could not explain, Emily Dickinson's verbal accuracy; *The Atlantic Monthly* noted the trenchant power of her style by calling it "a shaft of light sunk instantaneously into the dark abysm."[27] Most critics were content with bare phrases such as "intense concentration." The dividing wall between poet and public seemed particularly high at this point. *The Independent* pounced upon "a few serious misprints in the volume" which were actually examples of what Chadwick termed "great and often startling felicity of word and phrase."[28] Small wonder that the grammatical errors left uncorrected by Mrs. Todd offended most. A principal of Wellesley College asked Higginson to substitute "laid" for "lain" in the line "When one who died for truth was lain"; "To most of the educated people of New England, the confusion of *lie* & *lay* is condoned with some difficulty, and the writer of this note is the most sensitive, perhaps, with regard to a grammatical error of this nature, from the fact of her having known Miss Dickinson . . ." (MS-D57/To 296).

Critics paid equal attention to the thematic groups but rated them differently. The nature poems were widely approved. "Who has ever felt the charm of Nature more intimately than this poet?" asked *The Springfield Republican* on November 16, 1890. In the religious lyrics one sensed a pagan leaning which struck some as delightful, others as disquieting. Christina Rossetti, the orthodox Anglican, who had received a presentation copy from Niles, her American publisher, spoke in her letter of thanks of "a very remarkable work of genius,—though I cannot but deplore some of the religious, or rather irreligious pieces" (MS-D57/To 169). A more serious objection was raised in Boston. While Mrs. Todd was preparing the second series of poems for publication, she sent "God is a distant, stately lover" as a specimen to Samuel Barrows, who printed it in the April 2 issue of *The Christian Register*. Shortly after, he received letters of protest from two shocked readers one of whom, a Unitarian minister like Barrows, disparaged the poem as "one of the most offensive bits of contemptuous Unitarianism that I have met with." Barrows, who could not see why it should be "any more irreverent or daring than the metaphors used in the Song of Solomon" (MS-D57/To 365), as a progressive member of his creed defended Emily Dickinson in an editorial whose closing sentences called to witness a prominent quondam Unitarian: "Such a soul saw God, nature, and man at first hand, and made its own interpretation, its own alphabet and character. She wrote her own hymnbook and her own ritual; but we should as soon think of charging Emerson with irreverence as of so charging her." At any rate, the controversy led to the exclusion of the poem from the second series.

In the love poems readers were disturbed by the peculiar

nature of the sentiments expressed. "The love poems are written in the attitude of a worshipper and not of a lover," wrote Robert Bridges in *Life*. "It is not passion, but fervid loyalty that is depicted—and the chill of intellectual monasticism is in it." *The Critic* registered the absence of features essential to poems of this kind—"sensuousness and symmetry and melody."[29] Howells alone felt that "the heart of full womanhood" spoke in them.

The great number of poems quoted came as a confirmation of prudent editorial selection. Admirers would not miss a single one. "It is hard to find favorites, they are all so fine," *The Critic* déclared. For that reason, no consensus was reached. A few pieces attracting greater attention were "I never saw a moor" and, after Howells' appraisal, "Presentiment," also "I died for beauty," "The pedigree of honey," "The soul selects her own society," "I taste a liquor never brewed," and "Success is counted sweetest." The only exception was a dactylic nature poem entitled "The Sea of Sunset," which Mrs. Todd had, as a precaution, furnished with a rhyme in the second stanza:

> *This is the land the sunset washes,*
> *These are the banks of the Yellow Sea;*
> *Where it rose, or whither it rushes,*
> *These are the western mystery!*
>
> *Night after night her purple traffic*
> *Strews the landing with opal bales;*
> *Merchantmen poise upon horizons,*
> *Dip, and vanish with fairy sails.*

Louise Moulton ranked it with "the most polished gems" of the collection; *The Springfield Republican* cited it as "an example of what lyric elegance this writer might have accomplished had she chosen to do so"; even Lang, the malevolent Scotsman, grudgingly conceded that regarding the strength of this poem there "was poetry in the writer."

If the reviewers hardly came to terms with the poems separately, their attempts to assign them a place in the realm of literature, to discover similarities and establish possible influences, were bound to be unavailing. Of the person, one knew little more than that she had lived in seclusion; for the poet, one had Higginson's allusion to Blake. At first this sentence from the preface was much quoted; but only to Payne, writing in *The Dial,* did the suggestion seem evident enough to warrant the citation of "I died for beauty" as a characteristic example. Others thought the resemblance faint and doubted whether Emily Dickinson could be classed in any school. Dole found in her stanzas "a mixture of Blake, Emerson, and Heine—especially the last." The comparison with Emerson had been proffered earlier by Mrs. Moulton, who had declared Dickinson "his female counterpart," with this qualification: "But Emily Dickinson felt the pitilessness of nature, as, I think, Emerson never felt it." *The Critic* sensed an Emersonian influence behind "Success is counted sweetest." Thompson was most positive: "Much study of Emerson has colored and shaped her vision; it has also cramped her methods of expression. . . . She exaggerated the faults of Emerson's verse-style into absurdity." Others saw in Mrs. Browning's verses an almost equal neglect of rhyme; in her poem "Like trains of cars on tracks of plush," "a bit of poetic melodrama that Poe would have liked" (Bridges); in her religious pieces, especially her Sabbath poem, "pretty blasphemies which Thoreau would have gladly owned" (Chadwick). The remotest affinity, both spatial and temporal, was discovered by Thompson: "To me it is like nothing else so much as it is to a crude translation of some freshly discovered Greek lyrical fragments, the spirit of which, not the art, has been perfectly caught by the translator."

Though passing references to the Concord sage abounded, the kinship was never clearly defined. Wavering pronouncements are typical. Howells viewed in Emily Dickinson "a Blake who has read Emerson who has read Blake. The fantasy is as often Blakean as the philosophy is Emersonian; but after feeling this again and again, one is ready to declare that the utterance of this most singular and authentic spirit would have been the same if there had never been an Emerson or a Blake in the world. She sometimes suggests Heine as much as either of these; all three in fact are spiritually present in some of the pieces."

It occurred to hardly anyone to associate the poet with her New England homeland and its traditions. On the contrary, the biographer and historian William Roscoe Thayer, scion of a Brahmin family, wrote Higginson on March 24, 1891: "Surely our New England Calvinism never brought forth any other flower so sweet and un-Calvinistic. It's a miracle like that of young Keats coming out of the stables of London cockneydom" (MS-D57/To 302). After the appearance of Mary E. Wilkins' short story collection, "New England nun" became one of Emily Dickinson's standing epithets—when *A New England Nun and*

Other Stories was published at the end of March 1891 and the label was first applied (still enclosed by apologetic quotation marks) in *The Providence Journal* of June 14, the stress lay emphatically on "nun." Higginson himself had provided a cue in his preface: "She . . . was as invisible to the world as if she had dwelt in a nunnery" (v). Once again, Howells made a keen observation. "Such things," he commented on the death poem beginning "The bustle in a house," "could have come only from a woman's heart to which the experiences in a New England town have brought more knowledge of death than of life." In its insight, this is paralleled only by the testimony of Samuel G. Ward, an early Transcendentalist and member of Emerson's circle, who wrote to Higginson on October 11, 1891:

> She is the quintessence of that element we all have who are of Puritan descent pur sang. We came to this country to think our own thoughts with nobody to hinder. Ascetics of course, & this our Thebaid. We conversed with our own souls till we lost the art of communicating with other people. The typical family grew up strangers to each other, as in this case. It was *awfully* high, but awfully lonesome. Such prodigies of shyness do not exist elsewhere. We get it from the English, but the English were not alone in a corner of the world for a hundred & fifty years with no outside interest. I sate next to Jones Very for three years & he was an absolute enigma till he flashed on me with the Barberry Bush. . . . If the gift of articulateness was not denied, you had Channing, Emerson, Hawthorne a stupendous example, & so many others. Mostly it was denied, & became a family fate. This is where Emily Dickinson comes in. She was the articulate inarticulate. That is why it appeals so to New England women. (MS-D57/To 306)

This is a rare case of New England introspection which finds confirmation in a thought from Miss Freeman's story "A Village Singer" of the same year: "A New England nature has a floodgate, and the power which it releases is an accumulation."[30]

Little regard was paid to the person behind the poetry. Higginson's laconic biographical information was, for the most part, passed on to the readers without comment. But the very gaps in the record of her externally uneventful life encouraged speculations because of the joyous and sorrowful experiences expressed in the lyrics. These speculations took the form both of inferences drawn back and forth between life and work and of conjectures about a secret romance. Peripherally, the question of the unsettled authorship, denied by Mrs. Jackson, of the *Saxe Holm's Stories* series was revived since the tenor of some of the poems seemed to resemble the anonymous tales interspersed with verses. Had Emily Dickinson perhaps collaborated with Helen Hunt? Or, at least, had not Helen perpetuated her friend's memory in "Draxy Miller's Dowry," one of the stories?

Pondering over the interrelationship of person and poetry, critics reached sad results. "The impression made upon the reader, who interprets her life by her verse and her verse by her life, is that there could not well be any poetic wholes in her work," concluded *The Atlantic Monthly*, and *The Commercial Advertiser* dogmatized: "Extreme hunger often causes strange visions. That this hermitess never satisfied, perhaps never could satisfy, her craving for human companionship, may have first brought her into her strangely visionary state. Upon the theme of human love she becomes absurdly, if not blasphemously, intemperate. . . . Isolated from humanity, she cannot turn the current of her thoughts toward it except in intermittent galvanic shocks."[31] *The Literary World* compared her to Laura Bridgman, the blind deaf-mute New England woman who had died in Boston in 1889 nearly half a century after Dickens had written of the young girl in *American Notes,* and inferred "a case of arrested development" from "the pent-up and paralyzed inspiration" of her verse. "Here, surely, is the record of a soul that suffered from isolation and the stress of dumb emotion and the desire to make itself understood by means of a voice so long unused that the sound was strange even to her own ears." Twining, writing in *The Independent*, sought to explain the emotional tension of the poetry by the idea of a personality on the verge of insanity: "It is the delirium of a sane mind poised on a very serious basis of living and thinking." In a letter to Higginson, Thompson ventured even further: "Miss Dickinson's verse suggests to me a superb brain that has suffered some obscure lesion which now and again prevents the filling out of a thought—as if a cog slipped in some fine wheel just at the point of consummation" (MS-D57/To 303).

Compared with this biographical poring over her work, the intimations of a love affair as a turning point in the poet's life would be negligible had not the surmise of a "secret" remained an occasional center of attraction ever since. The fashion of blending fact and fiction, which had already set in during Emily Dickinson's lifetime, became irresistible to some. The issue was as yet not the identity but the mere existence of a lover. The natural starting point was the preservation of love lyrics that seemed to have much of the personal about them. "What Emily Dickinson says of love," stated *The Springfield Republican,* "has a peculiar interest, and it can hardly be forbidden that the reader should wonder what experience of her own she might have had to produce so exceptionally personal utterances." To no purpose did Mrs. Todd try to refute spreading rumors by supplying information in letters and lectures. On all sides distant relations and good old acquaintances felt called upon to publish their reminiscences in the daily press, and some reviews readily snatched them up. Besides, there circulated among old Amherst people a rumor brought forward as evidence against Mrs. Todd's protestations—an unconfirmed story of Emily's betrothal to a promising youth which had come to nought because her father had interposed his veto. Once the secret of the secluded life had been touched, the legend of the broken heart kept preying on curious minds. Curiosity formed an inseparable part of the price of posthumous fame Emily Dickinson had gained at "the Auction / Of the Mind of Man" (*Poems,* II, 544)—publication.

The most remarkable reminiscence of "Aunt Emily," seen from the viewpoint of a child, was written by MacGregor Jenkins, whose father Jonathan Leavitt had been pastor of the First Church of Amherst from 1866 to 1877. The most reasonable explanation of what turned the poet's life in upon itself was given by Howells, who perceived in this process "tendencies inherent in the New England, or the Puritan spirit."

On the strength of its higher pitch, only the British reception can safely be separated from the mixed chorus of voices, although it was prompted by American critics and had American reverberations. In the homeland, regional differences were hardly noticeable. Friends and foes were spread evenly over Boston, New York, Philadelphia, and Chicago. Only a few copies of the book had been sent to papers and stores in other cities. A single exception occurred in the Golden State. On February 24, 1891, Lavinia Dickinson had urged Niles to introduce the book in California (*AB,* p. 108). Notices appeared in *The Overland Monthly* and the *San José Mercury.* The review in the monthly founded by Bret Harte, in all likelihood penned by a Boston correspondent, did not depart from the usual. The newspaper critic, however, after quoting from Higginson's preface, picked a quarrel with New England: "After this elaborate flourish of trumpets, the reader on turning to the poems will be disappointed. The New England clique have a tendency to overpraise one another, and Miss Dickinson is an extremely New England poetess indeed. She has ideas which may be original but are certainly not novel, and she expresses them in a form of verse which may be novel but is certainly not poetical. The poems . . . read like the first random notes of a poem rather than of [sic] the poem itself, and appear to be fleeting ideas jotted down in a hurry with the intention of elaborating them later on."[32]

The initial success of the volume, material proof of which came in the form of handsome royalty checks to the poet's sister, had plucked up Lavinia and convinced her that "Emilies poems" had met the "cordial reception from the world" (AB, p. 105). Not even by Andrew Lang's scoffing was she to be diverted from her plan to have the poems reach England. Thus a few copies of the Boston edition crossed the Atlantic, and in the late summer of 1891, a London edition was brought out by Osgood, McIlvaine. (This edition was reprinted only once in 1905 by Methuen).

Although British criticism of American literature had entered quieter waters toward the close of the century, both condescension and animosity were revived because of the high claim made for Emily Dickinson by Howells, Higginson, and some of their compeers.

On January 2, 1891, the first to push forward to a violent attack was Andrew Lang, who vented his anger under the cloak of thinly disguised anonymity in *The London News*. The learned Scotsman, anthropologist, classicist, historian, journalist, novelist, and dabbler in poetry, who followed American literary activities with lively interest and formidable pen, had his favorites among the older Brahmin poets but was prepared to sacrifice "all the poetry all the presses of America have given to the world" for Homer's catalogue of the ships, a flippant aside which he allowed himself in *The Illustrated London News* on March 7, 1891. In the same year that he launched his tirades against Emily Dickinson, the *Atlantic* praised him for precisely those critical qualities which he entirely lacked in his skirmishes with the Amherst poet: "Not only can he put himself alongside of the author whom he is reviewing, which is the first condition of sympathetic criticism; he can put himself in his skin."[33]

An ironic title "The Newest Poet," an ironic distortion of Howells' words which had irritated him so much precede his central attack. He quotes the first stanza of a poem commended in "Editor's Study":

> *I taste a liquor never brewed,*
> *From tankards scooped in pearl;*
> *Not all the vats upon the Rhine*
> *Yield such an alcohol!*

and remarks: " 'Alcohol' does not rhyme to pearl. But Miss Dickinson is not to be regarded as responsible for mere rhymes. Nor for grammar! It is literally impossible to understand whether she means that she tastes a liquor never brewed at all, or a liquor never brewed 'from' tankards scooped in pearl. By 'from' she may mean 'in.' Let us give her the benefit of the doubt, and she still writes utter nonsense. It is clearly impossible to scoop a tankard from pearl. The material is inadequate." As neither Blake nor Emerson nor Heine were "idiots," Emily Dickinson is responsible for her own poetic sins. She is neither educated nor of sound mind.

"How many times these low feet staggered" turns out to be the second stumbling block. This "balderdash" is absurd; "low feet" is meaningless, let alone the conclusion "Indolent housewife in daisies lain": "This is no more English than it is Coptic." Missing rhyme, incorrect grammar, and obscure metaphors present insurmountable obstacles for the classical scholar with his classicist taste. Responding only with his intellect, he points up the examples given by Howells to demonstrate what is downright impossible. The knife of his intellect cuts another stanza to pieces:

> *New feet within my garden go,*
> *New fingers stir the sod,*
> *A troubadour upon an elm*
> *Betrays the solitude.*

"What in the world has a troubadour to do in New England? And why did he climb a tree? Or was he a bird? And how can solitude be betrayed by a troubadour, somewhere near Boston, in the foliage of an elm?" It is obvious that Emily Dickinson overstepped her bounds in transplanting the medieval Provençal bard into the New World and troubling him metaphorically for a feathered warbler.

37

He trips over the metaphor "startled grass" in "Presentiment." This is "mere maundering" as grass simply cannot feel the shock of surprise. Howells had better supply the poems with a running commentary. The final blow is simultaneously struck at Emily Dickinson, at Howells, and at America in general: "Of course the idea occurs that Mr. Howells is merely bantering; that he cannot really mean to praise this farrago of illiterate and uneducated sentiment. It is as far below the level of the Poet's Corner in a country newspaper as that is usually below Shakespeare. There are no words that can say how bad poetry may be when it is divorced from meaning, from music, from grammar, from rhyme; in brief, from articulate and intelligible speech. And Mr. Howells solemnly avers that this drivel is characteristic of American life!" After this dressing down all that remains is the ironic reference to the good taste of the poetess who never published her verse. There is nothing to be said against poetry of the portfolio, "but there is a good deal of harm in publicly praising as excellent and typical poetry, the trash which every editor of a magazine receives in bales." Howells' praise can only lead to the encouragement of poetasters.

The hollow truce that followed upon the high-strung scholar's first outburst was of short duration. On January 31, in a "literary causerie" held in London's *Speaker*, he skirmished afresh with America's "great lyrist," this time plucking to pieces "I died for beauty" (which, too, had been quoted by Howells).[34] On March 7 he engaged in a third battle. In his first review, he had defined poetry as "original, or at least . . . agreeable thought, musically and metrically expressed." According to this formula, of the four figures discussed in "Some American Poets"—Emily Dickinson, Thomas Bailey Aldrich, Sidney Lanier, Eugene Field —Aldrich came off best. Not only were his lyrics "beautiful and accomplished" (high praise), but "as pretty as if Paulus Silentarius had written" them (even higher praise). Also *The Little Book of Western Verse* written by Field, the humorist born in St. Louis, raised in Amherst, and living in Chicago, pleased him, for Field was an imitator of Horace. To Lanier he conceded genius and originality, but the Southerner had presumed in "The Crystal" to criticize Homer's style as "sandy," "drear," and "sleazy," an impertinence which branded him as a "blasphemer of Homer."

Emily Dickinson ranks lowest. That the poems had meanwhile reached a fourth edition is quite correctly explained in part by Howells' intercession. Lang categorically repeats the demand that poetry, if it is to exist at all, must have form, grammar, and rhyme when it professes to rhyme. Her deviation from correct usage gives him the opportunity to add a politico-cultural sarcasm: "We may be told that Democracy does not care, any more than the Emperor did, for grammar.[35] But even if Democracy overleaps itself and lands in savagery again, I believe that our savage successors will, though unconsciously, make their poems grammatical. Savages do not use bad grammar in their own conversation or in their artless compositions. That is a fault of defective civilizations." But his annoyance appears softened. While he still relies on the proven method of logically dissecting lyrical imagery, in leafing through the book, which he must have had procured in the meantime, he has "a puzzled feeling that there was poetry in her subconsciousness, but that it never became explicit." Still, "the true lyrical note" heard in "This is the land the sunset washes" and in "I never saw a moor" is a saving grace. The book as a whole, however, remains rather discouraging; it is "the fantastic, irresponsible note of a poet who was her own audience, and had constructed her own individual 'Ars Poetica.' "

The dispatching of review copies to the British press threw back a faint echo. On May 6 the London *Bookman* spoke highly of Emily Dickinson though, unfortunately, at the expense of American literature in general: "It is probable that the reputation which these poems have gained in their own land will be forthcoming here in due time. . . . Certainly America, generally sterile in poetical production, has produced nothing so truly poetical as these fugitive thoughts." In speaking of a "collection of verse more noteworthy for quaintness of phrase and odd unexpectedness of conceits than for the Blake-like quality which Mr. Higginson . . . discovers," *The Saturday Review* made shorter shrift of the lyrics.[36]

The weak response to the London edition characteristically rounds off what British critics had to say on the subject in 1891. *The Graphic* remained noncommittal,[37] but *The Saturday Review* judged the volume as fairly as *The Review of Reviews* and *The London Daily News* had unfairly.

In William Stead's monthly, the volume was summarily and flippantly dismissed: "The preface states that these poems were written with no idea of publication. . . . The quality of the verse is such as to make one wonder on what possible pretext the author's wishes were not observed."[38]

The critic writing in the *Saturday Review* could not resign himself any more than Lang to Howells' "very injudicious praise" and saw an undeserved merit implied in Higginson's phrase of uprooted poetry. Moreover, in a time when minor poets show remarkable mastery of form while lacking originality, there is the danger of overvaluing Emily Dickinson for her pronounced individuality. Nevertheless, he emphasizes two qualities in her work less denied than unrecognized by Lang: "Miss Dickinson's chief characteristics are, first, a faculty for seizing the impression or feelings of the moment, and fixing them with rare force and accuracy; secondly, a vividness of imagery, which impresses the reader as thoroughly unconventional, and shows considerable imaginative power." The poems do not remind him of Blake; they rather strike him as unmistakably American. Though the lines do not scan and lack grammatical correctness and, indeed, good taste, they express even in their very roughness ideas which make the reader listen attentively. Therefore, the reviewer's summing up is balanced: "The little volume contains much to exercise the satire and scorn of critics. The sublime in Miss Dickinson's poems comes sometimes dangerously near to the ridiculous; but any fair-minded reader will, nevertheless, acknowledge that there is something in her poems which cannot be found in the mechanical productions of mere verse-writers."[39]

The anonymous critic answerable for the notice "An American Sappho" in *The London Daily News* of October 3, 1891, availed himself of the two-fisted criticism tried and found reliable by Lang. For personal reasons presently to be discussed, Lang had crossed swords not only with Emily Dickinson but also with Howells. Similarly, this unknown last British foe picked for his second victim Higginson, who had just published in the October issue of the *Atlantic* a selection of Dickinson letters together with an account of his relationship with her. Like Lang, the critic aimed a sidecut at American literary taste ("'It takes all sorts to make a world,' in poetry as in other affairs, and in this world American taste has found a niche for Miss Dickinson"). While Lang had condemned rhyme, imagery, and meaning, he concentrated his attack on rhyme:

> She was emancipated, very. She had an extraordinary knack of avoiding rhymes which appear inevitable, as
>
> > *It's far far treasure to surmise*
> > *And estimate the pearl,*
> > *That slipped my simple fingers through,*
> > *When just a girl at school.*

Anybody, except Miss Dickinson, would have written "When just at school, a girl." Even Mr. Higginson sees this.

At first he confines himself to ironical comments on Higginson's essay so that the preceptor appears a fool and his charge a mental case. As a negative example of her art he quotes the hummingbird poem and goes so far as to claim "Why, anybody could write like Miss Dickinson"—an assertion he at once proceeds to prove by presenting the first stanza of "In the Garden"

> *A Bird came down the walk:*
> *He did not know I saw;*
> *He bit an angle-worm in halves*
> *And ate the fellow, raw*

and parodying it:

> *A trout came from under a stone,*
> *He never recked of a hook,*
> *He bit the worm to the bone,*
> *And I hauled him out of the brook.*

His defamations give way to concluding reflections which deserve to be quoted, since they mark the height of misunderstanding, unintentional as well as deliberate, to which Emily Dickinson was exposed in England (though not only there) during her "auction." A type of journalistic criticism has here erected its memorial:

> It is easy to see the interest of a character like this, but it is really next to impossible to see the merit of poetry like Miss Dickinson's. She had thought a great deal, she did little but think, yet the expression of her thought is immeasurably obscure, broken, unmelodious and recklessly wilful.
>
> Miss Dickinson in her poetry broke every one of the natural and salutary laws of verse. Hers is the very anarchy of the Muses, and perhaps in this anarchy lies the charm which has made her popular in America. . . . Fortunately that continent has a much more valid *raison d'être*.
>
> She seems to have been a kind of unfinished, rudimentary Brontë, and her character is so unusual and interesting, that it is a pity her rhymes should make matter for mirth. Yet it is impossible for most people to avoid laughing at what is, frankly, so laughable. Unless all poets, from the earliest improvisers to the Laureate, have been wrong in their methods, Miss Dickinson cannot possibly have been

right in hers. Compared with her, Walt Whitman is a sturdy poetical conservative. Her only merit is an occasional picturesque touch, and a general pathetic kind of yearning and sense of futility.

He can only warn Emily Dickinson's admirers not to become her imitators, for this would mean coming to the festival of the Muses without a wedding garment.[40]

Only two Americans took exception to the British slurs. Franklin Benjamin Sanborn, a survivor and literary executor of Emerson's Concord circle, who had once corresponded with Emily Dickinson in 1873, suspected Andrew Lang as the author of "An American Sappho" and weakly objected to his Philistinism. In particular, he demurred at the word "anarchy," "which is used in England to express all sorts of deviation from custom —highway robbery, mobbing the bishop of London, or refusing to wear a stove-pipe hat." Still, he conceded that the British critic had essentially been right; he even found fault with Higginson for his "venturesome" printing of parts of "his very intimate correspondence" with Emily Dickinson.[41]

The second protest was entered in the midst of the hostile London camp—but only into a diary. On January 6, 1892, precisely two months before her death, Alice James, the *chérie charmante* of a famous family, dictated into her journal: "It is reassuring to hear the British pronouncement that Emily Dickinson is fifth-rate—they have such a capacity for missing quality; the robust evades them equally with the subtle. Her being sicklied o'er with T. W. Higginson makes one wonder lest there be a patent flaw which escapes one's vision; but what tomes of philosophy *resume* the cheap farce, or express the highest point of view more completely than the following: 'How dreary to be somebody . . . .' "[42] This entry is the more surprising since Alice James's other remarks on American literature in her private record are confined to a sentence about Howells and a quotation from Aldrich.

Ludwig Lewisohn's résumé of the situation around 1890— that "few or none listened in those days to that voice"[43]—is wide of the mark, for Emily Dickinson's critical reception was quite lively. The tide of public interest reached its highest point around Christmas 1890, slowly ebbing away until the early summer of 1891. When it later became customary to refer to Emily

Dickinson's debut as the literary sensation of the 1890's, one no longer knew how exaggerated such a phrase was because, in the strictest sense, only the first volume of her selected poetry was, as a controversial literary discovery, a sensational event. Notices appeared in all important literary reviews except *The North American Review*, which in those years carried lengthy literary essays in place of columns on books and authors. The literary weekend sections of the great dailies responded with similar completeness.

Emily Dickinson's most influential advocate was Howells, her most prominent hostile critic Lang. Howells' attention had been drawn to the poems in good time by Mrs. Todd, although without her coeditor Higginson's sanction. "He is a dangerous friend," Higginson warned her on September 19, 1890, "often praising so whimsically (e.g. that turgid and imitative Cawain) that his praise rouses opposition as much as sympathy" (*AB*, pp. 64-65). Two aspects of Higginson's opinion are to be distinguished: Howells' exposed position in American literary criticism, and his understanding of Emily Dickinson. The public influence of a mind both respected and fought against was bound to have a detrimental as well as a beneficial effect on the poet's reception. Yet his praise was not as whimsical as Higginson had apprehended. Howells' sincerity has been questioned by scholars. Doubtless there were too many books to be reviewed for "Editor's Study," and it occasionally happened that he showed himself well-disposed toward a rhymester. All the same, he was disgusted with the mass production of mediocre verse. In May 1891, half jokingly propounding a Utopian scheme, he wondered "if the poets could not have a sort of spring and fall exhibitions, as the painters have. There might be a hanging committee or a literary tribunal answering to it, which could decide upon the different pieces of verse to be presented to the public." In Bellamy's commonwealth, there certainly would not be such "ruinous and wasteful form of publication for poetry as we now have it in these volumes of competitive verse." Until that happy moment, government control and a nationalistic production and distribution of poetry might perhaps best serve the purpose of saving paper and ink.[44] In his review of *Poems by Emily Dickinson*, not his benevolence but his perception surpassed that of his colleagues. His kindliness did not, even in part, take the form of flattery but rather moved him to study the newcomer's work without bias.

43

To dismiss Andrew Lang's belittlement of Emily Dickinson's poetry as British superciliousness would not be quite correct, for in general he was a more moderate judge in his humorously erudite editorials in the London press and in his numerous essays in American reviews. For his contemporaries his impressionistic criticism—much like Pater, he took criticism to be "the adventures of an ingenious and educated mind in contact with masterpieces"[45]—was at its best in his interpretation of the ancients and moderns. This, of course, with the characteristic exception of the seventeenth century in general and John Donne in particular. In his opinion, the great ages of literature were past, and the present age comparatively so unimportant that he gave free rein to his likes and dislikes. In the feud between the proponents of romanticism and realism he had sided with his revered compatriot Scott. To what extent previous battles with Howells were involved in his disparaging Emily Dickinson must be left undecided. Since Lang was more objective two months later, it is evident that his first and lowest rating was provoked by Howells' defense and based exclusively on the poems his opponent had quoted.

In addition to Howells and Lang, whose influence was directive in America and England, no special groupings among the critics can be ascertained. One might suppose that in the case of the Unitarian clergy the defense was more enthusiastic than in the case of any other group, for Higginson, Chadwick, and Barrows belonged to the professed advocates of the poet. One is tempted to speak of a Roberts Brothers group, since the names of Mrs. Moulton, Lilian Whiting, and Chadwick appeared on that publishing house's list. But their statements can only with difficulty be considered compatible. The distinguishing note of Emily Dickinson's literary debut lay in the predominance of extreme opinions and in the feeling that her poetry compelled the reader to assume an either-or attitude.

It speaks for the acumen of the majority of critics that they paid more attention to her poems than they did to the other volumes of verse waiting on their desks to be reviewed and noticed that she contrasted with Helen Cone, Annie Fields, Frank Sherman, Thomas Parsons, and other similar authors. When toward the end of 1890 *The Critic* consulted noted writers concerning the best five books of the last decade, two writers, Mrs. Moulton and Miss Woolsey, named Emily Dickinson.[46] But her work made demands which most critical readers would not or could not face up to and for which the contemporary critical standards proved too blunt. In spite of all admiration for the newcomer, they preferred ordinary people of familiar habit and average ability for daily companionship, as Barrows and others honestly admitted.

The predominantly optimistic prognoses for the survival of Emily Dickinson's work are a gauge of the reviewers' bewilderment because her art ran exactly counter to current aesthetic theory. While Arlo Bates and *The Springfield Republican* predicted only a tolerated place and a small reading public for her, *The Critic* was more confident, and Chadwick felt the book was "an argument for immortality." This was perhaps all that an intelligent contemporary could divine. Nevertheless, Howells, who since 1885 had surveyed the entire literary landscape of the United States from the "Editor's Study," made a weightier confession: "If nothing else had come out of our life but this strange poetry we should feel that in the work of Emily Dickinson, America, or New England rather, had made a distinctive addition to the literature of the world, and could not be left out of any record of it."

III

THE SECOND "AUCTION" (1891-92)

But then, Miss Dickinson was evidently born to be the despair of reviewers.[1]

THE SUCCESSFUL SALE of the first volume of poetry had sent the editors into ecstasy. It appeared to Higginson as though "we had climbed to a cloud, pulled it away, and revealed a new star behind it" (*AB*, p. 81). Even before the publication of the first selection, he had suggested to Mrs. Todd a second, the compilation of which was begun early in 1891. Ample material was available, for Mrs. Todd had in the meantime copied and ordered alphabetically no fewer than 1093 poems in addition to the verses contained in the first series. Higginson suggested that as little be changed as possible, since the public had already become accustomed to Emily Dickinson. Instead, he came upon the, for him, logical notion of titling the new book "Indian Pipe and Witch Hazel" (*AB*, p. 150). Mrs. Todd, however, dissuaded him from this fancy as from many of his somewhat clumsy titles for the poems.

In the preparation of the text, the editors, again probably mainly Mrs. Todd, proceeded more conservatively than in the previous year. Relatively fewer poems, namely 47 of 167 in comparison to 44 of 116, show textual changes. In order to create a text as even as possible, they combined different versions so freely that their procedure at times bordered on the jigsaw puzzle method.[2] Greater care than before is conspicuous in the case of deviations from the text. Before the editors altered words, they tried transposing them, especially when a rhyme was necessary.[3]

Thirty-six changes aimed at achieving a rhyme and sub-stituting indicative forms for the annoying Dickinsonian subjunctive. The other changes smoothed rhythm, syntax and diction.

In order to answer questions which had arisen and forestall objections, Mrs. Todd availed herself of her scrapbook of reviews in writing the first draft of the preface to the second volume, which was later rendered more precise by Higginson. Where the Colonel less than a year before still had had to woo the audience, she could reckon with a sympathetic circle of readers and predominantly well-meaning critics. She could even begin triumphantly with the statement that Emily Dickinson's simplicity had been victorious over the prevailing tendency toward artificiality. She added the letter of September 5, 1884, written to Emily Dickinson by Helen Jackson, whose high praise sounded more objective than any recommendation of Mrs. Todd.

Upon the suggestion of Higginson, Mrs. Todd met the objection of immaturity, which had been raised by the *San José Mercury*, by requesting that the poems be regarded only as rough drafts: "To what further rigorous pruning her verses would have been subjected had she published them herself, we cannot know. They should be regarded in many cases as merely the first strong and suggestive sketches of an artist, intended to be embodied at some time in the finished picture" (p. 5). Regarding the charge of formlessness, she was not able to counter with as much assurance, since form was for her also something external, something added as it were as a polish, which Emily Dickinson's verse exhibited only to an extent or not at all. Only the intrinsic skill of the diction could be opposed to this deficiency: "Like impressionist pictures, or Wagner's rugged music, the very absence of conventional form challenges attention. In Emily Dickinson's exacting hands, the especial, intrinsic fitness of a particular order of words might not be sacrificed to anything virtually extrinsic; and her verses all show a strange cadence of inner rhythmical music. Lines are always daringly constructed, and the 'thought-rhyme' appears frequently,—appealing, indeed, to an unrecognized sense more elusive than hearing" (p. 7). As with Mrs. Jackson's letter, this plea also argues indirectly. The form, which was judged inadequate according to what had been handed down or what was usual, resembles a new French manner of painting and the music of a fashionable German composer. This form consists in inner movement at the expense of external luster, in thought rhymes at the expense of the expected phonetic harmony.

Regarding the reproach for disrespectful treatment of religious themes, Mrs. Todd answered: "She touches these themes sometimes lightly, sometimes almost humorously, more often with weird and peculiar power; but she is never by any chance frivolous or trivial" (p. 7). Finally, she turned against the critics who had spoken of morbidness and melancholy and stressed concerning the talk of unrequited love that "she had tried society and the world, and found them lacking. She was not an invalid, and she lived in seclusion from no love-disappointment. Her life was the normal blossoming of a nature introspective to a high degree, whose best thought could not exist in pretence" (p. 7).

In the meantime Higginson wrote his second essay, which was once again intended to prepare for and call attention to the publishing of a volume of poetry. While "An Open Portfolio" had for the first time placed a greater number of poems before the public, a first sampling of the poet's correspondence followed in "Emily Dickinson's Letters."[4] As in Mrs. Todd's preface, the point of departure was the unexpected success of *Poems*—"almost without a parallel in American literature" (p. 444)—and unceasing reader requests for further biographical information. The reference to the latter point seemed necessary since the publishing of private letters almost exceeded the bounds of propriety. Higginson sketched the course of his acquaintanceship with the poet, including his visits in Amherst. He admitted that he was never able to comprehend his correspondent entirely—"even at this day, I stand somewhat bewildered" (p. 445). Further, he realized that his role as preceptor had soon come to an end: "I soon abandoned all attempt to guide in the slightest degree this extraordinary nature, and simply accepted her confidences, giving as much as I could of what might interest her in return" (p. 450). While Mrs. Todd spoke of a "normal blossoming," Higginson maintained the opposite: "The impression undoubtedly made on me was that of an excess of tension, and of an abnormal life" (p. 453). In the poems he found "irregularities," (p. 448), "obscurity" (p. 451), and "defiance of form" (p. 446). These qualities he traced back to her guiding desire for the most concise mode of expression.

Higginson's essay received much attention (cf. Sources, p. 322) and created interest in the new volume of poetry and a later edition of letters. *The Review of Reviews* called it "incomparably the best literary article of the month" and hoped for a Dickinson biography by the Colonel.[5]

The second selection of poems was delivered to the bookstores on November 9, 1891. The sales were good even if they did not match those of the first volume.[6] With the exception of the cover, which was now white with a light green spine and strip instead of gray, the layout corresponded exactly to that of its predecessor and generally found favor. The Indian Pipe put forth fancy blossoms variously identified as irises or as lilies of the valley. *The Literary World* recognized the design as the symbol for which it was perhaps intended and called it "the best criticism of Miss Dickinson's work."[7]

Compared to the first, this collection had been enlarged by one third. In the process, the sections "Life" and "Nature" grew from 26 to 57 and from 31 to 51 poems, respectively, while "Time and Eternity" (from 40 to 42 poems) and "Love" (from 18 to 16 poems) scarcely changed. The quality remained almost constant. The first poem ("I'm nobody! Who are you") and the last ("Lay this laurel on the one"), both of which stood out due to their positioning, attracted increased attention; regarding all others the statement was still valid that "one is prompted to quote the whole book."[8] Readers looked for the best examples but did not believe that they could do justice to the total effect of the volume. "Of the quality of these poems it is difficult to give an idea by the aid of selections," wrote a reviewer in *The Chicago Tribune*. "Their effect is cumulative."[9]

Once again the book was in most cases treated in omnibus reviews. While most critics were happy to be able to turn to Emily Dickinson, others proceeded to poets more perfect in form with a sigh of relief.[10] Once again the uncertainty of the attempts at characterization betrayed itself in designations such as "strange" and "queer." Nevertheless, expressions such as "force," "candor," "directness," "subtle charm," and Mrs. Todd's "simplicity" appeared with greater frequency and firmness. Once again one sought a footing by quoting from the preface, which occasioned fewer discussions than did Higginson's.

As in the previous year, the press responded promptly and spiritedly. Yet the attraction and the shock of the poetry were felt less strongly than in 1890, and after five months attention decreased. The first notices came from Springfield and Boston. The Springfield paper, which in the course of a year had visibly warmed toward the local poet, wrote on the day before the appearance of the book: "What is all that the makers of rondeaux and sonnets, who are so numerous, can do beside these irregular verses that throb with human and divine life? Criticise till you are gray, ye Zoiluses of dots and predicates and accurate rhymes, you will never know what makes Emily Dickinson a poet, since you do not demand ideas, but neat arrangements of words."[11] *The Boston Budget* struck an effusive note: "The first volume of those unique, wonderful poems . . . thrilled the reading world with a sense of surprise, delight and critical inquiry. Diamonds in the rough they were, but preëminently diamonds and not paste. The second series needs little heralding. The bare announcement of its publication will incite the eager response of thousands of readers in both this country and England."[12] In reality, there were far fewer readers in England than in the United States, and John Bull's critical echo regarding the second series of poems was completely lacking. The critics were also in complete disagreement about the reception of the first volume. If the majority spoke in terms of "well received," of "instant and hearty recognition and approval," and even of "admiration," there were other voices which remembered an extremely unfriendly reception. And the "eager response of thousands of readers" remained to be seen.

At first the critics drew comparisons with the first volume of poems. *The Springfield Republican, The Nation,* and *The Christian Intelligencer* considered the new poems quite as remarkable as the earlier ones; *The Literary World* saw its first impression deepened in every respect, but *The Catholic World* retrenched: "In this new volume the shocks of keen pleasure come less often, and lines that cling to the memory, and pictures that seize and pre-empt some hitherto unsettled corner in the brain, are indefinitely fewer."[13] Boston's *Courier* came upon "more of the faults and fewer of the virtues" than in the other volume, and *The Christian Register* concealed its disappointment behind polite verbosity: "We have wondered a good deal whether, if this second series had appeared first, it would have made the profound impression made by the first. We hardly think it would. To say that this is the gleaning after the other's reaping would be to differentiate it too widely from that for truth and for the honor it deserves. Possibly, to seem as good as the first series, the second must have been better. It is not quite so good."[14] *The Overland Monthly* was of the same opinion: "There is in it a too evident desire on the part of the compiler to meet the demand, rather than the higher canons of literary taste." In other words, it should have remained unprinted. That was exactly what the New York *World* thought: "It is questionable if the admirers of Miss Dickinson's experimental vagaries have done wisely in spreading her posthumous crudities before the public."[15] The gruffest rejection came from *The Critic*, whose reviewer experienced as paralyzing monotony what had pleasantly affected his colleague of *The Chicago Tribune* as a "cumulative effect": "A thought may be striking, but the stroke should not be fatal. After reading two volumes of Miss Dickinson's poems one gets exhausted, and a healthy mind begins to fear paralysis. There is too much of the same thing in them—morbid feeling, jerky and disjointed writing, and occasional faults of grammar. . . . It is their lack of grammatical correctness and their absolute formlessness which keeps them almost outside the pale of poetry."[16]

Mrs. Todd's suggestion that the poems be regarded as rough drafts had a beneficial influence on the criticism. With the notion of gaining an insight into the poet's workshop, the possibilities of explanation and familiarity with the work grew. The differentiation between sketch and finished picture stimulated *The Nation* to make the comment that a good poem is usually the result of long labor and reaches its highest degree of perfection by proceeding from the rough draft through an intermediate stage. The peculiarity of Emily Dickinson's compositions supposedly consisted in the fact that almost all had remained in that stage. "Up to the point where she left them, her chief solicitude had clearly been with the phrase, not with the verse or the line. . . . The minor changes required to perfect a rhyme or to avoid a repetition were sometimes postponed for some moment of leisure, it may be, or in other cases spurned as unimportant." The *Boston Transcript* also quoted the passage from the preface and further developed the idea of the "charm of the workshop—of the world behind the scenes." According to the reviewer, the charm of being able to watch the artist in her creative moments consisted in the proximity of the observer to the object observed. "The half-finished sketches of an old master, revealing where here a line was contemplated and there a line was erased, have a subtler fascination for latter-day artists than have all the treasures of the Uffizi." This is also true in the case of the New England poet and her verses: "Their very lack of finish has in it compensation, in added nearness to the singer's personality."

The passage from the preface once again allowed the question of form to arise incidentally, concerning which Boston's *Traveller* remarked: "Perhaps revision would have bettered the form, but might this not have been at the expense of strength?" Still, advocates like Chamberlain could now interpret the false or lacking rhymes, which so detracted from formal perfection, as simple omissions or as provisional features in lyrical sketches instead of attributing them to inability.[17]

In the renewed discussion of poetic form scarcely any progress became evident. Formal acknowledgment of the new Muse was tantamount to catching one's own shadow. The liveliness with which this very point was taken up again and again pointed to an unsolved and, for the present, insoluble problem. The familiar either-or attitude remained predominant. Howells' declaration that Emily Dickinson's work had an autonomous form had little effect. A few examples may suffice for clarification. *The Congregationalist* regretted: "It is a sad pity when the substance of true poetry is put at a disadvantage by the writer's recklessness in respect to form. . . . Her verses are fragmentary in thought and often clumsy in expression, and they pay small heed to rhyme and meter. Yet they are poetry. There is no denying that honestly." The structure of the poems displays an "intellectual," even a "moral defect" and represents a "permanent blemish." *The Chautauquan* found the extemporized verses "sometimes crude but always vivid" and said about the rhythm: "She runs over rhythm as a horse jumps a hedge, with a bracing if not smooth effect." *The Book Buyer* mentioned "a weird power and even fascination" in spite of the unusual form, and *The Christian Union* invited its readers: "If Miss Dickinson elected . . . to be 'nobody,' a fresh, unconventional, unhampered nobody, why, let us accept her as such, and admire her candid fancy with not too much reference to the great crudities of her work."[18]

A new formal association was discovered on December 26, 1891, in the *Boston Commonwealth*. Arthur Chamberlain, who as an advocate of Emily Dickinson took over the role previously played by Chadwick, rebutted the reproach of fragmentariness. According to him, the fragmentary character of the verse is an epigrammatic conciseness bordering on shorthand. "Indeed, many of the poems seem survivals from the 'Fantastic School' so-called, for strange comparisons and singular conceits abound; but they are not idle bits of laborious commonplace fretted into unwholesome prominence; they are rather descriptions of almost scientific exactness." Except for Higginson's allusion to "a curious seventeenth-century flavor" in the poem "A death blow is a life blow to some," which he had made in his essay of October 1891 (p. 455), this is the first general comparison with the form of the metaphysical poets, who were then better known by Milton's label and, as a group, were not exactly revered. This may be the reason why Chamberlain immediately precluded a too far-reaching comparison with a careful "but" in order to distinguish Emily Dickinson from the whimsical doings of the Fantastics and to show how suitably and precisely her art was capable of describing concrete objects. That such precaution was not ill-advised can be gathered from the catalogue of poetic vices compiled thirteen years previously by Moses Coit Tyler, who had denied John Donne and his compeers "harmony, taste, dignity, even decency" and had complained that Anne Bradstreet had become infected with this "literary disease."[19] Chamberlain also remained the only one during the reception of the second series who conceded that "each poem is a genuine whole," although he subsequently raised the question of literary form in general and tended to evaluate lack of rhyme as "a drawback to perfection . . . in these poems."

Chamberlain's parallel, which served the formal elucidation of Emily Dickinson's work, remained the sole new comparison. The search for similarities and possible influences abated. Mrs. Todd's allusion to impressionist painting was mentioned here and there, but her reference to "rugged" Wagner ignited no spark of recognition. Emerson, the favorite of the previous year, reappeared, but *Light* voiced a widespread opinion when it declared: "She has imitated no one, has invaded no one's domain."

Hardly anything new was said about the groups of poems. The critics still felt most at home with the nature poems. The small number of love poems was noticed, "as if the author's little tale of experience, in that direction, were soon told," as *The Nation* speculated on October 15, 1891. But the attempts to understand Emily Dickinson as a New England and American poet led one step further.

In order to appreciate the poet within her native tradition it seemed necessary to be acquainted with the region and its people. The Amherst student Schauffler, a Worcester periodical, and Chamberlain, the Boston critic, carried on Howells' and Samuel Ward's trains of thought. Schauffler referred to the "sturdy New England patriotism" in "My country need not change her gown" and recognized the portrait of a New England preacher:

> *He preached upon 'breadth' till it argued him narrow,*
> *The broad are too broad to define;*
> *And of 'truth' until it proclaimed him a liar,—*
> *The truth never flaunted a sign*

as "so typical of that large and ever-growing class of to-day, our would-be broad thinkers." At the same time, two attempts were made to explain Emily Dickinson's work biographically. *Light* relied on statements made by relatives of the poet still living in Worcester—presumably the sons of her uncle William Dickinson —and doubted that her poetic gift stemmed from the family of her father, "that sternest of Puritans": "Whence came this ability to express her thoughts in verse? Not even a Galton could find any reason for it among her paternal ancestors. Metered Psalms would include about all the poetry that they cared for; but when we turn to the Norcrosses, her maternal relatives, we find literary taste and activity that readily accounts for her own devotion. Not that the Dickinsons were not highly intellectual . . . but prose realities rather than poetic fancies filled their minds." Behind Chamberlain's reflections, which went the opposite way, lay a lecture given by Mrs. Todd on February 13, 1892, in the Kensington Hotel in Boston. In the lecture she had spoken about the strict, Puritan upbringing of the poet. "Calvinism is a somewhat gnarly tree," Chamberlain wrote, "but its core is as sound as eternal righteousness can make it, and the recent graft of liberal thought bears some wonderfully fine olives. This may explain that real reverence which underlies the most startling of Miss Dickinson's utterances. . . . Nor will it be difficult for the discerning mind to discover in that same Calvinistic inheritance the reason for the hatred of cant and sham which is conspicuous in all of Miss Dickinson's writings." While *Light* regarded the poet's paternal heritage as artistically barren, Mrs. Todd and Chamberlain saw her as an "orchid" grafted on the Puritan family tree, "another illustration of that sweetness which comes out of strength," as Chamberlain concluded.[20]

By linking her name with that of Walt Whitman attention was called to the problematic development of American literature. In 1891, shortly before his death, Whitman was no less notorious than he was admired. Although completely different from Emily Dickinson, his very controversiality sooner or later had to invite a comparison. In March 1891, *Scribner's Magazine* had found formal fault with both of them; *The Amherst Record* believed the genius of the good gray poet had found an echo among the Hampshire hills, "and yet not an echo, rather an answer." One month earlier Arlo Bates had been surprised that it had occurred to no one to consider the place of both in American literature since both belonged to the same class:

> They are both instances of the development of the sentiment and of the feeling so rapidly and so highly that the acquirement of a technique becomes impossible. It is a natural result of the hot-bed system upon which the intellectual development of this country has gone on. When one considers the brief time that has elapsed since Longfellow was the idol of the American public and reflects how he has taken his proper place, one is furnished with a sort of measure for the rapidity of the pace at which we have been going forward. To master the technical side of art, one must have the sensibilities under control, and it is difficult to master form in a society where everything is ripened so rapidly.
>
> In the case of both we have the melancholy spectacle of a mind gifted with great originality and with genuine imagination missing its best fruition through the failure to handle to the best advantage the art in which it worked.[21]

This comprehensive, though short, cultural-genetic attempt at explanation is an exception. The journalists of the early 1890's had little occasion in their book reviews to worry about the development of national literature. Even the literary historians' consciousness of living in a "national era" was not reflected in the handbooks. They subdivided the entire American literary scene into geographical and cultural sections and contented themselves with depicting the interrelationship and succession of the already famous.

What was actually new in the reception of 1891 and 1892 lay in another area. No matter how the critics evaluated Emily Dickinson, they began to think about the continued attraction of her verse for the readers. Each new printing placed before them the problem of the "secret of the magnetic charm her work undeniably has for the thoughtful reader," as the *Boston Transcript* stated. They tried to get at the bottom of this secret by studying her "methods" or by simply beginning to explicate individual poems.

In his long essay, Schauffler mainly investigated the method and the aim of her work. The method he considered just as natural as it was simple: "A striking thought would come to her mind; instantly it was jotted down . . ." (p. 175). In this way the poet collected hundreds of "untold, prosy thoughts, . . . almost too self-made for classification." And just as she had this one method at her disposal, she also had only one aim, "an aim which might well be called a strong, introspective thought-gathering." Hence her poetry is "a rare legacy of rare thought" (p. 176), which eludes a superficial formal criticism. On December 5, 1891, *Light* compared her manner of writing with the flight of the hummingbird described by her: "Like the humming bird . . . she goes from thought to thought; just a sip here and a dip there, the reader, all the time, admiring the implied thought, the scene just hinted at." For her, as for Poe, a long poem was an absurdity. Her brevity, achieved by omitting nonessentials, reminded *The Christian Register,* as it had Chamberlain, of "a compactness verging on an algebraic notation of ideas," of shorthand. The thought suggested that even her grammar, which remained a stumbling block, might obey the law of utmost succinctness. "Even her peculiarities of grammar," commented *The Nation* on October 15, 1891, "seem like mere short cuts or abbreviations, as when one takes notes in shorthand."

The attempts to penetrate deeper into this seemingly strange poetry led occasionally to beginning interpretations. They were restricted to the explication of verbal obscurities, since the critics thought that Emily Dickinson had worked on perfecting the language in the intermediate stage in which she had left her poems. *The Nation* quoted "Triumph may be of several kinds" as an example of "verbal felicities," yet there was only one interpreter who pointed out that the poet possessed what almost the entire reading world denied her—form. On December 19, 1891, *The Critic* had spoken of the first selection of poems as "a volume of curiously formless poems." On January 9, 1892, a New York English professor protested in a letter to the editor: "Miss Dickinson's poems may be formless, or they may be worded to so fine and subtle a device that they seem formless, just as the spectrum of a far-off star may seem blankness until examined with a lens of especial power." The aid of such a lens enabled him to recognize the spectrum of one of the poems ("I died for beauty") when he pointed out the close connection between thought content (the disturbed harmony of truth and beauty in this world) and the phonetic, rhythmic, and syntactic construction of the three stanzas.[22] Stoddard's attempt at interpretation remained an exception for a long time and would well have suited *The Explicator* even sixty years later.

The reception of the second series was predominantly friendly although critical opinion was divided about the prospects for the permanence of the work. The British camp was silent. Only Andrew Lang let himself be heard, this time because Higginson had irked him. Toward the end of 1891, the latter had published a collection of essays which had resulted from the endeavor "to assist in creating a modest and reasonable self-respect for American literature." In this collection, among others, Arnold's criticism of America was rejected and Kipling was commented upon. Nothing could come more opportunely for Lang. He poked fun at Higginson's "national self-consciousness" and his "strainings at the gnats of English colloquialisms while swallowing the dromedary of Miss Dickinson's grammar."[23] The most prominent opponent of Emily Dickinson in these months was the aging Thomas Bailey Aldrich. Reputed to be one of the great successors of the New England patriarchs, equally honored as a writer of prose, poetry, and criticism, he had passed as the touchstone of good taste during his editorship of the *Atlantic* (1880-90). As a poet and aesthete he represented a rigid formalism. "The things that have come down to us, the things that have *lasted*, are perfect in form," he once wrote to his friend Edmund Stedman. "I believe many a fine thought has perished being inadequately expressed, and I know that many a light fancy is immortal because of its perfect wording."[24] His overestimation of "craftsmanship" and "distinction of form" is encountered also in his poetry—as in "Art":

> *The workmanship wherewith the gold is wrought*
> *Adds yet a richness to the richest gold:*
> *Who lacks the art to shape the thought, I hold,*
> *Were little purer if he lacked the thought*

and in "On Reading—":

> *Great thoughts in crude, unshapely verse set forth*
> *Lose half their preciousness and ever must.*
> *Unless the diamond with its own rich dust*
> *Be cut and polished, it seems little worth.*[25]

On such aesthetic principles, Emily Dickinson had to founder. "*In Re* Emily Dickinson"[26] begins by declaring her work a poetic chaos. Through strict discipline she would have become "an admirable lyric poet of the second magnitude." In order to show how her poetry would have looked in that case, he makes use of the first stanza of "I taste a liquor never brewed," a poem which had already displeased others before him, tosses it until a rhyme falls out, and places it before his readers with the request not to accuse him of overrating Emily Dickinson. He changed

> I taste a liquor never brewed,
> From tankards scooped in pearl;
> Not all the vats upon the Rhine
> Yield such an alcohol!

to read

> I taste a liquor never brewed
> In vats upon the Rhine;
> No tankards ever held a draught
> Of alcohol like mine.

Aldrich was later repeatedly reproached for this well-known desecration, which exemplifies what he understood by form: rhyme, transparent imagery, logical succession of thought. In his version the ambiguous connection and the difficult image of the second line have vanished.

In his evaluation of Emily Dickinson he assumes a sympathetic-condescending tone, concedes to her "much fancy of a queer sort," but denies her imagination and, hence, true creative ability. He censures Higginson's friendliness, which he ascribes to his usual, out-of-place gallantry toward female poetic talents.[27] The tone of annoyance (he speaks of "whimsical memoranda," "eccentric, dreamy, half-educated," and so on) and the ironic-polemical jibes would have done Lang honor. His closing remarks resemble Lang's rejections and the anonymous writer in the March 1891, issue of *Scribner's:* "The substance is weighty enough, but the workmanship lacks just that touch which distinguishes the artist from the bungler. . . . If Miss Dickinson's *disjecta membra* are poems, then Shakespeare's prolonged imposition should be exposed without further loss of time, and Lord Tennyson ought to be advised of the error of his ways before it is too late. But I do not hold the situation to be so desperate. Miss Dickinson's verses have a queerness and a quaintness that have stirred a momentary curiosity in emotional bosoms. Oblivion lingers in the immediate neighborhood." With this condemnation Aldrich restores "the laws of gravitation and grammar" which she had set at defiance. His anonymous essay, which Higginson at first held to be the work of Agnes Repplier (*AB*, p. 187), would have had the same significance if the author had retitled it "*In Re* Thomas B. Aldrich," since it is a disguised self-justification. An affirmation of Emily Dickinson would have amounted to a rejection of his own theory and practice.

In the months of debate about the second selection of poetry falls a controversy which deserves brief mention. Miss Molly Elliot Seawell, a successful writer of short stories who lived in Washington, had categorically denied the female sex creative abilities in *The Critic* on November 28, 1891. This had aroused a storm of indignation which raged on in the letters-to-the-editor column until July 1892, and even yielded a letter from Dresden, Germany. On February 13, 1892, Emily Dickinson was cited as proof to the contrary. Higginson also argued against this thesis later, without, however, mentioning her. This once again lashed Miss Seawell into a fury. When the debate had progressed thus far, the ever-vigilant Andrew Lang strung his bow and simultaneously shot three poisonous darts at Emily Dickinson, at the Colonel, and at the young lady in Washington: "Miss Mollie [*sic*] Seawell is a young lady who sticks to her guns. Some months ago she boldly maintained the thesis that women, in art and literature, were no match for men. . . . But, lo! there came forth a champion from the camp of the men, the redoubtable Colonel Higginson, who was, as it were, the Columbus of Miss Dickinson, and discovered a continent of poetry where others had only seen a misty ocean of bad rhymes and bad grammar. The fair Penthesilea of common sense then girt on her armor, and she does battle with the Colonel in *The Critic*."[28]

Public interest in the second series of poems, as in the first, flagged after the lapse of a half year and was again revived only in the fall of 1894 by the publishing of the letters. To what extent private interest lived on can now hardly be determined beyond the acknowledgments and inquiries preserved in the Todd collection of the Amherst College Library. Yet there exist at least two testimonies from poets at the beginning and end of their careers, respectively. Young Edwin Markham, who was to become famous through "The Man with the Hoe" in 1898, wrote to a friend in 1892: "A new name has recently come into this kingly company. I refer to the Poems of Emily Dickinson, the Queen of the Quaint. Do you know of her? If not, arise at midnight, and go forth to find her books. She is quainter, if not stranger than Thoreau—than Landon—than Blake."[29] On March 14, 1893, the New England lyric poet Lucy Larcom wrote: "I have seen Emily Dickinson's poems, and enjoy their queer gleaming and shadowy incoherences. It does not seem as if her mind could have been fairly balanced. But her love of nature redeems many faults."[30]

Compared with her literary debut of 1890, the second appearance proceeded more equably and with less tension, not least because a British edition was dispensed with. Since the new poems resembled the old, people no longer took offense at the form. They remained welcome with friends. Yet even among the stalwarts a distinct fatigue became apparent which for the time being spoke against a third series of poems. The second auction had to content itself with a lower price.

The promotional efforts of the editors were restricted to six lectures by Mrs. Todd. The evening in Boston already mentioned was received with especial favor. Before a charged audience, of which Mrs. Moulton and Nathan Haskell Dole were a part, she read from unpublished letters and poems. She sought to counteract the current conception of Emily Dickinson as a disappointed, eccentric hermit by emphasizing her normally spent youth and by illustrating through anecdotes her humor. These efforts did little to the fabric of truth and fiction which had been woven not only in Amherst[31] but everywhere her poetry and life were discussed.

I V

WANING POPULARITY (1892-97)

We must look further west for the next harvest of letters. Meanwhile "requiescat in pace," Emily Dickinson, strange and lonely soul that you were![1]

FROM THE SUMMER OF 1892 until the fall of 1894 Emily Dickinson was scarcely mentioned in the press. On March 2, 1893, report came from Chicago that people in fashionable circles understood how to appreciate her poems in an "intelligent" manner by using them as social games. In October 1893 and 1894 comprehensive evaluations appeared in New Haven and Springfield, but contributed nothing new. Mrs. William Hawley Dickinson, the widow of a distant cousin of the poet who had died in 1883, published her reminiscences of Emily. Eight lectures of Mrs. Todd in small New England towns, Chicago, and New York round out the picture of these uneventful years.[2] A new impulse was necessary to bring the critical dialogue about Emily Dickinson into motion once again.

In her first enthusiasm about the external success of her work, Mrs. Todd had written to Higginson on December 16, 1890, that "some of Emilys letters *must* be published" (*AB*, p. 84). This was easier said than done. Many letters had been thoughtlessly destroyed by their recipients, and those which still existed were widely scattered. The difficult search, which began at the end of 1891, was often enough in vain, as it was for the letters to Helen Jackson which even the editor's trip to Colorado could not bring to light. Louisa and Frances Norcross, Emily's "little cousins," made only copies available. The letters to Susan Dickinson remained inaccessible. During the work on the edition of letters Mrs. Todd formed the plan of compiling a "Birthday

Book" of prose and poetry which was to contain a motto for every day in the year (*AB*, p. 201). As late as December 3, 1894, she wrote to Hardy of Roberts Brothers concerning an "Emily Dickinson Year Book": "My thought is that with isolated lines from the already published poems, many of which are perfect comets of thought, and some of these wonderful epigrams from the *Letters*, together with a mass of *unpublished* lines . . . I could make the most brilliant year-book ever issued" (*AB*, p. 311). This plan was realized much later by Helen Arnold's *An Emily Dickinson Year Book* in 1948.

The collection of letters was ready in the summer of 1893, but Niles advised putting off publication until the following year due to the depression (*AB*, p. 230). The two-volume edition of *Letters of Emily Dickinson* finally appeared on November 21, 1894, at the price of two dollars.[3] Mrs. Todd, who had worked without Higginson's assistance, was the sole editor.

The 345 letters are arranged in ten groups according to recipients. The accuracy of the text is difficult to judge, since most of the originals have been destroyed or are missing. In 77 letters considerable abridgments can be proven; 49 of the 58 letters to her brother are abridged. Since Austin also read the galley proofs, it cannot be determined who edited the text. These abridgments are insignificant in so far as they concerned affairs of everyday life, but these very omissions later contributed to the false conception of the poet's daily life as idle seclusion from the world. Emily Dickinson, who literally baked her father's daily bread, existed for critics and scholars as a hermit in the southwest room on the second floor of her parental home.

In the introduction Mrs. Todd adduced the urging of admirers and the necessity of correcting the one-sided conception of the person created by the poems as excuses for publishing the "deep revelations of a peculiarly shy inner life" (I, vi). "Emily Dickinson's verses, often but the reflection of a passing mood, do not always completely represent herself,—rarely, indeed, showing the dainty humor, the frolicsome gayety, which continually bubbled over in her daily life. The sombre and even weird outlook upon this world and the next, characteristic of many of the poems, was by no means a prevailing condition of mind; for, while fully apprehending all the tragic elements in life, enthusiasm and bright joyousness were yet her normal qualities" (I, v). In two places she compares the poet in her joyful self-sacrifice for the family and her simultaneous intellectual isolation with Emily Brontë. This seclusion determined her individual relationship to God and to society. She struck a critical, but not disrespectful, attitude toward her ancestral religion and observed the conventions of the world with amusement. Religious and social hypocrisy she rejected with determination.

Both volumes are furnished with a running commentary which includes biographical references, explanations of Emily Dickinson's epistolary quirks, and occasional comments on her verse and prose style:

> In the more carefully copied poems are many alterations, but it is a curious fact that not one change has reference to improvement in rhyme or rhythm. Every suggestion for a different word or phrase was in the evident hope that by some one of them the thought might be made clearer, and not in a single instance merely to smooth the form. (I, 268)
>
> Emily's prose style had developed its incisiveness—like her own thought, it went straight to the essence of things; and while still dressed in language sufficiently to pass in conventional places, it had gradually become divested of everything superfluous. (II, 367)
>
> Dr. Holmes somewhere says that rhymes "are iron fetters: it is dragging a chain and a ball to march under their encumbrance"; and if in Emily Dickinson's work there is frequently no rhyme where rhyme should be, a subtle something, welcome and satisfying, takes its place. (II, 439)

The critical resonance of the letters was weak, and the differences of opinion prophesied by *The Nation* were lacking. The announcements were generally uncritical and unoriginal, merely reporting and quoting. Mrs. Todd's introduction was accepted as authoritative.

The volumes were almost unanimously welcomed. *The New York Tribune*, which had already found fault with the poet and now fell on the letter writer with intensified dudgeon, was a characteristic exception: "We cannot say that the world of letters is greatly enriched by the publication of these two volumes. What is noteworthy in them could have been set forth easily in half the space. The range of ideas is high if narrow; there are repetitions in meaning and even in wording; and some of these halting and seemingly mystical phrases merely express what has been said better in many an ancient maxim and modern epigram. We are aware that in the vicinity of Boston vagueness is sometimes considered the mark of lofty intellect—an Olympian thundering behind the clouds; but the Boston 'fad' rarely takes rank as literature."

It struck several critics as embarrassing to see private letters exposed to the common view. "It is . . . a mean trick to publish private correspondence . . . of . . . poor little wayside, woodland Emily Dickinson," objected Mary Abbott, and *The Springfield Republican* felt "that the shy and elusive creature is intruded upon, and for our part, we are inclined humbly to beg pardon."[4] While looking around for comparable indiscretions, the critics remembered the *journaux intimes* of Henri-Frédéric Amiel, the pensive Geneva professor, and of Marie Bashkirtseff, the Russian princess who had died at an early age. The *Boston Daily Advertiser* emphasized the human value of the letters: "There may be extravagance in these letters, overstatement, but there is thought, high, subtle, delicate. These letters will be read, quoted, will find their place in books and selections. They will comfort bereaved ones; they will help, they will stimulate. These two volumes are among the books of the year."[5]

The arrangement according to correspondents found more criticism than praise. It reduced the autobiographical value of the letters since the history of Emily Dickinson's life receded behind that of her friendships. "Instead of having in unbroken order a series of documents illustrating the changing ideals and thoughts of the writer from early youth to maturity, one is presented with disjointed sequences, overlapping each other in several instances relating to almost identical epochs."[6] The grouping was considered unfavorable especially because readers regarded the volumes as "a companion to her poetry," "an admirable complement to her poems," and "very deeply interesting as reflecting Emily Dickinson." "It is chiefly as revelation of character that we attach importance to . . . the two volumes," wrote *The Outlook*.[7]

The aesthetic charm of the letters as literature had to give way to interest in, and mere curiosity about, the author. What readers had missed in the prefaces and essays of Higginson and had again and again publicly demanded and privately pleaded for since 1890, they now tried to read out of the correspondence as a source of biographical information. The equivocal personal background behind the poems had only heightened the suspense. Disappointment was not lacking. "Most of the letters are strangely impersonal," the *Boston Home Journal* determined, "coming from a recluse whose solitude must largely have been spent in introspection." "They do not give much biographic information," wrote *The Telegraph* in Philadelphia, "and indeed there was apparently pathetically little to give."[8] Those felt disappointed most who, like *The Book Buyer* and *Public Opinion*, had expected "the tangible solution of her many mysteries."

The conclusions drawn from the letters about the person of the author were for the most part contradictory. While Caroline Dall believed she recognized the "real Emily" in the childhood letters—"joyous, sportive, a bit priggish, very precocious, and quite willing to encounter the world's gaze"—most reviewers decided that the later letters were the characteristic ones. Several felt attracted by the human warmth of the writer; nevertheless, *The Nation* regretted: "Her attitude is depressingly superior. She does not abuse her neighbors enough to love them tenderly."[9] Humor predominated for the *Boston Home Journal*; Mrs. Jordan wrote: "One cannot help wishing that the writer's sense of humor had been more persistently indulged, or, perhaps, less persistently translated into paradox." *The Spy* and *The Literary World* did not entirely believe Mrs. Todd's assurance that "frolicsome gayety" was Emily Dickinson's element:

> Yet, self-sustained as she seems invariably to have been, one gets the impression that an unusual amount of sadness clouded her life.[10]
>
> . . . yet such sensitiveness as clearly was Emily Dickinson's means great capacity for suffering.[11]

The Dial declared that the morbid nature sporadically recognizable in the poems did not appear in the letters; the *San Francisco Chronicle* and *The Nation* maintained the opposite:

> The "Letters of Emily Dickinson" . . . furnishes as curious a study of morbid character as the journals of Amiel.[12]
>
> These letters . . . are suggestive studies in applied Lombroso.

The critics' fantasy dwelt most of all upon the riddle of Emily Dickinson's growing isolation from the surrounding world, a phenomenon which Mrs. Todd had interpreted as a natural development. In her withdrawn way of life, *The Literary World* saw an instinctive self-defense against the blows of fate. Mrs. Dall, who wrote from Washington, endeavored to arrange the letters and poems to form a "story" in order to prove the ex-

istence of the officially contested beau: "If we could have all
the letters written in 1854, during and after her visit in Washington, printed chronologically, I think we should be able to read
the story." She had the story from an unnamed relative of Emily.
" 'It was in Washington,' said her friend to me, 'that Emily met
her fate. Her father absolutely refused his consent to her marriage for no reason that was ever given.' " This passage contains
the beginning of the love legend later played up by Martha
Dickinson Bianchi, although it is here mixed with features of the
local Amherst version.

On the prose style the critics commented more in passing.
It showed "preternatural compression and point" and was "terse,
suggestive, original as her verse"[13]:

> It is the farthest possible remove from the delightfully
> diffuse correspondence of some of the famous letter writers
> of her sex, to the condensed, sublimated missives of Emily
> Dickinson.
>
> Words were no mere counters with her, but the coin of the
> realm; and she brought it to a rigid test.
>
> The poems and letters of Emily Dickinson were not the
> outcome of a narrow Puritan education . . . but rather of a
> prophetic insight. Some subtle instinct taught her that the
> last thought of the century would be—condensation.
>
> She aimed to reach the exact expression which she wanted
> to use, and she often dropped into verse in writing a letter.
>
> She was an impressionist of the first magnitude, and whatever
> was unconventional and went straight to its object drew
> her at once.
>
> She is still the poet in these letters of hers—responsive, elusive,
> suggestive, enigmatical often, yet always touching a deep
> spring in her reader's heart.[14]

Compression and concision were indeed the striking characteristics noted everywhere.

The prose diction with its kinship to that of the poems
suggested the designation "prose stanzas"; the occasionally under-
laid poetic rhythm was evaluated as proof of a natural talent for
writing verse. This rhythm reminded one of the descriptive passages of Blackmore's *Lorna Doone*. So the remark was obvious
that the letters presented the critic with the same problems as
the poems and that one could not make do with "well-worn
formulas that fit most books." And yet the reviewers generally

contented themselves with the store of formulas which had been applied to the poems since 1890.

One small controversy interrupted the almost unanimous praise of the prose style. *The Spy* had stressed the spontaneity of the letters, and *The Critic* carried the thought further by defining this term as "the need to speak." By contrast, the *New York Tribune*, *The Nation*, and *The Congregationalist* argued for the view that the facsimile of a rough draft of a letter to Helen Jackson printed in the second volume spoke for stilted affectation:

> We are inclined to doubt, however, whether the neatest strokes were quite unpremeditated. Some of them show a careful carelessness.
>
> In the longer efforts . . . there is a sense of strain and consciousness, not to call it affectation, as if the solitary instance of a rough draft adduced by Mrs. Todd were not the only one.
>
> If the existence of this corrected rough draft be proof of the habit of thus revising such familiar letters, the author can hardly be acquitted of some measure of intellectual affectation. . . . It is probable that she deliberately cultivated eccentricity.[15]

As in the evaluations of her stylistic art, comparisons and attempts at classification moved within the circle of what had been said about the poems previously. The rather superficial connection with her namesake Emily Brontë was repeated at times, but not explained. Twice there appeared a new comparison with Jones Very, whose posthumous volumes of poems (1883) and essays (1886) might still be weakly remembered. But here, too, the basis for comparison—originality and, hence, a difference in kind—was accidental.

The notes of uniqueness and commonness sounded with equal strength. "A personality is here revealed which has, perhaps, no counterpart in literary history," judged *The Boston Herald*, and *The Critic* followed: "Mrs. Todd . . . has given to American literature a unique book." The opposite side was represented by the Philadelphia *Public Ledger*, which placed the letters within the intellectual movement of Transcendentalism, and the *San Francisco Chronicle*, which spoke of the "outpourings of [an] emotional nature, held in close check by a cold New England temperament."

Between these extremes there began to emerge a new way of

thinking which no longer understood Emily Dickinson's life and work as fulfillment and refinement of the New England tradition, but as a protest against social and religious conditions. *The Boston Herald* was of this conviction: "She was eminently a religious person, but she took religion in her own way. It was not that of the narrow New England village where she lived, but the language of a free and liberal spirit, who believed that God was near and familiar and pervasive." *The Dial* developed the idea of the poet's partial break with the tradition of her native Pioneer Valley in greater detail:

> The conscience of New England half a century ago demanded much of its votaries and adherents. The limitations which it set about human intelligence and activity were many and certain. Its intense assurance of its own completeness and rectitude had its incommodities as well as its insights and rewards. To those who could acquiesce in its demands, it opened avenues to spiritual heights whence the outlook was large and superb, though the air might be somewhat thin for the health of daily life. At last, however, the burdens it imposed became too severe for a generation alive to much that was outside of its enclosed space, and the revolt began.
>
> It seems that valuable literatures usually begin with such revolts, and the stronger spirits, after considerable efforts and some suffering, throw off the fetters no longer endurable, and rejoice in the larger freedom which they have won. There are always, however, sensitive souls who feel that they must break with the traditions, but cannot find themselves wholly at home in the new and strange. Among the latter must be counted such writers as Emily Dickinson, as well as the Concord recluse, William Ellery Channing.[16]

Interest in the *Letters of Emily Dickinson* was exhausted within four months. Several lectures of Mrs. Todd in towns of Massachusetts produced no broad effect.

Between April 1895 and September 1896, when the third series of poems was published, only six essays and notices can be found (cf. Sources, p. 286). The editor herself began with a critical investigation which found its way into the first issue of a newly founded fugitive magazine after it had been rejected by *The Century*. A mainly biographical essay by Mary J. Reid strung together a baker's dozen of American woman poets, among whom were Helen Jackson, Celia Thaxter, Harriet Monroe, and Emily Dickinson, without establishing any connection between them. The attempt at a "Fresh Reading" in the Boston *Transcript* on July 11, 1895, contented itself, despite its promising title, with quoting nature poems and drawing on old critical sources. In the fall of that year, Mrs. William Hawley Dickinson once again took up her pen. For those among her readers to whom Emily Dickinson was still unknown, Grace Musser gave a short introduction to the work of the New England poet on September 20, 1896, in *The San Francisco Call.* Finally, in a review of the fragments of Sappho which had been translated into English by H. T. Wharton, Rupert Hughes turned against her exaggerated cult and proposed Mrs. Browning, Christina Rossetti, and Emily Dickinson as possible rivals, the last with an incorrectly quoted "fragment" and a reference to her "large pantheism and fellowship with nature."[17]

The critics mentioned Emily Dickinson's name in passing when the thin volume of poems by Stephen Crane, *The Black Riders, and Other Lines* (1895), ran the gauntlet of a predominantly hostile press and occasionally was decried as blasphemous. The boldness of the design reminded the reviewer in *The Atlantic* of an intellect like hers; the brevity and rhymelessness appeared to *The Nation*'s critic (very probably Higginson) "as of a condensed Whitman or an amplified Emily Dickinson."[18]

In this placid intermediate period a little-noted sidelight falls on Emily Dickinson's work and readers. Father Tabb (1845-1909), the Virginian lyric poet and wartime friend of Sidney Lanier, who became known through his *Poems* (1894) and *Lyrics* (1897), belonged with her admirers and was himself compared with her. On December 31, 1894, he wrote to John W. Chadwick, who was at the moment working on a review of his *Poems:* "Among my Xmas presents came a copy of Miss Dickinson's Poems, one or two only of which I had seen. I began at first to mark the thoughts 'that take one's breath away' & found I had 'italicized as 'twere' one half of the volume. I know not where so much before is said in such a compass. The thoughts project beyond the lines & leave the jagged ends. No wonder rhymes are missing" (*AB*, p. 315). In the last two sentences the writer himself falls into the characteristic Dickinson meter.

On May 23, 1895, Higginson compared "the celibate woman and the celibate priest" in the anonymous review column of *The Nation* because the work of both seemed to him to be curiously related: "There are pages here which might as well have appeared in either of her volumes—the same fine, shy, recluse observation of nature and of men, and the same terse brevity of utterance." As examples he quoted Tabb's "The Tax-Gatherer" as well as Emily Dickinson's and Tabb's hummingbird poems.[19] The comparison turned out in the New Englander's favor: "The woman's characterization is far more terse and vigorous, with more of motion and of color; she does not, like the man, sentimentalize a little bit over the blossom and the wooer, but who can help seeing the analogy?"[20]

In August 1896, *The Bookman* congratulated Tabb on the extraordinary success of his *Poems* and added: "Mr. Wilson, of the University Press, declares that with one exception never in so short a time they had to print so many copies of a first book by an American poet. The exception was Emily Dickinson; and it is a curious coincidence that Father Tabb should have said recently that 'of late American poets there is none worthy to go down to posterity except Emily Dickinson.'"[21]

On July 15, 1896, Tabb compared her with the well-known Boston lyricist Louise Imogen Guiney (1861-1920) and said of the latter: "She writes with ability but wears a 'learned sock' which mars her poetry. Miss Dickinson, on the contrary, with all her want of polish, 'teases out of thought' as does Keats' *Grecian Urn*, and is, I think, the strongest of the later Yankee bards." Until December 7, 1901, mention can still be found in his letters of his favorite poet whom he placed above the celebrated name of the day on the date mentioned above: "In my opinion Markham is a baby beside her; a quotation of hers has sometimes more in it than I have found in 'The Man with the Hoe.' "[22]

With this, a small circle closes which shows that Emily Dickinson lived on in the consciousness of the 1890's even if critics did not always write of her.

As early as July 1891 Mrs. Todd had begun the compilation of a third volume of selected poetry but did not discuss the matter with her coeditor until the fall of 1895. Since Higginson was sick, she alone took over the work as she had with the letters. The manuscript went to Roberts Brothers on December 31, 1895, but *Poems by Emily Dickinson, Third Series* did not appear until eight months later.[23] The short preface restricted itself essentially to an explanation of the reasons for another culling: "The intellectual activity of Emily Dickinson was so great that a large and characteristic choice is still possible among her literary material, and this third volume of her verses is put forth in response to the repeated wish of the admirers of her peculiar genius" (p. vii).

Textually, this volume was the zenith of "creative editing." Millicent Todd Bingham, who owned the manuscript of the third series, sought to conceal the number of changes made by her mother when she wrote: "My mother did alter the wording of some of the poems" (*AB*, p. 335). She cites five rather innocuous examples and adds an explanation which in reference to the first volume would have sounded genuine, but for the third seems threadbare: "In my mother's defense I should repeat that she did these things to protect Emily. The dose must not be too strong. Even after the smoothing-off process the waywardness of the poems was still offensive to many readers" (*AB*, p. 337). In reality Mrs. Todd, who was fully in command, took greater liberties than could previously be observed with the team of editors. She probably even devised most of the titles for more than half of the poems (92 of 168), although Higginson also contributed again.

Of the 168 poems no fewer than 89 deviate from Mrs. Todd's correctly made copies of the originals. Frequent omission of part of a stanza, of a stanza, even the omission of four stanzas are new above all. An explanation of the motives for the eighteen abridgments would require a special investigation. Did these verses belong for the editor to those "poems which could never be used entire" (*AB*, p. 311)? Or was it important to her—true to the statement of Mrs. Reid that "the last thought of the century would be—condensation"—to accent the epigrammatic qualities of Emily Dickinson even more strongly by such abridgments?

Although Mabel Loomis Todd valued grammatical correctness more highly than rhymes, she nevertheless snatched up her red pencil forty-three times in order to improve the art of her charge in this respect. Thirteen subjunctive forms were changed into indicatives. Five times a "be" became an "is," "are," or "was." The rhythm was found displeasing in two cases. In fifty-four instances small corrections were made which mean little, but sometimes allow the intention to be clearly recognized. The "ruddier Blue" in one spot seemed to have more meaning as "ruddier hue"; since blossoms can, by some stretch of the imagination, be "rowed" but never "sown," "And row my blossoms o'er" replaced "And sow by blossoms o'er"; "receipt" as a verb tasted too much of American business which explains why "A transport may receive us" seemed more pleasing than "A Transport may receipt us"; where Emily Dickinson had written "to take the trick," it could easily be transposed to the more idiomatic "to learn the trick." A further correction is suggestive:

> *Infects my simple spirit*
> *With Taints of Majesty*

became

> *It paints my simple spirit*
> *With tints of Majesty.*

Two word substitutions made an elegant painting metaphor out of an unpleasant sickness metaphor. In three poems the transpositions were considerable and distorting.[24]

This summary examination shows that Mrs. Todd went far beyond the earlier polishings. To types of changes deemed necessary in 1890 and 1891 out of consideration for the reading public she added new ones. Did she perhaps believe that through her long service to Emily Dickinson she had penetrated her work to such an extent that she could improve it? The doings of his "junior editor" did not, at any rate, escape Higginson. In his anonymous omnibus review in *The Nation* on October 8, 1896, he remarked: "It is noticeable, also, that in a few of the poems . . . there is an unexampled regularity of form, beyond anything to be found in the earlier volumes."[25]

One week before the distribution of the volume, the *New York Tribune* vented its general displeasure without taking up the poems, perhaps even without having read them at all:

> This is really too much. . . . While this may have some weight with "the admirers of her peculiar genius" who have asked for "more," we do not think it will appeal to a sober critic. . . . It is incredible, we repeat, that Mrs. Todd could have brought together enough verse to make a new collection. What she has really done, we suspect, has been to collect fragments or even complete poems which belong, as nine-tenths of Emily Dickinson's verses belong, to the sphere of casual, moody writing, to a class of verse which most poets . . . regard as mere trifles or experiments. Sometimes the genius, the great genius, can afford to print these trifles, once he has made his position secure; but a poet like

Emily Dickinson could never safely do any such thing. Her
vogue has passed—it was a temporary affair in its highest
estate—and now such reputation as she has among minor
lyrists is imperiled by the indiscretion of her executors.
Poor misunderstood authorship! How it must hunger in its
grave to be protected from its friends![26]

Other critics tuned their instruments to this dressing down of
both the editor and the poet. As they opened the book, astonishment at the large number of poems which had until then remained
unpublished was mixed with the presentiment that they might
not have been worth printing. "It was with misgivings that this
third volume of selections . . . was opened, misgivings that two
readings proved to have been only too well founded," stated the
Philadelphia *Telegraph,* whose critic resented Mrs. Todd's designation "admirers." In its place, he suggested "friends," since he
counted himself among the admirers without being able to ap-
prove of the new volume. Clarence Griffin Child also feared a
third series might mean a third-rate selection: "The fear is only
natural that the effect created by the previous volumes might
not be sustained and the admiration and love they excited be
chilled by dilution." The collection was considered a last harvest,
"a book of snatches and flashes rather than of complete embodi-
ments or thought-out or expressed ideas," which represented a
danger to the author's literary prestige since only few poems
equaled the best. "From each of the former volumes could be
culled a score of exquisite poems, but from this volume . . . but
seven," *The Telegraph* complained. *The Literary World,* which
had already been skeptical in 1890 and 1891, warned its readers:
"We recommend this book only to those who have liked its
predecessors."[27]

The attraction of newness had paled; in its place the impression of uniformity appeared the more strongly. Only a small
minority of voices, among which were *The Overland Monthly,*
The New York Sun, and the always enthusiastic Lilian Whiting,
welcomed the poems without qualification as an enrichment of
the canon:

There is no falling away in the originality and strength of
the selections in this later book, and at the same time there
is a lyric quality, a carefulness of finish . . . not found in the
earlier volumes. . . . The impression of the author given by
the first books was that she was not so much a writer of

73

poetry as one who had poetic thoughts, but without the power of giving them full expression. This third volume will go far toward removing the impression.

. . . whether she could have found in ordinary, regular methods of rhyming the vehicles which her thought required, whether she might or might not have been wiser had she omitted some strong expressions against orthodoxy, or whether she was irreverent at times or not, she is the solitary vital figure among American women who have ever appeared as versers, one of the four or five poetry-making women of the universe who have deserved universal recognition, and one of the chief poets of America.

There are books that are desirable, and a few that are indispensable, and it is perhaps among the latter that the lovers of poetic insight and philosophic thought will come to class the poems of Emily Dickinson.[28]

To most, this volume seemed a straggler—poorer, just as good, perhaps better than what people had read earlier by her. At any rate, it was easily classifiable since it was of the same species as the earlier ones and, depending on the value attached to her poetry, either a welcome or an infelicitous supplement. As a result the critics at such a late hour had little inclination to renew the debate. Merits and flaws were simply supported by quotations. Regarding preference for certain poems, the distribution of taste already observed once again made its influence felt. The poems "It dropped so low in my regard" and "There is no frigate like a book" found high praise, while the four-line poem beginning "Morning is the place for dew" was twice found fault with as an example of Dickinsonian obscurity. "When we come to such lines," commented *The Literary World*, "we feel ready to join the scoffers." And the *Chicago Journal* amusedly inquired: "Was the solitary poet wandering in mental nebula when she penned these words, or was her chirography an inscrutable mystery to her editor, who made what she could out of it?" Criticism and explanations exhausted themselves in occasional references to Emerson and Swinburne, in the statement that Emily Dickinson was a poet of the intellect and not of the heart, in the comment that the characteristic feature of the poems was their meter, in the rejection of the "shocking" grammar, in a short analysis of the metaphorical language of a poem. Concerning the intellectual heritage of the poet and the prospects for the permanence of her work, the reviewer of the *Chicago Journal* made some somber, dirge-like speculations:

> It is not probable that another sifting of her manuscripts will give Emily Dickinson's literary executors any more material worthy of publication, so that the time has come for the last word on this strange product of overcivilisation —for such, I hold, she was. She stands alone, apart from the other figures of our literature. She was not a part of a literary movement, nor do her poems mark an era. She is therefore a literary freak whose writings may tickle a jaded palate, but can have no permanent influence over a sane mind. Bloodless, disembodied, and unearthly, she represents the final effort of a once rich soil. New England brought forth Emerson, Lowell, Channing, Longfellow, Whittier, and the others of that splendid harvest of intellect, full-bodied, full-blooded, and strong. In a measure, the vitality has now gone out of the land, and in the gathering shade only the pale, sensitive, fragile Indian pipe blossom can push its waxen stem and flower, and Emily Dickinson, anemic, peculiar, burdened with too much genius, and too little flesh and blood, is the result.

As a center of culture, New England is leached out; Emily Dickinson, one of its overcultivated late blossoms, is given back to the past (cf. the epigraph of this chapter), and new lights are expected in the West.

The weak, colorless, and routine reception of the third volume of selected poetry is supplemented and balanced by four essays which surpass the small number of reviews in their extent and depth. They only concern themselves peripherally with *Poems* (1896); in the main, they deal with the problem of Emily Dickinson as it seemed six years after her appearance in American literature.

"Recent Poetry," the review Higginson wrote for the October 8, 1896, issue of *The Nation*, was his next to last comment on Emily Dickinson. As an aesthete, he had not changed his opinion even thirty-four years after his first acquaintance with his pupil. He spoke of the success of her poetry "in spite of all its flagrant literary faults." As an American, he resolutely came to her defense. With an eye toward *The Nation*'s overseas readers he took the icy reaction of British criticism in 1891 as an occasion to point out the inconsistent attitude toward her in comparison to Whitman—"The sole expressed objection to [her poems], in the English mind, lay in their . . . irregularities of manner; and yet these were not nearly so defiant as those exhibited by Whitman, who has always been more unequivocally accepted in England than at home"—and also to characterize her as a peculiarly American poet. He found a particular reason for British hostility in her use of native motifs. "What does an Englishman know of the bobolink, of the whippoorwill, the Baltimore oriole, even of the American robin or blue-jay?" he asked Andrew Lang without calling him by name. These natural poetic properties were recognized neither by the London press nor by certain American "cosmopolitans," who only acknowledged the conventional lark and nightingale. It was, however, becoming evident that the native poet was, in the last analysis, finding favor abroad. This was demonstrated by Whittier's popularity with British readers.[29]

Like Higginson, Bliss Carman began his essay in the *Boston Transcript* of November 21, 1896, with a glance backward at the "genuine sensation" of 1890. A Canadian by birth, coeditor of the semimonthly little magazine *Chap-Book*, and successful lyric poet, Carman had come to New York in 1888 and had joined the staff of *The Independent*. He clearly remembered the stormy enthusiasm with which the "chief," Maurice Thompson, had read from a new discovery, the poems of Emily Dickinson, to his coworkers. Thereupon Carman had immediately ranked the new book among the American classics. The volume of 1896 he welcomed as "the literary event of the season" and congratulated the readers of 1890 on their good taste. "It was only one more tribute to the New England ideal, the bent for transcendentalism inherited from Emerson; and, by the way, it was at the time another evidence of the alertness of the American reading public, and its sensitiveness to excellent originality." His explanation of Emily Dickinson as "a type of her race" and as a religious poet went beyond what Ward and Chamberlain had said earlier:

> It would never, I feel sure, occur to anyone with the least insight into the New England character, or the remotest inheritance of the New England conscience . . . to think of Emily Dickinson as peculiar, or her mode of life as queer. Somewhat strange as the record of it may show to foreign eyes, it was natural enough in its own time and place, though

sufficiently unusual to claim something of distinction even of itself. . . . And all the while, as we speak of Emily Dickinson's secluded life, . . . we should guard against the fancy that she was tinged with any shadow of sadness, or any touch of misanthropy or gloom. It seems rather that she must have had the sunniest of dispositions, as she certainly had the most sensitive and exquisite organization. It was not that the persons or fellows seemed to her superfluous or harsh or unnecessary, but rather that in one so finely organized as she must have been, the event of meeting another was too exquisite and portentous to be borne. . . .

She came of a race that was never at home in Zion, yet never was content out of sight of the promised land. It best suited their strenuous and warlike nature always to be looking down on the delectable Canaan from the Pisgah of their own unworthiness. Yet, however severe a face life wore to them . . . they were still making, though unwittingly, for the liberation of humanity. They were laying a substructure of honesty and seriousness, on which their intellectual inheritors might build, whether in art or politics. And their occupation with religion . . . has left an impress on ourselves, given us a trend from which we swerve in vain. And on every page of Emily Dickinson's poetry this ethical tendency, this awful environment of spirituality, is evident. Meditations of Psyche in the House of Clay; epigrams of an immortal guest, left behind on the chamber wall on the eve of silent departure, these brief lyrics seem.

As with Howells, long-standing familiarity with New England and its people may have made him capable of such insights and such identification.

Perhaps the most significant aspect of Carman's evaluation is an advance in the understanding of her rhyme technique. Full rhyme, handed down of old, he argues, represents only one possibility of audibly marking the lines. It is an arbitrary custom which harmonizes with "laws of poetry," but nevertheless does not itself make up the substance of the law. When Emily Dickinson deviated slightly from the generally practiced custom, she broke no law of poesy. She was free to rhyme "wine" and "unknown," since these partial rhymes fulfill the same purpose as full rhymes. She laid down a new rule for herself which she scrupulously observed. With this rule Carman is in subjective agreement: "It is wrong to say that she disregarded any law here. The question is rather: Did her new usage tend to beautiful results? For my part I confess that I like that falling rhyme very much." His appraisal of her entire work—"Emily Dickinson's contribution to English poetry . . . is by far the most important made by any woman west of the Atlantic"—agrees with his evaluation of her New England qualities and with his acknowledgment of her formal autonomy.[30]

Harry Lyman Koopman refrained just as little as Carman from pointing out flaws in Emily Dickinson's art.[31] In her inability to achieve "extended laborious architecture" Carman saw a serious deficiency which relegated her to the second rate. Koopman lamented her frequent bogging down in the half-said, in the mere impulse toward expression without the talent necessary for artistic realization, which sometimes ended in obscurities. Nevertheless, the same desire to understand and explain in retrospect runs through both essays. To both these poet-critics on the threshold of a new century the novelty, originality, and genuineness of her work seemed tantamount to a guarantee of its permanence. "Without waiting for any final decision, if such can ever be given, in regard to the excellence or faultiness of Emily Dickinson's peculiar style," Koopman carefully judged in the beginning, "we may even now venture the judgment that her name will henceforth hold a place in any list of the great woman writers of the world, and in any list of the great poets of her own country" (p. 82). He saw this claim substantiated in her double rebellion against tradition: in her formal revolt against the poetic usage of the nineteenth century, which she and other insurgents like Shelley, Poe, Swinburne, and Whitman undertook together, and in her intellectual rebellion against the Puritan heritage. In this respect she was related to Emerson and Thoreau —she came to a stop, in matters of form, halfway between "sternness and grimness" and "beauty" and, in content, between partiality toward authority and intellectual freedom (pp. 86-87). As "a free thinker on puritanic premises" she is an instance of "heredity by anticipation": "According to this principle, qualities that are to prevail in the future appear sporadically years, and often ages, before they become dominant" (p. 87). Without calling Koopman a prophet, one cannot deny the sensitivity with which he simultaneously related Emily Dickinson to her past and to the "scattered forerunners" of a future which he could only augur.

The clarification of Emily Dickinson's work after six years of journalistic criticism revealed itself in Carman's and Koopman's essays in fundamental reflections on the value of her poetry as permanent literature. This view is confirmed by perhaps the finest critic of Emily Dickinson in 1896: "She is the supreme lyrist of every-day life. She surely is, or must become, literature."[32] Rupert Hughes, who as a twenty-six year old classics scholar sat in judgment over all Western literature under the pseudonym Chelifer, had studied Emily Dickinson and her reviewers in detail since January 1896; he discussed the increasingly obvious tension between traditional and modern poetry, a tension which pivoted on the cardinal point of form: "The appearance of a new volume of Emily Dickinson's poems recalls the struggle between the Conservatives and the Liberals at the advent of her first volume. The good Tories simply dismissed her as hopelessly out of the pale—or pail?—of propriety. 'But note her ideas!' protested the Liberals. 'Bosh! they are mere oddity at best, and utterly spoiled by bad rimes, by incredible looseness of form! She is not worth serious consideration,' and so they dismissed her—from their own minds only. The more fools they!" (p. 541). Form is for Hughes, as rhyme was for Carman, the "etiquette" and not the law of art. If one pressed poetic inspiration into the Procrustean bed of iron convention, the form would degenerate to stiff pomp. The cogent examples were the "cage-birds," the "orthodox worthies" who could only move between the "golden wires of form." This group of poets dictated the laws of literature like oriental despots. An amendment to the artistic declaration of independence was necessary. The poet must be free to decide for or against such recognized forms as the sonnet or the rondeau, for the "orthodox" and the "outlaws" in literature have to go their own ways. This extension of artistic standards was intended to be in no way revolutionary, but only democratic, and the critic who judged exclusively according to his own favorite conceptions thereby exhibited his own intellectual confinement and poverty.

While Carman proved that Emily Dickinson had form in spite of her unique rhyming technique, Hughes's introductory demand that the prevailing stiff and normative poetics be dissolved serves in the second part of his essay to place her above the "cage-birds" and to elevate her to the level of the greatest thinkers of the world. "Form is a perennial delight, but it is not the only delight in art, and it is not the highest delight. The Idea

79

is surely a weightier matter" (p. 541). Higginson's decision, often repeated after 1890, was again made when Hughes enumerated a number of flawless poems, yet called Emily Dickinson generally "a grievous sinner against rime and meter" (p. 542), although he restricted this criticism: "Examples of her misrimes . . . are not so jarring in the context and under the predominating spell of the idea as when set apart" (p. 542). He then declared the poet along with Poe and Whitman to be one of the three American contributors to world lyric poetry. While Poe was only typical of Poe, the two others had common American characteristics: "Her outlook upon Death (and Walt Whitman's also) is so calm, so nonchalant; her pride so near Yankee brag; her seriousness so close to Yankee humor; so fond of every-day things, in short, so bigly democratic, that I feel in the poetry of both of them something markedly American, something majestic that belongs especially over here in our United States" (p. 543).

The reception of the edition of letters progressed quietly and equably, that of the third volume of selected poetry listlessly. After four and three months, respectively, the series of reviews, which in comparison with the years 1890 and 1891 had become shorter and shorter, broke off. Vehement debates no longer took place since the literary world did not see itself confronted with any new decisions. In 1894 the issue of form could not become acute; there was nothing to be scanned and no rhymes to be checked in the letters. Two years later, the critics avoided the question since it seemed to have been adequately discussed.

That a phase in the reception of Emily Dickinson drew to a close with the third volume was occasioned by the resignation of the editors. The reason lay, however, deeper. As long as a relatively uniform group of critics was always ready to reapply the old standards, further editions could only function as a confirmation of already established judgments. The brief, summarizing essays last discussed are a manifestation of the feeling that one could for the present close the case of the New England nun.

Part Two

REDISCOVERY

(1897-1930)

V

◇◆◇◆◇◆◇◆◇◆◇◆◇◆◇

THE LEAN YEARS (1897-1914)

◇◆◇◆◇◆◇◆◇◆◇◆◇◆◇

The muse sits neglected, if not forspent, in the hemicycle of the arts.[1]

LATE IN THE WINTER OF 1897 the long silence about Emily Dickinson began, only interrupted—for several months in 1914—by the publication of *The Single Hound*. Not before *Life and Letters* and *Complete Poems* appeared in 1924 did the critical dialogue, which has lasted ever since, again come into being.

The chief reason for the stagnation of her critical acceptance from 1897 until 1914 must be sought in the feud responsible for the suspension of editorial activity. The feud, which persisted for decades and which had a catastrophic effect on the fame of the poet during these years, had a bearing on the publication of the manuscripts, mentioned at the beginning of chapter II.

In the year of Emily Dickinson's death, the greater and by far better part of her poetry was in the hands of her sister Lavinia, the less significant part in Sue Dickinson's possession. The originals of the letters of which Mrs. Todd could gain possession were returned to their respective recipients after copies had been made. Until 1896 Mrs. Todd had borne the burden of the work; the profit had gone to Lavinia in accordance with the copyright laws. The publication of the first series of poems had led to a breach between Sue on the one hand and Mrs. Todd and Lavinia on the other. Soon thereafter the relationship between the latter two deteriorated. Austin Dickinson's attempts to mediate had little success. His intention of presenting Mrs. Todd with a plot of land from the Dickinson property in recognition of her work was forestalled by his death in 1895. To be sure, Lavinia signed the deed of gift in 1896, but initiated legal

83

proceedings in the same year, which canceled the gift and compelled Mrs. Todd to return the land in April 1898. There is no doubt that Mrs. Todd had considered a fourth and fifth selection of poetry as early as the beginning of 1896 and that she would have published volume after volume and exhausted the stock of poems before 1910. Instead, she withdrew, wrapped herself in icy silence until 1930, and, after her death in 1932, left it to her daughter to defend her and publish the remaining poems.

With Lavinia's death in 1899 the copyrights devolved upon Sue, who died in 1913 and left her legacy to her daughter. Martha Dickinson Bianchi renewed the rights to the collections edited by Mrs. Todd, which had run out in 1918, 1919, 1922, and 1924, respectively, and published the first three series of poems together with *The Single Hound* and *Complete Poems*.

A second reason for the neglect is Higginson's resignation as coeditor and promoter. Emily Dickinson's poetry had made a deep impression on him. She had been his greatest discovery, but one of many. It is characteristic of the busy man of letters that when reading the galley proofs in 1890 he could no longer remember whether he had visited the poet once or twice. Her posthumous fame, to which he had so decisively contributed, delighted him. One should not, however, overlook the fact that he was almost a seventy-year-old who had had a share in the rise of various poet friends and had learned in the process how quickly some of them again fell into oblivion. Emily Dickinson's work meant less to the aging man than to Lavinia and the young, enthusiastic professor's wife. Moreover, in questions of editing he had often been of another opinion than his coeditor and had done his best to keep out of the growing family discord after he had repeatedly offended and had recognized that "it is hard to steer safely among Dickinsons" (*AB*, p. 85). He had continued to follow the criticism. But in *Cheerful Yesterdays*, his autobiography written on a sick bed in 1895 and 1896 and published in 1898, he did not devote one syllable to Emily Dickinson. His collected works in seven volumes, also published in 1898, did not include the two essays of 1890 and 1891. The second essay was incorporated unchanged in his last collection, *Carlyle's Laugh and Other Surprises*, in 1909; the first was not reprinted until after his death. Higginson wrote briefly—jointly with H. W. Boynton—about his former pupil only once more in his literary history, as will be discussed.

Two further reasons, inherent in the times, are additionally responsible for the cessation of criticism. American literary criticism was still almost exclusively a journalistic discipline. New publications were routinely reviewed, but only reprintings of Emily Dickinson appeared. And verse found itself in decline. Around 1900, only in prose was the struggle between the old and the new, romanticism and realism, decided in favor of the realistic and true. The few significant poets wrote in isolation; they had no forum, no spokesmen, no audience worth mentioning, and, hence, no impact. Furthermore, the larger periodicals kept to ballads and sonnets, rondels and sestinas. Much passable poetry was written which people took notice of with just as much respect as boredom. Each year the two hundred obligatory volumes of poetry appeared. "When Yesterday Was Young," "Songs from the Capital," "Holiday, and Other Poems," "Easter-Song," "The Heart of a Woman," "The Soul's Progress," "The Blind Man at the Window," "Driftwood," "Heart Melodies," "Sweethearts Always," "Said the Rose" are a by no means unusual cross section of gilt-edged offerings reviewed in *The Dial* in the first half of the year 1907.

Poetry had played out its role in the intellectual life of the nation. "The taste for poetry is becoming a lost accomplishment," a critic wrote in 1898, and Jessie Rittenhouse stated six years later: "Poetry grows more and more an intellectual pleasure for the cultured classes and less and less a possession of the people." Another witness of literary happenings, who worked as a book dealer in Boston, explained in retrospect: "Poetry then seemed to be considered a completed aspect of literature, to be gathered up in stout, double-column volumes. A few new voices were just beginning to get a hearing, but were not an impressive sector in bookselling." Even a second "Ode to a Nightingale" would not create a stir, complained Stedman in *An American Anthology* in 1900 (p. xxxii). Whoever was still interested in poetry turned as a rule to an old favorite rather than a new voice. Many essays were written about the growing unpopularity of the craft. In 1905 *Punch* considered the case hopeless:

> *For men in these expansive times*
> *(Due, I am told, to fiscal freedom),*
> *Though earth were black with angels' rhymes,*
> *Dine far too well to want to read 'em.*[2]

In this stale climate, only poetry with a purpose attracted ephemeral interest. Markham's "The Man with the Hoe," in the

San Francisco *Examiner* of December 27, 1898, made him the Byron of a few months, a crowned workers' poet, but generally poetry passed as smugly bourgeois and third class, "the most timid, the most anemic, the most lacking in individualities . . . that any country has ever known."[3] American literature seemed in these years to consist in a dead vanguard. The first generation of poets—Bryant (1794-1878), Emerson (1803-72), Longfellow (1807-82), Whittier (1807-92), Holmes (1809-94), Lowell (1819-91)—was followed by a second, no less durable one with Stoddard (1825-1902), Stedman (1833-1908), and Aldrich (1836-1907) at the head, and after that, nothing.[4]

Two short dialogues from novels of 1904 and 1901 are perhaps still more revealing than the complaints and sneers concerning the condition of American verse shortly after the turn of the century. In the twentieth chapter of Jack London's *The Sea-Wolf*, Maud Brewster, the heroine and a poet, discovers that the hero, Humphrey Van Weyden, is "the Dean of American Letters, the Second." The following conversation ensues:

> "Humphrey Van Weyden," she concluded; then added with a sigh of relief, and unaware that she had glanced that relief at Wolf Larsen, "I am so glad."
>
> "I remember the review," she went on hastily, becoming aware of the awkwardness of her remark; "that too, too flattering review."
>
> "Not at all," I denied valiantly. "You impeach my sober judgment and make my canons of little worth. Besides, all my brother critics were with me. Didn't Lang include your 'Kiss Endured' among the four supreme sonnets by women in the English language?"

In this pleasant exchange of notes, which today comes close to being read as an unintentional parody of the late Victorian consensus of bard and critic, an easeful harmony still prevails. In Frank Norris' *The Octopus*, the respective positions of the Californian Mrs. Derrick, who holds with Pater, and the poet Presley from the East, who seeks new forms of expression, are clearly staked out:

> His indifference to "style," to elegant English, was a positive affront. His savage abuse and open ridicule of the neatly phrased rondeaux and sestinas and chansonettes of the little magazines was to her mind a wanton and uncalled-for

cruelty. . . . She could not see with him any romance, any poetry in the life around her, she looked to Italy for that. His "Song of the West," which only once, incoherent and fierce, he had tried to explain to her, its swift, tumultuous life, its truth, its nobility and savagery, its heroism and obscenity, had revolted her.

"But, Presley," she had murmured, "that is not literature."

"No," he had cried between his teeth, "no, thank God, it is not."[5]

The Presleys of those years, typically "in search of a subject," as the beginning of the novel says, who endeavored to include the shrill and discordant in the older Arcadian-sentimental version of poetic America, found few friends. As late as 1910, the critics and the readers, both of whom adhered to the old and did not see or did not want to see the new, were convinced of the torpidity of American literature. Neither Emily Dickinson, Crane, Moody, Robinson, nor Walt Whitman could rouse such an insensitive public.

Several literary histories bridge the transition to the new century and give information about the impression which the Dickinson criticism of the 1890's had left on the scholar.

Hans-Joachim Lang finds Emily Dickinson mentioned only seven times in manuals from the period between 1896 and 1913.[6] A reexamination of more than two dozen works published between 1895 and 1915, the first fruitful decades of American literary history, changes this conclusion but little (cf. Sources, pp. 298-99). Three things concern us: Which authors mention Emily Dickinson? How do they evaluate her work? In which greater historical perspective do they place the poet?

Just as with American criticism and aesthetics of the waning nineteenth century, the influence of Stedman's legacy must be estimated highly in the formation of the literary canon and of the critical terminology of the manuals in this transition period. His literary history, *Poets of America* (1885), and his anthology of 1900 were almost without exception taken by the historians as a basis for the newest poetry. Their divisions are reflected in most tables of contents. In 1913 John Macy was the first to break up the rigid pattern and change the emphasis by stressing Thoreau as the intellectual liberator, Whitman as the greatest poet, and Twain as the most significant novelist.

In *Poets of America* special chapters are devoted to Bryant, Whittier, Emerson, Poe, Longfellow, Holmes, Lowell, Whitman, and Taylor. A host of younger talents, who appear as an appendage in Stedman's and the other historians' manuals, follow the unchallenged veterans and patriarchs. Stedman's omnibus chapter XII ("The Outlook") treats seventy poets. As reasons for the deplorable "poetic interregnum" he adduces the war, the longevity of the great New England bards, diminishing public interest in poetry, and the switch of many poets to prose. Contemporary poets he characterizes as technically of high quality —"Scarcely one," he remarks humorously, "but turns you off his rondeau or ballade, and very cleverly withal"[7]—but monotonous and trivial.

Together with the tentative selection, the sensation of living in a twilight interval without signs of a new day, and the arrangement of the metrical newcomers in a predominantly cultivated and a rarer creative group, Stedman supplied the historian with an uncritical terminology which Fred Pattee, Katharine Bates, and others eagerly took up. The poet appears in the mind of the critic and historian as a craftsman, as a blossom in the garden, or as a wanderer on the slopes of Parnassus, where he picks the aromatic laurel, as singer, minstrel, musician, troubadour, part of a choir or body of singers which lets its ethereal and charming melodies echo afar. Finally, the poet appears as a light-footed bird, as a hermit thrush in the dog rose, united with other feathery singers to form an exulting choir which warbles sweet cadences with golden voices—a conglomeration of metaphors which in such doses borders on the ludicrous but which is quite characteristic and expressive of a decorative conception of art.

When Stedman published his comprehensive anthology in 1900, he felt that the "tyranny" of the older poets over the younger ones was more oppressive than it had been fifteen years before; he offset this by providing a collective chapter, "Second Lyrical Period," in which twenty poems of Emily Dickinson were included. Nevertheless, the tone of resignation had not changed.

According to scope and arrangement the handbooks can be divided into two types. Several restrict themselves to the great figures and avoid the mere enumeration of minor and later poets, in the case of the latter because of the lacking test of time. Howe and the pessimists Wendell, Woodberry, and Trent belong to this group. Emily Dickinson has no place in their books. Most

of the remaining literary histories, in which she assumes an inconspicuous marginal position, treat routinely many of the *minora
sidera* in the literary firmament and strive to evaluate them
provisionally.

Emily Dickinson is mentioned by Bates (1897), Bronson
(1900), Newcomer (1901), Abernethy (1902), Higginson
(1903), Halleck (1911), Cairns (1912), Long (1913), and Pattee
(1915). Abernethy, Bronson, Halleck, and Long grant her
scarcely a sentence; Higginson devotes one and a half pages to
her. Six times she appears in summary concluding chapters on
the "Later Activity" of the last generation (Bronson, Newcomer,
Halleck, Cairns, Long, Pattee), twice among the minor lyrists
of New England (Bates, Higginson). Abernethy places her in
the Hawthorne part of his chapter on Transcendentalism among
the minor figures of this movement, since Helen Hunt Jackson
was loosely associated with the Brook Farm group and Emily
Dickinson in turn with Mrs. Jackson. Thus, she is ranked as a
"belated Transcendentalist," which is incorrect historically but
not inept according to early criticism. One finds her most often
in connection with Sill, Aldrich, Stedman, Stoddard, Emma
Lazarus, and the "New England songsters"—Celia Thaxter,
Louise Moulton, and Mrs. Jackson. The latter forms a transition
to her in four instances, which is natural, since Higginson served
as a Dickinson source for Mrs. Jackson. Abernethy even quotes
him and dispenses with a judgment of his own: "Associated with
this group by the serious import of her work was Helen Hunt
Jackson . . . whose poetry 'unquestionably takes rank,' says
Higginson, 'above that of any other American woman, and its
only rival could be found, curiously enough, in that of her early
schoolmate, Emily Dickinson.' "[8] Newcomer proceeds in a very
similar manner when he writes about Helen Jackson: "She published a volume of verse in 1870; and it seems not too much to
say of . . . her poems . . . that they evince a higher imagination
than those of any other American woman poet except her fellow
townsman, Emily Dickinson."[9] While Taylor, Stoddard, Stedman,
and Aldrich are understood as a regional and stylistic group,
Emily Dickinson, like the vagrant Sill, wanders irrelevantly in
various contexts.

The difficulty of evaluating her corresponds to the uncer-
tainty about her rightful place. The first judgment is made by
Katharine Lee Bates: "From another Amherst woman, Emily
Dickinson, an elfish recluse in her father's house and garden,

have been wafted to the world a few showers of sibylline leaves more curious than anything else in our minor poetry. In demure and dashing strokes her letters vividly paint that typical New England household. . . . Safely cloistered in this environment, the shy little poet loved no words so well as *gallant* and *martial* and posed as roguish rebel against the traditional solemnities of Puritanism."[10] In language replete with dainty alliteration, four schemes of classification found in earlier criticism reappear: Emily the rogue, the rebel, the hermit, the mysterious seer. The author (1859-1929), a professor at Wellesley, who still made similar statements in 1925, does not take a stand. In this respect she resembles Bronson who, in connection with the rest of the New England poetesses, declares: "A rarer vein is that of Emily Dickinson . . . , whose condensed little poems on nature and life startle and stab by their erratic originality of thought and phrase."[11]

Newcomer goes into more detail, although he confesses: "Classification and comparison . . . avail nothing. She was modern; beyond that the chances of time and place do not signify; her life and poetry were equally remote from the ways of others." Her poems baffle him: "They seldom have titles, and sometimes no more words than poets three centuries ago put into their titles, for she pours her words as a chemist his tinctures, fearful of a drop too much. Two stanzas, of four lines each, imperfectly rhymed, are her favorite form. A fourteen-line sonnet is spacious by the side of such poems. Yet few sonnets have ever compressed so much within their bounds. To read one is to be given a pause that will outlast the reading of many sonnets." In assessing the content of her poetry he makes use of the lightning metaphor. The following "but" issues from the sense of form of the 1890's: "But stamped though they be with the celestial signature, they are but fragments, and in the temple of art, which keeps its niches for the perfect statue, they must shine obscurely."

The paragraph on Emily Dickinson in the joint work of Higginson and Boynton was very probably written by the former. For Higginson, as for Bronson, she is the "most remarkable," if the least intelligible, of the New England women. As "a strange, solitary, morbidly sensitive, and pitifully childlike poetic genius" she lived in a chosen home among the clouds. His verdict —the parting words with which he consigned her to the twentieth century—is the quintessence of an interest which had lasted for decades: "Emily Dickinson never quite succeeded in grasping the notion of the importance of poetic form. The crudeness which an Emerson could only mourn over, she could only acknowledge. With all its irregularity, however, her poetry preserves a lyrical power almost unequaled in her generation. In remoteness of allusion, in boldness of phrase, it stands at the opposite remove from the verse of Longfellow, for example; but if it can never attain popularity . . . , it is likely, in the end, to obtain the attention of the 'audience fit, tho' few,' which a greater poet once desired of Fate."[12]

Long and Halleck comment the most concisely of all. Long mentions only "the glittering fragments of poetry that strew the pages of Emily Dickinson" in his collective chapter "America Singing." Halleck offers a kind of appended Who's Who of the names disregarded in the text, in which Emily Dickinson is defined in telegraphese: "Author of unique short lyrics. *Poems.*" Cairns took slightly more trouble with the three volumes of verse: "Though uneven, as secret poetical work is almost sure to be, they show unquestionable genius. The author had humor, insight, and an unusual power of terse and well rounded expression."[13]

The last, scathing criticism of this period comes from Pattee, who had passed Emily Dickinson by in 1896. He designates her first as an "intense lyrist" (p. 220) and numbers her among the "distinctive poets of the era" (p. 222).[14] He does not seem to remember these labels on the page devoted to her work, for he fills it almost entirely with disparagement. He traces her popularity after 1890 back to Higginson's role as mediator; since he overestimates the friendliness of her critical acceptance, he feels called upon to do away with the supposed cult: "The poems are disappointing. Critics have echoed Higginson, until Emily Dickinson has figured, often at length, in all the later histories and anthologies, but it is becoming clear that she was overrated. To compare her eccentric fragments with Blake's elfin wildness is ridiculous. They are mere conceits, jottings of a brooding mind; they are crudely wrought and, like their author's letters, . . . they are colorless and for the most part lifeless. They should have been allowed to perish as their author intended."

Any mention of Emily Dickinson in the literary histories written during the twenty years which coincided with the subsiding of journalistic criticism is a matter of pure chance, in view of the abundance of competing names (Stedman's anthology alone contains 614 poets). Two thirds of the books are silent about her. The literary environments in which she is placed vary greatly. Characteristically, at this time she still cannot be classified. Aside from Newcomer's hint that she was "modern," familiar evaluations predominate. Where she is acknowledged, it is due to her power of expression. Now as before the form of her art arouses criticism. The spirit of this intermediate period manifests itself in adherence to what had already been established and in continual watchfulness for signs of a greater future.

More significant, perhaps, than some of the opinions quoted from the college manuals is a speculation of Barrett Wendell, the leading literary historian of the period, a speculation made in the face of the disintegration of the New England tradition. His theory of a possible literary flowering within a declining culture was applied—before him tentatively and after him in detail—to Emily Dickinson's work: "Artistic expression is apt to be the final fruit of a society about to wither. For generations, or perhaps for centuries, traditions grow until they reach a form which locally distinguishes the spot which has developed them from any other in the world. Then, at moments of change, there sometimes arises, in a race about to pass from the living, a mysterious impulse to make plastic or written records of what the past has meant."[15]

In 1936 the literary historian Percy H. Boynton wrote of Emily Dickinson that "from 1897 to 1909 there seems to have been no mention of her in print."[16] This remark has been refuted by the description of the critical reception of the third series of poems and by the examination of the literary histories of the transitional period. More than a dozen additional witnesses to the contrary could be adduced, although their cogency is admittedly weak; they merely show that she had not been entirely forgotten. These solitary voices issued from a time which even today is largely unexplored in the writing of literary history.

Two references are from the Middle and Far West. One is the essay "Emily Dickinson" in the June 12 and 19, 1898, issues of *Der Westen*. The other is the recollections of a former Amherst resident, the daughter of Samuel Mack, of a visit with Lavinia and Emily, which appeared in the *Sunday Oregonian* on March 18, 1899. These are a last echo of the widely diffused discussion of the preceding years. In the German-language paper, A.E. wrote with amusement about the embarrassment of the American critics who could not place Emily Dickinson within any school or group: "In literary history it must always all be labeled so neat and tidy, as in an apothecary's shop." He compared the Amherst poet with Annette von Droste-Hülshoff, translated three of her poems into German, and concluded: "Emily Dickinson must write as she wrote—to become what she is: up to now the most unique poet America has produced."[17]

In the new century two representatives of the old school were heard from first. The inclusion of a generous selection of the poems in Stedman's treasury marked the first appearance of Emily Dickinson in an important collection. The second critic who called the poet back to mind was Aldrich.

Just as Stedman had struck the literary balance of America toward the end of his life, Aldrich also pieced the most durable of his writings together in a complete edition. In the process he found the 1892 essay valuable enough for insertion in the ninth volume of his revised works.[18] Since the prophesy that Emily Dickinson would soon be forgotten had still not been fulfilled eleven years later, his rude tone is mitigated although she remains "un poète manqué." The reworked passages of the shorter new version show a gradual change in his opinion:

1892	1903
. . . her poetical chaos . . .	. . . Miss Dickinson's poetical mélange . . . (p. 83)
There are three or four bits of this kind in Miss Dickinson's book; but for the most part the ideas totter and toddle, not having learned to walk.	This is one of the ten or twelve brief pieces so nearly perfect in structure as almost to warrant the reader in suspecting that Miss Dickinson's general disregard of form was a deliberate affectation. (p. 84)

The poet who could not comply with the laws he had laid down for verse has become an artist who stubbornly insisted on her own principles of form. In 1892 Aldrich had quoted only one poem; now he cites a second ("This is the land the sunset washes"), which Lang also let pass, and grants it the "artistic finish" which he had previously categorically denied the poet. Ironically, this poem would also have been dropped as unpolished by Aldrich and Lang had not Mrs. Todd produced a rhyme with "bales" by changing "like Orioles" to "with fairy sails." The new image which simultaneously came into being may have moved Aldrich to designate the poem as "impressionist landscape" and attach a comparison: "The little picture has all the opaline atmosphere of a Claude Lorraine. One instantly frames it in one's memory" (p. 84).

Like the earlier characterization, an "eccentric, dreamy, half-educated recluse," the sharply delivered attack on Higginson is also missing. The original directness of the concluding judgment is dampened by being couched in a poet-bird metaphor which, within the store of critical language of the time, more than once suggests noncommittal politeness:

1892	1903
But the incoherence and formlessness of her—I don't know how to designate them—versicles are fatal.	But the incoherence and shapelessness of the greater part of her verse are fatal. (p. 85)
Miss Dickinson's versicles have a queerness and a quaintness that have stirred a momentary curiosity in emotional bosoms. Oblivion lingers in the immediate neighborhood.	Miss Dickinson's stanzas, with their impossible rhyme, their involved significance, their interrupted flute-note of birds that have no continuous music, seem to have caught the ear of a group of early listeners. A shy New England bluebird, shifting its light load of song, has for a moment been mistaken for a strange nightingale. (p. 86)

The remaining essays and notices published between 1898 and 1914 stem mostly from American and British enthusiasts who were discovering Emily Dickinson for the first time. Common to all of them is their fervor—two of them made pilgrimages to the poet's home—as well as their recourse to authorities and their partiality toward tradition.

In England it seemed impossible to find a larger forum for the American poet. On October 9, 1891, the London publisher James R. Osgood wrote a letter to Professor Todd in which he complained about the failure of the British edition and added: "Whether the book will make its way is a question which the future will decide. Meanwhile we do not feel encouraged to venture upon a second volume" (MS-D57/To 518). The matter rested there for twelve years until the Scottish narrator and critic Jane Helen Findlater came upon the poems and wrote to Mrs. Todd enthusiastically on December 15, 1903: "I have been immensely struck by their power and beauty, and am anxious to introduce them to English readers—for I do not think they are at all well known in this country. I gave the poems to my own publishers Messrs Methuen to read, and they are going to bring out an English edition of the book. But in the meantime I am writing an article on the poems for *The National Review* . . ." (MS-D57/To 500). To be sure, an unsuccessful reprint followed in 1905,[19] but the essay announced by Miss Findlater, who wrote regularly for *The National Review* in those years, did not appear.

Two noteworthy comments by British readers can be explained by special contacts with America. As author of the American Baedeker, James Fullarton Muirhead (1853-1934) was interested in American culture. In a travel book published in 1898 he interspersed informal literary talk with extensive comments on James, Howells, and Emily Dickinson. His unprejudiced assessment of "the essentially American nature of her muse" is new. For her mistakes parallels could be found in the annals of English literature, "but only in the liberal atmosphere of the New World, comparatively unshadowed by trammels of authority and standards of taste, could they have co-existed with so much of the highest quality." As an example he refers to her "ultra-American familiarity with the forces of nature." As a newly installed English professor at the University of Birmingham, John Churton Collins (1848-1908) was interested in Emily Dickinson professionally. When he penned the chapter "The Poetry and Poets of America" for a book of essays, he enlisted the aid of Stedman's anthology in order to find his way through the maze of later literature. For Emily Dickinson, Mrs. Thaxter, and Mrs. Jackson he reserved "honourable places" and wrote about the first: "She . . . is, in her jerky transcendentalism and strained style, too faithful a disciple of Emerson, but much of her work has real merit."[20]

From a third Englishman, William James Dawson (1854-c1928), a London Congregationalist clergyman with broad literary ambitions, we have an entirely personal testimony to his admiration for the poet. In 1891 he had brought back the first volume of selected poetry from a lecture trip to the United States and had learned to treasure the book as one of the few "dynamic" works "that really move the soul." Out of this tribute grew the judgment the implications of which he was scarcely aware in 1909: "I would cheerfully barter many pages of the poets counted greatest for a single page of Emily Dickinson. I have no doubt that many people will dissent from such a verdict, and call it exaggerated; but I find it quite insufficient to express my more than admiration for verse which has more power to quicken the poetic instinct in me than any other verse by an American author. Perhaps American critics have not yet quite understood how great a gift was withdrawn from the world when Emily Dickinson died."[21]

In addition to these British enthusiasts two Americans should be mentioned. Ella Gilbert Ives, who like Emily Dickinson had attended Mount Holyoke College, made an unsubstantiated assertion in the subtitle—"Her Poetry, Prose and Personality— Their Distinction and Growing Fame"—of her study, which appeared on October 5, 1907, in the *Boston Transcript*. Whatever the rank of the poet might have been in 1907, her fame had scarcely grown in the preceding ten years. The author adduced no signs whatever for growing fame and merely relied on the volumes of poetry and letters and on her knowledge of early Dickinson criticism, which she summarized for her readers:

> Many obvious, many contradictory things, have been said about this profound thinker and virile writer on a few great themes. Those who cling to the old order and regard perfect form essential to greatness, have had their fling at her eccentricities, her blemishes, her crudities; they place her with the purveyors of raw material to the artistic producers of the race. They deny her rank with the creators of permanent beauty and value. Others such as hail a Wagner, a Whitman, or a Turner, as an originator of new types and a contributor of fresh streams of life blood to art or literature, accept Emily Dickinson as another proof of Nature's fecundity, versatility and daring. All acknowledge in her elements of power and originality; but especially a certain probing quality that penetrates and discloses like an X-ray.

After this objective survey the conclusion is somewhat disappointing: "Granted that her poetry is uneven, so rugged of rhyme and rhythm that it jolts the mind like a corduroy road— I prefer it to a flowery bed of ease. Many can lull, but few can awake." Even Aldrich had admitted in 1892 that he knew of more important things that interested him less. Ella Ives takes up old strands without spinning them further. The poetry fills her with enthusiasm due to its electric shocks. Even the conception that the poems destroy old, favorite notions and call for a new system of weights and measures is not carried further. The next sentence states: "Perhaps there is nothing essentially new here."

Like Dawson and Ella Ives, Frederick J. Pohl (born 1889), who was an Amherst student at the time he wrote his essay, also made the Higginsonian decision in favor of Emily Dickinson despite the form of her poetry. "Where her technique falls far short of perfection, the clearness of the thought makes ample reparation."[22] He introduces his quotation of the hummingbird poem with the question: "Could a Coleridge or a Keats have done better?" (p. 49). That is, he asks himself like Dawson in a similar passage: Could two of the greatest romantic poets with all their formal perfection have written a better poem than did Emily Dickinson, the poet of intellection, with her deficient rhymes? He was the first to formulate the reason for such greatness with some clarity: "But the significant fact is that her thoughts were recorded as they occurred in her when engaged in household duties, so that we have the bare workings of her mind right on our printed page. This is why her thoughts are so valuable for us. They are the fruits of her experience, untouched by time or artificial polish" (p. 50). Here a conclusion is drawn with more anticipation than certainty: Stedman and other critics before him had frequently reproached third-rate rhymesters for practicing mere artistic finesse without having anything compulsive to express while Emily Dickinson avoided this pitfall by restricting herself to themes which everyday life in her immediate environment provided. Pohl finds a correspondence between her poetry and her religiousness by comparing her sacrifice of dogma in favor of a personal relationship to God with her sacrifice of formal correctness in favor of intellectual compression.

As in the case of American poetry of the twentieth century, one can also determine nothing less than a radical turnabout in critical thinking during the evaluation of Emily Dickinson. The creative and critical renascence, much commented on as a phenomenon, is often linked directly with the date of the founding of Harriet Monroe's *Poetry: A Magazine of Verse*, the first issue of which was published in October 1912, although most authorities are vague about the date. In the chronicle of Emily Dickinson's appraisal this time comprises the months between March 1912, when James Warwick Price's "Three Forgotten

Poetesses" was published in *The Forum*, and January 1913, when Martha Hale Shackford published a short essay in the *Atlantic*.[23]

Price, who had already written about Emily Dickinson in 1893, falls back on his earlier study and unites her with Amy Levy and Emma Lazarus under "secondary literature" which has its place beneath the "more glorious company" of the great poets, but is nevertheless worth being saved from oblivion. Martha Shackford begins with the statement: "Emily Dickinson is one of our most original writers, a force destined to endure in American letters" (p. 93). In the case of the three poetesses Price finds "a large possibility unfulfilled" (p. 376); Mrs. Shackford speaks of "persistent appeal," "the expression of vital meanings" and recognizes that "Idea and expression are so indissolubly fused in her work that every one of her phrases, her changing rhythms, is a direct reflection of her personality" (p. 94). Price quotes the opinions of Hamilton Aidé and "the venerable Thomas Wentworth Higginson"; Mrs. Shackford relies exclusively on her own opinion. She does not want to know anything about earlier criticism and rejects also a parallel—drawn shortly before by a reviewer—with Tabb, who had died in 1909: "Are we thus to lose the fine significance of poetic individuality? . . . Father Tabb's work . . . is full of quiet reverie, hers has a sharp stabbing quality which disturbs and overthrows the spiritual ease of the reader" (p. 93). She feels herself especially attracted by the honesty and aggressiveness of the poetry: "Compression and epigrammatical ambush are her aids; she proceeds, without preparation or apology, by sudden, sharp zigzags. What intelligence a reader has must be exercised in the poetic game of hare-and-hounds, where ellipses, inversions, and unexpected climaxes mislead those who pursue sweet reasonableness" (p. 93). She summarizes the quality of the work in three theses: "intensity of spiritual experience":

> Inquisitive always, alert to the inner truths of life, impatient of the brief destinies of convention, she isolated herself from the petty demands of social amenity. (p. 94)

"keen sensitiveness to irony and paradox":

> Since life seemed, to her, to move along wholly simple and direct ways, she delighted to accentuate the fact that out of apparent contradictions and discords are wrought the subtlest harmonies. (pp. 96-97)

"a dauntless courage in accepting life":

> Existence, to her, was a momentous experience, and she let no promises of a future life deter her from feeling the throbs of this one. No false comfort released her from dismay at present anguish. (p. 97)

Of incisive importance is her characterization of Emily Dickinson's imagery:

> Although her similes and metaphors may be devoid of languid aesthetic elegance, they are quivering to express living ideas, and so they come surprisingly close to what we are fond of calling the commonplace. She reverses the usual, she hitches her star to a wagon, transfixing homely daily phrases for poetic purposes. Such an audacity has seldom invaded poetry with a desire to tell immortal truths through the medium of a deep sentiment for old habitual things. It is true that we permit this liberty to the greatest poets, Shakespeare, Keats, Wordsworth, and some others; but in America our poets have been sharply charged not to offend in this respect. Here tradition still animates many critics in the belief that real poetry must have exalted phraseology. (p. 96)

As a poet of everyday life who knew how to transform common language into poetic coin, Emily Dickinson is balanced against the poetry of "sweet reasonableness" and "languid aesthetic elegance." The scale, at least for the person doing the weighing, bows down in favor of the New England poet. Her greater weight is substantiated, and the past itself is viewed critically. The end of a protracted period, which creatively and critically lived in the shadow of the century past, is reached.

During the eighteen years investigated in this chapter, time rather than criticism worked for Emily Dickinson. The old guard uttered last opinions which were enlightened by temporal distance; the historians gathered into their manuals what in this placid time had remained of Emily Dickinson's earlier fame; and solitary voices reminded their readers of her name. The supercession of retrospective criticism by a new outlook oriented toward the future came at a not entirely unexpected time: two months after the publication of Martha Shackford's essay, F. S. Flint formulated the three Imagist "rules" in *Poetry*. A comparison of these new aesthetic principles of a small group of poets with the work of Emily Dickinson and with Mrs. Shackford's opinion of this work shows us two things: first, that at the same time when the Imagists had programmatically made demands for direct statement, utmost linguistic economy, and new rhythms, American criticism had in at least one instance shown great receptiveness for a literature which approached these demands; and, second, that it could only be a short time until the Imagists themselves would discover Emily Dickinson.

V I

◇◇◇◇◇◇◇◇◇◇◇◇◇◇◇

IN THE SHADOW OF THE
"LITTLE RENAISSANCE" (1914-24)[1]

◇◇◇◇◇◇◇◇◇◇◇◇◇◇◇

*Present-day poetry is of two distant and widely dissimilar,
though sometimes converging, streams or orders. The first,
shaped by traditional influences and methods, may be either
of rhyming or blank verse nature, but must, at least in some
degree, conform to certain recognized modes and models. Its
formal antagonist, the poetry, real or debatable, reaching
its most characteristic development in the work of the
"imagistes" and their poetic kin, is reminiscent of the scholarly foreigner who, after spending some time in a busy newspaper office in perplexity remarked that "among American
journalists everything seems to be called a story but that
which really is a story, and that is called fiction." The distinctive poetry of the movement conforms to no rule, no
order, no model save that of the poet's personal and individual
taste.[2]*

THE SINGLE HOUND, a volume commemorative of the "romantic
friendship of my Aunt Emily Dickinson and her 'Sister Sue,' "[3]
was published three days before Amy Lowell's *Sword Blades
and Poppy Seed*, which marks the beginning of her experimental
period, and in that week in which the front pages of the newspapers still reported on the events of the War on the Marne and
the Masurian Lakes. This volume attracted the attention of only
a small group of readers and critics. The slight demand can be
gathered from the small numbers of copies printed: 595 were
published on September 19, 1914, an additional 293 on October
29, 1915. If it can be concluded from the number of copies for
sale that five and seven copies, respectively, were distributed to
review organs, the eleven notices mentioned in this investigation
(cf. Sources, pp. 305-6) might well be practically complete. Since

no more than 888 copies were printed, the book soon became a rarity for the bibliophile.

The Single Hound consists of 147 poems which Emily Dickinson had sent to her sister-in-law during the years 1858-86. They are frequently slightly varied versions of poems which she collected or sent to other correspondents. Only one poem had been previously published. Of 111 poems the originals are preserved, of 36 only Sue's copies.

From the greater fidelity to the text it can be determined how the mediatory role of Emily Dickinson's editor had in the meantime changed. The stanzas of thirteen poems are run together to form a continuous text whose blocklike arrangement conveys the impression of compactness. The 54 changes in 37 poems at first give rise to doubt concerning the correctness of Thomas H. Johnson's statement that the text of the volume is "refreshingly accurate" (*Poems*, I, xlvii). Yet it must be agreed to with certain qualifications. Four deviations are probably reading mistakes of the editor, who had to copy the difficult handwriting of her mother. Synonyms, other prepositions, and conjunctions are introduced in 44 cases. Types of corrections which predominated under the editorship of Mrs. Todd and Higginson are rare. One "be" became "is"; two subjunctives were replaced by indicatives; in one place the rhythm was smoothed; transpositions occur twice. The grammar was not improved upon: "Flinging the problem back / At you and I" in the last line of the poem "My wheel is in the dark" remained and was only normalized to "me" in later collections. The only instance in which a rhyme was achieved by transposition contrasts with another in which a rhyme was given up in favor of a word substitution.

Johnson explains Madame Bianchi's textual fidelity as follows: "By 1914 . . . Emily Dickinson's public had reached out far beyond New England, and her verbal and metric irregularities were recognized as essential to the form and meaning of her poetry, not wilful eccentricities. Therefore Martha Dickinson Bianchi . . . never felt under pressure to alter the text of a poem to smooth rhyme and meter" (*Poems*, I, xlvii). The history of the poet's reception is evidence against a broad circle of readers in the first fourteen years of the new century. It is more probable that the editor, who had published four volumes of her own verse since 1899 and had taken an active interest in the development of American poetry, placed her hopes in the general change of taste which had in the meantime set in. At a time when the public had abruptly become aware of a chorus of new voices—Lindsay, Pound, Williams, Robinson, Jeffers, and Frost had had volumes of poems published between 1909 and 1914 —she could confidently introduce a new voice to the chorus. Mrs. Shackford's enthusiastic essay may also have been involved in the intention to change as little as possible.

Corresponding to the poems directed next door to Austin Dickinson's house, the preface is tailored to Emily Dickinson's relationship with Austin's wife, Susan, and her children. The editor, who in a slightly exaggerated manner considered herself the savior of the poems, idyllizes the relationship between her mother and her famous aunt, which in reality, as she herself probably knew best, had become more and more strained over the years. "My revered Grandfather" (p. xi), who searched for his daughter Emily with his lantern, appears in passing as does also "our other faithful but prejudiced Aunt Lavinia" (p. viii). The sketch of Emily is drafted with an eye to Sue and is in addition stylized and simplified by the niece's perspective. When the poet died, Madame Bianchi was twenty; when she wrote her preface, she was looking back over a generation. From the child's point of view the aunt appears as a playmate and confederate; from the perspective of the young woman "her wit" and "her pitiless directness of thought" (p. vii) are admired. Although she protests against the interpretation of Emily the woman as "a rare strange being" and "a weird recluse" (p. vi), a general aura of the unreal slips into her ready-made portrait, perhaps due to the long period of time separating experience and recollection:

> She was of fairy lineage, akin to the frost on the nursery pane in Winter or the humming bird of Midsummer. (p. vi)
> . . . her way of flitting, like a shadow upon the hillside, a motion known to no other mortal. (p. vii)
> . . . as if she had been Hans Andersen's little Snow Maiden and might melt before our eyes if misunderstood. (p. ix)
> . . . her transition from arch to demure, from elfin to angelic . . . (p. xiv)
> She was not daily-bred. She was star-dust. (p. xviii)

The question of the lover, which had always been avoided by Mrs. Todd, was officially answered for the first time. Emily

Dickinson had not only a secret, but in addition many beaus all her life: "The list of those whom she bewitched . . . included college boys, tutors, law students, the brothers of her girl friends, —several times their affianced bridegrooms even; and then the maturer friendships,—literary, Platonic, Plutonic; passages varying in intensity, and at least one passionate attachment, whose tragedy was due to the integrity of the Lovers, who scrupled to take their bliss at another's cost" (xviii). This is the beginning of the legend which was enlarged in 1924 and 1929 and later dissatisfied biographers so much that they were stimulated to make their own fruitless speculations.

In her review of *The Single Hound*, Elizabeth Shepley Sergeant greeted Emily Dickinson as a precursor of the Imagists: "For starkness of vision, 'quintessentialness' of expression, boldness and solidity of thought, and freedom of form, a New England spinster . . . might give the imagists 'pointers.' "[4] The critic in *The Chicago Herald* was of the same opinion: "Emily Dickinson sang herself into silence before the dawn of the present era of picture-making rather than musical poetry, but some of these unconsidered soul-chips easily might be regarded as foreshadowing the newer birth." The editor of *Poetry* was most confident of all. "Emily Dickinson, New England spinster of the nineteenth century, was an unconscious and uncatalogued *Imagiste*," wrote Harriet Monroe. "She had the visual imagination, the love of economy in line and epithet, the rigorous austerity of style, and the individual subtlety of rhythm, demanded by the code of the contemporary poets who group themselves under that title."[5] With that pronouncement she granted her an honorary membership in the new Anglo-American poetic movement. The epithet "an early Imagist" held its ground in Dickinson criticism until 1930, in the literary histories even longer.

Harriet Monroe showed little inclination to go into *The Single Hound* in more detail. She praised the volume for the sake of a few poems. Like the other critics she quoted "Fame is a fickle food," "There is a solitude of space," and the four-line poem "Adventure most unto itself," which was placed at the beginning of the book for thematic reasons.

The majority of the small group of reviewers was not willing to see the new poems exhumed so effortlessly. It was doubted whether the publication of private verses written to a sister-in-law was advisable or even justifiable at such a late hour, a generation after the author's death. Ethel Colson would have liked to remand them to "their long cherished, lavender scented seclusion." Frederick Burrows, the editor of the *New England Magazine*, was astonished that a publishing house with the experience of Little, Brown & Co. had estimated the chances of sales high enough to undertake the printing. He raised an objection that had been brought forward in 1890: "If Miss Dickinson were living, the present volume would undoubtedly be received with a criticism more savage than is accorded to any but those essentially worth while."[6]

A form problem did not exist for the advocates of the new poetry, since their effort aimed at the abolition of compulsory rhyme as well as metrical and rhythmical fetters. Elizabeth Sergeant had made a positive value judgment with her reference to "freedom of form." But an unavoidable confrontation loomed ahead for those who continued to expect stanzas, rhyme, and rhythmic regularity. Ethel Colson, Burrows, and *America* sounded the traditional note:

> The body of the work is disappointing. Torn from their natural environment, . . . the fairy fragments seem lonely, are frequently obscure and often incomprehensible.
>
> Playing this hide-and-seek with her own soul, she meets the not wholly unmerited general verdict of being a mere eccentric, indifferent to good verse form, and not impeccable as to grammatical fundamentals—a fate almost tragic, when we consider that this person walked easily and as by native right of rank, in realms of thought not unknown to the few greatest.
>
> The reviewer gets the impression that Miss Dickinson might have made a name for herself in poetry if she had been willing to occupy herself with the technical rules of her art. These, after all, are of primary importance: they crystallize into beauty the trailing ghosts of the mind.[7]

For the last of these reviewers the literary sins were reason enough for rejection. Burrows understood the deficiency of form as the result of the New Englander's "inevitable obsession of phrase making," but nevertheless came out in favor of Emily Dickinson because of her "intensity, if not . . . finish and form." Elia W. Peattie and *The New York Times Book Review* simply accepted the inevitable. *The Springfield Republican* and *The Boston Herald* spoke in a familiar manner of "epigrams in verse," "gnomic wisdom," and "flashes born of brooding upon the web of life in the loom of time." Braithwaite, who since his founding of *The Poetry Journal* had been a member of the new movement but had soon been decried as sentimental and old-fashioned, bid Emily Dickinson welcome as "one of the great spiritual artists of the world." He admired her "distinction of expression and form," but neglected to substantiate this general claim.[8]

After the disappearance of the short-lived interest in *The Single Hound*, a second extended pause set in. Hesitantly after 1918 and more strongly after 1921 new voices became audible. The shuffling pace of the reception from 1915 until 1923 resembles that of the lean years. Madame Bianchi's edition did not stimulate a continuation of the criticism. Almost all of the essays written in the following years referred to the earlier volumes.

These were the years in which Emily Dickinson was once again discovered by admirers. "I chiefly taught myself by systematically reading through the alcoves of the almost unfrequented library," Austin Warren later recalled of his college years. "I remember discovering Emily Dickinson . . . ."[9] Among these admirers her name had a pleasant ring. "Year by year knowledge of her secret spreads, as friend whispers to friend and confides the inimitable poet to a new lover," Robert Hillyer wrote in *The Freeman* in 1922.[10] As the president of the New England Poetry Club, Hillyer himself contributed to the spreading of the secret on December 5, 1923, when he delivered a well-received lecture in the Boston Public Library and arranged there an exhibition of autograph poems and letters contained in the Higginson collection.[11] Later, in a poem of friendship to Robert Frost, he recalled a period of time spent with Frost about 1916:

> *From many conversations I remember*
> *One on a windy day in late November.*
> *The sly recluse of Amherst in those times*
> *Moved me, in spite of questionable rhymes.*
> *We talked of women poets, nothing else,*
> *From Sappho to our friend in Sevenels.*
> *"Miss Dickinson is best!" You shook your head.*
> *"Perhaps a genius, but mad," you said.*[12]

In addition to further changes in the critical and biographical image of Emily Dickinson during these quieter years, the attitude of the new anthologies and literary histories must be discussed. And it remains to be seen why the poet was passed over by the younger generation of critics after she had been apostrophized by Harriet Monroe in a conspicuous place as "modern."

The biographical portrait was further distorted in 1915 and 1919. In an essay published in *The Atlantic Monthly*, Madame Bianchi assumed the same tone as in her editor's preface of 1914. While Aunt Emily reappears as the children's boon companion, the feeling of oddness predominates in spite of familiar ties and daily association. The aunt is a freak, a "spider," "the little white moth, fluttering helplessly, all a-tremble, ready to die of the experience and be found on the floor next morning a mere hint of winged dust."[13] An essay of Gamaliel Bradford, which is based on Jenkins' reminiscence of 1891, treads exactly the same path but moves several steps further into the unreal. As a "white spirit of wonder and grace and fancy and mockery" Emily Dickinson glides past the backdrop of a gloomy and forbidding parental home. The old myth of a spiritualized nun opens and closes this psychograph: "One who, as a child, knew Emily Dickinson well and loved her much recollects her most vividly as a white ethereal vision, stepping from her cloistral solitude on to the verandah, daintily unrolling a great length of carpet before her with her foot, strolling down to where the carpet ended among her flowers, then turning back and shutting herself out of the world." That the rug used by the poet for gardening attains the length of a carpet in Bradford's mind shows how he stretches the meager facts with his fantasy.[14]

To the extent that the conception of a Puritan New England paled, the person and work of Emily Dickinson came into focus and detached themselves from their natural background. This process is observable in Bradford's sketch and in essays of three New England admirers.

Marsden Hartley, who wrote in *The Dial* in August 1918, remade Emily Dickinson in his own image.[15] Although he had attained the rank of *pictor laureatus* of Maine, he remained an amateur as a literary critic and did not wish to be more. The fresh and playful features of his subject attracted him:

> When I want poetry in its most delightful and playful mood, I take up the verses of that remarkable girl of the sixties and seventies, Emily Dickinson. (p. 95)

> She was the brightest young sister of fancy, as she was the gifted young daughter of the ancient imagination. (p. 96)

She is in modern times perhaps the single exponent of true
celestial frivolity. (pp. 96-97)

She was an intoxicated being, drunken with the little tipsy
joys of the simplest form. (p. 97)

Her poetry is transparent and akin to the metaphysical school:
"It was a charm unique in itself, not like any other genius then
or now, or in the time before her, having perhaps a little of
relationship to the crystal clearness of Crashaw—like Vaughan
and Donne maybe in respect to their lyrical fervor and moral
earnestness, nevertheless appearing to us freshly with as separate
a spirit in her poetry as she herself was separated from the world
around her" (p. 95). By comparing what Waldo Frank said
about Hartley and Hartley about Emily Dickinson the intellectual
affinity of the painter-critic and his picture reveals itself:

He is eclectic. But wher-
ever he goes he chronicles
not so much these actual
worlds as his own pleasure
of them. They are but
mirrors . . . for his own
delicate, incisive humor.
For Hartley is an innocent
and a *naif*. At times he is
profound. Always he is
profoundly simple.[16]

Here was New England, at
its sharpest, brightest, wittiest,
most fantastic, most wilful,
most devout, saint and imp
sported in one, toying with the
tricks of the Deity, taking them
now with extreme profundity,
then tossing them about like
irresistible toys with an incomparable triviality. (p. 96)

It is not surprising that Hartley, who according to Frank was in
quest of fairy creatures in the modern world, addressed himself
to the lighter, unproblematic side of the poetry and experienced
Emily Dickinson's world, like his own, as the tragicomic world
of a child.

Robert Hillyer and Herbert Gorman each celebrated Emily
Dickinson as his own discovery. Both were happy that the poet
had hitherto escaped all categories and was yet unknown in
college classrooms and halls of fame. Yet both were convinced
of her greatness as well as of her mounting fame. Hillyer hesi-
tates to answer the question "Was she a great poet?" because he
does not wish to have the word "poet" applied to a reputable
writer: "But there is only one American writer who, I am certain, can never, in any place, or in any manner, be subjected to
comparison; and perhaps that is another way of knowing
poetry."[16a] Gorman is more definite in his judgment: "Time

cannot but gather to her name as the years march by for the place which she secured for herself in the annals of American poesy is one which must remain forever. The conditions which made her, the philosophical atmosphere in which she came to maturity, have vanished. Her flowering was unusual, but one which might have been expected. She has become part of a great heritage."[17] Both apply to her the term mystic. But while Gorman declares her, without qualification, a mystic Hillyer immediately makes one restriction: "The immortality towards which Emily Dickinson turns so decidedly is no mystical merging of the many into the One—that subterfuge of the weak-spirited. Identity is the greatest boon, its preservation the soul's fiercest function." Her "mystical second sight" is balanced by her gift of precise observation.

For Gorman, a militant member of the "Younger Generation,"[18] the chain of tradition had broken in 1918. The grandfatherly generation of the "thrice honored Sacred Lamas of Literature"[19] had lost his respect. The only exception was Emily Dickinson. An investigation of her stylistic precision convinced him that she possessed that vitality which he demanded of literature but scarcely still found in nineteenth-century authors: "There is something extremely modern here, and it is astonishing to note how much Emily Dickinson anticipated certain genres of our own contemporary poetry. She possessed the precise eye that is so demanded by the imagists; she was never addicted to overelaborate trimmings; she never (or, at least, rarely) dropped into clichés or time-tarnished poetical phraseology. Most of all, she was essentially vital and always herself."[19a]

The quiet reception of the decade following the publication of *The Single Hound* closed with a strident and aggressive "Declaration" on the first page of a newly founded little magazine. In the December 1922 issue of *The Measure*, the editor, Kenneth Alling, inveighed against the modern would-be poets with the help of Emily Dickinson: "There is none of the poetry of Emily Dickinson, even the most casual jottings, that does not show the depth and incandescence of her soul. . . . If the general world held poetry in adequate regard, how could all the later brood of April fakirs be confounded by the songs that spring put forth in her? . . . She belongs to that exceeding few who are the aristocracy of time."[20] Here Emily Dickinson is not only completely affirmed and accepted—although "the form is sometimes exasperating"—but becomes a model for the moderns.

The investigation of her reception between 1897 and 1924

opens and closes with the questions why there was so little desire for critical involvement. One might have expected that after 1914 Emily Dickinson would have received greater notice from the younger in search of a new poetry than from the older critics for whom a great New England past still overshadowed the present. But there was nothing of the sort. Harriet Monroe's cry seemed not to have been heard by the readers of *Poetry*. The poems were rediscovered from time to time, read and guarded as gems, but only by a few. In the controversy about the new poetry carried on from 1912 to 1923 in the *Atlantic*, *The Bookman*, *The Dial*, *The New Republic*, *Poetry*, and *The Outlook*, one searches in vain for her name.

Amy Lowell, Louis Untermeyer, and Conrad Aiken certainly belonged to the readers of *Poetry* from its inception. All three were champions of the new poetry in the years during the war and shortly thereafter; all three were later closely linked with Emily Dickinson's rising fame; all three passed her by in their omnibus volumes *Tendencies in Modern American Poetry* (1917), *The New Era in American Poetry* (1919), and *Skepticisms: Notes on Contemporary Poetry* (1919).[21] These books may be considered representative of the attitude of other poet-critics who had their first volumes of verse published before 1918 and then later wrote about Emily Dickinson, such as Amy Lowell (born 1874), Alfred Kreymborg (1883), Louis Untermeyer (1885), John Gould Fletcher (1886), Clement Wood (1888), Conrad Aiken (1889), Genevieve Taggard (1894), Mark Van Doren (1894), and Stephen Vincent Benét (1898). Their books show that the poet-critics were at war with one another. They employed their pens in the "life-and-death struggle among the poets," as Aiken complained, and in so doing, each review changed under the writer's hands to an open attack and a concealed "apologia pro specie sua."[22] For the time being, the new poetry laid claim to all the critical powers of the participants. Untermeyer celebrated its liberation from false "puritan" standards and from the incubus of Stedman's *An American Anthology* —"this gargantuan collection of mediocrity and moralizing"— and its return to "actuality," "heartiness and lustihood," and, most of all, to "democracy."[23] With unmistakable intention, Amy Lowell grouped in her book six poets by pairs in a line of development which proceeds from the literary evolutionists Robinson and Frost through the revolutionists Sandburg and Masters to the highly advanced Imagists H. D. and J. G. Fletcher.

Aiken skeptically turned against such enthusiasm, deplored the predominant aesthetic relativism, and dryly commented on Amy Lowell's construction: "So far as truth is concerned, her evolutionary order might be inverted" (*Skepticisms*, p. 254).

Aiken and Amy Lowell make only passing references to America's poetic past. Untermeyer considers a background sketch appropriate to define the new spirit and distinguish it from the old. In the process he carefully walks in the footsteps of Van Wyck Brooks's *America's Coming-of-Age*, applies his formula of the polarity "highbrow-lowbrow" in American life and thought, and closes with a hymn to Whitman as the first useful American poet whose work made a harmonious national ideal possible. He quotes the half dozen "Our Poets" whom Brooks had dismissed as relics and finds them "colonial" and "unhuman." Like Brooks, Untermeyer does not even name Emily Dickinson.[24]

Taken together, the books of Amy Lowell, Aiken, and Untermeyer reveal four attitudes toward the literature of the past which helped to form the Dickinson image of the 1920's: first, the view of Whitman as a pioneer of the modern era, as whose countertype Emily Dickinson later emerges; second, an impressive ability to apprehend the peculiarities and values of poetry congenial to the pathetic ego of the critic; third, the inclination already observed in Hartley and Hillyer to reinterpret and to blur the limits set by time, space, and personality; fourth, an unwillingness to understand and appreciate the past in its own right.

The acid test of this attitude is Amy Lowell's critical and creative involvement with Emily Dickinson during her years of struggle for the cause of Imagism and shortly thereafter.

In a lecture on "The New Manner in Modern Poetry" held before the Boston Round Table Club on April 8, 1915, she referred to American verse at the time of her famous ancestor James Russell Lowell and, with the exception of the two unappreciated geniuses Poe and Whitman, rejected it as imitative. At the end of the Civil War, poetic activity was inert. "Inert, that is, save for one still, small voice. One little voice which was the precursor of the modern day. A voice considered only as bizarre and not at all important, by its contemporaries. I refer to Emily Dickinson, who is so modern that if she were living today I know just the group of poets with whom she would inevitably belong."[25]

On January 4, 1916, she spoke before the Roxburghe Club in Roxbury, Connecticut, on "American Poets of Today." In the introductory historical part of the lecture the same names and accusations appeared. Once again Emily Dickinson was mentioned with Poe and Whitman as forming the trio of the great exceptions. This time she went into more detail concerning Dickinson:

> Strangely enough, there started up in New England a rare (if it had not really existed I should have said an "impossible") anomaly. A true pagan poet shut up in the cage of a narrow provincial Puritanism. But the odd part of this poet was that the cage was not merely the exterior one of family and surroundings, it was the cage of her own soul. I refer, of course, to Emily Dickinson. She was a pagan if ever there was one, but she was also a sincerely religious woman. This led her to address poems to the Deity in so joyous and familiar a strain that her first biographer wrote many pages to explain her seeming irreverence. But really there was no explanation except the one I have given. But one cannot help feeling that sincere though her religious attitude certainly was, it was due partly to early education, and partly to atavism (her father was a minister), while her own peculiar, personal characteristic was the pagan one. I have often wondered whether this duality of temperament was not responsible for the shyness and elusive quality which she is said to have had in a marked degree. In wider surroundings might she not have developed into a greater poet and a more tranquil woman? It is significant that those of her poems most prized by her contemporaries are the ones we care least for today.[26]

On March 20 and 27, 1918, she delivered two lectures on "Imagism Past and Present" in the Brooklyn Institute. The first explained the principles of this school with examples from the past, above all Theocritus, Blake, Coleridge, and Emily Dickinson, who, as she said, all wrote at the end of a literary epoch and enlivened the poetry of the time by turning back to reality. The names chosen occasioned the drawing up of a genealogical table in which Emily Dickinson becomes the direct descendant of Blake and Coleridge. Since Dickinson is not only a descendant but also a precursor, Amy Lowell once again refers to her intellectual and religious dissociation from the New England tradition and the possibility of a more fruitful creative development under more favorable circumstances. The conception of

Higginson as a jailer who made his protégée a captive joins the notion of the bird locked "in the cage of a narrow provincial Puritanism."[27] Nevertheless, his 1890 preface was good enough to serve her as a prerequisite for proof that Emily Dickinson possessed Imagistic qualities. What Higginson had defended as "flashes of wholly original insight" and "rugged frame" she simply explained, with reference to points three and four of the Imagist manifesto,[28] as the hard poetry demanded by Flint, Pound, and herself. "The exact word, the perfect image, that is what makes these short poems so telling."[29] As a precursor she evaluated Emily Dickinson on the basis of her usage, her dissatisfaction with contemporary meters and the occasional use of free verse, and her "unrelated" method of writing—"that is, the describing of a thing by its appearance only, without regard to its entity in any other way."[30] The example chosen for clarification is "A route of evanescence."[31]

The rejection of nineteenth-century American literature with the exception of the triad of poets recurs for a fourth time in *A Critical Fable* (1922). The interlocutor of the "I," James Russell Lowell, expresses his astonishment at such a devaluation since his own verse satire of 1848:

> *"Your strange estimation has made me quite jealous*
> *For those of my time whose secure reputations*
> *Gave us no concern. These are trifling vexations,*
> *But they itch my esteem. Is there really not one*
> *You sincerely admire?" "Yes, Miss Dickinson,"*
> *I hastily answered. At this he stopped dead*
> *In his walk and his eyes seemed to pop from his head.*
> *"What," he thundered, "that prim and perverse little person*
> *Without an idea you could hang up a verse on!*
> *Wentworth Higginson did what he could, his tuition*
> *Was ardent, unwearied, but bore no fruition."*[32]

The last discussion of Emily Dickinson was of a personal nature. In the poem "The Sisters" a new trio is assembled. All three of the "little family / Of singing sisters"—Sappho, Mrs. Browning, Emily Dickinson—are "great." But none of the three actually has a word for the "I" of the poem. The guilt in the case of Emily Dickinson lies not only with "Queen Victoria," but also with Martin Luther and the Church Fathers

> *Who draped their prurience like a dirty cloth*
> *About the naked majesty of God*

and who let Emily Dickinson's soul starve in Amherst. The connecting link between her and the "I" is represented, characteristically, by a hummingbird, which the Amherst recluse is watching when the "I" visits her in a dream. The element of separation lies in the gesture of despair with which Amy Lowell locks Emily the woman back up in the cage of her time from which she formerly would have liked to free her.[33]

The Dickinson biography, which was mentioned as early as 1922 in letters and was planned despite the difficulties to be expected in procuring material from two hostile camps, was never begun. Amy Lowell died in 1925 three months after the publication of her *John Keats*.[34]

The Bostonian encountered Emily Dickinson during her sorties into the nineteenth century, in which she hoped to uncover the roots of the new poetry. She was less interested in her as an artist of her time than in what she could contribute to a better understanding of the Imagists. When Amy Lowell snatched the poet out of her habitat, Emily had to appear as an intimate sister; when she later considered her in her environment, she often lost patience with her eccentricity, her Puritan heritage, and her passive submission to an "atavism." Then an assenting answer from one of her guests at Sevenels was needed to cause the lady of the house to do an angry about-face and cry: "Emily Dickinson was one of the great poets."

What Untermeyer and Aiken had failed to do as critics of Emily Dickinson until 1919, they made up for as editors of anthologies (cf. Sources, pp. 274-75). With a reference to their "almost carved lines," Untermeyer included three poems in the first edition of his *Modern American Poetry* (1919). Aiken proceeded much more generously in his *Modern American Poets* (1922), a collection intended for British readers, in which, as the only premodern, Emily Dickinson is represented by twenty-three poems. He justifies her inclusion with the statement that she deserved more notice than had been accorded her, that a voice of an older generation makes a wholesome contrast to the modern authors, and that "in any case I cannot conceal my feeling that Emily Dickinson is one of the most remarkable American poets, and that her poetry is perhaps the finest, by a woman, in the English language."[35]

Most of the early critical outlines and anthologies of contemporary poetry set the beginning of the modern era in the year 1900, with which Stedman had concluded his selection. The arbitrariness of this date caused anthologists to make exceptions. When they prepared an expanded new edition of *The New Poetry: An Anthology of Twentieth Century Verse in English* (1917) in 1923, Harriet Monroe and Alice Henderson felt compelled to remark that the new poetry had already gotten underway in the nineteenth century and that the omission of one name was particularly regrettable: "Emily Dickinson . . . achieved a vivid directness and compactness worthy of the imagists, as well as a very personal technique which searched for hidden, rather than obvious, delicacies of assonance and rhythm." Although the subtitle did not allow her to be included, two poems were quoted in the introduction.[36] In the same year a second exception was made when Leonora Speyer and Alfred Kreymborg compiled *An Anthology of Contemporary Verse* at the request of the German publisher Kurt Wolff in Munich. In addition to Aiken, Frost, Eliot, and their contemporaries, Emily Dickinson is represented by six poems.

That her verse had in the meantime become important enough for inclusion in anthologies and no longer appeared here and there in a collection of nature or love poems is confirmed by the college anthologies after 1915 (cf. Sources, p. 274), but especially by *Century Readings for a Course in American Literature* (1920) by Fred Lewis Pattee, who remained her declared enemy during his lifetime. He inconsistently admitted eleven of her "fragments, lyrical ejaculations, childlike conceits, little orphic sayings often illogical and meaningless."[37]

Acknowledgment in literary histories came at about the same time. The years from 1915 to 1921, from Pattee's *A History of American Literature since 1870* to the printing of the third volume of the *Cambridge History of American Literature*, led out of the impasse of the college handbooks (cf. Sources, p. 299). There is a significant decrease in age from Brander Matthews through Percy Boynton to Norman Foerster—sixty-six, forty-four, thirty-four—at the time of each of their publications, which amounts to no less than the difference between two generations.

Matthews omitted Emily Dickinson in the revised new edition of *An Introduction to the Study of American Literature* (1918) just as he had in the first edition of 1896. Having dedicated books to Andrew Lang and Higginson and taken Aldrich as a literary model, Matthews contented himself with the enumeration of more conservative "women writers" in his concluding chapter XIX, "Other Writers." The new verse disquieted him because of its technical anarchy. In Percy H. Boynton's *A History of American Literature* (1919), too, the chances of happening upon Emily Dickinson are slight since the book is restricted to major authors. For the "Later Poets," chapter XXIX, there remains little and for Dickinson no room.

The Cambridge History of American Literature marks the end of a period in the writing of American literary history and a new beginning. Of the phalanx of worthies only a dozen names remain in the chapter "Later Poets" written by Norman Foerster for the third volume. The New York group, especially, has shrunk, while Emily Dickinson has grown in importance. All of these later lights are "minor"; all belong to the experimental phase of the second half of the century when literature espoused either beauty or life. Aldrich, Taylor, Stoddard, Stedman, and Gilder represent the "poetry of beauty" which was to continue a great tradition but suffered from the taint of mechanical repetition and mannerism; Emily Dickinson with her perceptiveness for genuine experience and her aesthetic deficiencies represents the "poetry of life." Her increase in stature since 1890 seems so significant to the author that he places her at the beginning of the chapter and opens and concludes the three pages devoted to her with references to this upgrading:

> None of these has gained more in time than has Emily Dickinson. Despite her defective sense of form, which makes her a better New Englander than Easterner, she has acquired a permanent following of discriminating readers through her extraordinary insight into the life of the mind and the soul.[38]

Her place in American letters will be inconspicuous but secure. Her formless verses are counterbalanced by the flashes they contain. Whimsicality was the characteristic feature of the person and the work: "That was her guiding divinity, Whim in a high sense: not unruliness, for all her impishness, but complete subjection to the inner dictate. She obeyed it in her mode of life, in her friendships, in her letters, in her poems. It makes her poetry eminently spontaneous—as fresh and artless as experience itself—in spite of the fact that she was not a spontaneous singer."

The tradition of the older handbooks was upheld by the outlines of Haney and Hastings, both of which were published in 1923 (cf. Sources, p. 299). Both mention Emily Dickinson without, however, contributing a new point of view.

Owing to the tension between the older and newer criticism, the critical reaction to *The Single Hound,* though weak, was a turning point in the course of her reception. The poetry was for the first time fully embraced by reviewers; it was placed beside the art which the Imagists sought to create. For most critics, however, the way in which this "gifted and somewhat eccentric lady"[39] had written remained questionable.

Did Emily Dickinson belong to the nineteenth or the twentieth century? Miss Monroe's opinion was propagated in Amy Lowell's campaign for Imagism and logically led to Alling's déclaration in an avant-garde literary journal: the poet was reinterpreted as a premodern. The traditional attitude, which still dominated the reviews of 1914, became weaker, although it lingered in literary histories until 1921.

These antithetical attitudes are reflected in two poems of 1917 and 1916. The placid reminiscence of an Amherst citizen begins:

> *The robins still in Amherst*
> *Keep punctual to the dawn,*
> *And still officious bumble-bees*
> *Patrol the candid lawn.*

"And still" recurs in the same place in the next three stanzas. The poet leaves Emily Dickinson in her familiar environment of the "Pelham hills," which she could see in the east from her window. On the other hand, Carl Sandburg is concerned with her legacy:

> *You gave us the bumble bee who has a soul,*
> *The everlasting traveler among the hollyhocks,*
> *And how God plays around in a back yard garden.*[40]

The editors of modern poetry had to face the dilemma of her historical position. The new critics could for the time being still evade the embarrassing situation, since they were completely occupied in attempting to orient themselves in the exciting "little renaissance" in the midst of which they actively stood.

REHABILITATION (1924-29)

*Poor Emily who could not write like Lowell and Long-
fellow! She could not. She wrote in secret, for herself alone,
and now we find her, in the company of the maddest and
most stubbornly realistic men, Blake, Shakespeare, and
Browning.*[1]

THE THREE NEW PUBLICATIONS of 1924 scarcely enriched the
Dickinson canon. Moreover, Emily Dickinson still appeared in
the mended Victorian garb which had been placed around her
shoulders by her first editors. Nevertheless, the time had been
well chosen by Martha Dickinson Bianchi for her *The Life
and Letters of Emily Dickinson*. Flagging critical interest had
been stirred up and kept alive, and younger critics sat in the
reviewer's chairs and guaranteed a broader and friendlier reception than that of ten years earlier. The opposition to American
literature of the nineteenth century had diminished. The anthologists had been compelled to cross the magic border of 1900
in order to get to the springs of the modern age. On this side of
the century mark the poetic renaissance seemed, in the perspective of 1924, a part of the most recent past which invited
criticism and comparison. The discovery of new geniuses continued and became the object of parody, since people recognized
how carelessly the term was applied. Old rediscoveries like Blake,
Hopkins, Donne, Whitman, and Crane were taken more
seriously.

Emily Dickinson was a genius among others. In one of Burton Rascoe's weekly columns in the New York *Herald Tribune*,
she appeared in 1922 in a catalogue of his thirty-five favorite
authors, which extends from Sappho and Anacreon through

Villon, Shakespeare, and Goethe to E. A. Robinson and H. D. On the occasion of a visit with Archibald MacLeish and E. E. Cummings in Paris, he reported two years later in the same place: "Coming out of the train I had been counting up our lyric poets of the first order since Poe—Emily Dickinson, yes, on the evidence of two or three lyrics alone—Sarah Teasdale, darn near it, darn near first rank anyhow, maybe first rank— Edna St. Vincent Millay, absolutely, because she is one of the few poets who have been able to breathe life into the sonnet since Shakespeare . . . ."[2] The staccato monologue continues. It was considered the epitome of the hectic New York literary spirit of the day by the chronicler of the decade.[3]

This spirit of unrest, of precipitate evaluations, of enthusiastic demonstration of sympathies, of feverish joy at discovery and of the rejection of everything dusty left its mark on the criticism of Emily Dickinson in the years of her rehabilitation, especially in 1924, when people believed the poet was being rescued from long oblivion. They thought they finally possessed the collected works in one volume and could comfortably survey all she had written. The feeling that the editor had led them around by the nose set in only five years later when "further" poems followed the "complete" poems and these in turn were later followed by more and more.

The collection of letters, which critics misunderstood to be a biography, was published by Houghton Mifflin in April 1924. It was followed in July by Little, Brown's edition of *The Complete Poems* and in October by *Selected Poems*, edited by Conrad Aiken and published in London by Jonathan Cape.

Madame Bianchi's "biography" became a financial success.[4] The editor had made an easy job of the work. Without mentioning the name of, let alone a word of thanks to, her predecessor, she had the material collected by Mrs. Todd reprinted as *Letters*, in chronological order and with the addition of several unpublished letters to Sue's children. For the first part, *The Life*, she supplied a biographical sketch, full of flaws and distortions.

That the biographical study of Emily Dickinson continued to revolve around the vague allusions of the niece and the misled speculations of the critics is an irony for which Martha Dickinson Bianchi is responsible. The unreal features of this life given in the preface to *The Single Hound* could not but encourage Gamaliel Bradford. His psychograph was again criticized by the niece, as were the conjectures of other critics. She spoke of a public "which has, doubtless without intention, misunderstood and exaggerated her seclusion—amassing a really voluminous stock of quite lurid misinformation of irrelevant personalities. She has been . . . even betrayed by one American essayist of repute to appear a fantastic eccentric." The critic of 1924 who perused the eight short chapters of the biographical part in the hope of discovering "the real Emily" must have already had his doubts when he read in the preface: "However the present volume may lift the veil, or presume to lead her shy reality into the light of mortal dawns again, Emily alone supplies the only clue to herself, the articles of her Faith." The pervading solemn tone and the continual self-adulation of the author of *The Life* as "the sole survivor of her family," "the last living member of her own family," must have appeared similarly strange. The doubts of reviewers must have become stronger when they found "intimate" letters from the years 1853 to 1855 mentioned which had been "too sacred for revealing" (p. 44) and when the poet was characterized as an unreal being about which the "frail incidents of her days" could tell nothing:

> She had the soul of a monk of the Middle Ages bound up in the flesh of Puritan descent. (p. 95)
> Like Saint Francis, she might have preached to the birds, and included not only "Sister Lark," but Bumble Bee, in her sermon. (p. 96)
> She had the inhuman, elfin strain that has nothing whatever to do with man-made rites or professions. (p. 97)

Her death was the "setting free" of "a winged thing" (p. 101).

Still, the reader learned something about her ancestors, her youth and school years (including her "revolt" at Mount Holyoke), later friends and acquaintances, as well as about social life in Amherst. Moreover, the veil was reluctantly but dramatically lifted in the fifth chapter, "The End of Peace,'"—the legend of 1914 was expanded. The two short paragraphs were accepted at face value in the following years since they seemed to be from a trustworthy source:

> Certainly in that first witchery of an undreamed Southern springtime Emily was overtaken—doomed once and forever by her own heart. It was instantaneous, overwhelming, impossible. There is no doubt that two predestined souls were kept apart only by her high sense of duty, and the necessity

for preserving love untarnished by the inevitable destruction of another woman's life.

Without stopping to look back, she fled to her own home for refuge—as a wild thing running from whatever it may be that pursues; but only a few days later Sister Sue looked up from her sewing to see Lavinia, pallid and breathless from running, who grasped her wrist with hurrying hand, urging: "Sue, come! That man is here!—Father and Mother are away, and I am afraid Emily will go away with him!" But the one word he implored, Emily would not say. Unable to endure his life under the old conditions, after a short time he left his profession and home and silently withdrew with his wife and an only child to a remote city, a continent's width remote, where echo at least could not mock him with its vain outcry: dying prematurely, the spell unbroken. p. 47)

The publication of *The Complete Poems of Emily Dickinson* took shape in a similarly uncomplicated manner. Only five unpublished poems were added to the three series of the 1890's and to *The Single Hound*. Like *Life and Letters*, the book went through several printings and into a London edition.[5] In the introduction, which omitted the names of Mrs. Todd and Higginson, the volume was designated as "a final complete edition" and was recommended to all who otherwise never read poetry: "The scoffers, the literary agnostics, make exception for her. She is also the poet of the unpoetic, the unlearned foreigner, the busy, practical, inexpressive man as well as woman, the wise young and groping old, the nature worshiper, the schoolgirl, children caught by her fairy lineage, and lovers of all degree" (p. ix).

With the *Selected Poems of Emily Dickinson*, Aiken fulfilled a wish which had been uttered twice in the previous year.[6] He had greater difficulties to overcome. His plan met first, as he later reported, with the threefold resistance of the critics, of the publishers, and especially of Madame Bianchi.[7]

The introductory essay ("Preface") is the showpiece of Dickinson criticism in the 1920's. In its effect, it is almost comparable to Higginson's 1890 foreword. There were reasons why Aiken published it twice before it served as an introduction in October 1924. With the first publication in the April issue of *The Dial*, he anticipated Madame Bianchi's editorial activity;

with the reprint in the London *Bookman* in October he called attention to the forthcoming anthology. The greatest notice was taken of the preface, from which the following quotations derive. The psychological approach, the sober weighing of failure and achievement, the sparse, intentionally personal praise supplied more food for thought than the effusive words of the niece.

He can only ascertain, but not explain, that Emily Dickinson must have sustained a deep psychic injury. Mrs. Todd's protestations and Madame Bianchi's legend only permit conjecture. From the intellectual barrenness of Amherst he concludes that, in the middle of a time of literary flourishing, the poet lived in a vacuum, that she suffered from this sterility and, of necessity, narrowed the circumference of her life: "One must assume that she found in her immediate environment no one of her own stature with whom she could admit or discuss such things; that she lacked the energy or effrontery to voyage out into the unknown in search of such companionship; and that, lacking this courage and wanting this help, she became easily a prey to the then current Emersonian doctrine of mystical Individualism" (p. 12). Her person and work are regarded as the "most perfect flower of New England Transcendentalism": "In her mode of life, she carried the doctrine of self-sufficient individualism farther than Thoreau carried it, or the naïve zealots of Brook Farm. In her poetry, she carried it, with its complement of passionate moral mysticism, farther than Emerson: which is to say that as a poet she had more genius than he" (p. 14). In her withdrawal, he sees protest, but also exhibitionism. "Vanity is in her letters—at the last, an unhealthy vanity. She believes that anything she says, however brief, will be of importance; however cryptic, will be deciphered. She enjoyed being something of a mystery, and she sometimes deliberately and awkwardly exaggerates it" (p. 13). Her compression of Emerson's gnomic style to an epigrammatic symbolism results in obscurity as well as felicitous simplicity. The concluding evaluation resembles Higginson's. Despite her disregard of "grammar, rhyme, metre" (p. 21) she wins her readers over:

> The magic is terse and sure. And ultimately one simply sighs at Miss Dickinson's singular perversity, her lapses and tyrannies, and accepts them as an inevitable part of the strange and original genius she was. The lapses and tyrannies become a positive charm—one even suspects they were de-

liberate. They satisfied her—therefore they satisfy us. This marks, of course, our complete surrender to her highly individual gift, and to the singular sharp beauty, present everywhere, of her personality. These two things cannot be separated; and together, one must suppose, they suffice to put her among the finest poets in the language. (p. 22)

Nobody doubted that an attempt to write the life of Emily Dickinson would encounter great difficulties and that the niece —as eyewitness, relative, and heir to the estate—was the natural biographer. Yet the opinions concerning the author of *Life and Letters* differed widely (cf. Sources, pp. 314-15). Several voices, among which were those of Ethel Parton, Stephen Benét, Gamaliel Bradford, and Katharine Bates, were full of praise. Benét declared the work the Book of the Month, underscored its "reticent excellence," as did others after him, and thought that "her biographer succeeds in giving a portrait of her far finer and more vivid than portraits which the historians of many more noisy existences have achieved."[8]

The band of the dissatisfied, led by Herbert Gorman, Rolfe Humphries, Genevieve Taggard, Edward Sapir, George Whicher, and Newton Arvin, found much to object to: the *Life* scarcely contained new material; the mystery was not solved; the person remained a pale shadow; the author passed by important crises; she behaved as though ecstatic and treated her subject as if she were writing a holy book. These critics were well aware of the history of publication and the feud between the Todds and Dickinsons. Humphries and Miss Taggard cited *Letters* (1894), reproached Madame Bianchi for her omissions and inaccuracies, accused her of unfair behavior toward Mrs. Todd, and found fault with Sister Sue's being pushed unduly into the foreground. The demand to report either all or nothing about Emily Dickinson grew out of the realization that the *Life* could at best be considered a rough draft. Scandal and anecdotes were no substitute for biography.

The accusation of distortion exceeded the reproach for sketchiness. For the young Amherst lyricist Rolfe Humphries the long known old wives' legend now served up as a biography rhymed with the retouched frontispiece: "She has become . . . a Mysterious Recluse, subject of solemn gossip and celibate admiration; a New England female saint, prized possession of serious folks—and their spiritual descendants—who feel that there was in her something queer not to care for their black-mittened, small-college-town diversions. How much more queer it would have been if she had. Emily Dickinson deserves a better memorial."⁹ Genevieve Taggard described the book as "only a mundane reproduction along familiar lines" and became indignant at its onesidedness as well as at its gaps: "Where are the bold and capricious and impassioned colors that lie so marvelously beside the nun-like gray and spiritual azure of her nature? Not here. This is the supreme irony of the book: Emily's family still has her under lock and key; so far as such devices are powerful at all, they are still, forty years after her death, the chief concern of this single surviving Dickinson. Reticence, good taste, Amherst sensibilities—all the forces that stifled and warped the living girl are here again, silencing the events of her life and destroying her letters, as perfect in many instances as her poems."

Comments like those of Benét, Boynton, Parton, and Bates show how the schematic, hermit-like portrait, which was pilloried by the more discerning, could affect trusting souls. They all accepted the blanched picture and concluded that Emily had lived as a "gay and normal personality" in a serene, understanding environment. "How vividly that family circle is drawn in a few elfish strokes," exclaimed Katharine Bates, and added with alliterative gusto: "Emily Dickinson is the perfect flowering of a rare but recognizable variety of the New England gentlewoman of the past—the lily-of-the-valley variety, virginal, sequestered, to the passing eye most delicate and demure, but ringing all the while spicy bells of derision and delight."¹⁰

While these uncritical minds contented themselves with leading their readers past the obligatory stations of Emily's normally spent youth with its tragic Washington and Philadelphia finale, others were taken aback when they compared letters and life. Howsoever Madame Bianchi had sought to attune the correspondence to the tone of her biography—people noticed the difference. "The visual image one has of her from the memories of that time is of something delicate, white, and flitting, almost floating; but the mental impression one takes of her intellect is rather of something forcible, virile, not to say 'gritty,'" wrote one critic. Another stated: "One could not easily reconcile this morbid and cloistral figure of the legend with the arrogant, racy, ironic, and almost Shakespearean Emily of the poems and letters. One has been tempted to wonder whether Taine's 'milieu' and 'moment' may not here too have had their relevance; and whether

Emily may not have been but one more American artist 'compensating' for the inadequacy of her environment."[11]

The "secret" provoked some to venture interpretations of their own to explain what they thought the biographer had concealed. In the episode of 1854 Gorman saw "the complete outline of a tragedy" and demanded that "it is from that crisis in her life that the critic must build Emily Dickinson."[12] According to Keys the fate of the misunderstood genius had overtaken the poet just as it had Henry Adams; according to Colton, nothing more than a constant striving for happiness lay behind the mystery. Genevieve Taggard assumed that a chain of associations existed between the lover and his death on the one hand and the role of God, father, and death in her work on the other.

In contrast to the general biographical curiosity, of which the letters were a greater source than the introductory biography, concern with the prose was negligible. In addition to the mystery pervading her life, only her religiousness, which was interpreted as a protest against the Puritan tradition, was of interest. John Gould Fletcher, following Madame Bianchi's suggestion, made Emily Dickinson a sister of St. Francis and a martyr who bore her renunciation heroically. Kathérine Brégy interpreted the poet as a seeker who, bored by her paternal religion, became an essentially Catholic thinker: "In fact, without the slightest familiarity with Catholic doctrine, Emily Dickinson seems to have felt intuitively both the sacramental possibility of love and the impossibility of achieving this through the destruction of other lives."[13]

Madame Bianchi tried to repay the malcontents in their own coin when she accused "certain critics"—by which she meant Herbert Gorman and Arthur Colton—of a desire for mere sensation. In a letter to the editor of *The Saturday Review of Literature* she wrote on August 2, 1924: "What more do they want to know,—unless it be the name of the man she loved, and his street number?" There was nothing else to be told. "It is disappointing to admit that there was no jealously guarded mystery, no scandal, no vulgarity, nothing sensational. It was all helplessly true and simple and mighty."[14]

When the complete poems were published in July 1924, there was great astonishment that the Amherst recluse had been able to remain an unknown for so long despite her early popularity. She reminded one of Hopkins and even more of the recent rediscovery of Blake. The temptation to draw the poems also into the arena of biographical inquiry was great. "Here is written out clearly the story of a hopeless love," exulted *The Christian Science Monitor*.[15] Yet, in the course of the months the number grew of those who left off speculating and contented themselves with finding Emily Dickinson in her poems. Reviewers pointed out her stature, removed her from the past, regarded her in the light of the most modern American lyrical achievement, and endeavored to explain her genius.

In most reviews astonishment took the form of spontaneous upgrading. Her fame was considered a *fait accompli*. E. L. Pearson called the poems "perhaps the best and most important book published in America this month"; E. Merrill Root spoke of "one of our three or four American poets"; Whicher of "a New England classic."[16] Arvin declared: "She belongs now to the ages." Benét was more explicit: "Time cannot diminish, but only makes more apparent, what she had and did not claim. She may never be a universally popular poet—her thought has burrs for the lazy—but she will always be a great one." The critics compared her with other writers and placed her next to or above Elizabeth Browning, Christina Rossetti, and Charlotte Brontë. Only *The Literary Digest* and Colton were less convinced of her rank.[17]

Through his familiarity with the poetry of the little renaissance, the reader of 1924 had come closer to Emily Dickinson. "The unconventionality of her form does not jar upon us, familiar with Sandburg's shredded prose, Vachel Lindsay's jazz and Amy Lowell's polyphonic experiments, as it jarred upon many in 1890."[18] The tendency to measure Emily Dickinson according to modern standards was increasingly accompanied by an inclination to hold her up as a mirror before contemporary poetry. To some she appeared the sole genuine Imagist. At the same time she continued to exist as a precursor of the free verse movement.

For those who had a quarrel with modern poetry, and particularly with Imagism, she served as a weapon to express their discontent. "Emily Dickinson may be safely approved by the modern readers of freak magazines," wrote Pearson in *The Outlook*, "for she was often a bad metrician and a worse rhymster; as with Whitman, they will love her best for her faults." E. Merrill Root went furthest in this direction in *The Measure*. His opening remark that Emily Dickinson was great simply because she had something to say, and not a gaudy way of saying nothing, is barbed. The targets are Untermeyer and, above all, Amy Lowell, "a pseudo-poet"; the arrows are Emily Dickinson and Walt Whitman:

Emily Dickinson . . . was a sister of Whitman. Miss Lowell is fond of claiming Whitman as her literary grandfather. Untermeyer even suggests that Emily Dickinson was a forerunner of the imagists—which is like making Christ the forerunner of John the Baptist. Imagine it! Amy Lowell a child of Whitman! Why, she is not redly human; if you cut her, she would not bleed—she would exude spiritual ichor, like one of Milton's angels. . . . In the first place, Emily Dickinson gives us depths; Miss Lowell gives us surfaces. (p. 16)

Emily Dickinson shows a sense of humor while Amy Lowell does not; with the one, form is a necessary expression of inner energy, with the other, an intellectual toy: "Miss Lowell is interesting as a sort of literary sword-swallower, a literary double-headed calf in a side-show. Emily Dickinson is interesting in the same noble and human way as Christ or Joan of Arc or Nietzsche" (p. 18).

In Root's battle against Amy Lowell the end result was that Emily Dickinson was assured of her stature and timelessness and of being a Whitman parallel. With a sharper eye, the German-American linguist Edward Sapir set himself the task of playing off her achievements against the suspiciously regarded literature and culture of the day. For him she is at once the destroyer of a belated romanticism and the harbinger "of a spirit that has not yet succeeded in shaping itself. In the wiser chronology of the future history of American literature she is likely to be counted the spiritual successor, and possibly destroyer, of our . . . cerebralists and vendors of 'jeweled bindings.' " She is the founder of a not yet organized "primitive" school. She lived intuitively, turned her back on the materialism of the Gilded Age, and drank very sparingly of the stream of contemporary literary culture. "Hence all her poems, the very poorest with the fine and beautiful ones, are protected from the slightest alloy of sham. Where she failed . . . it was never because her vision was unsure, but over and over again because she had no tools ready to hand. Yet so ardent was her spirit that an almost comic *gaucherie* in the finding of rhymes could not prevent her from discovering to us the promise of a fresh, primitive, and relentless school of poetry that is still on the way." The American poetic renaissance did not prove to be a rebirth, but merely a shrill cacophony. The Whitman tradition with its sentimental glorification of democracy and its insistence on the mystical beauties of an externalized world had led to a deterioration of poetic values. A renewal could only be effected through a return to "unhampered intuitive living" and "spiritual passion," as they are foretokened in Emily Dickinson's life and work.[19]

The predominating concern with Emily Dickinson the person and the attempts to place her work in, or in contrast to, modern literature brought about a loss of historical perspective. In May 1925, a young English professor in Amherst, George Whicher, called attention to the deceptiveness of such thinking. Her seclusion was just as normal as Thoreau's and Hawthorne's. She was neither an intellectual outsider nor a contemporary of the critics of 1924, but "a vestal of the New England hearth":

> By noticing her daring sallies and ignoring the steadiness of her reliance on heaven we underestimate the sincerity of her poetry. Her distinction lies in the completeness with which she conserves the spirit of Puritanism in its period of fine flower. She is Puritan in every fiber, . . . Puritan in her reticence and her pungent idiom, in her passion for renunciation, in her habit of humorously watching her mind at play, in her preoccupation with death and eternity, in her whimsical familiarity with God, in her deep and ardent loyalties.[20]

Hardly any progress was made in the comprehension of Emily Dickinson's art, a fact which can be gleaned from the critical terminology. Enthusiasts continued to speak of "flawless diamonds glistening always with undiminished brilliance" and "flashes of genius like streaks of lightning in a murky sky." Kathérine Brégy took over Higginson's term "spasmodic" as *le mot juste* for the poems, "since they vary all the way from the old rhetoric of the poetaster to free verse and a distant anticipation of what is now called imagism" (p. 351). Arthur Colton, Allen Nevins, and Walter Yust fell back into old trains of thought. For Howard Mumford Jones, writing in *The New Student*, there existed no doubt that she had not been an accomplished artist, but "a sensitive spirit artistically endowed." "Her poems are like nothing so much as they are like the notebooks of a Leonardo da Vinci—full of fugitive and imperfect glories. The verse cries out for the labor of the file" (p. 12). That did not sound much different from what the Boston *Transcript* had written concerning the half-finished sketches of an old master on December 9, 1891.

In *The Outlook* of April 23, 1924, Ethel Parton had spoken of "a marked revival of interest" in England in Emily Dickinson's work,[21] and several reviewers repeated the phrase. In reality, nothing more had appeared than an essay in the London *Spectator* of January 6, 1923, which was occasioned by Aiken's anthology *Modern American Poets*. The merit for having given British Dickinson criticism a small nudge in 1923 and an enduring impulse in 1924 falls to Aiken's anthologies.

The assessment by the lyric poet Martin Armstrong in *The Spectator* of January 6, 1923, was that of an enthusiast who had come upon the poems in Aiken's collection and had then read the Dickinson volumes that had been published up to that time. He suggested that the poet would "gain enormously by careful selection" and praised her "great concentration of meaning and a gift for arresting and dynamic epithets and verbs—a short-circuiting, as it were, of emotion and meaning." Aiken's judgment that "her poetry is perhaps the finest, by a woman, in the English language," was affirmed by Armstrong's "I quarrel only with his perhaps" (p. 23).

An English admirer of the New England poet expressed himself with almost as much enthusiasm in *The Vote*. He linked her name loosely with Crashaw and Vaughan and hoped for further English editions "when a public is found for Emily Dickinson in England."[22]

At first, the British response to *Selected Poems* resembled that given in 1891, in its national prejudice, harsh judgments, insistence on "craftsmanship," and method of dissecting individual poems and stanzas. Yet it ended on a friendlier note. Aiken's guarded introduction aroused less controversy than had Howell's and Higginson's appraisals.

Harold Monro followed Andrew Lang's example by first pulling the work to pieces and then making a conciliatory gesture:

At a first impression, Emily Dickinson's tiny lyrics appear more like jottings of a half-idiotic school girl than the grave musings of a fully educated woman. This kind of verse, I thought to myself, may go down in America, but, when imported to England, we inevitably apply to it the test of comparison with the poems of Emily Brontë, Christina Rossetti, Mary Coleridge, Michael Field. Her poems are splendid blunders. How much better they could have been if she had specialized in her craft. She was intellectually blind, partially deaf, mostly dumb, to the art of poetry. Consequently seven out of ten of her lyrical jottings are plain failures.

He found her style "clumsy," her language "poor," her technique "appalling," her grammatical errors inexcusable, her few rhymes "unnecessary," yet admitted that "her worst is as distant from her best as the half-idiotic schoolgirl from, let us say, Keats." That is, Monro in the end let himself be moved to something approaching Aiken's subjective praise. Oxymora like "splendid blunders" and "splendid awkwardness" are his highest praises after he had progressed in the art of understanding her.[23]

The formula "perfection in imperfection," which a long leading article, "An American Poetess," in the *Times Literary Supplement* found for Emily Dickinson's style, also contains contradictory terms. Still the reviewer endeavored to apply his formula. As an epigrammaticist, Emily Dickinson concerned herself with different aspects of truth and registered the fleeting impressions pouring in upon her with uncompromising precision. The problem of the meaning of form was of secondary importance. She understood it only partly. The thought and its poetic representation are two things. Mastery of both would be a "double perfection" seldom encountered in her work. Instead, she was an expert at "perfection in imperfection" which consists in the use of dissonant rhymes like "pain" and "suffering" in the stanza

> *The heart asks pleasure first,*
> *And then, excuse from pain;*
> *And then, those little anodynes*
> *That deaden suffering*

to underscore meaning. This imperfect rhyme technique "becomes almost a device."[24]

The critiques of Monro and the *Times Literary Supplement* provoked a retort in an essay on "The Irregularities of Emily Dickinson" by Susan Miles.[25] Since Emily Dickinson's rhymes are so hopeless from a conventional point of view that they cannot possibly be explained by mere incompetence, Susan Miles tries to show that they perform an artistic function. The technique of awakening expectations with a rhyme scheme and then disappointing them is in itself ambivalent since it depends on what the artist wishes to express:

If he wishes to give expression to a consistent belief in a world where not a worm is cloven in vain and not a moth with vain desire is shrivelled in a fruitless fire, he does artistically well to construct a volume of neat stanzas where "sin" rhymes with "in," "fall" with "all," "night" with "light," and "ill" with "will." If he has had an impression of a universe where all discord is harmony not understood, all partial ill is universal good, he will adequately express that impression in trim heroic couplets, rhyming "be" with "me" and "curse" with "worse" in undeviating regularity. As a matter of fact, neither Pope nor Tennyson nor any other poet ever had a wholly consistent impression of such a world. And when these poets were not actively believing in a dove-tailed universe their rhymes ceased to resemble a game of ping-pong played by expert and cautious children. (p. 146)

For Emily Dickinson the world consisted of parts which often did not exactly fit together, and she tried to convey this impression in her poetry. "She pondered a tremendous scene, and a little madness in her rhymes was a part of her expression of it" (p. 147). The central argument of the essay is the statement: "If we study the irregularities of Emily Dickinson's rhymes, in nine cases out of ten we shall see that she is expressing some notion which implies defeat, incongruity, suspense, failure, struggle, frustration, disillusion, thwarting disruption, or escape. In the tenth case we may assume either a flaw in Emily Dickinson's technique or obtuseness in ourselves" (p. 147). The result was now and then three-quarters rhyme, sometimes half-rhyme, often nonrhyme. The irregularities are less frequent in the nature poems than in those which have human nature as their subject. Rewritings to create full rhymes can only lead to changes for the worse. This is demonstrated by the author in the case of twelve entire poems. With her capacity to convey aesthetically the impression of a disrupted world, Emily Dickinson belongs, with Thomas Hardy, to a small group of poets. Her irregularities are artistic necessities.

Susan Miles's interpretation is not only an answer to previous British criticism, but also a plea for an organic conception of art which puts an end to the duality of form and thought content by recognizing in the one a correlate of the other. Logically, she last turns against the idealistic aesthetics of Lascelles Abercrombie's *The Theory of Poetry* (1924), which perceives in each poetic work, by virtue of its form, an ideal version of a desired world.

The rediscovery of Emily Dickinson in 1914 and 1924 had not led to a better understanding of the poet in her time and region. On the contrary, she had been more and more strongly wrested from her world. "Puritan" had ceased to be a recommendation for writers. Emily Dickinson was converted into a premodern or a modern and thereby a phenomenon which was almost incompatible with mid-nineteenth-century Amherst. Madame Bianchi had only supported this impression. The old discussion of the poet in her native tradition, initiated in 1891 by Samuel G. Ward and continued by Schauffler, Chamberlain, Arlo Bates, and Carman, had been interrupted in the new century. Only one episode interested her readers in the 1920's: the incident at Mount Holyoke College, where she was said to have publicly defied Mary Lyon. This was played up as a sign of her dissent, as a case of the individual's rebellion against the group.[26]

After Whicher's allusion to the Puritan vestal in May 1925, Allen Tate was the first to discuss Emily Dickinson as "the special case of nineteenth-century Puritanism." What Susan Miles had contributed to the partial defense of the poet, Tate sought to contribute to the determination of her place in literary history.

Tate begins by taking stock of the previous criticism, the confusion of which he attributes to the fact that "her problem" had been misunderstood. The problem is her position in the crumbling structure of the New England ideology. She lived during the crisis of the final disintegration of the old theocracy and of the rise of industrialism. Until around the middle of the century Puritanism had been a controlling force which lent to the individual a tragic-heroic stature and "dramatized the human soul." After the softening of the great idea, a process hastened by Emerson, a secularized culture remained from which any possibility of tragedy had vanished. In Hawthorne alone the vision of a tragic Puritan world lived on; in his work alone man is still measured by a great idea outside himself and is declared imperfect. For Emerson man is greater than any idea and is potentially perfect; there is no struggle, since the possibility of tragic error is excluded. After Emerson New England literature lost its vitality except in Emily Dickinson. She stands midway between retrospective Hawthorne and prospective Emerson and also in the transition to James's stoicism, which caused Hawthorne's view of life to shrivel to the dimension of the individual conscience. Like Shakespeare, she was born into a time counterpoised between an old and a new order. Puritanism was for her no longer impersonal dogma, but personal confession and the pulse of her life. By virtue of the historical situation her work is free of systematized ideas and all didacticism. She is separated from Hawthorne, the master of the idea, by her inability to apprehend and analyze abstractions. Although both equally affirm tradition and its values, she looks—instead of contemplating—and fetches the Puritan drama down from the intellectual stage upon which Hawthorne had placed it. Mastery of the world through renunciation is the true import of her decision in favor of seclusion. This motive is identical with the doctrine of Mather and Edwards, with the meaning of fate in Hawthorne's work, and with the main artistic concern of Henry James.[27]

With the exception of the studies of Lois Leighton Comings, Allen Tate, Walter Rollo Brown, and of the literary histories still to be investigated, the years before the appearance of *Further Poems* yielded no new point of view. *Life and Letters* inspired three reminiscences. A granddaughter of a former president of Amherst College wrote about a visit with Lavinia Dickinson; Clara Green remembered serenading the poet, "a tiny figure in white," when she was a child and, in opposition to Madame Bianchi's presentation, confirmed the old local legend of a frustrated engagement; Lawrence Abbott, who had been a student at Amherst from 1877 to 1881, recollected the recluse as " 'queer,' a mysterious member of the aristocracy of that college community."[28]

The noteworthy evaluations of Abbott, Trueblood, Hunt, and Roberts also showed no progress. Abbott stated "that Emily Dickinson was not a technician." Charles K. Trueblood found that "she was evidently inattentive to the more or less 'artistic' arts of metrical and phrasal music." Percival Hunt, to be sure, began his radio lecture with the assertion that "Emily Dickinson is one of the greatest American poets," but then merely spoke of "intensity," "compact fire," "condensation and flash." The British journalist Richard Ellis Roberts (1879-1953), who had become acquainted with the work of Emily Dickinson about thirty years earlier, praised—corresponding to the title of his essay "Uncut Stones"—the unpolished epigrams for their high themes.[29]

"When the literary history of our generation is written," readers of the February issue of the New York *Bookman* in 1924 were told, "there will be a curious chapter devoted to the vogue of the anthologists in this decade, and of the character of their achievement."[30] As tentative critical selections, the anthologies of modern poetry which mushroomed after 1918 exercised as great an influence on the writers of literary history as had the collections of Stedman and others around the turn of the century. The literary historians saw themselves confronted anew with the problem of somehow classifying Emily Dickinson.

Understandably, no great surveys of literary history were written in the 1920's, since the critics had only just begun to revaluate the past and had not yet paved the way far enough ahead. A new phase in the writing of literary history, initiated by Parrington, did not reach its zenith until the early 1930's. The usual college handbooks continued to prevail. In addition, there were surveys of modern poetry and works censuring contemporary American culture written in the guise of literary histories. To the first group belong the books of the Van Dorens (1925), Leisy (1929), and Pattee (1930); to the second those of Weirick (1924), Wood (1925), and Kreymborg (1929); to the third those of Brown (1929) and Josephson (1930; cf. Sources, p. 299). The two works published in 1930 are here treated with the rest since Josephson's, as will be shown, is rooted entirely in the spirit of the 1920's and Pattee's is a continuation of his literary history of 1915.

Bruce Weirick's *From Whitman to Sandburg in American Poetry*,[31] the first of the three outlines of modern verse written by poet-critics, appeared in February 1924, and could not make use of the editions of that year and their critical reception. Weirick's sympathies appear in the title, his antipathies in the preface: "The world of Longfellow and Holmes, Whittier and Lowell and Bryant, is become a relique. It was a derivative and sterile culture" (p. x). He illuminates the scene with the lamp which Van Wyck Brooks had used in *America's Coming-of-Age*. In the process he chances upon Whitman as the emancipator from barren Victorian convention and godfather of a flourishing school of poets. Whitman is not only contemporary but also timeless. As a "cosmic" personality he is placed alongside other "Olympians" such as Homer, Christ, Buddha, Sophocles (p. 12). The poetic renewal in the spirit of Whitman took place in the Midwest and culminated in Sandburg, the greatest American poet since the death of the master, a "clay-foot Titan" who "stalks with Cyclopean steps" (p. 210). Tired, anemic New England, which even Robinson and Frost had failed to enliven, is played out against the "poetry of Titanism" (p. 220).

To fill up the barren "Period of Reconstruction" between 1870 and 1890, Weirick avails himself of the old handbooks and readily adopts their idiom: "Here, still flourishing, is a whole host of minor poets, capable of a few sweet notes, poets whose highest aim is a neatly turned sonnet to Tennyson, or some ballad to the Venus of Milo. The products of a cultivated society, these poets write about equally well" (p. 94). One and a half pages are devoted to Emily Dickinson, who is preceded by Aldrich and followed by Sill. What the author has to say about her is almost entirely borrowed. First, there is a quotation from Aldrich, then the worn reference to Helen Hunt. For conclusion there is a poem ("I'll tell you how the sun rose") and the off-hand evaluation: "A reader who spends a half-hour now and then with these three quiet volumes of Miss Dickinson will find much to charm and interest and little to cast aside. One predicts permanence for this sly poet" (p. 97).

Weirick's book is a history of Whitman's influence. He shows little patience for anything which does not fit into the tradition of the far-reaching, robust, and revolutionary.

The objection raised in *The Outlook* that Wood had done injustice to the New Englanders, would have more justly applied to Weirick.[32] Clement Wood at least singles out Emily Dickinson, Robinson, and Frost for close treatment in *Poets of America*.[33] Before he proceeds to eight notable figures of the present, his succession of chapters runs: Poe, Whitman, Adah Isaacs Menken, Lanier, Emily Dickinson, Robinson, Frost. Among these seven, the Camden and Amherst poets receive especial emphasis. Emily Dickinson "wrote many more enduring poems than any of these except Whitman; she never sagged as low as each of them did" (p. 94). In contrast to Bryant, Whittier, Lowell, Holmes, and Longfellow, who are brushed aside as imitators on one page of the introduction, she belongs to the "poetic innovators" (p. 67).

A genuine tension exists between the external course of life of the "shrinking seer," who lacked "the advertising flair" and "the exhibitionist desire" (p. 82), and her inner rebellion which is reflected in her verse as an artistic revolt against the conventional.[34] "All the more astonishing that this singer wore the modern gown so long before it grew to be the healthy style" (p. 94).

The least original of the trio of poet-critics is Alfred Kreymborg. His dithyramb *Our Singing Strength*,[35] a book written with verve but lacking discrimination, refers directly back to Amy Lowell's and Untermeyer's outlines without going any further. Praise for the dead and flattery for the living replace selectivity and criticism. The barely recognizable basic conception is evolutionary; the figures of the past are precursors and prophets. One third of the book is devoted to the period from the beginnings to 1900, two thirds to the generation thereafter. Kreymborg's view of Emily Dickinson resembles that of Gamaliel Bradford. In his enthusiasm—"Only ecstasy can follow her ecstasy" (p. 195)—he surpasses Hartley and Hillyer:

> One gives in to the drunken girl and goes drunken with her. (p. 193)
>
> Walt and Emily, along with Forefather Emerson, are the great American rebels; and the woman is fully the equal of the males. (p. 193-94)
>
> Gayety, sunlight, audacity, are the salient motives of her music. (p. 195)
>
> Her joyousness is amazing in view of her Puritan background. To this freedom she was led by her master: the serene and equally eccentric Emerson. (p. 196)
>
> The air for which one yearns comes through the open window, not of the Menckens, but of the Emersons and Dickinsons. (p. 196)
>
> Nothing in poetry can be more tedious than the cosmic utterance. Emily, too ecstatic to drag any one mood too far, was blessed with that antidote against the cosmic: the comic. (p. 204)

His only objection involves the old reproach for deficient formal perfection, but it is immediately recanted: "In a world so full of perfect poets, let us have at least one irresistibly imperfect" (p. 205).

Carl and Mark Van Doren's *American and British Literature since 1890*[36] differs from Weirick and Wood in its critical distance from the Whitman tradition, from Kreymborg in its omission of all nonessentials, from all three in its historical perspective. To be sure the emphasis lies "upon the modern elements, whether ideas or forms, in recent literature" (p. v). Nevertheless, the few nineteenth-century poets treated retain their places in their times. Emily Dickinson is not a precursor, but an American classic. Among the lyricists, only nine exemplary figures are stressed. James Whitcomb Riley, the popular bard, and George Santayana, the pure aesthete, are followed by Dickinson, the archetype of the "irreducible" writer: "In particular she dispensed with the customary poetic padding. She stripped her verse to the bone, as if nothing but the essential idea or the essential image were important. . . . She survives because she is . . . without false colors likely to fade" (pp. 8-9).[37]

Emily Dickinson's conspicuous rise in public esteem in the 1920's had not failed to catch Fred Lewis Pattee's notice. While he had dismissed the poet with a few sentences in *A History of American Literature since 1870* (1915), he pronounced her the "most noteworthy" talent of the "transition poets" in 1930 and devoted four pages to her.[38] He fills two of them with a biographical sketch and begins discussing her work with a hardly flattering quotation from Moody comparing her verse with potatoes forgotten in the corner of a cellar which sprout toward a few incident sunbeams. He proceeds by indirection in other respects too. The "crudely wrought" of 1915 becomes: "Judged by the Victorian standards under which the lyrics were written, there is in them everywhere scorn of conventional technique, a 'revolt against the trammels' of fixed forms and canons" (p. 198). Four sentences later he stumbles over her "slovenly rhyming" and thus identifies himself as a Victorian. Finally, he makes her responsible for the "rebellion against law and order" in modern versification (p. 199). What follows is a swipe at the " 'new' school of innovators" and thus reluctant praise of Emily Dickinson: "Her transcendental glimpsings, her Emersonian flashes, her uniqueness of imagination, her visionings, they did not, perhaps could not, see or feel. It was only her lofty carelessness with the materials of poetry, her seeming revolt against the trammels of the older forms, that made her for them an inspiration" (p. 199). For Pattee the Victorian she revolts *de facto*; for Pattee the enemy of a new poetic anarchy she only appears to revolt. His divided allegiance makes Emily Dickinson at once the weapon and the target of his criticism.

The total rejection of 1915 is mollified: "Her final place among the poets is still open to question. The sensation occasioned by the discovery of her work has hardly yet subsided

enough to allow cool analysis. Already it is seen that the enduring part of her poetry is embedded in much that is childish,
much that must be dismissed as jingling nonsense" (p. 199). Poets
of the old school like Edith Thomas, Lizette Reese, and Clinton
Scollard remain more familiar to him since they are "a stabilizing
influence in an age of riot and experiment" (p. 210).

An inspection of the cultural criticism published by Ran-
dolph Bourne, Waldo Frank, and Harold E. Stearns between
1919 and 1928 discovers no mention of Emily Dickinson. She
only appears in the seventh chapter, a reprint of a 1928 essay,
of Rollo Walter Brown's *Lonely Americans*. Her case substantiates his theory of the intellect. In Matthew Josephson's *Portrait
of the Artist as American*, which exemplifies, with the aid of
nineteenth-century literature, the dilemma of the American
writer, she plays a greater role.[39]

Josephson's *Portrait*, a book at the turn of the decade, re-
flects the spirit of the past years. As a restrospect, a lamentation,
and a vague admonition, it must be seen against the background
of its author's years abroad and of his partisanship with the
younger generation. It is written in the spirit of Brooks, Weirick,
and Wood: "After we have pruned away the débris of provisory
reputations the names that remain, of Emily Dickinson and
Henry James, of Ambrose Bierce, Lafcadio Hearn, and Stephen
Crane, suggest a slender but genuine contribution to culture"
(p. xvi). Can art exist in democratic society? The negative
answer to this question is the theme demonstrated by these
writers, to whom, in the Gilded Age, only the choice between
isolation and flight from America remained.[40] After the happy,
decentralized youth of the republic, the turning point came in
1865. Henry James, the protagonist of the book, fled to Europe,
that is, he decided in favor of "civilization" and against "the
brassy show of existence which passed for life in America" (p.
98). His example was followed by Crane and, more radically,
by Hearn, who rejected the Western World altogether. Writers
who remained at home were silenced (like Melville), fell into
disrepute (like Whitman), bowed to the time (like Adams and
Howells), became "hardened and weather-beaten survivors"
(like Twain and Bierce), or withdrew (like Emily Dickinson)
into "an interior life of terrible isolation" (p. 173).

The astonishment and incredulity with which the public
received Emily Dickinson in 1890 fills Josephson with indignation: "To have withheld her literature from her contemporaries

strikes us as a severe judgment of her age and a profoundly right one. For everything that she wrote was posthumous and clearly designed to appear after her death" (p. 173). She does not appear rooted in her environment; her visions remind him (with Madame Bianchi) "of some possessed medieval saint rather than of the reasoning New England conscience" (p. 174).

Josephson's criticism of Emily Dickinson is less interesting than her position in his entire sketch. The melancholy spectacle of the artists after the Civil War resembles a "pattern of flight." "They were divorced from the spirit of their times . . . and each in turn searched for a certain romance, for the richness of traditions, for a gentler civilization of which the signs . . . were not visible in the immediate landscape" (pp. 289-90).

Even before 1924, Whitman, whose fame had been promoted by the activity of his following, had been recognized as the greatest genius of the nineteenth century. That Emily Dickinson now became his "sister" and that Kreymborg rather lightly spoke of "Walt and Emily" is, from the vantage point of those years, a proof of her growing popularity.

The explanation of Emily Dickinson's art did not keep pace with her rise in esteem. As a craftsman she had been most strongly criticized in England; as a craftsman she was first restored to her rights in England. Susan Miles's essay remained without immediate effect in America, just as did Tate's attempt at historical interpretation which consciously combatted the critical trend.

It was to be expected that the criticism of the 1920's, which proceeded militantly against the American literary past, should combine a reinterpretation with the rehabilitation of Emily Dickinson and create an Emily who was to have nothing, or only very little, to do with Amherst and New England. One would rather have settled her in the Middle Ages than in the nineteenth century. In the first place, she was a genius—modern and, at the same time, timeless; in the second, she was an American—a rebel against tradition and a victim of her age.

VIII

◇◆◇◆◇◆◇◆◇◆◇◆◇◆◇◆◇

FAME AND MELANCHOLY
RENOWN (1929-30)

◇◆◇◆◇◆◇◆◇◆◇◆◇◆◇◆◇

Emily has been given us as friend, as member of the Dickinson family, as "genius"; she was all these and more. No one has written her down as artist, with all the aches and ecstacies to which that quickened flesh is heir.[1]

THE YEARS 1929 AND 1930 FORM A UNITY in the intensification of critical attention to, and public interest in, Emily Dickinson. They differ in that in 1929 attention was chiefly devoted to the poet's work, while it centered on the person in the centenary year.

Further Poems of Emily Dickinson: Withheld from Publication by Her Sister Lavinia, edited by Madame Bianchi and her collaborator, Alfred Leete Hampson, was published by Little, Brown in Boston on March 16, 1929, and by Secker in a London edition in October. The sales exceeded those of all earlier editions. By October 1930, 12,465 copies had been printed. The editors had provided for publicity. Selected verses appeared in February and March in one British and four American journals (cf. Sources, pp. 271-72). Moreover, the editors had the publishers come out with a press announcement on January 25 and had advance copies examined by Untermeyer and Hillyer. Both experts were not chary of their praise. Untermeyer proclaimed that the poems were "extraordinary as biography and magnificent as literature." In the same Associated Press announcement Hillyer stated: "The discovery of the poems sets a new date in our literary history. Unlike so many discoveries of new material, this one has brought to light not remnants, but a collection of poems written at the height of power. They are a treasure trove from Emily Dickinson's genius at its best."[2]

140

The editors' desire to appeal to the largest possible audience may have moved them to attempt to meet the readers halfway. This attempt was made in a very arbitrary manner by means of numerous textual changes and by a layout whose irregularity was probably intended to look modern.

Emily Dickinson had often written her verses down as she found room on a piece of paper, without consideration of metrical form. The editors went to work with similar freedom when they rearranged 106 of the 175 poems. For example, the third stanza of " 'Why do I love' you, sir" is rendered as follows:

> *The lightning never asked*
> *An eye*
> *Wherefore she shut when*
> *He was by—*
> *Because he knows*
> *She cannot speak,*
> *And reasons not contained*
> *Of talk*
> *There be—preferred by daintier folk.*

The poet had written:

> *The Lightning—never asked an Eye*
> *Wherefore it shut—when He was by—*
> *Because He knows it cannot speak—*
> *And reasons not contained—*
> *—Of Talk—*
> *There be—preferred by Daintier Folk—*
>
> (*Poems*, no. 480)

With the simultaneous deletion of many stanza breaks, the strategy of the blocklike arrangement tried for the first time in 1914 was continued.

These optical manipulations distorted the structure of the poems: 145 textual changes in 96 poems, not counting reading mistakes, put a wrong construction on phrases, sentences, often entire poems, and exceeded the liberties which Mrs. Todd had allowed herself in 1896. Old types of corrections recur in the avoidance of the subjunctive in fifteen instances, the normalization of forms such as "ourself" in eight, and the smoothing of the rhythm in three. The foregoing of additional rhymes, which probably were no longer felt to be as important in 1929 as they had been a generation earlier, is the only exception. The broadest area of changes is once again the insertion of synonyms and the substitution of words which change meaning. The resulting deviations stretch from nuances to nonsense. Emily Dickinson's

To interrupt His Yellow Plan

barely differs from Madame Bianchi's

To intercept his yellow plan.

A change of tone is effected by

You'll find it when you come to die

in the place of the original nonchalant beginning

You'll find it when you try to die.

The alteration from

As Birds—that tumble from the clouds

to

As birds that tremble from the clouds

effects a change of meaning.

Heaven is sky of earth

for

Heaven is shy of Earth—

is destructive of meaning because it is meaningless. The semantic field formed by "shy," "bashful," and "to hide," in which Heaven plays the part of a courted lover, has become irrelevant.[3]

These few examples show clearly enough a paradoxical attitude on the part of the editors. They presumably wanted Emily Dickinson to appear, at least optically, as a modern, but they did not venture to let her diction pass uncensored. They tailored a garment according to the latest fashion and trimmed it with Victorian lace. That readers and critics accepted it was due to their never having seen the poet in her proper dress.

Emily's sister, who had been designated as "our other faithful but prejudiced Aunt Lavinia" in 1914, appeared in the subtitle as the black sheep of the family. She had to bear the reviewers' foreseeable indignation concerning the long delay of the publication. With this subtitle Madame Bianchi acted not only unfairly toward the innocent aunt but also imprudently.

Shortly after, the general interest in Emily Dickinson brought to light the essay of Nathan Haskell Dole in *The Book Buyer* of May 1892, in which unmistakably stood: "There are at least 1200 poems catalogued, and no one knows how many more in a mass of notes and manuscripts found among her possessions—enough to make several stout volumes." To what extent the sub-title was incidentally intended as an advertising stunt, is unimportant. The introduction nevertheless permits the conclusion that *Lavinia Dickinson* was meant as an excuse and *Withheld* as a measure designed to arouse curiosity.

The introduction does not answer the obvious question as to why the poems had been held back: "When the little, un-explored package gave up these poems of Emily Dickinson which her sister, Lavinia, saw fit never to publish, it was for one breath-less instant as if the bright apparition of Emily had returned to the old house. . . . It is possible that these were intended for another volume in the series already published. It is certain that to destroy them would be a heresy to the faith of her following" (p. v). The numerous verses scattered through the introduction must have astonished the attentive reader who read them again in the text: they all differed in punctuation, many in the division of lines, some even in the text. The fifty-six love poems, which form the conclusion and culmination of the book, are offered as "an almost unbroken narrative of Emily's own experience, from the first sight of the man she had heard as a stranger preach-ing in Philadelphia, on through their mutual bewilderment, certainty, and renunciation" (p. xvi). Nothing more stood in the way of identifying this lover with the noted preacher Charles Wadsworth.

It is sadly ironic that *Further Poems*, the most deficient of all Dickinson editions, had the greatest literary success. By 1929 reviewers were grateful for the publication of anything that came from Emily Dickinson's pen. The volume was repeatedly regarded as the most significant contribution of the year to American literature. It appeared three times in the nonfiction bestseller list of *New York Herald Tribune Books*. More than half a dozen poems were dedicated to the poet. Conrad Aiken saw his former intercession confirmed: "By just so much more evidence, we see that her claim to first rank is no accident; that her power was an extraordinarily individual and consistent one; that her range—particularly if we consider in this new collection the magnificent series of love poems—is a good deal wider than we had supposed it to be."[4]

Only few protested against the opinion of the majority that the poems enriched the canon, that even each fragment had to be welcomed. Clara Green regarded many of the verses as fragments or discarded drafts and deplored their publication. Lavinia had been right in her judgment if she did, indeed, set aside these attempts. Anna Mary Wells went one step further and compared poems which said the same thing. She concluded that, due to the progressive thinning of the stock, Emily Dickinson's work had been published "in exactly a descending order of merit." *Poetry* was disappointed: "They are mainly the sort of poem which every author leaves out of his published volume—unfinished, hasty, not always musical."[5]

Despite the subtitle Madame Bianchi did not succeed in making Lavinia Dickinson another Cassandra Austen. While the informed among the critics had rebelled against the biographer in 1924, they now reproached the editor. The threadbare explanation in the introduction was not able to deceive. Louis Untermeyer was the first to ask the questions which were often repeated by others: "In all these years did Mrs. Bianchi, who inherited and lives in the Dickinson home, never make a thorough search of the relics? Did Lavinia actually 'suppress' these poems, and if so why did she keep them where they could be found? If Emily's sister hid them, as the publishers imply, because the love-poems are too frank, how are we to account for the withholding of a hundred 'general' poems on poetry, prisons, birds, flowers, women, creation, God?"[6] Rolfe Humphries, who had already taken *Life and Letters* to task, found the subtitle "downright malicious." To vindicate Lavinia he cited parts of a letter which she had written to Higginson on December 23, 1890. In these passages disappointment that Susan Dickinson had so little supported the publication of the poems is clearly evident.[7] He himself had also taken the trouble to ask the editor about the "discovery" and had received the evasive answer: "The poems were for the most part found in a small trunk long overlooked as holding only old papers of my grandfather's. The first one dropped out of a volume of Emerson's essays—which set me guessing." Humphries accused the family, which had kept Emily Dickinson under lock and key for so long, of the New England "sin of covetousness" and asked: "Are we to expect additional volumes?"

Other reviewers found other reasons to object. Spencer complained about the punctuation, which distorted the meaning, and saw "stupidities on every page," above all in the typographical arrangement. Hillyer declared that in 1921 he had seen the original of the poem "I never felt at home below," which was printed on page 43. In his brief essay "Emily Dickinson and Her Editors," Aiken cited all these complaints and demanded a corrected new edition. Madame Bianchi, who occasionally showed fight, could object but little to all this.[8]

In comparison with the reaction to *Complete Poems*, the public reception of the *Further Poems* took a quieter course in spite of stronger interest and growing displeasure with the editor. *The Christian Register* and Untermeyer fell into the temptation of reading the love poems as a coherent story. "Emily tells the whole story of her love, her first rebellious desire, her inner negation, her resignation, her waiting for reunion in Eternity," Untermeyer wrote. The temptation to classify Emily Dickinson as a modern abated. Occasional references to her being a precursor were balanced by an increasing inclination to return her to the nineteenth century or to settle her in the seventeenth.

The critical examination of the artist continued to be stagnant. Susan Miles was not mentioned, since her analysis was probably not known. Kreymborg again went drunken with the little tippler: "One wishes, if one could, to turn rowdy with her, to go reeling about the thoroughfares of respectability, whether on earth or in heaven, and to knock all the planets and the Creator a little lop-sided." Hutchison wrote: "She is never an artist"; Hillyer took offense at the "false" rhymes, Helen Chadwick at the indifference to form; Babette Deutsch used the time-honored metaphor of the diamond in the rough.[9] So much the more astonishing is the growing certainty with which these and other voices pointed out Emily Dickinson's greatness.

Hillyer:

> Her work is gradually being recognized as the most interesting poetry America has produced.

Babette Deutsch:

> It is not every generation, it is not every century, even, that poets of Emily Dickinson's calibre are to be met with.

Hutchison:

> Emily Dickinson presents as fascinating and as tantalizing a figure as will be found in the entire history of English letters.

Mark Van Doren:

> She is so much the best of women poets, and comes so near
> the crown of all poetry whatsoever, that her art . . . has
> been little talked about.[10]

New critical impulses came from three directions and together established Emily Dickinson as a metaphysical poet.

The first impulse came from Hutchison and Mark Van
Doren. Regarding the poem "A wife at daybreak I shall be,"
Hutchison commented: "The intellectual will be found to outweigh the emotional." Van Doren fixed Emily Dickinson more
precisely as a poet of the intellect, of the spirit, and of wit:

> My point in general is that she wrote with brains, as all good
> poets do, and that she is to be appreciated in the brain or
> not at all.

> Her love is vastly less interesting than what she said about it.
> Expression was her master first and last; if she renounced
> anything it was in favor of words . . .

> Wit is the word, I think, which sums Emily Dickinson up
> —and we must go back through several centuries of usage to
> find its full content. In the seventeenth century it meant
> the point at which imagination and idea, passion and under-
> standing, experience and form met in good poetry—it meant,
> in short, good poetry. Emily Dickinson has wit in one of
> the richest combinations that I know, and therefore I call
> her one of the best poets.

The second impulse resulted from a consideration of her
diction and her metaphorical language, based on micro- and
macroscopic comparisons once again understood as a natural
emanation of her personal experience. Spencer, Babette Deutsch,
Hillyer, and Mumford expressed their opinions concerning this
"verbal genius":

> But this very application of a homely and familiar word
> ("nicknamed") to unknown and illimitable things ("eter-
> nity") is one of the individualizing features of Emily Dick-
> inson's style, and when it is successful, is responsible for
> some of her most vital and moving poems.

> But it is in her discovery of the right, the perfect word,
> that she shows herself the mistress of her art. With the

shrewdness of the metaphysical poets of the Seventeenth Century, she mixes high abstractions and vulgar commonplace in a divine brew. She can carry the freight of a whole lyric in a line, in an adjective.

The single word as she wrote it received the impact of her entire personality. . . . One thought she passionately held to: that the things of earth, however microscopic, are essential parts of a design too vast for contemplation, yet dependent on the smallest tendril for its fulfillment. She is content, therefore, to refer to the great her absorption in the little, finding her universe at the end of the microscope no less than at the end of the telescope; indeed, losing the sense of measured space as much as mortal can.

Emily Dickinson shows us life through a spiritual microscope; every tiny globule of experience becomes enlarged a hundred diameters.[11]

A third impulse came from the mystical note perceived in the love poems. It did not generally lead to comparisons with the religious poetry of Herbert and Crashaw, but nevertheless suggested these comparisons among others. Anna Mary Wells cited "A wife at daybreak I shall be" "because it shows rather clearly the union of her thwarted love with a mystical devotion." *The Christian Register* called Emily Dickinson one of the great mystics of all time: "These fifty-six poems constitute valuable contributions to the literature of mysticism of all lands and ages. They are comparable to the Confessions of Saint Augustine, or St. Theresa, or the poems of Madame Guyon."[12] Hutchison compared her with "the four great mystics in English poetry," Herbert, Vaughan, Crashaw, Alice Meynell, and added her to them. He, too, cited "A wife at daybreak": "Sacred and profane love, to use terms honored by tradition—the commingling of the two, till that which is sacred and ethereal and formless takes corporeal form, and that which is, or would have been, corporeal, becomes wholly spiritualized, is the last distillation of mysticism. In these stanzas Emily identifies the renounced lover with the Christ, and the Christ becomes her lost lover on earth; both are one, and each is both." The reviewer of *The Springfield Republican* uttered similar thoughts: "Richard Rolle of Hampole, Traherne, Crashaw, Francis Thompson, Gerard Hopkins, are in truth the line in which Emily Dickinson has descended. And this hard and intense school of mysticism explains the enigma more correctly than would reference to the meters and themes of, say, Browning and Tennyson, or Longfellow and Felicia Hemans."[13]

Emily Dickinson as a poet of the intellect, as a literary artist able to fuse the incongruent, as a mystic—these tendencies are conspicuous in the reviews of *Further Poems*. The comparisons with the religious poets grouped with John Donne are not yet more than allusions. Only two reviewers were more explicit. Spencer pointed out the connecting link with the aid of "I make his crescent fill or lack": "There is here the same development of thought through imagery, the same use of metaphor in a structural, not merely an ornamental, manner which we associate with metaphysical verse. The moon is to this poem just what the pair of compasses is to Donne's 'Valediction Forbidding Mourning.' Without the image the thought and emotion would not be fused into unity; the image is both a poetic mortar and a short cut to communication" (p. 499). Catherine Tolles devoted an essay to the subject in which she drew parallels to Donne and Emerson. The quintessence of the metaphysical attitude is the discrepancy between life as appearance and experienced truth. Emily Dickinson's poetry is an attempt to join truth and observation, which she never quite succeeded in doing, although she always patiently tried anew. From this—her view of life—follow her microscopic, almost scientific, observation, which amazedly discovers continually increasing intricacy and diversity, and the macroscopic view of an all-encompassing law, the great unity at the base of all things. In common with Donne are her break with tradition at the dawn of a new era of scientific discovery, the interplay of erudition and imagination, and the capacity for cold self-analysis. Similarities with Emerson are seen in her striving for self-sufficiency, in her intellectual isolation, and in her ability to apprehend the extraordinary in the ordinary. She is philosophically related to the latter, psychologically to the former.[14]

In the centennial year the reviewers' pens were so strongly preoccupied by two biographical revelations and an old Amherst citizen's reminiscences that hardly any intellect and ink remained for the collected *Poems* which appeared in the fall of 1930. The commemorative year occasioned various ceremonies and exhibitions, feuds and flat statements, and a grandiose parade of editors and critics, but not what one would have expected of it: reflection on the poet's work, about which everything ultimately revolved. In November, when the great hubbub was over, Whicher placed a quatrain on the title page of his Dickinson *Bibliography* as a silent commentary:

Fame and Melancholy Renown

Funny to be a Century
And see the people going by,
I should die of the oddity,
But then I'm not so staid as he.

However, the fact that legend and sensation-mongering had run amok stimulated cooler minds to criticize the criticism and to rescue Emily Dickinson from the hands of niece, speculators, and journalists. Hence, the centennial marked not only a sensational culmination of her fame and melancholy renown, a culmination which included a novel and a play about her life, but also effected a sudden turnabout. Henceforth, the pace was set by academic criticism.

The books of Josephine Pollitt and Genevieve Taggard— *Emily Dickinson: The Human Background of Her Poetry* and *The Life and Mind of Emily Dickinson*, which were published in New York in January and May—were revelations in so far as they each introduced a lover of Emily by name; they far exceeded *Life and Letters* in their scope and thoroughness, although they had been written without the cooperation of Madame Bianchi. Miss Pollitt had not even received permission to quote from the poems and letters. Neither author laid claims to exclusiveness. "My interpretation of Emily Dickinson and of the influences upon her, is offered as a suggestion," wrote Miss Pollitt in her preface (xi); Miss Taggard expressed the conviction that Emily Dickinson could only be found in her own words:

. . . Emily, where are you?

Go to her verse, reader,
To the great verse.
Here is nothing of hers.

She will elude us all . . . (p. viii)

Both biographers could construct their suppositions only with the help of a weak framework, namely the poet's trip to Washington and Philadelphia and her second letter to Higginson, which allusively and misleadingly spoke of "a terror—since September" and mentioned the "friend, who taught me Immortality," the "Tutor," and "one more," who "left the Land." The undated poems, the originals of which could naturally not be examined, had to supply further support.

The candidate of Josephine Pollitt, who incidentally was the first to declare Madame Bianchi's "preacher" to be identical with Charles Wadsworth, was Major Hunt, the first husband of Emily's childhood friend Helen. The chief piece of evidence was a letter written by Higginson to his wife shortly after his visit with the poet in 1870, which contained the ominous sentence: "Major Hunt interested her more than any man she ever saw" (p. 120). Several dates in the lives of Hunt and Emily Dickinson coincided: he met her for the first time in Washington, visited her without doubt in 1855, possibly in 1856 and 1857 also, was inducted in September 1861 ("I had a terror—since September"), and met with a fatal accident in the fall of 1863. The course of the questionable friendship is sketched "as I believe it happened" (p. 127). Circumstantial evidence is seen in autobiographically interpreted poems, in the assumption that Helen became suspicious and wrote *Mercy Philbrick's Choice* as a *roman à clef*,[15] and in the influence of Hunt the natural scientist on her "discipline of expression" and her military metaphors (p. 209).

The candidate of Genevieve Taggard was George Gould, a classmate and close friend of Austin Dickinson. Her piece of evidence was an affidavit received in 1929 from an unnamed correspondent who claimed to have it from Lavinia Dickinson "that the man Emily Dickinson loved and renounced was Mr. George Gould . . . and . . . that Emily Dickinson's father forbade the match" (p. 109).[16] Miss Taggard had followed the trail of the Amherst legend and had only in conclusion found a confirmation of her supposition: "This revelation, from Vinnie, via one other person, is the simple fact we have so much needed to know in order to simplify Emily Dickinson's life, cluttered as it now is with absurd and unnatural suppositions" (p. 110). Miss Taggard's evidence inspires still less confidence than Miss Pollitt's: first, the unfounded assumption that there was a meeting in Philadelphia; second, the assumption that a ten-year correspondence ensued, which was carried on through two discreet middlemen; third, poems with which Emily accompanied Gould on his long European tour; fourth, her emotional crisis of 1862, which is ascribed to Gould's marriage. An indirect confirmation of the probability of the Gould theory is seen in the elemental relationship between father and daughter, which on Emily's side was characterized by vacillation between defiant resistance and deferential subordination, on Edward's by an ever-growing jealous striving for absolute control over his daughter's life, "as a planet relates its motions to the central sun. By this we may observe that the relationship between Emily and her father was a primitive one" (p. 87). This primal relation affected all later acquaintance-ships (with Bowles, Wadsworth, Holland, Lord): "A masculine friend always turned out to be a foil of Edward, as if Emily must test his opposite and find, if possible, the better clime of another person to which she might migrate" (p. 189).

Both biographies corrected false dates, pointed out the sig-nificant roles of Lavinia as preserver and Mrs. Todd as editor of the work, and freed Emily Dickinson from the spell of the omni-present "Sister Sue" in *Life and Letters* by allowing other figures such as Humphrey and Hunt, Wadsworth, Bowles, and Higgin-son to come into their own as friends and critics.

MacGregor Jenkins' *Emily Dickinson: Friend and Neigh-bor*,[17] a slim volume, had little to add to his 1891 essay. The result of his childhood memories and his later reflection was a "Miss Emily" who almost exactly resembled Madame Bianchi's "Aunt Emily."[18] He endeavored to dispose of the Dickinson myth,[19] but became entangled in contradictions and thus contributed to the myth himself. Although he describes Miss Emily as "a very real and very human friend and comrade" (p. 31), on the next page "She always impressed us as a bird poised for flight"; "a lunar moth" (p. 35) contradicts the "very normal" (p. 37). His at-tempt to describe her verse culminates in statements such as:

> Emily Dickinson was leading an exquisite, vibrant life, not as a morbid recluse, as some would have it, but as an en-thralled observer of all the great things that make the soul a soul. . . . (p. 21)

and

> She was sensitized to life in a different key, the whole cadence of her being was quicker, she felt acutely things that were but dull intimations to most people. She responded to a wholly different set of stimuli and her reactions were individual reactions, not herd or clan reactions. In this lay the whole difference. (p. 145)

Like Genevieve Taggard's biography, Jenkins' memoir was pub-lished in May.

The waves of public excitement spread far; they reached Fort Worth, Texas, on July 13, the shores of Hawaii on July 19. Sensational headlines such as "Amherst, Brave Amherst," "Emily Dickinson Unveiled," "Man Emily Dickinson Loved,"

"Recluse because She Didn't Like Own Appearance" carried the poet's name over the entire country.

Jenkins' book, the least pretentious of the three, elicited little contradiction. Even if it was only a drawn-out version of the essay and in its attitude a product of the past century, the few additional letters it contained were nevertheless welcomed. The biographies were received with mixed feelings, while there was a storm of indignation against Madame Bianchi. Whicher compared the carefully guarded family secret with a citadel defended since 1924 by the unaccountable reticence of the niece and made her responsible for the poet's thwarted love gaining more prominence than it deserved. Aiken spoke of a Dickinson scandal. Granville Hicks accused Madame Bianchi of delaying tactics: "If [she] knows his name she is under heavy obligation to reveal it. If she does not she should admit her ignorance and lend her assistance to every earnest effort to discover the truth."[20] While the protest against the treatment of Emily Dickinson as an exclusive family possession became general, the two "unofficial" biographers indirectly gained sympathy for their laborious detective work. If Miss Taggard's book came off comparatively better in the process, it was because her thesis sounded more plausible and appeared to have been advanced with less claim to exclusiveness (Leonard Humphrey also remained a possible beau), whereas one sensed the nonsense of the true story magazine in Miss Pollitt's construction. The sleuthing seemed to have led to a dead-end, and the witnesses were ready to poke fun at the detectives. "From the same materials as sound a case might be built against the Reverend Charles Wadsworth," remarked Linscott regarding Josephine Pollitt's argumentation, and Untermeyer scoffed at Genevieve Taggard's use of legal metaphors in the poems as proof of a father complex: "It would not be difficult to plot the curve of a devotional vocabulary pointing to ministerial preoccupations, or compile an imposing array of horticultural terms to prove that she was in love with the (as yet unnamed) town gardener."[21]

Since the naming of Wadsworth by Miss Pollitt, three candidates were in the field. The trio occasioned the supposition among the sober-minded that there possibly had been no lover at all. "She was romantic, imaginative, probably highly sexed," mused Frances Robbins. "Young men were not unwelcome in her father's house. Four or five men charmed and inspired her in her youth. May she not have created a composite picture of them and endowed it with life?"[22] Untermeyer did not quite seem to remember his biographical reading of the love verses in *Further Poems* when he advanced a similar hypothesis: "It was an age of rhetoric. Male friends could write 'We loved each other at first sight . . . we seemed to fuse into one.' Emily herself used the word 'love' indiscriminately—especially for those who stood in the relation of teacher to her. Whoever it was who came, saw, and captured Emily, he may have been quite unconscious of his conquest. . . . As likely as not he went off, married, and speedily forgot the rather plain girl with her fancy phrases. It may have been nothing to him; to Emily it was All." Mrs. Todd confirmed this train of thought by referring to her introduction to *Letters* (1894), in which she had rejected any dramatic attempt to explain the quiet life of the poet.[23]

Such critics were joined by others who, weary of the flood of biographical revelations, exclaimed with Frances Robbins: "How foolish, after all, to care!" and reminded their readers that Emily Dickinson meant more than a biographical riddle. Most of the reviewers shared the conviction that a definitive life had yet to be written. That, however, had already been mentioned by Josephine Pollitt at the end of her book: "One hundred years after her birth this poet's life is still in a half-shadow. An Emily Dickinson mystery is being perpetuated. There is confusion in interpretations of her . . ." (pp. 319-20).

In 1929 the time had been reached when people began to be astonished when they did not find Emily Dickinson in an anthology, a literary history, or a reference work. Thus, in his review of March 16, 1929, Untermeyer had noted her absence in *The New International Encyclopaedia* of 1914 and the *Encyclopaedia Britannica* of 1926, and Hutchison had traced her absence in Barrett Wendell's literary history of 1900 and in Quiller-Couch's *Oxford Book of English Verse* to the simple fact that she had been unknown to the authors. It was natural that the poet's increased fame stimulated investigations of her early reception.

The first step, taken by a young student of English literature in her master's thesis in 1927, was "Early Criticism of Emily Dickinson," by Anna Mary Wells, who cited the essays of Aldrich and Higginson, pointed out Howells' key role in the early 1890's, and defended the much-abused Colonel (whose biography she was to write forty years later) against the accusation that he had not understood Emily Dickinson's work.[24]

The second step was taken four months later by Mabel

Loomis Todd. In "Emily Dickinson's Literary Début" she informed the public about her editorial activities, Higginson's enthusiasm for the poems, and the confusion of the reviewers. By referring to Lavinia Dickinson as the driving force behind the scenes, she intensified the critics' previous displeasure with Madame Bianchi's misrepresentation.[25]

The third consisted of two bibliographical inventories. One, compiled by Alfred Leete Hampson for the Hampshire Bookshop in Northampton, was published in May 1930, the other, compiled by George Whicher for the Amherst Jones Library, in November. Hampson's list confines itself mainly to the years 1924 and 1929 and is full of gaps and errors. The situation at the beginning of the centennial year is grotesquely exaggerated: "New books seem to roll off the press almost daily in the sudden enthusiasm for this neglected poet." Whicher's somewhat more comprehensive and much more accurate compilation threw strong light on the years of Emily Dickinson's literary debut.[26]

It would probably be correct to date Emily Dickinson's national fame from the year 1930. The press of the entire country took notice of the "pilgrimages." Commemorations took place on November 8 and 9, 1929, in South Hadley, on May 10, 1930, in the Hampshire Bookshop, and on December 10, 1930, in the Jones Library. Exhibitions were organized in the Jones Library and the Yale University Library. The parties marched separately to these occasions: Todd ceremonies, from which Madame Bianchi remained absent, included the Alumnae Weekend Conference at Mount Holyoke on the Founder's Day of the college and the memorial ceremony at the Jones Library on the occasion of Emily Dickinson's hundredth birthday. Bianchi celebrations, at which Mrs. Todd and her following did not appear, included the events in Northampton and New Haven. Emily Dickinson's candidacy in the election for the New York Hall of Fame for Great Americans may also be regarded as a sign of her national fame.[27] She also found her way into the *Encyclopaedia Britannica* and the *Dictionary of American Biography*.[28] Henceforth, her work was no longer in danger of being overlooked.

The feeling predominant among her admirers in the centennial year was that a new chapter in the history of the poet's criticism had begun. Few were, however, as optimistic as Genevieve Taggard who wrote: "The beginning is made. Emily Dickinson is downstairs again. She will become part of American life, American thinking, American living."[29] The conspicuous lead of her high popularity in relation to the lagging understanding of her work and the even more humiliating backwardness of the editions elicited comments on the oppressive situation. In view of the commemorative celebrations Granville Hicks was agitated by unpleasant feelings: "The situation is this: apparently less than one half of Emily Dickinson's poems have been published; those that have been published have been edited arbitrarily and perhaps stupidly; important facts regarding her life have been concealed. This is a situation so appalling as to be almost ridiculous. Here is America's greatest poet, and here is a large and appreciative audience for her poetry entirely at the mercy of a woman who, much evidence goes to show, is unworthy of such a responsibility. In countries whose inhabitants are more demonstrative and more deeply concerned about literature than we there would be riots and mass meetings. In the United States we calmly invite Mrs. Bianchi to be the principal speaker at centennial celebrations."[29a] Babette Deutsch also doubted the competence and sincerity of the niece and asked herself whether "Last Poems," "Final Poems," and "Ultimate Poems" were still to be expected.[30] In his review of July 5, 1930, Untermeyer warned of uncritical overestimation of the poet: "Emily Dickinson's work, independent of her legend, having gone through periods of mystification and patronization, is now entering a stage of sanctification. . . . After the years of neglect, one can sympathize with the overcompensatory breathlessness. But are there no reservations? Was Emily Dickinson always a great poet?" Obviously not. To the catalogue of her mistakes belong "the impulse to point every adjective," "her habit of acting coy among the immensities," "her impulse to pirouette before the mirror of her soul," and "her frequent failure to differentiate between inspiration and whim." A point of attack for critical investigations is seen in that her work was not a spontaneous creation but "the labor of a craftsman" and therefore "subject to the laborer's file."

In the preface to his bibliography, Whicher disassociated himself even more strongly from the reviewers' indiscriminate admiration and suggested a virtual course of study: consideration of Emily Dickinson's independence:

> Instead of claiming her at once as a "mystic akin to Emerson" or "the feminine Walt Whitman," let us have the patience to study her own pattern. (p. 11)

consideration of her Puritan heritage:

The simple and central fact about her is that she lived in
Amherst during the middle of the nineteenth century. This
meant that she came into a Puritan heritage at the moment
when it was becoming invalid. (p. 11)

consideration of the main theme of her work:

The most striking theme of her poetry is the Puritan theme
of renunciation. It occurs again and again, studied from many
angles.... No writer has so deeply and piercingly laid bare
that quality in the New England character which enables
it to invert suffering into a kind of joy, to welcome defeat
for the sake of the increment thereby added to the soul,
and to project satisfaction beyond the bounds of life. (p. 13)

The first who set about carrying out this program was Whicher
himself.

The most remarkable aspect of the British critical reception
in 1929 and 1930 is a drift toward the American opinion of the
New England poet—her acknowledgment as "certainly one of
the greatest women poets who ever lived" and "the most original
of American poets."[31] "The greatness outweighs any lawlessness
or harshness," wrote a reviewer concerning *Further Poems*.[32]
The main reason for her mounting fame on the other side of the
Atlantic may be seen in Aiken's selection of poetry; the main
proof of this development, in a series of well-meaning notices (cf.
Sources, p. 309). Even J. C. Squire, the leading conservative
critic who in his *London Mercury* followed American literary
doings with more blame than praise, became a deferential admirer: "These poems are one of the important literary discoveries
of our generation. I dislike superlatives. Time is long, and space
wide, and words like 'great,' 'marvellous,' 'profound,' and 'un-
surpassed' do not easily come to my pen. However, that first
sentence may stand: it is meant. Emily Dickinson was not one
of the world's great poets, but she was a very good and a very
individual one."[33]

This British *rapprochement* was, however, not an assimilation. The London critics remained cooler than their American
colleagues in 1930 and never quite forgot the old problem of
craftsmanship. Naturally, even Squire thought that "it would be
a mistake to admire her for her slipshod artistry, her wild shots,
her obscurity, her ineffective pseudo-rhymes. . . . What we must
admire is the force of her personality and the delicacy of her
perceptions."

In the shift of interest from the work to the person and in the increasing number of reviews, the criticism during both the years investigated here followed a straight course until August 1930, when the excitement gradually ebbed away. The centenary edition of the poems, a mere cumulation of the five earlier volumes, was scarcely noted when it appeared in November. The few critics were cross because Madame Bianchi had made no attempt to arrange the verses chronologically.

Despite the additional information about Emily Dickinson's life the mystery remained unsolved. The three rival candidates as lovers and the fourth possibility that no lover at all had existed fitted like interchangeable pictures into the frame of a few dates and suppositions. It was consistent with the development of events in 1930 that the year ended with a novel and a play about Emily Dickinson. MacGregor Jenkins, who had declared in his memoir that "no biographer can go far from the facts as known, for biography is not fiction" (pp. 143-44) and who is said to have pilloried Miss Pollitt's biography as "precisely the sort of book that might have made the poet kaleidoscopic with rage,"[34] wove from the threads of his memory *Emily*, not fact but fiction. Susan Glaspell's three-act play *Alison's House*, which was stimulated by the Dickinson criticism of that year, was concerned with the question of whether the family of a deceased poet possesses a monopoly on her life's work. It was played for the first time on December 1, 1930, in the New York Civic Repertory Theatre and was so successful that it yielded the playwright the Pulitzer prize for 1931.

Part Three

CONSOLIDATION
(1930-62)

IX

ACADEMIC CRITICISM (1930-62)

> *Emily Dickinson's inflated popularity has reached its high-water mark, has already dropped and will continue to fall, to the sober level of her proper place. She is no longer a discovery. She is now established as one of the three great poets of the nineteenth century in America. Some persons will continue to think that she is without question the greatest poet produced in our country so far. She will always have friends in excess of her established position; but she will never again have serious detractors.*[1]

AN ACCOUNT of Emily Dickinson's critical reception must follow the rhythm of the reception. After 1930 the rhythm changed from irregular to flowing—the predominantly journalistic criticism being superseded by academic research and interpretation. Until 1930 each new edition of poems or letters had caused a more or less violent wave of reviews. After the centennial year the criticism was directed chiefly by the application of new critical methods. Emily Dickinson had arrived. Scholarly notes, articles, and monographs assumed the role previously played by notices in the daily and weekly press. With the exception of the year 1945, when once again a situation with controversies and ill feeling arose, and of the year 1955, which yielded the critical edition of the poems, the earlier spontaneous manifestations of enthusiasm and antipathy gave way to sober discussion. Book reviews supplemented the process of evaluation but no longer determined it.

A manner of presentation which surveys greater periods of time would seem to correspond to this alteration in the tone and course of the critical debate. The metaphors of the unexpected breaking of a "literary ice-jam" and the "late thaw of a frozen image," used by Whicher in 1950 and by Jay Leyda in 1955 to characterize the importance of the donation of the Dickinson papers to Harvard and the appearance of the variorum edition,[2] apply more to the entire period from 1930 to 1962 than to the first half of the 1950's. The thaw, which consisted in a continual growth of the canon, an increase in knowledge about the person, and in a more thorough explication of the poetry, set in immediately after 1930. It may become necessary to date the beginning of a fourth phase of the criticism from the second half of the 1950's, but this phase is still developing.

The dual process of transmitting Emily Dickinson's poetic estate was grotesquely reduced to the question of which of the parties would survive the other. Martha Dickinson Bianchi possessed the rights for all unprinted material. At her death in 1943 the rights and manuscripts were transferred by will to her collaborator Hampson. In 1950, the papers were bought by a Manhattan bibliophile, Gilbert Holland Montague, who presented them to Harvard University. For the Todd party that meant a blocking of all editions of material held back after 1896, a questionable legal situation from 1943 to 1950, and great difficulties thereafter.

Madame Bianchi published the following volumes: *Emily Dickinson Face to Face* (1932), *Unpublished Poems of Emily Dickinson* (1935), and *The Poems of Emily Dickinson* (1937). The first book was little more than a remodeling of *Life and Letters*, full of errors, distortions, self-praise, and the familiar tone of hushed reverence. It continued the one-sided portrayal of the "elfin, mischievous strain" in Emily Dickinson and, in the preface contributed by Hampson, smote those "rank outsiders" who had dared to write about the life of the poet. Lavinia received greater emphasis. The printing of 118 unpublished letters to Sue was more significant. Untermeyer welcomed the book as "the most explicable as well as the most nearly complete portrait yet drawn"; the scholar Morris Schappes, who had shortly before examined the text of the edition of letters of 1924, pointed out mistakes and found little new.[3] A biography of Lavinia, announced in the preface, was never issued.[4]

To offer "unpublished" poems again in 1935 had an embarrassing effect after the scandal created in 1929. Perhaps this was why the editors contented themselves with a mere variation of the threadbare explanation given before. In a parenthesis it is simply stated: "—disclosed during the exhaustive examination of the Dickinson family papers made obligatory by the increasing posthumous fame of the poet—."[5] The poems, which were for the most part of little significance, were combined in 1937 with those in the Centenary Edition under the title *The Poems* . . . . The echo created by both editions was weak; old demands were categorically repeated. Nevertheless, the collection of 1937 with its 909 poems formed the basis of Dickinson scholarship for the next eighteen years.

The second line of the transmission of the texts was extended in 1931. Shortly before Mrs. Todd's death an expanded new edition of the out-of-print letters was published. It was enriched by 130 passages omitted in 1894 and by six letters to Charles H. Clark which cast new light on Emily Dickinson's relationship with Wadsworth.[6] After the editor's death on October 14, 1932, the possibility of publishing the remaining material resting in the legendary camphorwood chest depended on the survival of the Todd party. Only in the preface to *Ancestors' Brocades*, written in October 1944, could Millicent Todd Bingham state—not entirely without malice—that "Emily Dickinson's family is now extinct" (p. ix) and then conclude the work of her mother in three steps. The first was publication of 668 poems as *Bolts of Melody: New Poems of Emily Dickinson* (1945) and a gleaning which supplied lacking stanzas of fifty-six poems that had been published only in part.[7] In spite of the standardization of orthography and punctuation *Bolts of Melody* was of a textual precision not previously achieved and was in keeping with the introductory affirmation that "in no single instance have I substituted a word or a phrase not suggested by Emily herself" (p. xi). The second step was *Ancestors' Brocades*, that detailed history of publication in the years 1890-96 which is often cited in this study and which was to serve as a vindication of Mrs. Todd against the Dickinsons. For the last time and with greater clarity than ever before, this book made the feud public and occasioned indignation as well as sneers such as

> *Martha died and Mabel died,*
> *But Millicent now enters*
> *With fresh supplies of manuscript*
> *Assembled for the printers.*[8]

While the poems, which were generally found fragmentary and disappointing, attracted little notice, the revealing volume by

Mrs. Bingham led to partisanship (especially of Aiken against Madame Bianchi and of John Erskine against Mrs. Todd), shook the critics' confidence in Mrs. Todd and Higginson as editors, and induced a scurrilous flight of Bernard DeVoto's fancy, which will be dealt with.

The last step was the publication of the letters in Mrs. Bingham's possession. The reason for withholding these letters is obscure, in spite of Mrs. Bingham's assurance: "Bequeathed to me by my mother, . . . they had come to her in the early 1890's as a gift from the recipient, Emily's brother Austin. . . ."[9] *Emily Dickinson's Home* was ready for print in 1950, but could not be published until five years later due to Harvard's contestation of the copyright, and only then because Mrs. Bingham stubbornly insisted on her rights. In the meantime *Emily Dickinson: A Revelation* (1954) was published. As in the case of the poems, a gleaning of "Prose Fragments of Emily Dickinson" followed.[10] *Emily Dickinson: A Revelation* contains drafts of fifteen letters to Judge Otis P. Lord from the years 1878-83 which reveal the "last great love of her life." While the poet's friendships with other persons in each case only touched "a separate 'apartment' of her nature," the sole "master passion" is seen in her inclination toward Lord: "Only at last, in Judge Lord, did all tenderness converge and fuse."[11] The letters printed as the "Revelation" comprise only a small portion of the thin volume. Three fourths of the contents—"The Challenge," "The Search," "The Findings," "The Approach"—are devoted to a biographical sketch of Lord and to a description of the work which the book had caused the editor. *Emily Dickinson's Home*, a carefully documented family history in which Edward's and Lavinia's letters to Austin are published for the first time, is considerably richer in material.

New material flowed more sparsely from other sources. In 1932 six poems emerged from Higginson's literary estate in the Boston Public Library. In the same year a letter fragment was discovered by John Howard Birss in an auction catalogue of 1909. A year before, two grandchildren of Eudocia Flynt presented to the Yale Library two letters of Emily Dickinson to their grandmother. The publication, in part, of a letter of the poet to the well-known Unitarian clergyman, Edward Everett Hale, unexpectedly threw strong light on Emily Dickinson's "tutor," Benjamin Franklin Newton. One day three letters to Mary Haven fell out of a secondhand copy of the first selection of poetry. Fourteen letters to Henry Vaughan Emmons came to light in 1945. (Cf. Sources, pp. 272-73). In 1951 the granddaughter of

Josiah Holland made the greatest contribution to this third strand of textual transmission. She edited sixty-five letters, together with thirty already published by Mrs. Todd, as *Emily Dickinson's Letters to Dr. and Mrs. Josiah Gilbert Holland*. These letters, all dated exactly, were textually reliable.

With Montague's donation of Madame Bianchi's estate to the Houghton Library, the reluctant provision of access to Mrs. Todd's Dickinson papers by her daughter, and the naming of a noted literary historian as editor, the way was cleared for the critical edition of the poems in the summer of 1950. Thomas H. Johnson underscored the importance of the event: "Certainly not in this decade, perhaps not in this half-century, has a more fortunate event—one long hoped for—occurred in the history of American belles-lettres." If he underestimated the amount of work to be accomplished—"Johnson . . . expects to prepare three or four volumes within three years," *The Publishers' Weekly* reported on June 3, 1950—it was mainly due to problems of dating, which Mrs. Todd and Madame Bianchi had never really tackled.[12]

Johnson's edition marked the beginning of a new period in the history of Dickinson criticism. *The Poems of Emily Dickinson* (1955) became the model of a critical edition. The canon had only been insignificantly expanded to a total of 1775 by the addition of 41 unpublished poems. One hundred fifteen poems remained undated due to missing autographs and other clues. The nearly chronological arrangement permitted conclusions about the poet's development and the extent of the "creative" editing of previous editors for the first time. *The Letters of Emily Dickinson* (1958) could lay less claim to finality, although, like *The Poems*, it was considered definitive and was unanimously acclaimed. "One feels virtually certain," Johnson wrote in the introduction, "that more Dickinson letters will eventually come to light, though painstaking search over a period of several years has not turned them up" (I, xxiii). There were more irretrievably lost letters than there were lost poems. Johnson's investigations, however, enlarged the collection by approximately one hundred letters to a total of 1049.

In the criticism of Emily Dickinson the person, the year 1930 had the effect of a shock. That the first unretouched portrait of the poet was not published until 1931 seemed almost symbolic. Mrs. Todd, who used it as a frontispiece for her edition of the letters, recommended in the introduction a return to the sources.

This return, which ended in three biographies and a documentary work, took the form partly of demythologizing and partly of enriching Emily Dickinson's personal history by several new features. An investigation of the year spent at Mount Holyoke showed that its founder and head, Mary Lyon, was more human than had previously been assumed. The picturesque scene of Emily's rebellion had probably not taken place. The investigation also proved that the poet's religious sincerity had not been unique: "She shared the scrupulous honesty of the forties which refused to accept anything but the most positive inner conviction as proof of conversion."[13] Other studies drew attention to the friends of the poet and indicated that she had lived with closer connections to the world than had been supposed. Her relations with the Hollands and the Bowleses, with Newton, Higginson, and Helen Hunt Jackson, even with Irish-born Maggie, the house servant, came to the fore. Leyda was right in supposing that "the total reality of Emily Dickinson's circumstances . . . is the best of all levers to pry off accumulated speculation and romancing in order that we may see what sort of woman it was who wrote those poems."[14] The attempts to arrive at the truth through new evidence logically led from Mrs. Bingham's *Emily Dickinson's Home* to a compendious documentation, *The Years and Hours of Emily Dickinson*, which was compiled on the spot from Amherst documents, press notices, genealogies, memoirs, letters, and diaries. The author, Jay Leyda, did not regard his work as a substitute for biography but as a compilation of sources for a future, more realistic life and, in the meantime, as "the next . . . step in combatting the biographical simplification that only recently has begun to yield to the correction of factual scholarship."[15]

The letter to Hale about Newton, which had turned up in 1933, proved to be momentous in the fight against the love legend. "The information supplied by this letter," wrote Whicher, "put an end to all speculation on the subject and opened a new chapter in the poet's biography." Whicher identified Newton as the "friend, who taught me Immortality" and stressed his significance for Emily Dickinson's decision to devote her life to poetry.[16]

In Whicher's *This Was a Poet*, the individual biographical studies which had been made up to that time were combined with supplementary information to form a balanced life history which placed the father as cardinal fact near the center, without making him a concealed lover as Genevieve Taggard had done, pushed Sister Sue to the periphery as a pseudo-sister, and removed all lovers from the circle. Newton and Wadsworth were credibly fixed in their roles as intellectual adviser and spiritual friend. The Wadsworth legend of Madame Bianchi was finally buried in 1949 when Whicher looked up his son, the coroner Dr. William S. Wadsworth, in Philadelphia: "The picture that emerged, as we talked through an hour, was that of a man utterly consecrated to his ministry, happily married and devoted to his family, finding complete fulfilment in his marvelous power to uphold and strengthen the wavering souls of his flock. In such a career there was not the slightest room for a wayward inclination. One could see how Emily Dickinson could idolize such a man, but what could she have meant to him?"[17]

Richard Chase and Thomas H. Johnson hardly went beyond the line drawn by *This Was a Poet;* indeed, the listlessly written biographical part of Chase's *Emily Dickinson* (1951) is based entirely on Whicher. Johnson's interpretative biography, published simultaneously with his edition of the poems, did not search for new material, but followed the inner development of the poet's life. Of the three biographical chapters—"The Valley," "The Family," "Friends"—only the first is original. It makes Emily Dickinson's religious conflicts more understandable by relating them to the "difficult ideals" of the Pioneer Valley. The biography is appropriately one of omissions since former speculations are quietly passed by. Johnson is quite aware of this and refers the reader to the work of his predecessor: "George Frisbie Whicher's . . . work will continue to be a guide to others as it has been to me."[18] Work-oriented biographical interpretation was continued in Theodora Van Wagenen Ward's studies collected in *The Capsule of The Mind* (1961).

Side by side with sober biographical research the quest for the identity of the lover continued. Rebecca Patterson retraced the steps of Kate Scott, a close childhood friend of Susan Dickinson, and believed she had found in her an answer to the riddle. She accused Madame Bianchi of camouflaging tactics by having pushed Wadsworth forward, associated the geographic symbolism of the poems with Kate's trips, and used the love verses to construe an abnormal tête-à-tête between Emily and Kate which she supposed to have taken place in 1860.[19] The book met with unanimous, vehement criticism. Whicher called it "probably the worst book on Emily Dickinson yet written, and that is saying a good deal."[20] Later, two critics elevated Samuel Bowles to the rank of a lover. David Higgins supposed that the small group of "Daisy" letters was addressed to Bowles; Winfield Scott went further by trying to show that all dates and allusions which had earlier been connected with Hunt, Gould, and Wadsworth, would apply as well to the editor of *The Springfield Republican*.[21] These speculations were joined by two psychoanalytical studies. In a group of love poems Griffith saw an unconscious fear of everything male and explained the neurosis by noting that the few male persons in Emily Dickinson's life had left her in the lurch: her father failed her in that he did not reciprocate her affection, her brother in that he married, the critic Higginson through his condescension, finally even God in that he remained silent and beyond reach. A year later Anna Mary Wells made an amateurish attempt to render the poet's life in the form of a clinical report to prove that she was for a time psychopathic and was treated in Boston for this.[22]

The image of Emily Dickinson and her family experienced perhaps its greatest distortion in 1945 at the hands of Bernard DeVoto.[23] In *Ancestors' Brocades*, which was often far removed from the pretended "objective factual account" (p. xviii), Millicent Todd Bingham had in defense of her mother first played off Susan Dickinson against Lavinia and then Lavinia against Mrs. Todd, and had unveiled both sister and sister-in-law of the poet as furies filled with irreconcilable hatred for each other.[24] DeVoto took this vindictiveness as a clue to the earlier family history, a story of terror which might have been most fittingly written by a Dostoevski:

> The house was a crucible for the distillation of terrors and hatreds more intense than any our literature has chanced to embody elsewhere. (p. 603)
> Millicent Todd Bingham . . . has made it possible for the first time to define the hatreds rioting in that house where Atreus and Emily Dickinson and the Furies all lived together. (p. 604)

The poet's withdrawal from the world is a "transcendental fairy tale," the Wadsworth legend a "Victorian love story": "It will not do, gentlemen. This is a more tragic, more terrible, more triumphant story. This woman came to hold the infinite in her hands. It was not put there by love of a married parson denied her by her father—she brought it back out of hell." As a result, he construes Emily Dickinson as "the supreme poet of hate."[25]

Whicher, who had not at all approved of Mrs. Bingham's misrepresentation of Lavinia and had called it "a blow below the belt," reacted with uncommon asperity and irony to DeVoto's "preposterous notions."[26]

In spite of a new spirit of objectivity the old impressionistic criticism, the intuitive, personal response to Emily Dickinson's work, flared up from time to time. At first, the enthusiasts predominated, but from the end of the 1930's to the beginning of the 1950's a new skepticism spread.

In 1934 Desmond Powell celebrated Emily Dickinson as "one of the most original love poets in our language," although he was convinced that there was no penetrating her art by formal analysis. In 1937 William Van Wyck took refuge in a metaphor: "She is a volcano erupting in a colossal block of ice. None of the strength of the eruption, none of its beauty is lost, but due to the glacial coating, all terrors are gone and we may enjoy a mighty spectacle attended by none of its usual terrors." In 1942 Donald Connors saw the significance of the poet in the ethical value of her work: "Stopping by the landmarks of her poetry, we find ourselves uplifted by her life poems, moved by her love poems, and taught to see more clearly by her poems on nature and immortality."[27] Nine years later, in the time of "the cold war and the moral problem,"[28] Richard Chase clearly stressed Emily Dickinson's new relevance to contemporary experience:

> Her sense of the anguish of personal existence and of the precariousness of human life recommends her to a time in which new philosophies of existence have come forcefully to our attention. Her vigor, her curious and reconnoitering mind appeal to a period which has been given too much to apathy and suspicion of the spirited imagination. Her rigorous psychology and her sense of the virtue of definition, of intellectual severity, of the exclusions which the mind must make if it is to preserve its precarious "economy," of the powerful consequentiality of fact and circumstance, of the hostility or indifference of the universe to man—all these attitudes recommend Emily Dickinson to an age which is seeking secular modes of thought more severe, more realistic, more durable than the easier optimisms which have sometimes characterized American intellectual life.[29]

Those who regarded Emily Dickinson highly were confronted with old and new skeptics. Sir Herbert Read and Fred Lewis Pattee numbered among the last old-school critics. Read, who reviewed a London reprint of the Centenary Edition, was greatly disappointed. He regretted that misunderstanding enthusiasm had put a private talent on public display. The monotony of the poems resulting from "poverty of technique" especially repelled him: "It would not be unfair to compare these poems with the works of a painter who had all his life painted small pictures of similar subjects in one color with one texture. The eccentricity of tec' nique, when we see it in bulk, is evidently not one of design, but rather of incapacity, of insensitiveness, of incredible naïvety in thought and expression." He let "a kind of cryptic economy of statement" pass as the only merit of her manner of writing.[30]

Pattee's displeasure was also directed against Emily Dickinson's admirers. Even in 1937, the seventy-four-year-old critic had not entirely made up his mind about the stature of Emily Dickinson: "Is it safe even now to try to determine her quality?"[31] Whereas he had resigned himself to her increased fame in 1930 and had partly revised his opinion of 1915, he now relapsed into his extreme conservatism.

Again he attains his goal of unmasking Dickinson by indirection. The first attack is made through Melville, who had been problematic for him throughout his life: "The rocketing of an American writer long unknown into sudden perihelion is by no means a unique phenomenon. On the contrary, it is the American literary way. Note the swift change in the stellar magnitude of Melville. Note the men who, rejected by their own generation, now head the roll of our American classic creators: Whitman, Poe, Thoreau, and, in his early period, Emerson. Rebellion against the conventional estimate appeals to American readers, and if there be in addition a mysterious personality presenting a problem seemingly insoluble, then awaken the masses" (p. 180-81). The second attack takes aim at Emily Dickinson but, as in 1930, indirectly through the verdicts of the old guard—Arlo Bates, Aldrich, Andrew Lang—whom he quotes with relish, whereas he is amused at Howells' benevolence and young Stephen Crane's enthusiasm. Pattee's concluding remarks reproach Emily Dickinson for dilettantism, immaturity, and deficient logic:

> She knew no better. She simply wrote in any jumble of form that came to her pen. (p. 194)

> Why then start her poem in conventional form and then suddenly switch it into chaotic formlessness? . . . Rhyme in poetry is by no means a necessity, but by every law of

harmony and commonsense when one begins a poem with a
definite rhyming system it must follow throughout the same
system or else give the sense of discord or even shock the
reader. Were she a conscious rebel she would have thrown
off completely shackles of uniform rhyme and stanza form
and expressed herself in free verse. Either all or nothing.
(pp. 194-95)

But her poetry? Always as I read it I think of Higginson's
impression of her childlikeness. The originality of it is the
originality of wondering childhood, and so in its comparisons
and analogies. (p. 197)

These old objections are joined by a new factor: Emily Dickinson could find a public only during a literary ebb. "At no other
time in the history of our poetry could she have come with the
same effect" (p. 184).

Read's and Pattee's reservation lingered on both sides of
the Atlantic, in England more strongly than in America. Admittedly, there were advocates among the British, but the three
new volumes of poetry of 1935, 1937, and 1945 awakened without fail the desire for a new anthology. "It is the only form,
in England at any rate, which would make any appeal to a larger
public," wrote a critic in 1937 who generally expressed himself
disapprovingly: "How monotonous I find her flowers, her bees
and bobolinks . . . , how empty her love poems—a love more
guessed at than known or wanted. Even the visions of death and
eternity . . . seem the product of a curious musing, as though
here, too, the point was that experience could be forestalled."[32]
Moreover, the selected hymns of praise of American critics which
Bianchi and Hampson had imprudently quoted in the preface of
each new edition irritated British ears, since they were considered representative of the American consensus. "Such fulsome
panegyrics," wrote Edward Sackville West in *The New Statesman and Nation*, "have made the achievement of this genuine,
but very limited and capricious, muse necessarily difficult to
assess, since a word in dispraise will almost certainly be taken
(especially in the U.S.A.) as a sign of brutal insensibility."[33]
These hymns annoyed W. Somerset Maugham also;[34] they
prompted a reviewer in *Scrutiny* to remove Emily Dickinson
from the pedestal on which Chase had placed her and assign her
"a minor if (on the strength of a few poems) secure position
in literature."[35]

James G. Southworth and Thornton Wilder numbered

among the later American skeptics. For the former, Dickinson had not become a great artist because she had not comprehended the Antaean myth. By uprooting herself, as it were, through her very seclusion she forwent a fruitful contact with life and remained emotionally immature. "She demanded for herself a too rarefied air, and her poetry suffers for it."[36] The comparison with Dickens' Miss Havisham obtrudes itself. Southworth feels more at home with Robert Frost, who had grasped the significance of the myth: "She is as truly New England as Mr. Frost; but it is a phase of New England that only one with New England roots can fully understand, a casual visitor never" (p. 27). This native Michigander ranks himself among the casual visitors.

In the reflections which occurred to him while preparing his Charles Eliot Norton lecture on Emily Dickinson, Thornton Wilder also found some things to object to in the poet's person which had had a disadvantageous effect on the artist. His main reservations are directed against the tone of affected modesty perceivable in letters and poems: "We have heard this tone before. It belongs to women who in childhood have received too heavy an impress from their relation to their fathers. It may be called the tone of *misplaced coquetry*. Its general character is that of archness. . . . It has certainly no place in mature friendship."[37] Nevertheless, the symptoms of "childhood fixation" and of "*arrest in her development*" are not crucial for Wilder. He attempts to understand Emily Dickinson within the context of the lecture series which dealt with "American characteristics." In his Thoreau lecture he had remarked that the American is rootless, "disconnected from place, distrustful of authority, thrown back upon himself."[38] His critique of Emily Dickinson also culminates in an evaluation of the specifically American characteristics of her work:

> Americans can find no support for their identity in place, in time, or in community—they are really in relation only to Everywhere, Always, and Everybody. Emily Dickinson is a signal illustration of this assertion. The imagination of this spinster withdrawn into a few rooms in Amherst was constantly aware that the universe surrounded every detail of life. . . . In this constant recognition of the immensity of dimensions of time and place, she is the least parochial of American poets and exceeds even Walt Whitman in imaginative sweep. . . . The problem of American lone-

liness . . . is the problem of "belonging." . . . Emily Dickinson, in all appearance the loneliest of beings, solved the problem in a way which is of importance to every American: by loving the particular while living in the universal. (pp. 47-48)

After 1955 objections became rarer. When a reviewer of *Letters* (1958) sympathized with Higginson's designation "partially cracked poetress" and regretted that his "lungs are not designed for prolonged stays in such a rarefied atmosphere,"[39] ten other members of his guild showed heartier constitutions. When in 1961 an annoyed Whitman fanatic fell into the cadence of Andrew Lang, applied his methods of dissection, attempted to ridicule such Dickinson interpreters as Austin Warren and Allen Tate, derided Emily Dickinson as "an injured rag doll of lyricism spilling sawdust," and predicted her "decline on the critical stock market,"[40] he stood completely alone. His very reproach that Emily Dickinson was "admired now to the point of silliness by those who should know better" was no longer true after 1955, when the often effusive admiration of an Untermeyer or a Van Doren had abated.

The contribution of the New Criticism to the explication of Emily Dickinson's work began in the mid-1930's. The understanding of her art was considerably furthered by the investigations of Tate, Blackmur, and Winters. They constituted an influential trio. Tate's essay of 1928 was reprinted in *The Symposium* in April 1932 in a slightly expanded form. Blackmur's and Winters' studies appeared in 1937 and 1938.

R. P. Blackmur's essay "Emily Dickinson: Notes on Prejudice and Fact" first removed a set of dangerous prejudices before proceeding to the facts. The first prejudice—that Emily Dickinson was a great poet—he traces to Conrad Aiken. He makes Madame Bianchi responsible for the second—that her artistic revolt against the conventions of poetry was absolute—and continues: "Emily Dickinson never knew anything about the craft of verse well enough to exemplify it, let alone revolt from it. . . . [She] did not abandon rhyme so much as she failed to get that far—her lines strike *as if* they intended to end in rhyme; and her assonances seem frequently incomplete substitutes for rhyme and not assonances at all."[41] The third prejudice—the linking of Dickinson with great writers (such as Goethe) or great intellectual movements (such as mysticism) by means of unexpanded comparisons—he substantiates by citing Ludwig Lewisohn's *Expression in America*. The fourth prejudice—the regarding of the poet as a fatal event in cultural history—is ascribed to Allen Tate. At the bottom of all these prejudices lies a false conception of the nature of poetry: "The greatness of Emily Dickinson is not . . . going to be found in anybody's idea of greatness, or of Goethe, or intensity, or mysticism, or historical fatality. It is going to be found in the words she used and in the way she put them together; which we will observe . . . as a series of facts about words." To illustrate this assertion Blackmur quotes "Renunciation" and suggests: "Let us provisionally inquire what it is in the words that makes poetry of the statement about renunciation."

The following interpretation was cited in 1941 by John Crowe Ransom as exemplary of the new method of criticism.[42] What the poet succeeded in accomplishing in this poem by virtue of her aptitude for language usually miscarried, which is why two thirds of her poems are to be discounted as mere exercises. To discover the reasons for such failure Blackmur pursues contextual studies of the words "plush" and "purple" and catalogues Emily Dickinson's vocabulary. With the help of "plush" and "purple" he explains her "habit of so employing certain favorite words that their discriminate meanings tend to melt into the single sentiment of self-expression" (p. 344); with the aid of the catalogue he shows that her art stranded wherever she failed to activate her small, abstract, rigidly compartmented vocabulary by the more extensive homely vocabulary derived from her personal experience. After the critical examination of several such failures the concluding evaluation follows as a "fact":

> I think it is a fact that the failure and success of Emily Dickinson's poetry were uniformly accidental largely because of the private and eccentric nature of her relation to the business of poetry. She was neither a professional poet nor an amateur; she was a private poet who wrote indefatigably as other women cook or knit. Her gift for words and the cultural predicament of her time drove her to poetry instead of antimacassars. Neither her personal education nor the habit of her society as she knew it ever gave her the least inkling that poetry is a rational and objective art and most so when the theme is self-expression. She came, as Mr. Tate says, at the right time for one kind of poetry: the

poetry of sophisticated, eccentric vision. That is what makes her good—in a few poems and many passages representatively great. But she never undertook the great profession of controlling the means of objective expression. That is why the bulk of her verse is not representative but mere fragmentary indicative notation. The pity of it is that the document her whole work makes shows nothing so much as that she had the themes, the insight, the observation, and the capacity for honesty, which had she only known how— or only known why—would have made the major instead of the minor fraction of her verse genuine poetry. But her dying society had no tradition by which to teach her the one lesson she did not know by instinct. (pp. 346-47)

The starting point of Yvor Winters' deliberations was, as in the case of Blackmur, the deplorable popularity of the poet, which he attributed to the glorification of her vices. Like Blackmur he concerned himself chiefly with the flaws. Even more sharply than Blackmur he tried to separate the chaff from the grain, for "probably no poet of comparable reputation has been guilty of so much unpardonable writing."[43] In contrast to Blackmur, however, he does not gain any insight into what separates the best from the worst: "Her best poems . . . can never be isolated certainly and defensibly from her defects; yet she is a poetic genius of the highest order, and this ambiguity in one's feeling about her is profoundly disturbing" (p. 150). As flaws, he tries to isolate her tendency toward "silly playfulness" (which is why he finds "I like to see it lap the miles" an "abominable" poem) and toward "obscurantism." "Playful" and "serious," "irresponsible" and "responsible" become the criteria of his ethical judgment of the work. The playful element, which is reflected in metrical singsong, in poetic nursery jargon, and in forced obscurity, is irresponsible and morally contestable. Emily Dickinson displays a sense of responsibility only in her allegorical presentation of timeless themes. As a result the poems on death and immortality as well as all those which are concerned with "the definition of moral experience, including the definition of the difficulties of comprehension" (p. 152), are stressed as the most valuable. In some of them the flaws recede almost entirely; three —"A light exists in spring," "As imperceptibly as grief," and "There's a certain slant of light"—which belong among the best poems in English, are metrically analyzed. The final judgment is pronounced according to aesthetic, not ethical, points of view:

> Of all great poets, she is the most lacking in taste; there are innumerable beautiful lines and passages wasted in the desert of her crudities; her defects, more than those of any other great poet that I have read, are constantly at the brink, or pushing beyond the brink, of her best poems. This stylistic character is the natural product of the New England which produced the barren little meeting houses; of the New England founded by the harsh and intrepid pioneers, who in order to attain salvation trampled through a world which they were too proud and too impatient to understand. In this respect, she differs from Melville, whose taste was rich and cultivated. But except by Melville, she is surpassed by no writer that this country has produced; she is one of the greatest lyric poets of all time. (p. 165)

In the period immediately following the studies by Blackmur and Winters the greatest energy was expended in the explication of individual poems. Fittingly, Cleanth Brooks and Robert Penn Warren began with an interpretation of "After great pain a formal feeling comes" in *Understanding Poetry* (1938), the anthology for college students which was to become very influential in spreading the new critical methods. Soon not a year passed but that several poems were analyzed in *The Explicator*. General assessment was replaced by individual explanation—true to the motto of this periodical that "the last verse . . . is not yet sufficiently explicated."

The specialization of research and criticism which began in 1931 and grew stronger after 1941 increasingly involved a splintering of interests. Parallels and influences were discovered, comparisons were drawn, Emily Dickinson's religion and her theory of poetry were investigated. Almost all these endeavors can be pointed out much earlier as tendencies; now old opinions were confirmed, supplemented, modified, rejected, discovered anew. A study of the poet's critical reception cannot be concerned with the pursuit of particulars, which would be the object of a report on research, but only with the recording of trends.

The least progress was registered wherever critics traced influences and parallels. The nets hopefully cast out were pulled in empty. Biblical echoes could indeed be easily pointed out, but the investigation of influences, such as the metaphorical language of Wadsworth's sermons, the terminology of Sir Thomas Browne, the verse form, rhyme technique, and themes of Isaac Watts, did not lead far and at best evinced a highly individual, condensed assimilation:

> Some of these resemblances give the impression that, in her immensely receptive and active mind, she is revolving a new idea derived from her reading and registering, like marginal notes, her reaction to it.
>
> It is a tribute to her originality that her debt to Browne cannot be more specifically determined.
>
> It is rather difficult to lay examples of the two poets side by side, for Emily Dickinson's fire of imagination far surpasses Watts's modest talents.[44]

The comparisons made with various poets of the late eighteenth and of the nineteenth centuries also bogged down at the very outset, since they rarely amounted to more than superficially drawn parallels. That Emily Dickinson was separated from Christina Rossetti, the first significant religious woman poet of England, by a wide gulf, the orthodox Anglican herself had indicated in her letter to Thomas Niles in 1891. "Between these two women no comparison need be forced," wrote Morton Zabel in 1931. "They lived in different worlds, but each found in isolation the fulfilment of high lyrical impulse."[45] The more detailed comparisons with Poe, Thoreau, Blake, the Brontës, Annette von Droste-Hülshoff, Emerson, and above all Whitman scarcely seemed more cogent: they yielded almost nothing but differences.

While the search for parallels ended altogether in an acknowledgment of the poet's originality, the endeavor to link her with the metaphysical tradition received new stimulus from Cleanth Brooks's *Modern Poetry and the Tradition*, which also opened a new chapter in Donne criticism. According to Brooks the emergence of modern verse necessitated a critical revision of the entire poetic tradition: "One cannot participate fully in the poetry of John Crowe Ransom . . . and continue to enjoy Shelley on the old basis."[46] The ironic and structural use of metaphor and wit in modern poetry in a manner comparable to the seventeenth century supplies the basis for a broad definition of metaphysical poetry as "a poetry in which the opposition of the impulses which are united is extreme." With this definition as a norm Brooks experimentally constructs a new tradition in his tenth chapter: "Notes for a Revised History of English Poetry." This tradition begins with Herrick, Donne, and Browne, skips over neoclassicism, romanticism, and Victorianism as for the most part devoid of psychological conflict, and continues in Frost, Eliot, Auden, and others. Concerning Emily Dickinson and Hopkins, Brooks says: "One would like to comment on Gerard Hopkins and Emily Dickinson as poets who transcended Victorianism, pointing out that their poetry, significantly, is characterized by the use of vigorous metaphor, the incorporation of the difficult and unpoetic, and the use of dramatic shifts of tone. (One notices too that they incur from conventional readers the charge of obscurity.)"

Brooks's ideas were tentatively applied by Eunice Glenn in 1943. She begins with a characteristic censure of the "romantic criticism" to which the New England poet had been subjected and with a demand for close study. In order to show Emily Dickinson's kinship with the metaphysical group she analyzes four poems of increasing complexity.[47] "Title divine is mine" is characterized by "paradox and the skillful control of tone" (p. 579); "He put the belt around my life" by "complexity of tone" (p. 581); "I cannot live with you" by "extremely ironical implications concerning the Puritan view of life and sense of love" (p. 584); "Because I could not stop for death" by "unification of heterogeneous materials" (p. 586). The second poem is compared with Donne's "Valediction Forbidding Mourning," the third with Marvell's "The Definition of Love." The summary shows the proximity of the author to her master, Cleanth Brooks: "She does not use disparate materials sparingly as the romantic poet is often inclined to do. And her liberty in the use of words would hardly be sanctioned by the typically romantic poet. . . . This kind of unity, or reconciliation that we have been observing at work in these poems is chiefly responsible for their success. Proof of this is found in the fact that the few poems of Emily Dickinson's that are not successful show no evidence of the quality; and some others that are only partially successful show less of it. In this sense we are justified in referring to Emily Dickinson as a metaphysical poet" (p. 588).

Emily Dickinson's stylistic connection with the metaphysical school was strengthened by Joseph Duncan in 1959. He describes her art as "the best example of poetic work which, though apparently not directly influenced by the metaphysical poets, is strikingly illuminated when examined in terms of metaphysical techniques."[48] Similarities and differences become apparent, first, in the poetic transformation of her experience into mathematical and spatial quantities:

> Although in reducing ideas and feelings to bare abstractions she approached the geometrical figures of Donne and Marvell, she went much further, and retained a detached scientific view more consistently. (p. 79)

Second, in the use of sacramental symbolism:

> In contrast to her scientific approach, Miss Dickinson's second controlling interpretation of her material was rooted in traditional Christian symbols and correspondences. Her affinities with the metaphysicals would suggest this incarnational and sacramental approach, and it occurs boldly enough —but with her own distinctive flavor. (p. 82)

Third, in her use of everyday metaphors:

> The vast reservoir of the ordinary provided Miss Dickinson, as it had Herbert, with many characteristic figures. Circuses, guns, clothing, and household affairs became charged with meaning in her poetry. (p. 84)

In addition to the comparisons, the poet's equivocal religious attitude formed another complex of interest. The contradictory coexistence of skepticism and childlike faith in poems and letters continued to lead to incompatible conjectures. Mary James Power devoted an entire book to arguing that Emily Dickinson had had a propensity for the dogma of Catholicism, a thesis first advanced by Kathérine Brégy in 1924. This book, written with the cooperation of Madame Bianchi, elaborates the idea that "Emily's recusancy to the generally accepted creed of New England, her regard for doctrine . . . , her predisposition to Catholic thought, her *jeu d'esprit* in a biased age, her whimsey, her drollery, her exaltation of death, her informality with Divinity give her the happy distinction of the *rara avis* on this side of the water; she was the *Phoenix among the Puritans*, as Gerard Manley Hopkins was the *Phoenix among the Jesuits*."[49] Although R. P. Blackmur attacked the previously popular epithet "mystic," it was repeatedly taken up again until Sister Mary Humiliata explained that it did not apply to the life and work of Emily Dickinson.[50]

These investigations, which penetrated into particulars, were combined in the syntheses of Whicher, Wells, Chase, Johnson, and Anderson.

Like the biographical part of *This Was a Poet*, the critical part offered no sensations, but a level-headed interpretation based on previous work with the notable exclusion of the criticism of the 1920's, except for Susan Miles's and Allen Tate's studies. Whicher reminded his reader that the poet was not to be understood as a contemporary, but as a confluence of the three streams of Puritan tradition, Yankee humor, and spiritual unrest typified by Emerson: "What she actually represents is the last surprising bloom . . . of New England's flowering time."[51]

Henry W. Wells's *Introduction to Emily Dickinson* switched the emphasis completely. While Whicher had interpreted the poet in terms of her heritage, Wells attempted to show how she left sex, personal ties, and provincial world behind her by virtue of her genius, how she ascended from the personal to the universal: "Both the thought and art of Emily Dickinson's poetry belong in their essence to the literatures of the most remote and ancient peoples. They signify an advanced civilization rather than any qualities fundamentally American."[52] She belongs to world literature, not to New England and America: "She stands in company with the chief poets, seers, mystics, and visionaries, far more nearly than with those men and women to whom she wrote actual letters" (pp. xvi-xvii). As a universal genius, she is simultaneously childlike and mature, poet and thinker, mystic and stoic, romantic and gifted with scientific vision. She resembles many of the great from Sappho and Anacreon through Angelus Silesius and Goethe to Sandburg and Cummings: "Emily Dickinson was a reincarnation of masters long dead and a prophecy of masters to come" (p. 132). Analogies, not influences, interest Wells in his intention to "deliver Emily from the claws of personal interpretation and to place her personality upon a more distinguished height, not of Amherst Hill, but of Parnassus" (p. xvii). The pendulum which in the case of Whicher had swung back swings forward again. Parallels to the "Emily" conception of the 1920's in the spirit of Burton Rascoe, John Gould Fletcher, and Louis Untermeyer are obvious.

In Richard Chase's *Emily Dickinson*, written for the American Men of Letters Series, her work is understood as a great symbolic construction, as a ritual act which gave her the strength to bear life: "In Emily Dickinson's poetry . . . there is but one major theme, one symbolic act, one incandescent center of meaning. Expressed in the most general terms, this theme is the achievement of status through crucial experiences. The kinds of status our poet imagines are variously indicated by such favorite words as 'queen,' 'royal,' 'wife,' 'woman,' 'poet,' 'immortal,' and 'empress.' The kinds of experience which confer status are love, 'marriage,' death, poetic expression, and immediate intuitive experiences which have the redemptive power of grace. . . . Each 'estate' involves its own renunciation, except for one: immortality. And each of the crucial experiences which confer the different kinds of status is a type and emblem of one of them: the coming of death."[52a] The application of this formula to a considerable portion of the poems constitutes the new approach of this study, which is otherwise indebted to Whicher and Wells.

The critical section of Thomas H. Johnson's *Emily Dickinson: An Interpretive Biography* went so little beyond Whicher that Charles R. Anderson's *Emily Dickinson's Poetry: Stairway of Surprise* (1960), a brilliant interpretation of a hundred of her best poems, became the first comprehensive study of her work.

Whicher's unremitting reference to Emily Dickinson as the product of her time and place resounded through research and criticism as a thorough bass. From 1925 until his sudden death in 1954, his essays and reviews counterbalanced the tendency to emphasize the timeless, the eternal in her work. In his "Centennial Afterthoughts" of 1931, he lifted her out of the "sawdust pile" of the later poets included in Stedman's *An American Anthology* and juxtaposed her to her countertype Whitman: "These two writers defined the poles of national feeling in their time as Franklin and Edwards defined the cleavage in American thought a century earlier."[53] This is a revealing statement in three ways. It applied to the nineteenth-century Van Wyck Brooks's cultural antinomy of highbrow and lowbrow which he had seen personified by Edwards and Franklin, who divided the eighteenth century between them; it upgrades Emily Dickinson historically and puts her on a level with Whitman, which signifies a departure from the cult of the Whitman tradition of the 1920's; it anticipates what Philip Rahv later defined as the dual tradition of the "redskins" and the "palefaces."[54] "Since recent poetry, in so far as it has any intellectual substance, has aligned itself, now with one, now with the other of the contrasting attitudes represented by Whitman and Emily Dickinson, the development of these basic and still valid modes of endowing life with meaning is from our point of view the main achievement of poetry in the later nineteenth century" (pp. 94-95). What distinguished these poets from the Stoddards and Stedmans was "a fresh interpretation of experience" (p. 95). Emily Dickinson's individual struggle to preserve self-respect and personal integrity, which the ivory tower poets avoided, was "a tiny part of the greater conflict going on elsewhere": "The accidents of her experience paralleled and intensified many fold for her the predicament of her generation. There were no palliatives at hand, and in any event she was not one to accept compromise. She faced the realities of her situation and worked out a personal adjustment to them according to the pattern of her need. That was exactly what her more literary contemporaries were failing to do" (p. 96).

Whicher's polarization of Emily Dickinson and Walt Whitman was repeatedly, though less expressly, taken up, modified, discovered anew. Blackmur contrasted both with Longfellow and Poe, who did nothing to revitalize the flaccid verse language around the middle of the century.[55] When Henry W. Wells published a history of American poetry in 1943, the sequence of chapters (Freneau, Poe, Whitman, Emerson, Emily Dickinson, Melville . . .) appeared to blur the key position of both, but the introduction stressed Whicher's and Blackmur's thoughts: "In studying the continuity of our native tradition, Whitman and Emily Dickinson become the two most important figures of the last century."[56] In 1952 Thornton Wilder wrote: "Walt Whitman and Emily Dickinson seemed to be at every moment advancing into new territories in relation to writing; the time for them had not come to consolidate what they had acquired, to establish their limits and to construct their conventions." One year earlier, a carefully evaluating Richard Chase had said that "she stands, perhaps with Whitman, at the top of the American achievement in poetry."

The main result of the academic evaluation after 1930 was the more serious consideration of Emily Dickinson the artist. Even her name was used more cautiously. "Miss Dickinson" and the familiar "Emily" slowly vanished. The impersonal "Dickinson," her own signature in several letters to Higginson after 1866, appeared to do her more justice, even though its use was partly conditioned by the practice of *The Explicator*. Moreover, one found that the "lion of biography"[57] lay between work and reader, that, for the understanding of the poetry, the previously customary equation of the prosaic, historically determinable "I" of the letters with the dramatized, fictive "I" of the poems was untenable. One recalled that the poet herself had warned Higginson in one of her first letters: "When I state myself, as the Representative of the Verse—it does not mean—me—but a supposed person" (*Letters*, II, 412). The "I," the protagonist of the poems, became "ED *poeta*, not necessarily the same person as the Emily Dickinson known in Amherst,"[58] a prima donna, a princess, who had worn a mask since 1861 and spoken through it.

X

LITERARY HISTORY (1931-51)

It is a principle that shines impartially on the just and on the unjust that once you have a point of view all history will back you up.[1]

THE LITERARY events of the early 1930's during which not less than half of the handbooks and outlines treated below appeared, were characterized by a landslide of intellectuals toward the left, the withdrawal of leading critics from the scene, and the massive appearance of Marxist criticism, which offered the advantage of consistency in a time of helplessness and of searching for standards. Although the object of controversy, the Marxists were taken seriously by the academic forum. Their mistakes were obvious, but their claim to be able to extend historical lines of development from the past through the present to the future had something attractive about it.

While the critical reception of Emily Dickinson remained unaffected by the ideological fluctuations of the time, her evaluation in literary history was necessarily drawn into this process of revaluation.

Until 1915 Dickinson had appeared to the historians of American literature as a minor figure at best. Not until 1921 did Norman Foerster assign her an "inconspicuous but secure" place. Thereupon she was demoted by Weirick and Pattee to the group of would-be poets, while Wood had put a "modern gown" around her. Finally, the Van Dorens and Kreymborg had become aware of her rising fame. Even so, the work most influential on the writing of literary history in the 1930's, Vernon L. Parrington's *Main Currents in American Thought* (1927-30), did not even mention Emily Dickinson by name. The reasons for her omission in the unfinished third volume, *The Beginnings of Critical Realism in America,* can be gathered from the basic concept of the entire work. Parrington wanted to furnish proof of a continuous tradition of Jeffersonian liberalism; to this end he singled out whatever documentary evidence he could find in American literature taken in the broadest sense. As the New England writers of the time of the Civil War and after contributed little to his thesis, they were not taken into consideration. Only Aldrich is cited as an example of a genteel author. The literary historians of the 1930's entered upon an unwieldy Dickinson inheritance.

Carl Van Doren's *American Literature: An Introduction*[2] is a direct continuation of Matthew Josephson's *Portrait of the Artist as American.* The intellectual depression in the wake of the financial slump had driven him, as it had Josephson, to take stock of what was left of tradition. For him, too, tradition had become questionable, but he wrote from a later standpoint, without a thesis and without searching for what was congenial in the past. His vignettes published in 1933 were the result of his reorientation. His reformulation of the title to *What Is American Literature* in 1935 expresses even more strongly the quest for constant values.

The canon is reduced to all but the essentials. Only a handful of authors meet this qualification. In the Colonial period are Edwards and Franklin, in the national period Paine, Irving, Cooper, in the continental period Emerson, Thoreau, Poe, Hawthorne, Melville, in the "imperial" period Whitman, James, Twain, Howells, Dickinson—with the exception of the "critical" period fifteen enduring figures altogether.[3]

Emily Dickinson stands on the threshold of the new, "critical" era. She is set off by Van Doren from that last generation of the nineteenth century for which literature had become "not so much a series of special triumphs as a moral process" (p. 67). Her fame has outstripped that of all contemporaries. Biographical facts are irrelevant, since her life fulfilled itself in ever diminishing circles: "In the last of them she lost the timidity with which she viewed the outer universe" (p. 68). And just as her internal and not her external life is significant, so also is her vision, and not the form of her poetry: "She might, having got her image, have gone on like most poets and rounded it to a form already devised. Instead she chose to let the image make its own form with the quick words she had found for it. She did not so much cut her poems to the bone as leave them as they were, without adding the customary flesh. Her work approaches poetry's irreducible minimum, which is poetry's immortal part" (pp. 68-69). Her abstract metaphors prove to be "only the symbols of her experience. . . . Everything in it is achingly alive" (p. 69). Her provincialism, which she carried to extremes, verges on universality.

In his consternation at the helpless role of the individual in relation to changing social forces, Josephson had written a jeremiad on the artist's plight in America. For Van Doren, the historical question is almost entirely lacking. The figures outlined in brilliant sketches represent a critical selection which is not grounded historically.

On the other hand, the then Marxists V. F. Calverton and Granville Hicks see the individual as agent in the historical process. They programmatically demanded intervention from the artist in this process and the reform of existing conditions. In Calverton's *The Liberation of American Literature*[4] the emphasis still lies on the theoretical corroboration of the Marxist doctrine of literature: the Colonial complex and the Puritan myth had to be sloughed off before the liberation of American literature, starting from the West, could ensue. Whitman and Twain are the first significant authors. Robinson is a precursor of the proletarian revolution. Dickinson is not even mentioned once. New England is Calverton's hostile citadel and does not exist as a literary tradition. In the only place which would have offered the opportunity to refer to Emily Dickinson he writes: "Prior to Robinson's appearance on the American scene in 1896 . . . poetry in this country had lost the place of significance which it had possessed earlier in the century" (p. 415).

A year later Granville Hicks could no longer squeeze by Emily Dickinson, although the novel is, as a matter of principle, of greater importance to him than poetry.[5] He forces the literary development since the middle of the nineteenth century into the Procrustean bed of one question: to what extent have the writers given expression to the forces which have formed American life? These forces are the growing industrialization and the social problems resulting from it. His ideal author is, or becomes, a proletarian. As might have been expected, the balance is depressing: three hundred pages of settling accounts with bourgeois authors until he, like Calverton, finds in John Dos Passos the only man to his taste. In order to construct in conclusion the great tradition announced in the title he has to come down a peg or two, however, and fetch into the temple those whom he had previously damned. The chosen few are Whitman, Howells, and Bellamy, Garland and Norris, Herrick and Phillips, Sinclair and London; these nine are revolutionaries and pioneers even if they still succumbed to the enticements of the bourgeoisie and capitalism. Where is Emily Dickinson?

We find her together with Sarah Orne Jewett and Henry James in a group of fugitives, which reminds one of Josephson: "We can understand why flight, born of a desire to escape from a scene too unpleasant to contemplate and a situation too complicated to understand, was so common in the Gilded Age. It remains now for us to ask ourselves what, in its happiest form, flight could do for a writer" (p. 100). On the seven pages devoted to her a general dilemma of Marxist literary history reveals itself: the poet has only a negative function in his system, though Hicks is not blind to her greatness. His dual standards of social and artistic significance drive him into a corner. He acknowledges her as "the most distinguished poet of her generation" (p. 126), and even more: "She reminds one . . . of the greatest poets" (p. 128). In comparison with her the polite poets like Aldrich, Stedman, and Gilder, who wandered beaten paths and wrote like slaves for a well-to-do public, rank much lower: "To compare Emily Dickinson's poetry with the verse of her contemporaries is almost to deal with incommensurables" (p. 129). Longing for individual expression, she was forced into solitude: "Her age spoke in her poems only negatively, only in their omissions. The positive content comes from Emily herself, from her observations and from the influence of her childhood, which was of another age" (p. 128). Hicks praises her poetry for its "vitality" and "aliveness," for its quality of Emersonian self-reliance and Thoreau-like art of extracting meaning from the simplest events in nature. Everything in her work is "immediate, personal, and honest" (p. 130).

After such sincere, if reluctant, praise, Hicks pronounces his sociological standard judgment as in the case of Melville, Hawthorne, and James; but this, too, is qualified: "And yet the poetry of Emily Dickinson is undeniably fragile and remote. The discovery of her work is, for any sensitive reader, an exciting event. . . . But, close as her life comes to the lives of her readers, it touches them at very few points. . . . The fact that she would not publish her poems during her lifetime . . . indicates . . . that she was aware of the impossibility of coming to terms with her own age" (p. 130).

While Hicks the critic had designated Emily Dickinson as "America's greatest poet" in the centennial year, Hicks the Marxist historian reduces her to the Platonic half of a poet. The other half is Whitman: "Emily Dickinson complements Walt Whitman, and the two of them, one feels, might make one poet. Where Whitman was merely expansive Emily Dickinson was intensive, but where she was narrow he was broad. . . . As one weighs the faults and merits on both sides, one sighs with Emerson: 'So many promising youths and never a finished man!' " (p. 130).

Hicks cannot cope with Dickinson. He gets out of his dilemma with an embarrassed quotation. His system crumbles. Although he admires her aliveness and vitality, he does not recall these qualities when, at the end of the book, he assembles his great tradition: "Comparing . . . Robert Frost with Emily Dickinson, we realized that it has been increasingly difficult for those who ignored industrialism to create a vital literature" (pp. 301-2). In his treatment of Emily Dickinson, personal sympathy recedes in favor of the Marxist conception of literary history.

For Ludwig Lewisohn, whose *Expression in America*[6] is psychoanalytic in its approach, literature is expression of experience, a liberation from the bonds of inhibiting tradition. In deriving the quality of the artist from the quality of the person he applies simplified Freudian ideas. After he has unmasked the writer, he strives to salvage the permanent part of his work. His method is as willful as it is unhistorical; it ignores dates, connections, and the influences of time and environment on the writers whom he understands as autonomous personalities.

In his reconstruction of a usable past Lewisohn writes off the great New England writers as rhymesters. Only Emerson, who in the underbrush of this group stands out as a tree, is saved for posterity in spite of his low vitality, with the hopelessly inhibited Thoreau. Surprisingly, Emily Dickinson emerges clearly and undiminished from her time and place; by comparing her to Goethe Lewisohn pays her the highest tribute of which he is capable. He is able to do this because he concedes independence to her as a genius and isolates her from the bête noire of the Puritan tradition.

He deplores the Dickinson cult and fears a sharp reverse if blind admiration is not checked by reason. "It is time, above all, for anthologists to disengage her clear and lovely successes and

not perversely display her as, perhaps, a powerful psychologist
—she was often that—but as a writer of slovenly and grating
verse" (pp. 357-58). In addition to Emily Dickinson's numerous
fragments, he numbers among the failures those poems in which
art and expression suddenly broke down as in the last two lines
of the stanza

> *To lose one's faith surpasses*
> *The loss of an estate,*
> *Because estates can be*
> *Replenished—faith cannot.* (p. 358)

The abundance of her poetry can endure this retrenchment:
"Her very great lyrical qualities of spiritual integrity, of cosmic
quaintness and of moonstruck charm would but shine forth more
triumphantly if ill-advised admirers did not too often leave
obscure her successes and display her failures" (p. 359). Lewisohn
sees her successes in her epigrammatic conciseness, in the heroic
note through which she enriched hackneyed love poetry, in her
kinship with the "intense mystical poets" of the seventeenth century, and in her delight in mockery, which is reminiscent of
Heine: "Thus Emily runs true to the form of the higher creative
spirits whose power is measured by intensity and not by wealth
or multiplicity of experience. The wonder is not that she was a
great poet amid the poverty and narrowness of her experience;
the wonder is that there was born in that Amherst house so great
a poet that she needed only that house and the seasons and a few
books and one supreme and unfulfilled passion to make her one
of the very few great women poets of all literature" (pp. 362-63).

Emily Dickinson assumes a special position; she stands up
to Lewisohn's test better than any other figure of the nineteenth
century by virtue of her intensity, her uncompromising attitude,
and the harmony of experience and expression. Not even Melville
passes uncensured.

In Van Wyck Brooks's *New England: Indian Summer,*
1865-1915,[7] which is a melancholy farewell to a culturally de-
pleted region, historical scholarship is replaced by pastiche. The
Dickinson chapter is colored with gossip and legend. The forbidding father, the hospitable son form a transition to Emily, the
shy recluse, to her little letters to her friends and—of course, one
is tempted to say—to her love affair. Her relationship with Higginson and his visit in Amherst yield two pictorial pages, anecdotes concerning her eccentricity fill a third. For Brooks, Emily's

chestnut headband, her oxalis plants, and her watering pot are just as important as her verse. He considers it obvious that the recluse was a poetic genius. When he comes to discuss her work toward the end of the chapter, he does it indirectly by looking over the shoulder of the artist at her "solitaire," her writing: "And she labored over her phrases to make them right. Were they all her own? Were there echoes in them, or anything of the conventional, the rhetorical, the fat? Were they clear, were they exact, were they compact?" (p. 326).

For a moment Brooks lifts her out of the retrospective, epigonal period of the crumbling Puritan tradition, points to her as a pioneer of a later poetic renaissance, and puts her carefully back into her narrow world. Biography and criticism blur in his glimmering, elfin portrait: "Her poems were packed with meaning; and, swiftly as her images changed, they were scarcely able to keep the pace with which her mind veered from mood to mood, from faith to mockery, from mysticism to rationalism, through ecstasy, disillusion, anguish, joy. These poems were fairy-like in their shimmer and lightness, they moved like bees upon a raft of air; and yet one felt behind them an energy of mind and spirit that only the rarest poets ever possessed" (p. 328). This description seems remarkably antiquated; it corresponds indeed to the tenor of the book, but much less to the state of Dickinson criticism around 1940.

The academic literary historians reacted just as promptly as did the Marxists to the creative and critical revolution of the two previous decades. Under the influence of Parrington's trilogy they sought to redefine American literature according to the criteria of closeness to life, social relevance, and the specifically American.

The first of the new handbooks of the 1930's is Russell Blankenship's *American Literature as an Expression of the National Mind.*[8] Of the New England writers only the Transcendentalists appeal to the author. Since he can link Emily Dickinson neither with them nor with the younger generation of poets (Aldrich, Stedman, Gilder) whom he excluded as imitators, he places her at the head of a list of names which contains a dozen representatives of the new poetry: "Although Emily Dickinson died twenty-six years before 1912, she belongs to the school of contemporary poets in both spirit and technique" (p. 576). This association shatters the chronology. Therefore, her dates are of little importance. Blankenship's attempt at historical explanation remains unsuccessful: "Emily Dickinson took the stuff of her poetry from her personal experiences. Although she was born in the full flood of the romantic revolution . . . she seems to have absolutely nothing in common with the writers of her time. She is wholly original—a primitive, some have called her. Her ideas cannot be linked up with those of other poets and her verse form is just as truly her own. It is not correct to say that she turned her back on current literature and philosophy, for she seems never to have been aware of their existence" (p. 577). For Blankenship she is a timeless classic who had nothing in common with her century: "It is her reduction of life to its lowest terms and the statement of those terms in short jets of unmistakable poetry that has made her an American classic. Her poetic technique or the lack of it is not material to her accomplishment or influence. The important thing is her way of phrasing in an impromptu fashion, almost carelessly, audacious imaginative flights that have at their core the love, desire, and fear that have been felt by all men. She is forever contemporary. Her banishment of the trivial and the transitory in favor of things elemental will make her contemporary with countless unborn generations" (p. 579).

The dilemma of doing justice to Emily Dickinson in a system influenced by Turner, Beard, and Parrington appears perhaps most clearly in Thomas H. Dickinson's *The Making of American Literature*.[9] Not only is she placed in "The Frontier Period (1855-98)," but, moreover, this chapter deals with "The Decline of New England Literature" and "The Decline of Poetry." Since Emily Dickinson, with Whitman and Twain (particular subchapters are granted only to these three), nevertheless belongs to the frontier period, she fits into the conception of the book neither as a poet nor as a New Englander. The explanations necessary in both cases are unconvincing, since they practically assert that due to the posthumous publication of her work no Emily Dickinson had actually existed before 1890.[10] As an exceptional phenomenon in Thomas Dickinson's historical framework she is simply declared "one of the great poets of the modern world" (p. 603) and characterized in a manner similar to that of Blankenship: "Emily Dickinson is now recognized as the true herald and precursor of the modern poetic renaissance. More than Whitman she represents the qualities that the poets of the twentieth century strive for. This being the case, it is probably fortunate rather than otherwise that her poems were not published during her lifetime. They would not have been understood" (p. 599).

The same grouping and accentuation of Whitman, Emily

Dickinson, and Mark Twain is to be found in A. C. Ward's *American Literature, 1880-1930*.[11] These writers, who are bracketed as "Three Voices" (p. 33), freed America from the incubus of Europeanism which had until that time weighed upon the literature of the new continent. Common to all three is an independent vision which, if advantageous from a twentieth-century point of view, implied the danger of a new barbarism: "In their several ways, Whitman and the other two were barbarians. If for convenience and at the moment they conformed, their influence was ultimately a disintegrating one. They are spiritual anarchists who throw the individual person back upon the necessity of discovering a standard of values relative to himself and the Eternal; whereas the traditional or conventional order postulates a standard, relative to the community and the Eternal, to which the individual entity must conform under whatever pains of self-adjustment or, often, of maladjustment. The conflict, in short, is between culture and nature, between conformity and the protestant spirit" (pp. 64-65).

Emily Dickinson and Whitman are seen in a complementary relationship "as if he were the positive and she the negative pole in a single circuit—the circuit of the passionate self" (p. 43). Dickinson's role in the American literature of the late nineteenth century is singular, but significant: "She was the antithesis of the hurried pushing America which forced itself onward to unique material prosperity and had no time to stabilize its mind and soul. Living in a generation that was becoming increasingly gregarious and veering toward an idea of heaven organized chiefly for 'stout fellows,' 'good mixers,' Rotarians and Elks. . . . Emily Dickinson appears to a later age as both a rock and a lighthouse withstanding and warning against an idea of heaven which has turned out to be very hell" (pp. 46-47). If, in another place, the poet is a barbarian for Ward, the Englishman, her role as an outsider in the above-quoted context is used for massive criticism of American conformity. "If the United States had gone the way of Whitman and Emily Dickinson it might have become one hundred per cent. human, instead of (while clamouring to become one hundred per cent. American) becoming neither human nor American but merely one hundred per cent. bemused and stultified" (p. 47).

In 1936 Percy H. Boynton wrote the last large-scale one-man literary history in the old style. His *Literature and American Life*[12] is more scholarly and less biased than the handbooks of Blankenship, Dickinson, and Ward. In the twelfth chapter, "Deferred Reputations," of the third part, "The Recent Past," Emily Dickinson is treated along with Bierce, Hearn, and Adams according to the extrinsic criterion of authors who failed to win their audience during their lifetime. Boynton is intentionally conservative in his rejection of the "romance fabrication" by biographers in 1930, in his reference to her Calvinist heritage and her regionalism, and in his critical examination of her careless prosody. His parallels are original. He finds earlier instances of the poet's "utterly unorthodox and profoundly religious" attitude: "It was the New England whimsy, covertly expressed, that Sarah Kemble Knight confided to her diary . . . . It was the skepticism of Mark Twain offset by the faith Mark Twain yearned for. It was the contempt of Thoreau when he said of this theological deity that men had 'somewhat hastily concluded' that it was their chief end to glorify God and enjoy him forever" (p. 695). On the basis of temperamental affinity he draws a comparison with Emerson which two years later won Whicher's approval: "Comparison of these two compounds of convention and revolt shows that she played on a wider keyboard than Emerson did in his published poems; at times she was more piquantly irreverent, and in her reverential moods she was more content to use the locutions of the Calvinists. But a fair comparison would liken the unrestraint of Miss Dickinson's poems with the unrestraint of Emerson's journals. Emerson's comments on his reverend grandfather's prayer for rain, on eugenics among the Brook Farmers, on the prosperous Unitarian tone of 'In Memoriam,' prove to be quite in Miss Dickinson's mocking vein" (p. 696). He illustrates the occasional identity of the style of both poets with two striking examples. Although Emily Dickinson read Emerson's *Poems* when she was nineteen, he sees no reason to assume conscious or unconscious imitation.

In *The Literature of the American People*,[13] the more scholarly but less pretentious of the two handbooks of the postwar period, Clarence Gohdes fell back into the chronicle style of the old college manuals since he could not otherwise cope with the "multitudes of fledglings" (p. 721) among the "New Voices in Verse." After he has mentioned numerous lesser lights, he continues with an impartial account of Emily Dickinson, based on research done in the 1930's and characterizes her as "quintessentially a New Englander" (p. 729).

In *Literary History of the United States*[14] the straitjacket of the cyclical structure is clearly noticeable in the classification of Emily Dickinson. Emerson, Thoreau, Hawthorne, Melville, and Whitman, the quintet canonized by F. O. Matthiessen in *American Renaissance,* brought the first literary fulfillment. Whitman is seen in the introduction as a "pivot"—the key figure in the entire history of American literature. Since the beginning of the second cycle is tantamount to a new start, a period in which great literature is not yet again possible, Emily Dickinson stands out but little in the second part ("The Sections") of the second book. She is treated with Lanier in the fifty-fifth chapter "Experiments in Poetry." At first it seems as though, in accordance with the title, the same tendency to break old forms and search for new ones links both poets. Both are then unequivocally enough defined as "the rebels" (II, 899) and "the heralds of great changes impending in the poetry of America" (II, 901). It turns out, however, that the actual counterpart of Emily Dickinson is not Lanier but Whitman, whose work had marked the closing of the first cycle twenty-six chapters earlier:

> In the emergence of the new poetry Lanier typifies its uneasiness rather than its rebirth. Like Emily Dickinson and like Whitman, he felt the trammels of established verse, but, unlike them, he never truly initiated new forms. (II, 901)

> Together, she and Walt Whitman . . . represent the farthest pioneerings of the nineteenth century American mind in the trackless regions of spirit, in so far as they are reflected in poetry. (II, 907)

Not only in these passages by Stanley T. Williams, but also in other places in *Literary History of the United States* Dickinson and Whitman—and not Lanier—are bracketed as experimenters and breakers of tradition, for example, by Spiller (I, 378) and by Thorp (II, 825). Joining the Southerner and the New Englander under the concept "experiment" was a makeshift, since Lanier, in the last analysis, remained a Tennysonian while Emily Dickinson disassociated herself from a Victorian verse tradition which no longer corresponded to her experience of life: "In her half-rhymes, her irregularities of speech and rhythm, her spasmodic quality, she mirrored the incongruities and frustrations of human experience; the awkwardness in her poetry became a metaphor of life itself" (II, 901). Lanier and Emily Dickinson cannot be hitched to the same yoke.[15] The placing of both figures in the beginning of the second cycle creates difficulties which manifest themselves in contradictory terminology. At first Williams speaks of "the revolts of Sidney Lanier and Emily Dickinson" and "the rebels' bold chants" (II, 901); he revokes this claim in accordance with the plan of the entire work when he writes at the end of the chapter that "their restlessness was a symptom, not a rebellion" (II, 915-16).

While the literary historians regarded Emily Dickinson's place in American literature as secure, they ironically could not define it more closely. With the exception of Gohdes and Boynton, they exhibit a remarkable tendency to avoid history by ignoring the simple circumstances of time and place. Van Doren, Lewisohn, Blankenship, and Thomas Dickinson look upon the poet as an exceptional phenomenon; they isolate her and let her exist in a vacuum. Lewisohn is silent as to her locus, Van Doren summarily relates her to a period already past, Blankenship sees her as a harbinger of a period not yet begun, Brooks does both. Thomas Dickinson endeavors to obscure historical facts, since she is for him, as for Hicks, an annoying flaw in the system. The historians cannot bring the New Englander into harmony with the New England of the 1860's and 1870's except as an irregularity or as a solitary voice of the future—who, with Whitman, was one of the small group of "Sowers and Pathfinders," as Lewisohn titled his Dickinson chapter. She can be interpreted as a symptom, but not as a great poet in the Amherst of the Gilded Age.

RETROSPECT

Criticism has condemned whatever was, from time to time,
vital and fresh in literature; it has always fought the new
good thing in behalf of the old good thing; it has invariably
fostered and encouraged the tame, the trite, the negative.
Yet upon the whole it is the native, the novel, the positive
that has survived in literature.[1]

THE STUDY OF THE FAME OF AN AUTHOR is a special type of
literary biography which consists in the interpretation of the
writer and his work "as they are mirrored in the minds and hearts
of his readers, contemporary and posthumous."[2] The tracing of
an author's reputation is mainly concerned with the more important question of what goes on in the minds of his readers; we
have little knowledge of what moves their hearts. Nevertheless,
one should not quite forget the readers' spontaneous reactions
which are reflected in letters of thanks to the editors of the
poems[3] and in dedicatory poems. An early example may be cited
here as one of many:

> *I hold her volume in my hand,*
> *With half my mind I snatch its words:*
> *(The other half enough affords*
> *For listening and answer bland).*
>
> *She was a woman, too, it seems,*
> *Whom life not wholly satisfied;*
> *She loved: more heartily, she died;*
> *To die's the keener in her dreams.*

And I, who flagged, my zeal renew:
The trivial's phantom-terrors flee
This witness of reality.
I can live more since death's so true.[4]

Such documents offer clues to the mirroring of the work in the hearts of the readers and to the meaning which Emily Dickinson had for many of them. What is preserved of her noncritical reception is briefly discussed in the Appendix.

The critical response to Emily Dickinson up to 1897 forms a self-contained unity. At the end of the century, the poet's small niche in the pantheon of American literature seemed secure. What had seemed novel, strange, and provocative in the first volume soon lost its sting, since the critical labels could be re-applied to the poems of the second and third series. Emily Dickinson had ceased to be a discovery.

The sparseness of evidence for the first decade of the new century renders it difficult to answer the question as to the date at which Emily Dickinson became a rediscovery. For Stedman and the literary historians about 1900 she still lived on as a minor lyricist by virtue of the initial success of her work. Ella Gilbert Ives (1907), W. J. Dawson (1909), and James Price (1912) also still remembered her. Owing to their age and taste they belong to the original group of readers. Their judgments scarcely deviate from those passed on the poet in the 1890's. One must assume that during the decade and a half after 1897 many more recalled Emily Dickinson, although evidence is lacking.

The change from recollection to rediscovery begins with Martha Hale Shackford's realization that a comparison of Dickinson with John B. Tabb was irrelevant since her work possessed greater vitality than his. After 1914 her work was inserted into new frames of reference, changed and transformed by new use. To an increasing degree it was accorded a new reality. It had reached a stage at which it could be reinterpreted by the adherents of the Imagists and their foes, by the advocates of modern poetry in general and their opponents, and even by the cultural critics.

Since a date seemed useful, the beginning of the second phase of the critical reception was set in the year 1897. Naturally, this phase did not suddenly become apparent, but emerged as part of a continuous development. The supersession of the older critics by the younger took place gradually. About 1914 the opposing forces of conservative and progressive criticism were balanced; then the younger critics prevailed. This does not mean that all representatives of the earlier group fell silent, for Katharine Lee Bates was still heard from in 1925, Richard Burton in 1930, and Fred Pattee in 1937; nor does it mean that the younger critics developed new points of view throughout. Those who had all too willingly thumbed their noses at Aldrich and his like unwittingly accepted the deficient terminology of their elders and inherited a goodly portion of their standards of value, that is, of their helplessness when it came to an aesthetic justification of Emily Dickinson; nor were the younger critics more congenial to the New Englander. On the contrary, despite the growing lapse of time the poet seemed more congenial to them. They were the first to make come true W. H. Auden's dictum that a dead man's words are "modified in the guts" of those living— they reinterpreted Emily Dickinson. Many of the tensions and antinomies in Dickinson criticism from 1914 to 1930 are due to the coexistence of both groups of readers separated by a generation. In 1924 Aiken was thirty-five years old, Gamaliel Bradford was sixty-one; in 1930 Pattee was separated from Josephson by thirty-six years and Mrs. Todd from Genevieve Taggard by thirty-eight years.

This significant transition from the first to the second generation of readers and critics was a gain for Emily Dickinson's reputation, especially since her work profited from the change in taste taking place at approximately the same time. When poet-critics came to reject " 'the sublime' / In the old sense"[5] and welcomed the rediscovery of "the beauty, the dignity, I might almost say the divine core, of the casual and commonplace,"[6] they were ready to rescue the few genuine poems they still found in the almost thousand pages of Stedman's *An American Anthology*.

The confused decades from 1900 to 1930 were followed by a period of consolidation and steadily increasing scholarly concern with Emily Dickinson. The first interest of the universities evinced itself in master's theses, of which at least seven were written between 1918 and 1929 and at least fourteen more from 1932 to 1942 (cf. Sources, pp. 297-98). Most of these were little more than poor copies of what journalists had written. In 1937 Blackmur's remark that "on few poets beyond the first bloat of reputation has so little work been done" was still more than justified, for academic work began late and hesitantly. Two dissertations in progress in 1932 and 1936 on "The Prosody of Emily Dickinson" and "The Diction and Imagery of Emily Dickinson" were dropped.[7] A comparison of the number of doctoral dissertations written in the United States between 1933 and 1948 about American authors illustrates the lag of Dickinson scholarship: thirty-eight treated Emerson, twenty-nine Melville, twenty-eight Whitman, twenty-three Hawthorne, twenty-two Twain, fifteen Howells, fourteen Poe, fourteen James, twelve Thoreau, ten Lowell, none Emily Dickinson; seventeen other writers were dealt with, among others, Higginson in three dissertations.[8] Considering this state of affairs it was understandable that Emily Dickinson was passed by when scholars of the Modern Language Association had to agree on the writers to be included in *Eight American Authors: A Review of Research and Criticism*.[9] Of the two criteria for selection, "intrinsic worth" and "the significance of the biographical and critical writing that has been done on them and their work" (p. vi), the first could at best be applied to Emily Dickinson. The waste of energy on biographical speculation and the chaotic state of editions, chronology, and text, which the first close readers such as Gay Wilson Allen and Blackmur found especially oppressive, were mainly responsible for this delay.

The criticism of Emily Dickinson's poems and letters in periodicals and newspapers needs explanation only for the 1890's. If her work was scarcely mentioned between 1897 and 1914 and between 1915 and 1924, it was because she was little known. The weak reaction to *The Single Hound* was brought about by the small edition and the few copies distributed for review. The broad echo in 1924 and in 1929-30 resounded to the Pacific. After 1930 each book by and about the poet was noticed in numerous newspapers and periodicals. A reference to the years in which the important scholarly periodicals *The New England Quarterly* (1927) and *American Literature* (1928) were founded will suffice to establish the beginning of the academic discussion; the key years 1939, when John Crowe Ransom founded *The Kenyon Review*, 1943, when *The Explicator* was called to life, and 1944, when the old and venerable *Sewanee Review* underwent a critical metamorphosis under the editorship of Allen Tate (1944-46), are significant for the interpretation of Emily Dickinson's work by the New Criticism.

In the 1890's newspaper notices were both friendlier and more uncritical than reviews in periodicals. In Boston the *Trav-*

eller, Budget, Herald, Courier, Transcript,[10] *Beacon,* and *Daily Advertiser* took an active interest in the volumes of poems and letters. In Philadelphia the *Public Ledger, Telegraph,* and *Evening Bulletin* concerned themselves above all with the letters. In New York the *Tribune* expressed itself just as adversely as the *World* did approvingly while the *Times* and *Commercial Advertiser* reported neutrally. In Chicago the *Tribune, Evening Post,* and *Inter Ocean* reacted particularly in 1896. Amherst's *Record* and Springfield's *Republican* reported on and summarized the evaluation of the local poet throughout the country rather than following it critically.

The attitude of influential periodicals was of greater moment. The Big Four of the decade kept themselves aloof from contemporary poetry and replaced criticism with uncritical acceptance of the established canon and with reminiscences and biography. Their attitude toward Emily Dickinson corresponds essentially to this policy. In its monthly "Comment on New Books," *The Atlantic Monthly*, the most pretentious of the group, mentioned the first selection of Emily Dickinson's poetry only briefly[11] then printed her letters to Higginson, who had been one of its liveliest contributors under the editorship of Lowell, Fields, and Howells, and finally gave its former editor Aldrich the opportunity to advance his demurrer. Howells' *Harper's* essay was published in his department "Editor's Study," which served him mainly as a battleground for the cause of realism and only rarely as a place to review recent verse. Without Howells, who as a noted novelist and friend of the great New Englanders was more tolerated than liked, the periodical would probably have passed Emily Dickinson by. After Charles Dudley Warner had succeeded to "Editor's Study," she was not mentioned again until 1945. *The Century Magazine* did not refer to the new poet at all and also rejected Mrs. Todd's critical study, which she then placed with *The Bachelor of Arts*. Not even individual poems were welcome. "We thank you very much for sending us these poems of Emily Dickinson's, which we regret to find not available for use," a coeditor wrote to Mrs. Todd on December 27, 1895. "The fact of it is we must confess not to caring very much for her literary work . . ." (MS-D57/To 364). How brusque this rebuff was can be judged by taking into consideration that the Todds and the editors of *Century* had been on good terms since 1889, for Professor Todd had published various astronomical articles in this periodical. In *Scribner's Magazine* the troublesome New Englander occasioned a traditional discussion of form and substance in poetry.

Among the literary journals, *The Literary World* remained censorious; it only warmed up to the letters. The Chicago *Dial*, "a journal with Standards,"[12] which had earlier heaped venom and malice on Whitman, gave noncommittal reviews written by its coeditor William Morton Payne; but once again the letters found approval—that of Louis James Block, an immigrant Austrian poet. The New York *Critic* showed itself better disposed; it was heard from often and compensated for its disapproval of the second series of poems by printing Francis H. Stoddard's letter to the editor.

The book trade journals—John Wanamaker's *Book News* in Philadelphia and Scribner's *Book Buyer*—described and explained without evaluating. In the weekly reviews—Boston's *Commonwealth* and New York's *Nation*—the cause of Emily Dickinson was represented by Arthur Chamberlain and Higginson. Of the denominational journals the leading Unitarian publication, *The Christian Register*, strongly favored the poems and letters; *The Catholic World*, *The Independent*, and *The Congregationalist* remained skeptical.

During the time of Emily Dickinson's debut the critical keynote was sounded by a handful of prominent reviewers, among them Howells and his antagonist Lang, Higginson, Arlo Bates, and Aldrich. The lines between conservatives and progressives seemed clear-cut from the very outset. It was Arlo Bates who had almost predicted Howells' intercession when he wrote in the *Boston Courier* on November 23, 1890: "There will be those, indeed, who will contend that the book is better for having disregarded technical form, or at least no worse. It is not wholly impossible that in the Editor's Study something looking in this direction will some day see the light."

Higginson's role was by far the most significant. That this reputable man of letters was coeditor of the first two volumes of poetry made many reviewers reflect further on her merits. His opinion of his protégée's talent never changed. He did what he could for the dissemination of her work, commented on it, supported it privately, and defended it against the denigrations of the British. With his penchant for aphoristic brevity in his own prose, he again and again became enthusiastic about the style of the poems. He changed less in them than he was reproached for. If he thought he had to make allowance for their form, one should not demand more acumen of an individual than of the whole tribe of critics of the 1890's.

In its broad effect Howells' double role as mediator and critic was second only to that of the Colonel; in his comprehension of Emily Dickinson he was superior to Higginson. He enlivened the critical debate, and he recommended the poet to his friends. As late as 1898 Emily Dickinson is mentioned and quoted in a letter to Mark Twain.[13] Best known is that evening in April 1893, on which he read from her poetry to young Stephen Crane and thus induced him to try his own hand at verse. Howells differed from his conservative colleagues mainly in his view that literature should not persist in its indebtedness to great models of the past, but should progress with changing political, social, and religious circumstances. He believed in the "new good thing," whereas Higginson always struck a conciliatory attitude toward old and new. Howells watched the development of American literature throughout his life, registered new impulses, and sought to classify them for his readers. His receptivity to free verse, which can be traced from 1888 to 1917, is an example. He could never entirely overcome his aversion to this "shredded prose," yet he tolerated Whitman, Amy Lowell, and John Gould Fletcher. It is understandable that his friends often disapproved of his progressive attitude. "I honestly think his mind unbalanced," T. B. Aldrich confided to George Woodberry in 1892. "Certainly Howells is making a pathetic spectacle of himself these days."[14]

Andrew Lang, a contributor to many American periodicals, especially *Scribner's Magazine*, was highly respected in the United States. That Howells or Higginson were Dickinson adherents was all that was needed to prompt him to take a stand. His invectives resounded through America long after; in England they probably had an effect on the volume published by Osgood, McIlvaine: the sales were so slow that a reprint or a new edition was out of the question. If Lang's views concerning Emily Dickinson were supercilious, they did not differ much from the British critics' conviction that America had a multitude of minor poetic talents.

Aldrich's attack, Arlo Bates's skepticism, and Mrs. Todd's biographically informative and corrective activity also had a noticeable effect on early Dickinson criticism.

Arthur Chamberlain, a Bostonian, John Chadwick,[15] and Nathan Dole,[16] who are comparable to Higginson in their understanding and sympathy, and three enthusiastic ladies are among the lesser critics of Emily Dickinson in the 1890's. Mrs. Moulton could hardly put her admiration into words in *The Boston Herald;* Lilian Whiting[17] was full of praise; Mary Abbott[18] at first seemed positively affected by the poet's letters to Higginson, but then apostatized. In *The Chicago Times-Herald* on December 8, 1894, she considered it "a mean trick to publish private correspondence," and in 1896 she was repelled by the language of the poems.

Three critics of the older generation, Katharine Lee Bates (b. 1859), Bradford (b. 1863), and Pattee (b. 1863) carried the Dickinson image of the 1890's far into the next century. The pioneering essays of Martha Hale Shackford and Susan Miles were not heeded. The most influential figure during the second phase of the criticism was Conrad Aiken. His anthology contributed decisively to the rise of Emily Dickinson's reputation in England, where he had already been known through his "Letters from America" to the readers of *The Athenaeum* and *The London Mercury*. The skepticism predominant in Aiken's early criticism and also perceptible in his essay on Emily Dickinson was a pronounced relativism based on his study of the new psychology. Since, for Aiken, the work of art was deeply rooted in the personality of the artist, he concerned himself just as much with these roots as with the finished work. And since the value of the work depended on its effect on the complicated psychological make-up of the reader, there existed in his estimation no possibility for the critic to judge the work objectively.

Next to Aiken, a large group of stalwarts, headed by Untermeyer and the Van Dorens, should be mentioned. Their enthusiasm never flagged. Carl Van Doren and Untermeyer edited Dickinson anthologies as late as 1948 and 1952. The only backslider among the group was Robert Hillyer, who had rediscovered Emily Dickinson earlier than most of his contemporaries and had been instrumental in the spread of her name in New England. The passage quoted in chapter VI from his *Letter to Robert Frost*, which renders Frost's early opinion of Dickinson, is followed by an afterthought from the perspective of 1936:

> *Alas for Emily, alas for me,*
> *That now I go much further than agree:*
> *Once irresistible, now merely coy,*
> *Her whims, her verbal airs and graces cloy.*[19]

None of the leading Dickinson scholars after 1930 made his influence felt through his enthusiasm. They were very much less interested in advertising than in explanation and rectification. That three Melville scholars (Chase, Leyda, Anderson) turned to Emily Dickinson is no accident. In the entire history of Emily Dickinson's critical reception a loose formation of "redskin" and "paleface" camps is recognizable. Critics in the camp of Whitman and his tradition had little taste for Dickinson throughout. Examples reach from John Nist (1961) back to Bruce Weirick (1924). The adherents of the "thin, solemn, semi-clerical culture of Boston and Concord" passed Whitman by. Higginson who, like Emily Dickinson, disliked Whitman's manner, is an early example.

Until 1897 conservative aesthetics admitted three attitudes toward Emily Dickinson's art which are perhaps most clearly embodied in the judgments of Aldrich, the reviewer in *Scribner's Magazine*, and Lilian Whiting: first, a hostile attitude dictated by the intellect, which insisted on the following of established rules and rejected Emily Dickinson as a hopeless dilettante; second, a neutral attitude consisting of a mixture of rational reservations and intuitive approval; third, sheer enthusiasm which pushed aside or ignored formal objections. Other standards than those of "form and substance" in a broad sense were scarcely applied. For Chamberlain, the poems fulfilled Arnold's requirement for poetry as "a criticism of life." Maurice Thompson compared them with the lyrics and epigrams of the *Anthologia Graeca*. Aldrich thought he was saying something especially detrimental about Emily Dickinson when he granted her a grotesque fancy but denied her imagination. In doing so he did not distinguish himself from other critics who talked of flashes of lightning, rays of light, missiles, shorthand, or the song of the lark. "The poems . . . shoot up high into the sky and drop thence a few notes of uncommon melody, and the song ends, sometimes broken, generally too soon," is a typical opinion of 1890.[20] The lightning and light metaphors are particularly transparent in that they contrast the intensive but ephemeral effect of Emily Dickinson's art with the weaker but more constant fire of customary poetry. In other words she was an expert at the lighter, more superficial, sometimes even trivial though witty game of the charm of words without having a sense of form. Hence such designations as "obscure," "seer," "epigrammaticist" which predominated from 1862 to 1897.

The attempts to reclassify Emily Dickinson in the new century can be explained with the help of several catchwords—"Immortal Lady," "epigrammatic Walt Whitman," "Puritan metaphysicist," "Amherst recluse," "Feminist"—which Catherine Tolles enumerated in her essay of April 1930. The first three concerned primarily the poetry, the last two the person.

"Immortal Lady," the least definite of these designations, connected two areas of association. By virtue of her genius she seemed immortal especially to the critics of the 1920's. The stinginess of the first reviewers was compensated by the slow dialectic of time. As an immortal Emily Dickinson was on a par with the classic authors, but also with other "immortal" rediscoveries. She was compared with many from both groups. Whitman never had to be rediscovered because he had never been forgotten,[21] but Thoreau, whose reputation had suffered seriously under Lowell's derogatory essay, was rescued from near-oblivion by the literary historian John Macy in 1913 and by many after 1917.[22] Henry Adams and Gerard Hopkins followed in 1918, Melville in 1919,[23] Crane in 1923,[24] Sarah Orne Jewett, whose sudden fame was owing to Willa Cather's judicious selection, in 1925. In 1924 the sparks of a new British enthusiasm for Blake arced to America.[25] As a lady, Dickinson was compared with other "immortal ladies," most often with Sappho, Christina Rossetti, and Mrs. Browning. "Immortal lady" was little more than a tribute to Emily Dickinson's fame.

The formulation "epigrammatic Walt Whitman" had deeper and more lasting consequences. At first it merely referred to what one regarded as permanent in nineteenth-century American poetry. In the course of the upgrading of both poets, "Emily's" work emerged as the opposite pole to the work of "Walt." The parallel itself is old. As early as 1891 Arlo Bates had linked both names, and five years later Rupert Hughes conjectured that the work of both would be America's most original contribution to world literature. Still, few critics were broad-minded enough to be able to feel equally sympathetic to both. Most Whitman adherents passed Emily Dickinson by, and vice versa.

Emily Dickinson had gone through an equally long and similarly sporadic development as a "Puritan metaphysicist." Since Chamberlain had apologetically placed her in the "fantastic" school in 1891, this school, especially John Donne himself, had come into favor. To be sure, Pattee still spoke disparagingly of "mere conceits" in 1915. But the change in taste and the concomitant reinterpretation of Emily Dickinson had not proclaimed themselves accidentally two years earlier when Martha Shackford, without expressly naming the metaphysicals, emphasized the poet's use of irony and remarked that in her verse "out of apparent contradictions are wrought the subtlest harmonies." In her review of *The Single Hound* Elizabeth Sergeant was the first to mention Donne's name—when she perceived "echoes of Donne's rhetoric and abstract vocabulary" in Emily Dickinson's poetry. Hartley and Gorman were not sure of the similarity. The change to greater certainty came in 1924. Thereafter, fleeting comparisons with Donne, Vaughan, Herbert, and Crashaw became more frequent. The interpretation of Emily Dickinson as a metaphysical poet culminated temporarily in the critical debate of 1929 and in the inclusion of selected poems in Genevieve Taggard's anthology *Circumference*, titled with a key word of Dickinson's.[26]

All attempts at classification developed before the centennial year—Catherine Tolles could have added "New England mystic" as a fifth catchword to her list—at first held their ground after 1930. In 1947 Emily Dickinson seemed so versatile to Henry Wells that she appeared to dissolve in a multiplicity of analogies with poets of all times and places. Yet a change soon set in. The demodernization had progressed far in the 1930's. The designations "Imagist," "precursor," "mystic" became rarer. The Whitman parallel persisted. The insistence on her metaphysical qualities encouraged the New Critics to interpret her in terms of that tradition. "Obscurity," the charge frequently heard in the 1890's, became a challenge. In 1960 Charles R. Anderson saw his task as "star[ing] a hole in the page until these apparently cryptic notations yield their full meanings."[27]

Previous studies in the history of American literary criticism can help us little in attempting to explain why the first readers rejected Emily Dickinson as an artist. At most they give information about the Coleridgean aesthetics of Edmund Stedman whose "pronouncements were accepted during the eighties and nineties as those of a literary arbiter."[28] Yet with his much-quoted definition—"Poetry is rhythmical, imaginative language, expressing the invention, taste, thought, passion, and insight, of the human soul"[29]—which subordinated form to content, Stedman as a theoretician could have found little fault with Emily Dickinson. On the contrary, she would have had to gain, since he characterized the rhymesters of his time as skilled but uninspired and traced their "over-refinement" to a lack of suitable themes. "If, then, the people care little for current poetry, is it not because that poetry cares little for the people . . . ?" he had written in 1885. "Busying itself with intricacies of form, and sound and imagery, it scarcely deigns to reach the general heart. Your skill is admirable, say the people, and of interest to your own guild, but we ask that it shall be used to some purpose."[30] Art had a wider meaning than technical refinement. The root of the problem lies in the mechanical separation of form and content. Like his close friend Aldrich, Stedman was capable of writing in *Poets of America* that "a faulty poem or picture may be great because a great thought or character is in it" (p. 458). His critical practice is indeed far removed from his theory; its key-word "workmanship" and the concomitant critical metaphors, which attribute decisive importance to formal aspects, were considerably more influential than Stedman's theory.[31] The poet is a craftsman who ascends to the rank of a master after a long apprenticeship; he dexterously files and polishes his raw material with utmost care until he has created a finished piece. Accordingly, poetry is the product of melted down and recast metal, a hewn and polished block of marble, a cut jewel. However Stedman might deplore the creative ebb and the degeneration of poetry to shallow perfection, "workmanship" remained the hallmark of poetic achievement.[32]

With Stedman the critics of the fin de siècle knew what they could expect from a poem in respect to form, and the poets who set great store by succès d'estime lived up to their expectations. Arlo Bates's *The Poet and His Self*, which—also with Roberts Brothers' imprint—was reviewed in the same weeks as Emily Dickinson's second series of poems, showed not only talent but "genius," was "clever and facile," contained "the always clean verse," and had "the genuine ring."[33] Emily Dickinson did not possess such merits. As her poems did not have the brilliance of gems, the thought was near at hand that they were merely fragments.

A vicious circle resulted from this conception of form. The discussion of *Poems* again and again proceeded through two stages and back to the starting point. Owing to their growing aversion to chiseled verse, most reviewers were ready to acknowledge Emily Dickinson because she appeared to possess all poetic attributes except rhyme and grammatical correctness. Her work suggested that "form" was, after all, something superficial, external. Such reasoning was countered by the warning not to overestimate substance. The high opinion of her originality, one argued, was easily understandable in an age of facile imitation.

In the last analysis, however, only the formal perfection demanded by the wisdom of all times guaranteed permanence.

Emily Dickinson's lack of form was explained as inability, lack of training, primitiveness, indifference, or compulsion to break existing bonds. Her advocates from the beginning regarded her as a poet of the intellect and closed their eyes to what they considered to be her mistakes. This tendency, which can be observed as early as in the comments of Susan Dickinson, logically led to Rupert Hughes's declaration that Emily Dickinson belonged to the great thinkers of the world. Mrs. Todd's suggestion that the poet had bogged down in an intermediate stage of her work seemed plausible. The unanimous belief of friend and foe that the law of form was not to be flouted and that Emily Dickinson as an artist was at best an interesting outsider testifies to the sway Stedman's practical aesthetics held over the reviewers of the decade. That she possibly had a claim to form of her own kind was a supposition which gained some ground in the course of the years but never became a shared conviction. Samuel Barrows indirectly pointed up the possibility of different types of poetic form through a *concordia discors* justifiable in music. That, however, did not mean the dissolution of current aesthetic laws, but only their extension in the sense of an "elasticity of orchestration" conceded by *Scribner's Magazine*. Nor does the standpoint reached by Carman and Hughes—that form is the etiquette of art and a drag on the genius—represent a break with tradition, but only a high degree of disgust in view of the nadir to which English and American poetry had sunk. The mechanical thinking in terms of form, substance, and workmanship was too deeply rooted to secure greater resonance for voices like Howells and Stoddard. In contrast to the novel there was no poetic movement against tradition and hardly a major critic outside of the tradition. A criticism oriented toward the third-rate in contemporary verse and schooled on the great models of the past could cope neither with Whitman nor with Emily Dickinson.

The situation of the 1890's does not lack a trace of irony. The same reviewers who had pilloried the overrefinement and intellectual impoverishment of poetry finally turned back to this very poetry after attempting to give Emily Dickinson her due; the same poets who were indefatigably on the lookout for "the Poet who is to come,"[34] automatically overlooked the volume with the six pipe-shaped flowers on its cover which lay on their desks among those of the minor poets.

For literary criticism between 1890 and 1897 Emily Dickinson's work was a challenge which led in many cases to statements of principles. It is hardly permissible to ignore this as the literary historian of the decade did or to dismiss her early critics as obtuse.[35] The aversion to the immediate past which set in shortly after 1900 and the subsequent identification of the waning nineteenth century with imitative poetry on the one hand and the conspicuous struggle for the cause of realism in fiction on the other has blocked the view of the quieter but no less significant discussion of such new poets as Emily Dickinson, Stephen Crane, and E. A. Robinson.

How explain that Emily Dickinson's work met with predominantly well-disposed readers and critics after 1913 without being vindicated artistically? That the iconoclastic critic Kenneth Alling chose the term "exasperating" when he mentioned the question of form? That Conrad Aiken passed over the "lapses and tyrannies" with a sigh? That another critic of 1924 could rejoice that Emily Dickinson had torn loose from "a mean bondage to poetic form," but immediately suspected that "her revolt may have cheated her of supreme artistry"?[36] That the quintessence of all considerations up to 1930 appears to be Kreymborg's paean on the little tippler?

American criticism of poetry in the 1890's had had at its disposal a set of rigid norms which enabled it to give the grounds for a judgment. After the old idealistic aesthetics had been rejected by poets and critics of the younger generation, a period of confusion ensued. In the new poetry's years of struggle, the Imagists and their opponents were concerned with slogans and victory, not explanation. The criteria according to which poetry was judged in the 1910's were more subjective than those applied two decades earlier. The uncertainty of the statements about Emily Dickinson are symptomatic of her critical reception from 1914 to 1930—still practically unexplored. Only a few of the more skeptical minds raised objections. Aiken's remark that "our criticism is still a rather primitive parade of likes and dislikes"[37] characterizes the embarrassing situation. His reviews before 1924 are a gauge of the deeply rooted relativism and the groping for new guiding principles,[38] as are also the commentaries of other critics;[39] E. E. Kellett's *The Whirligig of Taste*[40] concludes with the observation that "the one thing certain is that there is no certainty."

As a result, an astonishing addiction to an outmoded aesthetics is evident in Emily Dickinson's reception from 1897 to 1930. The conservative older critics worked consciously, the progressive younger critics just as often unconsciously with the traditional tools of their trade. In the essays of Alling, Armstrong, Aiken, and others, the same subjective displays of sympathy as had been voiced by Higginson and his contemporaries are observable. The continuity manifests itself also in the stereotyped craftsman and lightning metaphors which reappear until after 1930.

The growing acknowledgment of Emily Dickinson was an act of habituation rather than a result of investigations of her poetry in order to determine its artistic value. Familiarity with her work grew in proportion to the development of sensitivity for modern verse. The view already expressed in 1890 that she was a great verbal artist consolidated itself through Pohl (1910), Price (1912), Hartley (1918), Armstrong (1923), and Aiken (1924) and contributed to the fact that she could be classified with some precision as a metaphysical in 1929. The form problem was not solved; it simply dissolved as it appeared less acute than it had to the first readers. Emily Dickinson became an artless artist, which some lamented and others welcomed after they had inverted the critical signs. At any rate the disparity between her fame and its justification about 1930 was considerable.

The case of Emily Dickinson as a critical stumbling block would have to be included in the as yet unwritten history of British and American literary aesthetics of the last hundred years. The old-guard position was effectively buttressed by schematized treatises on poetry, the most influential of which was Francis B. Gummere's *Handbook of Poetics for Students of English Verse*.[41] Although Gummere conceded that "the lyric has its choice of a hundred forms, or may go further, and invent a new form" (p. 41), his poetics is a closed system. Later treatises such as Edmund Holmes's *What Is Poetry?* (1900), H. C. Beeching's *Introduction to the Study of Poetry* (1901), Bliss Carman's *The Poetry of Life* (1905), William Allan Neilson's *Essentials of Poetry* (1912), Max Eastman's *Enjoyment of Poetry* (1913), Theodore Watts-Dunton's *Poetry and the Renascence of Wonder* (1916), and John Livingston Lowes's *Convention and Revolt in Poetry* (1919) did not lead out of the impasse. They occasionally quoted Dryden's dictum of the slavery of rhyme, Gray's opinion that the necessity of rhyming is a great obstacle to preciseness of expression, and pointed to the offenses of Burns, Tennyson, and Mrs. Browning. Nevertheless, complete harmony prevails:

Rhyme reduplicates the metric pulse when feeling runs strong . . . . It is neither a conventional ornament, nor a mnemonic device, nor esoteric, nor ephemeral in poetry. It is as native to a rhythm that flows high as whitecaps to the ocean.

Rhyme . . . offers the poet something craggy for his mind to break on. And whether they take the form of rhyme or metre, or of something else, I confess a firm belief in the tonic properties of crags.[42]

Even two declared spokesmen of the new poetry followed these views of the elders. In *An Introduction to Contemporary Poetry*[43] Marguerite Wilkinson asks: "What does rhyme add to poetry?" and arrives at the conviction: "Rhyme, after all, like rhythm and imagery and symbolism, is something which contributes to the strength of a poem." Clement Wood, who published *The Craft of Poetry*[44] in 1929 "for those who aspire toward expression in poetry or light verse," made concessions to "polyrhythmic" poetry in reference to Whitman as well as to "off rhymes" and "sour" rhymes only because Emily Dickinson had probably invented this "sophisticated ultra-modern technique" and passed it on to Edna St. Vincent Millay, Elinor Wylie, and other new poets.

Only in the third period of her critical reception was the artist Emily Dickinson vindicated by the New Criticism, which was just as little concerned with form in the old acceptation as were the critics who had influenced this movement. The new critics were interested rather with the analysis of a work of art as a structure of tensions. Emily Dickinson's use of "false" rhymes was finally analyzed with the help of an aesthetic tradition which goes back at least to 1880, when Sidney Lanier's *The Science of English Verse* was published. This prosody illustrates his own poetic practice with the thesis that the laws of music and verse are identical and that time and not accent is the most important rhythmic element. In 1901 J. P. Dabney, tired of the old textbooks on metrics, took up Lanier's idea of *The Musical Basis of Verse*.[45] The decisive question of the necessity of correct rhyme is denied by an argument from analogy. Just as tonal completeness is achieved in music when a cadence ends on the third or fifth of the tonic, repetitions of related vowels in poetry are similarly tonally satisfying. John Keats and Emily Dickinson are adduced as examples of the use of such "imperfect authentic cadences" (p. 106). It is well known that Dabney's argumentation was not heeded for a long time. As late as 1919 Harriet Monroe, in a plea for greater formal freedom, complained after referring to the wealth of forms in music that "one is often moved to wonder at the narrowness of the field still generally accorded to poets as compared with the ample kingdom reigned over by the other arts." The composer, the painter, the sculptor enjoy freedom. "But the poet!—his domain was rigidly bounded by the ancients, and therein must he follow appointed paths."[46] The comparative aesthetic argumentation was applied to Emily Dickinson only in 1937, when T. Walter Herbert not only developed a typology of her "near-rimes," but also distinguished between the occasional false rhymes of earlier poets and her conscious use of imperfect rhymes: "I use the word *near-rime* instead of *false rime* because the latter term applies definitely to unsuccessful attempts to produce perfect rimes; whereas the writer of near-rimes, not failing to do what he attempts, rather attempts a different thing."[47] The aesthetic justification of this practice resembles Dabney's: "Surely if music, whose coherence depends exclusively upon associated sounds, continues to charm while its rules allow more latitude than two-thirds identity in a qualitative pattern, poetry may follow in the same path" (p. 434). As a second justification he adduces the great rhythmic flexibility of verse encountered since ancient times: "The near-rime offers for quality of sound just the escape from absurdity and monotony which Chaucer's, Milton's, Pope's devices achieve in rhythm. Just as two consecutive lines of good poetry, though built of the same fundamental pattern, are rarely allowed to be identical in rhythmic outline, so in near-rime two consecutive end-sounds, though fundamentally similar, are rarely allowed to be identical in pronunciation. Near-rimes give the coherence of associated sounds, and the comfortable effect of echo, without the jingle to which Milton objected" (p. 440).

Emily Dickinson's work appeared to many readers of the first and second periods of her evaluation as an " 'impossible' anomaly," as Amy Lowell had said. As a historical irregularity it assumed an outside position at the end of the nineteenth century and a middle position between old and new during the first third of the twentieth. For the first generation of readers it meant a double problem, since it offended aesthetic as well as historical rules; later, the aesthetic crux diminished while the historical problem continued to exist.

The uncertainties of the 1890's in the formal evaluation of Emily Dickinson's poetry and its stylistic, historical, and regional classification are reflected in the spate of college handbooks. In seventeen literary histories written before 1915 Dickinson was not mentioned; in nine she assumed a secondary position among later authors treated marginally. The predominant schematization according to time, rank, place, genre, and sex caused her to appear as one of the later, minor singers of her region. The criticism of her poetic achievement was based, as might have been expected, on the preceding commentary by reviewers and did not proceed beyond it. For Alphonso Newcomer alone, she did not fit into the staked out territory of the manuals. For him she was a "modern," untouched by the chances of time and place. The influence of these handbooks on the writing of American literary history cannot be overestimated when one sees how eagerly the younger reviewers of Emily Dickinson's poetry paged through them and then considers that even Bruce Weirick relied on them in his discussion of the poets less interesting to him.

The revaluation of nineteenth-century American poetry from 1915 to 1930 is complex in its effects on Emily Dickinson's fate in literary histories. The old handbooks had derived their standards from the flowering of New England poetry around 1850, which was followed by a "twilight interval," a period of imitation. The new outlines by Amy Lowell, Untermeyer, Weirick, Wood, and Kreymborg centered on the recent poetic renaissance. Their sketches are evolutionary. As a result Emily Dickinson's place in the handbooks around 1900 was among the weak successors of a great period, in the newer works among the very few precursors.

The changes in emphasis led to a revaluation of poets. In the poet-critics' surveys "since 1900," the old phalanx of New England greats dropped lowest, while the minor talents of the succeeding generation were either decimated or omitted. Emily Dickinson indirectly gained from the loss of respect for the "thrice sacred Lamas"; she gained directly through her association with the modern movement.

Thus, the historians failed to place her historically regardless of whether they related her to the "latter-day Puritans" (Foerster), the "great American rebels" (Kreymborg), the "irreducible poets" (Carl and Mark Van Doren), or to the exiles (Josephson). She remained an anomaly; however, historians and critics tended to enclose her existence in a vacuum. Newcomer had already done that, and Amy Lowell, Aiken, and Genevieve Taggard[48] followed his example.

The difficulties of placing Emily Dickinson historically continued in the handbooks of the 1930's and 1940's, although historians became conscious of her significance in the American literary tradition and began to interpret her as the sum of the artistic possibilities inherent in the New England soil.

In the decade following A. H. Quinn's *The Literature of the American People* (1951) no great literary histories were written. Nevertheless, a new pattern of thought, which might influence the writing of literary history in the future, began to appear in Dickinson criticism. The poet moved ever closer to what Matthiessen called America's renaissance. Admission to the American Parnassus had been denied her in the 1930's by the socio-economic character of the handbooks and in the following decade by Matthiessen's influential period history. In 1956 Lewis Leary wrote of the collected poetry that "it establishes her as responding to the same forces of unrest and exploration which were responsible during the middle decades of the last century for the writings of Emerson, Thoreau, Hawthorne, Melville, and Whitman, in the first great upsurge of literature in the United States. It is fitting that she should thus be placed with authority among them."[49] Shortly thereafter, another critic arrived at the same conclusion: "These years have seen a sixth writer added with equal surety to the peerage, and therein lies a new chapter in the history of American literature."[49a]

That such ideas spread becomes evident in Roy Harvey Pearce's *The Continuity of American Poetry* (1961), the only history of the genre worth mentioning since Henry W. Wells's *The American Way of Poetry* (1943). Pearce, who sees the continuity of American poetry in its antinomian impulse and in the incapacity or unwillingness of the poets to acknowledge America's system of cultural values, conceives of the renaissance about 1850 as a double flourishing: the popular New Englanders Bryant, Longfellow, Lowell, Holmes, Whittier, and Lanier the Southerner belong to the secondary tradition, the major poets are Poe, Emerson, Whitman, and Emily Dickinson.

The person behind the poetry continued to be an object of speculation for a long time, since little was known about Emily Dickinson's life. Still, the three biographical works of 1930 would have found no broad response if they had not been caught by the boom in biography of the time. "Anyone with spare time and access to a public library can now publish a biography," Henry Seidel Canby scoffed in 1929.[50] The flood of biographies of statesmen and writers—Lytton Strachey, Emil Ludwig, and

André Maurois were among the leading authors—was strongest in the second half of the 1920's, and the public was then most receptive to such products. An expert differentiated between the three types of fictionalized, debunking, and psychoanalytic biography.[51] MacGregor Jenkins' reminiscence belonged to the first type, Josephine Pollitt's book combined features of the first two, and Genevieve Taggard's of all three types.

The change in the conception of the person is more significant than attempts to solve the mystery by identifying the lover. Like the poetry, the person was reinterpreted. Old stereotypes of Emily Dickinson as an eccentric recluse lived on in Katharine Lee Bates's idyllization, in Madame Bianchi's soft-spoken presentation of her aunt, and in Bradford's soul portrait. For them as well as for Hartley and Hillyer, Emily Dickinson remained an anchoress to whom one paid attention since she had written good poems, but one did not take her quite seriously as a human being. To those who rejected the Bianchi still life, "Emily" became so familiar in the 1920's that they patted her on the back. "She would have appreciated the current slang about 'snakes' hips' and 'bees' knees' and 'cat's pajamas,'" a critic remarked in 1924.[52] To others she seemed an escaped Puritan, a rebel against religious and social conformism, a courageous individualist who renounced her paternal religion to find her own God. To still others she appeared pitiable. "But such a little world! Such a pity that one with so capacious and faring a soul should not have lived a life more expansive!" Rollo Walter Brown exclaimed in 1928.[53] Amy Lowell had probably been the first to express this thought. Finally, a few pointed out that any pity was misdirected as Emily Dickinson had lived a rich life.

Even if the speculators' *furor poeticus* never entirely flagged, this last view of a minority before 1930 became the shared conviction of most critics during the third period of her evaluation. The romantic interpretation of Edward Dickinson as the prototype of the unfeeling Victorian father and the sentimental attitude toward "Emily" diminished. "Emily the Elusive," the guest from fairyland, began to descend to earth.

Madame Bianchi had worked herself into the role of the last of the Dickinsons to such an extent that she could not become the first of the biographers. She had experienced only a part of her aunt's life, owned only a part of her literary estate, and could not achieve the necessary objectivity because of lack of distance, family pride, and false discretion. Powerless against the research done by "outsiders," she sought in vain to assist her side to success by supporting the publications of a small group of "insiders"—Jenkins, Mary James Power, and Laura Benét.

If the history of the critical opinions of a work, an author, or of an entire period does not take the shape of a dialectical process in which the truth slowly unravels through thesis and antithesis, it is probably mainly because the critical dialogue of decades and centuries is not a logical argumentation in which answer follows question and antithesis follows thesis in such a way that a higher unity results. Moreover, the total meaning of a work of art, being inexhaustible, is never brought to light. Finally, there are established views which time does not over-turn. Thus, at least two threads run through the tangled first century of Dickinson criticism: that of her stylistic strategy of surprise—"the friction of disappointment on delight," as a Southern poet expressed it in 1891, or "as of a ceiling being re-moved above our heads," as Thornton Wilder experienced it exactly sixty years later—and the conception of her short, witty, sharply pointed verse as intellectual poetry. "She sharpens and refines what in others remains inchoate and crude," wrote Henry W. Wells in 1947, probably without knowledge of Susan Dick-inson's obituary of her sister-in-law. Both qualities, the first one of form the other one of substance, warrant permanence. And it is Emily Dickinson's artistry and humanity which appeal to recent scholarship. "My own prediction is that Emily Dickinson will grow stronger with the years as we continue to outdistance the sentimentalities that still cling to her," said one of the leading Dickinson scholars in 1963: "Her eccentricities will fall into perspective. We will become increasingly aware of the tough-ness and sinew of her poetry, its range and versatility, its chal-lenge to our understanding. We will test our knowledge of humanity against hers and find that we can learn on almost every front. Far from the little figure of frustrations and renunciations and regrets, we will come to see her as a poet of great strength, courage, and singleness of purpose."[54]

APPENDIX

THE NONCRITICAL ACCEPTANCE

THIS STUDY BEARS OUT THE TRUTH expressed by Emily Dickinson in "The poets light but lamps" a century ago. Without doubt the decisive contribution to the growth of her reputation falls to the share of journalistic and academic criticism, although the noncritical acceptance of person and work is not to be underestimated. Whicher's *This Was a Poet* may come much closer to the truth than MacGregor Jenkins' *Emily*, but the novel has probably had a broader effect than the biography.

Emily Dickinson's fate in anthologies of American poetry seems most closely related to her critical reception for the anthologist, by his choice, performs a critical act indicative of his taste and often the taste of his time. Accordingly, her appearance in a variety of anthologies has been traced up to 1930. The two most influential collections, Stedman's *An American Anthology* and Untermeyer's *Modern American Poetry*, testify to early esteem on the part of the leading genteel critic as well as to the rise of her reputation with the best-known collector of modern verse, about whose practice Robert Hillyer commented in *A Letter to Robert Frost*:

> *Taste changes. Candid Louis Untermeyer*
> *Consigns his past editions to the fire;*
> *His new anthology, refined and thrifty,*
> *Builds up some poets and dismisses fifty.*[1]

Emily Dickinson was not among the fifty. From the first to the fifth revised edition of Untermeyer's anthology the number of her poems included increased from 3 (1919) to 6 (1921), 13 (1925), 30 (1930), 32 (1936), and 37 (1942).

As a glance at the titles of early collection shows (cf. Sources, p. 273), the editors of special anthologies had taken notice of her nature and love poems as well as of her humor and her verses for children several years before she appeared for the first time in a general anthology of American poetry.

In all, we find her represented in 45 works with 287 poems from 1891 to 1930. Eleven anthologies with 34 Dickinson poems and 34 anthologies with 253 Dickinson poems were compiled during the first and second periods of her reception, respectively. The percentage of different poems chosen by 1897 is considerably higher, with 30 out of 34 in contrast to 109 out of 253, that is, the consensus of the editors in their selections increased considerably from 12 percent to 51 percent. If one adds to the 45 anthologies two of the more significant later publications—Harry Hayden Clark's *Major American Poets* (1936) and F. O. Matthiessen's *Oxford Book of American Verse* (1950), which include 40 and 48 Dickinson titles, respectively—the following list of frequency results (the first number gives the date of the first publication of each poem, the numbers following are the publication dates of the anthologies in which the poem appears):

1890 "I never saw a moor" 1896, 1900, 1905, 1919, 1921, 1925, 1925, 1925, 1927, 1929, 1930, 1936.

1896 "My life closed twice before its close" 1898, 1900, 1905, 1922, 1925, 1925, 1927, 1927, 1929, 1930, 1936, 1950.

1890 "Because I could not stop for death" 1896, 1898, 1905, 1922, 1927, 1927, 1927, 1930, 1936, 1950.

1890 "The sky is low, the clouds are mean" 1900, 1919, 1921, 1925, 1925, 1927, 1950.

1890 "The soul selects her own society" 1894, 1925, 1925, 1927, 1927, 1929, 1950.

1890 "I died for beauty, but was scarce" 1912, 1922, 1923, 1925, 1927, 1936.

1890 "These are the days when birds come back" 1898, 1905, 1905, 1921, 1925, 1927.

1891 "A bird came down the walk" 1912, 1922, 1927, 1930, 1950.

1890 "The bustle in a house" 1896, 1925, 1927, 1927, 1950.

1890 "Alter! When the hills do" 1900, 1925, 1927, 1927, 1929.

1891 "I like to see it lap the miles" 1921, 1925, 1925, 1936, 1950.

1890   "If you were coming in the fall" 1891, 1894, 1905, 1930, 1950.

1891   "Just lost, when I was saved" 1900, 1920, 1925, 1927, 1927.

1890   "Our share of night to bear" 1897, 1900, 1925, 1927, 1929.

1891   "God made a little gentian" 1899, 1900, 1922, 1927.

1890   "Have you got a brook in your little heart" 1891, 1891, 1905, 1927.

1896   "Heart! We will forget him" 1900, 1925, 1927, 1936.

1890   "I taste a liquor never brewed" 1925, 1929, 1930, 1950.

1890   "If I can stop one heart from breaking" 1896, 1901, 1912, 1913.

1891   "Of all the souls that stand create" 1900, 1927, 1927, 1936.

1890   "Safe in their alabaster chambers" 1893, 1927, 1927, 1950.

1890   "There's a certain slant of light" 1925, 1927, 1936, 1950.

1891   "They dropped like flakes" 1896, 1898, 1900, 1927.

An additional 27 poems were chosen three times, 37 twice, the rest once. Before we evaluate this list, it is advisable to consult modern Dickinson anthologies. Charles R. Anderson states in the preface to his critical study, *Emily Dickinson: Stairway of Surprise:* "Her really fine poems do not seem to number more than a hundred, her great ones about twenty-five." The 103 poems fully quoted in the text form "a select anthology of her best poems."[2] If one compares the titles chosen by James Reeves for *Selected Poems of Emily Dickinson* (1959) with those chosen by Malcolm Brinnin for *Emily Dickinson* (1960), 56 duplications result. If one consults Anderson's critical selection, 23 poems remain which appear in all three books:

1891   "A bird came down the walk" (A).

1891   "A narrow fellow in the grass" (A).

1891   "Ample make this bed" (A).

1890   "Because I could not stop for death" (A).

1896   "I felt a funeral in my brain" (A).

1896   "I heard a fly buzz when I died" (A).

1891   "I like to see it lap the miles" (A).

1891   "I read my sentence steadily."

1890   "I taste a liquor never brewed" (A).

1891   "It was not death, for I stood up" (A).

1890   "Mine by the right of the white election."
1890   "My cocoon tightens, colors tease" (A).
1891   "Of all the souls that stand create" (A).
1890   "One dignity delays for all."
1891   "Safe in their alabaster chambers" (A).
1891   "Our journey had advanced" (A)
1896   "Split the lark and you'll find the music" (A).
1896   "The bat is dun with wrinkled wings" (A).
1890   "The soul selects her own society" (A).
1891   "There came a day at summer's full" (A).
1890   "There's a certain slant of light" (A).
1924   "Title divine is mine."
1896   "What soft, cherubic creatures" (A).

All 23 of these poems are in Thomas H. Johnson's *Final Harvest* (1961); not less than 19 (designated by A) were in Aiken's *Selected Poems of Emily Dickinson* (1924). The two preceding lists contain 23 poems each, with 8 duplications. The total number of poems chosen more than three times by 46 anthologists between 1891 and 1950 as well as by Reeves, Brinnin, and Johnson amounts to 38.

Not less than 37 of these 38 poems, which have proven the most permanent over a long period of time, had already been selected by Mrs. Todd and Higginson: 18 for the first series, 12 for the second, 7 for the third. Only "Title divine is mine," the manuscript of which was in Madame Bianchi's possession, was published for the first time in *Complete Poems*. This substantiates unequivocally the good taste of the first editors, the decline in quality of the second and third series of poems, and that the critics of the 1890's already had the best poems of Emily Dickinson under consideration.

The temporal distribution of the first list is not entirely balanced. It is conspicuous that four easily intelligible poems which rhymed throughout—or almost throughout—were no longer chosen after 1913, 1927, 1929, respectively: the admonishing "Our share of night to bear," the idyllic "Have you got a brook in your little heart," the slightly sentimental "If I can stop one heart from breaking," and the patriotic "They dropped like flakes." On the other hand, some poems emerge late; just as the list in general projects slightly into the third period of the poet's reception. Four of the eight poems which also appear in the second list are decidedly modern: "A bird came down the walk" (after 1912), which separates the worlds of nature and man in the unsuccessful attempt of the "I" to approach a bird in the garden; the railroad poem (after 1925), her ironic and ambiguous contribution to the theme of technology; the metaphorically bold, bacchanalic "I taste a liquor never brewed," which was often misunderstood by early critics; and the difficult love poem "Of all the souls that stand create" (after 1900). These modern poems can be supplemented by five more which were first noticed in the 1920's and which are all in the anthologies of Aiken, Brinnin, and Johnson, as well as in Anderson's critical selection:

1891 "Ample make this bed" 1923, 1925, 1950.
1890 "Apparently with no surprise" 1925, 1927, 1936.
1891 "There came a wind like a bugle" 1922, 1950.
1896 "What soft, cherubic creatures" 1929, 1936.
1891 "A route of evanescence" 1925.

These are a Puritan death fantasy, two poems on the destructive powers of nature, a caustic satire on the hollowness of small-town ladies, and Emily Dickinson's favorite poem, which she dispatched at least six times to friends, the example par excellence of a poem with an omitted center.

The numerous poems dedicated to Emily Dickinson stand on the borderline between rational criticism and emotional reaction. Often written in the form of a sonnet, mostly of little artistic value, yet at times coming from well-known poets such as Sandburg, Amy Lowell, Hart Crane, William Rose Benét, Robert P. T. Coffin, Mark Van Doren, Joseph Auslander, and Yvor Winters, they reflect in a manner similar to the anthologies the ups and downs of the critical discussion. As early as 1891 five such tributes appeared; they were joined by only twelve more in the long span from 1892 to 1924 and by no fewer than eighty in the period from 1925 to 1949 (cf. Sources, pp. 277-82).

In the earliest of these verses, personal recollection of the deceased poet dominates. Emily Fowler Ford, who had come to Amherst at the age of thirteen and had lived there for six years (1839-45), wrote a poem in 1891 in which she referred to a visit in the Dickinson home on July 15, 1862, at which the poet did not receive her:

> *Friend, you thought*
> *No life so sweet and fair as hiding brought,*
> *And beauty is your song, with interlude*

Of outer life which to your soul seems crude,
Thoughtless, unfeeling, idle, scant of grace;
Nor will you touch a hand, or greet a face,—[3]

The early reminiscences were later increasingly joined by expressions of admiration and gratitude, by appreciations of her nature poetry, by appeals to her as a congenial mind, by musings on her life, by derision of her first biographers but also by censure and (unsuccessful) parody. Wallace Gould lamented in 1929 that she did not run away with "him," the lover described by Madame Bianchi, but instead gambled away her talent in small experiments:

You could have sung the love songs of our racial dawn.
   Ah, but no,
you gave us epigrams in rhythm, saws that the town wag
   could have uttered—

What he had hoped of her, was "that eternal cry / just as it is, virile, simple, direct, / . . . Yankee love / with all its native jest, its classic force / its transcendental plainness."[4]

The artistic side of her work was commented on especially by the early versifiers. Thus, a student at Iowa College, Mary Bowen, wrote at the end of a sonnet:

The hand of Nature touched thy tunéd heart,
   And, lo, thou utter'st in simple strain
A song, too thought-rich for a fettered art,
   Yet bearing ever Nature's sad refrain.[5]

Another admirer, J. William Lloyd, would not be outdone by the student; in one of his rather jolty *Wind-Harp Songs* a goodly portion of the Dickinson criticism of the 1890's is reflected:

   Emily Dickinson
   It seems to me you sing a song
   That startled every one;
   Odd intergrowth of heathen
   And New England Puritan.

   Your art is like a Japanesque;—
   Perspective and detail
   Are very independent,
   But the picture pleases well.

Suppose a Quaker wood-bird
To throw a parrot wing,
Talk Manx and Hindostanee,
And then go back and sing

Weird bits and beautiful,
A Concord touch or two,
Lyric thought, so stated
As no one else dare do.[6]

The novels and dramas written about the life of the poet were of considerably greater influence than the lyric tributes. Helen Hunt Jackson's "Esther Wynne's Love Letters" and *Mercy Philbrick's Choice* (1876) can scarcely be related to Emily Dickinson even if several reviewers of 1890 and 1891 supposed such a relation existed and Josephine Pollitt construed the novel as a *roman à clef*. The story was published in December 1871, in *Scribner's Magazine* as the conclusion of the first series of *Saxe Holm's Stories*. It deals with the discovery of several of Esther's love letters and poems to a supposedly married recipient and is possibly based on Amherst gossip about Emily Dickinson of which the author may have been aware. The interspersed sentimental lyrics weakly recall Emily's early style. The small town Penfield in *Mercy Philbrick's Choice*, the first volume of the No Name Series, seems to be modeled on Amherst, but the action fits Helen Hunt's life to a nicety, for Mercy is a young widow (like the author), who comes from Cape Cod (Newport) to Penfield (Amherst) and, after a romance with cowardly Stephen White, leaves again in order to become a great poet.

The three novels (two of which were written primarily for children and adolescents)—Jenkins' *Emily* (1930), Laura Benét's *Come Slowly, Eden* (1942), and Jean Gould's *Miss Emily* (1946) —were entirely in the Bianchi tradition and carried the uncomplicated and slightly heroized Dickinson image of *Life and Letters* into the 1940's. Jenkins and Laura Benét enjoyed the cooperation of the poet's niece; Jean Gould drew her information chiefly from Jenkins' *Emily* and from *Miss Emily*.

Four plays were richer in conflict. The attempt to dramatize Emily Dickinson's life is repeatedly evident in the 1920's, for example in Amy Lowell's and Wallace Gould's dialogue poems or in an anonymous review which appeared in the March 1924 issue of Houghton Mifflin's *The Piper*. Here the reader comes upon a spring scene in an "old-fashioned garden at Amherst," which begins as follows:

> Emily: *My life closed twice . . .*
> Sue: *Emily, it is spring once more . . .*
> Emily: *Morning might come by . . .*[7]

What is only hinted at here through the dramatization of passages from the poet's letters was translated into action by Susan Glaspell in her above-mentioned three-act play, by Elva Knight in "Bulletins from Immortality" (1932), by Vincent York and Frederick J. Pohl in *Brittle Heaven* (1935), and by Dorothy Gardner in *Eastward in Eden: The Love Story of Emily Dickinson* (1945).

Elva Knight, whose unpublished play "in three brief acts" was put on at Elmira College, had collected her material by questioning old Amhersters and consequently brought onto the stage the local rumor of the lover who had been turned away by a jealous Edward Dickinson. The family tyrant puts his foot down at the end of the first act: "You cannot escape your greatest duty in this world—obedience to your Father's will!"[8] *Brittle Heaven* makes use of the theory of Miss Pollitt (who had in the meantime become Mrs. Pohl). The stichomythic use of aphorisms from the letters and poems of Emily Dickinson in the crucial love scene with Hunt spoils the play, for it transforms the lovers into a ludicrous pair of prudent parrots. Dramatically the best of the four plays, *Eastward in Eden*[9] depicts the growth of the friendship between Emily and Charles Wadsworth, their love, and their renunciation. It even found Whicher's approval. "Dorothy Gardner has beautifully accomplished the impossible," he wrote in the preface of the book, published four years after the first performance. "Her play presents with sympathy and invincible dignity the essence of an unfulfilled romance which conceivably might have served to heighten to tragic intensity a New England girl's instinctive powers of poetic expression."

Artistically related to the dramatic attempts is the dance "Letter to the World" performed by the modern dancer Martha Graham in 1941 and reproduced in 1947 and 1952 (cf. Sources, p. 323). The artist, herself a New Englander and a direct descendant of Miles Standish, had already represented themes of New England's Puritan past in "Lamentation" and "Salem Shore." The role of Emily Dickinson is divided into the speaking, historical Emily and a silent, gesturing figure that seems to be the invention of Emily's soul. Embodied by Jean Erdman and Martha Graham, both sides of Emily's character dance through a symbolic sequence of childhood adventures ("Let us play yesterday"), anticipation of love ("Dear March—Come in"), and certainty of death ("Looking at death is dying") in the omnipresent shadow of the figure of the Ancestress (Jane Dudley), a symbol of Puritan conscience.

In addition to these creative interpretations of the poet's life through the medium of the novel, the play, and the ballet, a strand of the noncritical reception of her poetry which reaches back to 1896 may be mentioned. By 1951 fifty-six of her poems had been set to music. Among the texts most frequently chosen, sentimental pieces such as "If I can stop one heart from breaking" and "Poor little heart" stand out (cf. Sources, pp. 275-77). The first poem was included in *The New Hymnal for American Youth* in 1927. The composer Aaron Copland in 1947 combined ten poems with an instrumental "Preface" and "Afterthought" to form a secular cantata for four-part chorus of women's voices and small orchestra with incidental soprana and contralto soli.

The poet's gift for making her nephews and niece and their young friends her confederates and for sending them letters and poems through which they felt privileged runs through the reminiscences of Madame Bianchi and MacGregor Jenkins. "She has a child's ignorance of the world, a child's imagination and love of color," wrote *The Chicago Tribune* on December 12, 1891. The first of her young readers were Susan Dickinson's children. For Edward (1861-98) she wrote eight poems, for Martha (1866-1943) and Gilbert (1875-83) two each. In 1891 two poems from Mrs. Todd's collection of manuscripts appeared in *St. Nicholas*, a monthly magazine for children, before they were published in the second selection of poetry. In the following years eight pieces were first printed in *The Youth's Companion* (cf. Sources, p. 271). Mary I. Lovejoy included "A drop fell on the apple tree" in her *Nature in Verse: A Poetry Reader for Children* (1896), and William Rose Benét's *Poems for Youth: An American Anthology* (1925) contains three Dickinson titles. In 1934 Alfred Leete Hampson edited *Emily Dickinson: Poems for Youth*, a well-received collection of seventy-eight poems with illustrations by George and Doris Hauman.

Jenkins' *Emily*, written for adults, is today, appropriately, in the juvenile departments of municipal libraries, as are the novels by Laura Benét and Jean Gould. Charlie May Simon,

John Gould Fletcher's wife, included a story of "Emily Dickinson" in her *Lays of the New Land: Stories of Some American Poets and Their Work* (1943). The New England poet also appears among the fictive pairs of great figures from the past in Hendrik Willem Van Loon's *Lives* (1942), a humorous modification of the genre made famous by Landor: "And Now a Rather Strange Combination, EMILY DICKINSON and FRÉDÉRIC CHOPIN, But Emily Has the Time of Her Life, and Chopin Shows Also What He Can Do with a Minnie-Piano," runs the subtitle of chapter XVIII. The attempt to translate Emily Dickinson's poetry into the idiom of American youth has progressed farthest in a comic, "The Railway Train by Emily Dickinson," in which every two lines of "I like to see it lap the miles" are illustrated by cartoons of the fabulous locomotive.[10] Two essays on the poet appeared in 1957 in a Boston magazine for children. The author of "Emily Dickinson and Children" noted the "amazing quality of eternally fresh perception which makes one identify Emily Dickinson with youth. She looked at the world each day as though she had never seen it before."[11]

ABBREVIATIONS

The following frequently quoted titles have been abbreviated in the Notes and in the Sources:

I. Books

> AB   Millicent Todd Bingham, *Ancestors' Brocades: The Literary Debut of Emily Dickinson* (New York, 1945).
>
> DAB   *Dictionary of American Biography*, ed. Allen Jones and Dumas Malone, 21 vols. (New York, 1928-36); *Supplement One* (New York, 1944).
>
> ED   *Emily Dickinson: A Collection of Critical Essays*, ed. Richard B. Sewall (Englewood Cliffs, N.J., 1963).
>
> Letters   *The Letters of Emily Dickinson*, ed. Thomas H. Johnson, associate editor Theodora Ward, 3 vols. (Cambridge, Mass., 1958).
>
> Poems   *The Poems of Emily Dickinson: Including Variant Readings Critically Compared with All Known Manuscripts*, ed. Thomas H. Johnson, 3 vols. (Cambridge, Mass., 1955).
>
> RED   *The Recognition of Emily Dickinson: Selected Criticism since 1890*, ed. Caesar R. Blake and Carlton F. Wells (Ann Arbor, 1964).

II. Periodicals

> AGQ   *The Amherst Graduates' Quarterly*
>
> AL   *American Literature*
>
> AM   *The Atlantic Monthly*

B	*The Bookman* (New York)
BB	*The Book Buyer*
C	*The Critic*
CR	*The Christian Register*
CSM	*The Christian Science Monitor*
CW	*The Catholic World*
E	*The Explicator*
HLB	*Harvard Library Bulletin*
HM	*Harper's (New Monthly) Magazine* (until 1900 *Harper's New Monthly Magazine*, thereafter *Harper's Magazine*)
I	*The Independent*
KR	*The Kenyon Review*
LM	*The London Mercury*
LW	*The Literary World*
MHAQ	*Mount Holyoke Alumnae Quarterly*
N	*The Nation*
N&A	*The Nation and Athenaeum*
NEQ	*The New England Quarterly*
N&Q	*Notes and Queries*
NR	*The New Republic*
NYHTB	*New York Herald Tribune Books*
NYTBR	*The New York Times Book Review*
O	*The Outlook (and Independent)* (1893-1928 *The Outlook*, 1928-1932 *The Outlook and Independent*)
PMLA	*PMLA: Publications of the Modern Language Association*
PW	*The Publishers' Weekly*
SM	*Scribner's Magazine*
SR	*The Sewanee Review*
SRL	*The Saturday Review (of Literature)* (until 1951 *The Saturday Review of Literature*, thereafter *The Saturday Review*)
TLS	*The Times Literary Supplement*
UKCR	*The University of Kansas City Review*

Abbreviations

YC	*The Youth's Companion*
YR	*The Yale Review*

III. Newspapers

ARec	*The Amherst Record*
BGl	*The Boston Globe*
BHer	*The Boston Herald*
BTr	*Boston Transcript*
HCour	*The Hartford Courant*
NYHTr *NYTr*	*New York Herald Tribune*
NYTimes	*The New York Times*
SFChr	*San Francisco Chronicle*
SRep	*The Springfield Republican*
Sun	*The New York Sun*
SUnion	*The Springfield Union*
World	*The New York World*

IV. Other Abbreviations

n.d. = not dated; n.p. = not paginated; Sources (with page number) refers to the list of sources at the end of the book.

Names of months have been shortened as follows: Ja, Fe, Mr, Ap, (May), Je, Jl, Au, Se, Oc, No, De.

Manuscripts from the Emily Dickinson Collection in the Robert Frost Library of Amherst College are referred to by the identification number of the collection (MS-D57) followed by the number of the respective manuscript (e.g., MS-D57/To 303).

NOTES

CHAPTER I

1. From a letter of June 7, 1862, to Higginson. *Letters*, II, 408. Cf. Abbreviations on pp. 227-29. Volume and page numbers in the text of this chapter refer to *Letters*.

2. David A. Wasson, "Modern Poetry," *The Galaxy*, III (1 Ap 1867), 786.

3. *Ibid.*

4. *The Centennial Edition of the Works of Sidney Lanier*, ed. Charles R. Anderson and Aubrey H. Starke (Baltimore, 1945), IX, 413.

5. Cf. "Tabulation of Recipients," *Poems*, III, 1197-1200. Of other acquaintances, Mrs. Jackson received 11 poems, Niles 7, Mrs. Todd 6.

6. Information on Emily Dickinson's tutors is found in George F. Whicher, "Emily Dickinson's Earliest Friend," *AL*, VI (Mr 1934), 3-17, and Jay Leyda, *The Years and Hours of Emily Dickinson* (New Haven, 1960), I, lxv, xliv-xlv, lxix.

7. Higginson (1823-1911), born and buried in Cambridge, Mass., Unitarian minister in Newburyport and Worcester, ardent champion of abolitionism and women's rights, became colonel of the first regiment of Negro volunteers during the war and, after 1865, devoted himself to his literary career. A friend of the prominent New England poets, he wrote biographies of Longfellow, Whittier, and Margaret Fuller. He encouraged a host of young, especially female, talents, among them Celia Thaxter, Elizabeth Stuart Phelps, Mrs. Jackson, and George E. Woodberry. He himself felt like a celebrated horse "which had never won a race, but which was praised as having gained a second place in more races than

any other horse in America." The scattering of his gifts was the reason both for his literary key position during the last third of the century and for the rapidity with which he was forgotten immediately after his death. Only in recent years has his role as Emily Dickinson's preceptor rescued him from oblivion. Cf. Anna Mary Wells, *Dear Preceptor: The Life and Times of Thomas Wentworth Higginson* (Boston, 1963), Van Wyck Brooks, *New England: Indian Summer* (New York, 1940), pp. 129-33, and M. A. deWolfe Howe in *DAB*.

8. "I do not see how there could possibly be a list of the dozen masterpieces of the world's literature, of which at least one half should not be Greek." "A Plea for Culture," *AM*, xix (Ja 1867), 32. The three subsequent page numbers in the text refer to this essay.

9. "Letter to a Young Contributor," *AM*, ix (Ap 1862), 403-5.

10. The poems included in the second letter were: "There came a day at summer's full," "Of all the sounds despatched abroad," and "South winds jostle them."

11. Opinions differ about the tone of the correspondence. Cf. *AB*, pp. 166-68, Thomas H. Johnson, *Emily Dickinson: An Interpretive Biography* (Cambridge, Mass., 1955), pp. 110-17, and Theodora Van Wagenen Ward, "Emily Dickinson and T. W. Higginson," *Boston Public Library Quarterly*, v (Ja 1953), 3-18.

12. The reading was sympathetically received by the Boston ladies. The second unknown authoress was Higginson's sister Louisa, who had died in 1873. Cf. Wells, pp. 239-40.

13. Ward, p. 3.

14. Helen Maria Fiske Hunt Jackson (1830-85), daughter of the professor of moral philosophy and metaphysics at Amherst College and a childhood acquaintance of Emily Dickinson, began to write poetry after the death of her first husband, who was killed in a wartime accident in 1863. In 1884 she won international fame as "H.H." and "Helen of Colorado" with her historical romance of Indian life in California, *Ramona*. Her novel *Mercy Philbrick's Choice* (1876) was later interpreted as a *roman à clef* about Emily Dickinson. After her second marriage in 1875, she lived in Colorado Springs. Cf. Louise Pound in *DAB*.

15. Niles (1825-94), who was in charge of the first two selections of Emily Dickinson's verse, joined the publishing house of Roberts Brothers in 1863 and was instrumental in the rise of the firm. Though preferring conservative poets, he went out of his way to publish great talents such as Christina and D.G. Rossetti, William Morris, and Swinburne. Of American authors, he helped Louisa

Alcott, Helen Jackson, E.E. Hale, and Arlo Bates. Cf. Raymond L. Kilgour, *Messrs. Roberts Brothers Publishers* (Ann Arbor, 1952), passim.

16. Mrs. Todd (1856-1932), now known only as Emily Dickinson's editor, was a writer in her own right. While engaged in preparing the poet's manuscripts for the press (1886-96), she took part in two astronomical expeditions of her husband to Japan and published a volume of her own poetry, a popular astronomical book, as well as numerous essays and reviews. Cf. George F. Whicher in *DAB* and Nathan Haskell Dole's obituary notice in *SRL*, IX (19 No 1932), 260.

17. Leyda, II, 361, 377. In the second entry, the misspelt reference seems to be to the character in Dickens' *Great Expectations*.

18. Alterations can be proved in five of the seven poems (*Poems*, nos. 214, 216, 228, 986, 67). Possible changes in nos. 3 and 324 are no longer verifiable because of the loss of the originals.

19. Opinions differ about the corrector's person and the number of alterations. The changes are probably, but not certainly, Niles's, since he was editor both of the volume and the whole series, although Higginson's copy (in the Galatea Collection of the Boston Public Library) has a note in his own hand reading: "Emily Dickinson / altered probably by Mrs. Helen Hunt." Of the six alterations listed by Johnson, only four are to be found in the text of the poem as printed in *A Masque of Poets*.

20. *Works of Sidney Lanier*, IX, 39-40.

21. Martha Dickinson Bianchi, *Emily Dickinson Face to Face: Unpublished Letters with Notes and Reminiscences* (Boston, 1932), p. 27.

22. *Emily Dickinson's Letters to Dr. and Mrs. Josiah Gilbert Holland*, ed. Theodora Van Wagenen Ward (Cambridge, Mass., 1951), p. 25.

23. Cf. *LW*, IX (10 De 1878), 118: "If anything in the volume was contributed by Emerson, we should consider these lines upon 'Success' most probably his."

CHAPTER II

1. Maurice Thompson, "Miss Dickinson's Poems," *America*, v (8 Ja 1891), 425.

2. *Emily Dickinson Face to Face*, ed. Martha Dickinson Bianchi (Boston, 1932), pp. 163-64.

3. Robert Escarpit, *Das Buch und der Leser: Entwurf einer Literatursoziologie* (Cologne, 1961), p. 69.

4. Thomas H. Johnson, *Emily Dickinson: An Interpretive Biography* (Cambridge, Mass., 1955), p. 93.

5. Of the following numbers, the first refers to the page in *Poems* (1890), the second to the number in *Poems* (1955), the third to the line(s): in 22 (371) 11 a missing relative pronoun was added; in 55 (640) 10 colloquial "broke" was changed into "broken"; in 106 (258) 2 idiomatic "Winter afternoons" was converted into "On a winter afternoon"; in 119 (449) 7 "Themself are one" yielded to "the two are one"; in 129 (622) 25 "Love too blest to be" replaced "Love too best to be"; in 145 (596) 10 Mrs. Todd wrote "I never can decide" for "Ourself cannot decide."

6. 33 (650) 3.

7. *Check* = "baggage check," occurring as an Americanism since 1845 (according to *A Dictionary of Americanisms on Historical Principles*, ed. Mitford M. Mathews [Chicago, 1951]), may have sounded too unpoetic. Examples are 57 (640) 45; 19 (90) 7; 93 (975) 5; 126 (1052) 8.

8. Examples are 16 (172) 12, 22-23; 23 (371) 24; 138 (712) 9; 139 (712) 16; 80 (647) 7-8.

9. Thomas Wentworth Higginson, "An Open Portfolio," *The Christian Union*, XLII (23 Se 1890), 292-93; *Poems by Emily Dickinson*, ed. Mabel Loomis Todd and T.W. Higginson (Boston, 1890), pp. v-vi, iv.

10. Arlo Bates (1850-1918), born in Maine, went to Boston in 1876 and had gained a reputation as a critic and writer of short stories, novels, and dramas before he was appointed professor of English at the Massachusetts Institute of Technology in 1893. Cf. Charles Noble in *DAB*.

11. Roger Burlingame, *Of Making Many Books: A Hundred Years of Reading, Writing and Publishing* (New York, 1946), pp. 272, 274.

12. The first edition of 500 copies, published on November 12, 1890, was followed by a second (380) on December 16, and by a third (500) on December 27, 250 of which were wrongly bound. This put the total sale at 1380 copies at the end of 1890. Encouraged by mounting sales, Niles planned to popularize the book by putting it in a simpler dress and reducing the price from $1.50 to $1.25. This was done from the fourth edition on (issued on January 29, 1891, followed by a fifth on February 17, and a sixth on March 11). On July 16, 1891, *The Nation*, announcing an eighth edition, added a canard: "An Arabic translation made in Syria has passed through several editions" ("Notes," LIII, 48). The hoax was reprinted by *The Critic* on July 18 ("Notes," XIX, 36). The eleventh edition was printed at the end of 1892, the sixteenth in 1898. The seventeenth,

issued in 1904, was reprinted for twenty years. In 1898, when Roberts Brothers was taken over by Little, Brown, 7850 copies had been sold. Between 1899 and 1925, another 3820 copies were printed. The rumors afloat in the early 1890's of more than 12,000 sold copies (cf. "Literary Notes," *I*, XLVI [14 Je 1894], 771) are totally unfounded and were possibly spread, just as the announcement of the Arabic edition, for advertising purposes. Also, Higginson's entry on the inside cover of his copy deposited in the Boston Public Library—". . . it sold some 10,000 copies without especial effort . . ."—is misleading.

13. "Some Books of Verse," *The Overland Monthly*, XVII (May 1891), 549-50; "Miss Dickinson's Poems," *The Providence Journal*, 14 Je 1891.

14. William Morton Payne, "Recent Books of Poetry," *The Dial*, XI (Fe 1891), 313; "Talk about New Books," *CW*, LII (Ja 1891), 600-604; Samuel J. Barrows, "Emily Dickinson's Poems," *CR*, LXX (30 Ap 1891), 274.

15. Droch [= Robert Bridges], "The Poems of Emily Dickinson," *Life*, XVI (27 No 1890), 303-4.

16. *Boston Post*, n.d., quoted in "What the Critics Say about Emily Dickinson's Poems," *ARec*, 3 De 1890.

17. "Literary Notes," *NYTr*, 4 Ja 1891; *The Providence Journal*, 14 Je 1891; Thompson in *America*, V (8 Ja 1891), 425; Arlo Bates, "Miss Dickinson's Poems," *Boston Courier*, 23 No 1891.

18. Noah Brooks, "Books of the Christmas Season," *BB*, VII (De 1890), 521; "Emily Dickinson's Poems," *LW*, XXI (6 De 1891), 466; MS-D57/To 303.

19. Louise Chandler Moulton (1835-1908), born in Connecticut, held literary salons in Boston and London and was famed as a lyric poet. From 1886 to 1892, she contributed a weekly "Letter on Books" to *The Boston Herald*, part of which was her notice "The Wonderful Poems of Emily Dickinson" on November 23, 1890.

20. "Literary form, as used by others, she regarded little, but in her own sight she was rigorously bent to express herself just as she did, having her own standard of rhythm, or perhaps we should say of music, and her own choice of words" ("The Literary Wayside," *SRep*, 16 No 1890).—"She had almost no criticism, and was absolutely untrammeled; so that the verses are sometimes almost formless, while at other times they show great capacity for delicate and sweet melody, suggesting the chance strains of an Aeolian harp. But in compass of thought, grasp of feeling, and vigor of epithet, they are simply extraordinary, and strike notes, very often, like those of a deep-toned organ" (Recent Poetry," *N*, LI [27 No

1890], 422-23).—*The Catholic World* wrote: "Now and then there is . . . a perverse failure to use a rhyme that was almost inevitable and would have been appropriate, concerning which one finds it at the moment not so easy to restrain the pedagogic instinct; but, on the whole, here is a poet who knew so well a mind so well worth knowing, that one ends by accepting her experience of it as it stands, and being grateful to the editorial wisdom that left it unamended."

21. J.W.C. [John White Chadwick], "Poems by Emily Dickinson," *CR*, LXIX (18 De 1890), 828.

22. Nathan Haskell Dole, "Literary Topics in Boston," *BB*, VII (De 1890), 546.

23. Henry Park Schauffler, "Suggestions from the Poems of Emily Dickinson," *The Amherst Literary Monthly*, VI (Je 1891), 87-90.

24. William Dean Howells, "Editor's Study," *HM*, LXXXII (Ja 1891), 318-20.

25. "Form and Substance," *SM*, IX (Mr 1891), 395-96.

26. [Lilian Whiting], "Poems," *The Boston Budget*, 23 No 1890.

27. "Comment on New Books," *AM*, LXVII (Ja 1891), 128-29.

28. [Kinsley Twining], "Poems by Emily Dickinson," *I*, XLII (11 De 1890), 1759.

29. "The Poems of Emily Dickinson," *C*, XVII (13 De 1890), 305-6.

30. Mary E. Wilkins, *A New England Nun and Other Stories* (New York, 1891), p. 28.

31. "Grim Slumber Songs," *The Commercial Advertiser*, 6 Ja 1891.

32. "Miss Dickinson's Poems," *San José Mercury*, 19 Ap 1891.

33. *AM*, LXVIII (May 1891), 707.

34. A.L. [Andrew Lang], "A Literary Causerie," *The Speaker*, III (31 Ja 1891), 135-36.

35. Alluding to Emperor Sigismund who, at the Council of Constance in 1414, is said to have replied to a prelate criticizing his Latin grammar: "Ego sum rex Romanus, et super grammaticam." [Andrew Lang], "Some American Poets," *The Illustrated London News*, XCVIII (7 Mr 1891), 307.

36. "Poems by Emily Dickinson," *Bookseller*, no. 402 (6 May 1891), 447; "New Books and Reprints," *The Saturday Review*, LXXXII (18 Jl 1891), 94.

37. "As a matter of fact, the verse is not always readily intelligible; still there can be no question that the late Miss Dickinson possessed the poetic temperament and insight into some of the sor-

rows and mysteries of life. Nevertheless there is a sense of incompleteness about her work as if the thought were dashed off and committed to her portfolio in a hurry." "Recent Poetry and Verse," *The Graphic*, 12 Se 1891.

38. "New Books of the Month," *The Review of Reviews* (London), IV (Se 1891), 308.

39. "A Poet and Some Others," *The Saturday Review*, LXXII (5 Se 1891), 279.

40. "An American Sappho," *The London Daily News*, 3 Oc 1891.

41. F. B. Sanborn, "The Breakfast Table," *Boston Daily Advertiser*, 27 Oc 1891.

42. *Alice James, Her Brothers, Her Journal*, ed. Anna Robeson Burr (New York, 1934), pp. 248-49.

43. Ludwig Lewisohn, *Expression in America* (New York, 1932), p. 301.

44. *HM*, LXXXII (May 1891), 964.

45. Quoted in Roger Lancelyn Green, *Andrew Lang: A Critical Biography* (Leicester, 1946), p. 173.

46. "The Best Five Books of the Decade," *C*, XVII (27 De 1890), 339. Sarah Chauncey Woolsey (1845-1905), from Cleveland, Ohio, was known as a lyric poet and essayist under the pseudonym Susan Coolidge.

CHAPTER III

1. Arthur Chamberlain, "The Poems of Emily Dickinson," *Boston Commonwealth*, XXX (28 De 1891), 7.

2. A good example of this combinative manner of editing is *Poems by Emily Dickinson*, ed. T.W. Higginson and Mabel Loomis Todd, second series (Boston, 1891), pp. 126-27 (= *Poems*, no. 1466). Cf. *Poems*, III, 1016-17, and *AB*, pp. 160-61. As these combinations are not changes of the text, they were not included in the list.

3. In the case of *Poems* (1891), p. 228 (= *Poems*, no. 237), ll. 13-16, the transpositions concern an entire stanza, with one instance of rewriting.

4. Thomas Wentworth Higginson, "Emily Dickinson's Letters," *AM*, LXVIII (Oc 1891), 444-56.

5. "Emily Dickinson," *The Review of Reviews*, IV (No 1891), 459.

6. At first, the book sold "like 'Hot Cakes'" (Hardy of Roberts Brothers to Higginson on November 13, 1891 [MS-D57/To 181]). After the surprisingly good sales of the first selection the printing

was doubled to 1000 copies. The first printing was exhausted on November 13, 1891. "This evidences a sudden popularity quite unprecedented to which praise and censure alike have probably contributed," surmised *The Nation* ("Notes," LIII [19 No 1891], 391). The second printing of 1000 copies appeared on the same day; a third and fourth printing of 1000 copies each became necessary in December. Total sales can be estimated at 7500 copies. For purposes of publicity, Hardy mentioned a figure which was too high when he spoke of 7000 copies of the second series which had been printed until June 1894 in comparison with 12,000 copies of the first ("Literary Notes," *I*, XLVI [14 Je 1894], 771). These exaggerations led to mistaken conceptions. Anna Mary Wells, *Dear Preceptor* (Boston, 1963), p. 290, still overstates the total sales as 19,000 copies of both series by the summer of 1894. A combined edition—*Poems by Emily Dickinson: First and Second Series*—was published in 1893 (500 copies) and was enlarged two years later by 500 more.

7. "Poems by Emily Dickinson," *LW*, XXII (19 De 1891), 486.

8. "Books and Bookmen," *Light*, IV (5 De 1891), 322.

9. "Second Series of the Poems of Emily Dickinson," *The Chicago Tribune*, 12 De 1891.

10. "So from the realistic literature of the age, the 'novels written with a purpose,' the poems metrically correct and unimpeachable as to rhyme, it is pleasure to turn to the verse of one who wrote without the ever-present fear of critic's condemnation" ("Emily Dickinson's Poems, Second Series," *ARec*, 2 De 1891).—"It is a relief to turn to the writings of Mr. Gilder. His thoughts are not the less fresh and significant for being subdued to the usages of musical rhythm" ("Poetry," *The Congregationalist*, LXXV [31 De 1891], 459).

11. "The Literary Wayside," *SRep*, 8 No 1891.

12. "Emily Dickinson's Poems," *The Boston Budget*, 15 No 1891.

13. "Talk about New Books," *CW*, LIV (De 1891), 448.

14. "Miss Dickinson's Poems," *Boston Courier*, 22 No 1891; "Poems by Emily Dickinson," *CR*, LXX (31 De 1891), 868-69.

15. "Recent Verse," *The Overland Monthly*, XIX (Fe 1892), 218-19; "Poems by Emily Dickinson," *World*, 6 De 1891.

16. "Recent Poetry and Verse," *C*, XIX (19 De 1891), 346.

17. "Recent Poetry," *N*, LIII (15 Oc 1891), 297; "Library and Foyer," *BTr*, 9 De 1891; "A Second Series of Remarkable Poems," *Boston Traveller*, 28 No 1891.

18. "Talk about Books," *The Chautauquan*, XIV (Ja 1892), 509-10; "Volumes of Poems," *BB*, VIII (Ja 1892), 650-51; "Recent Books of Verse," *The Christian Union*, XLV (18 Je 1892), 1212.

19. Moses Coit Tyler, *A History of American Literature, 1607-1765* (New York, 1878), I, 282.

20. Henry Park Schauffler, "Second Edition of Emily Dickinson's Poems," *The Amherst Literary Monthly*, VI (No 1891), 179; "Emily Dickinson," *Light*, IV (12 De 1891), 349; Arthur Chamberlain, "Emily Dickinson—Poet and Woman," *Boston Commonwealth*, XXXI (20 Fe 1892), 6-7.

21. Arlo Bates, "Literary Affairs in Boston," *BB*, VIII (No 1891), 417.

22. Francis H. Stoddard, "Technique in Emily Dickinson's Poem's," *C*, XX (9 Ja 1892), 24-25. The author (1847-1936), who came from Middlebury, Vt., had attended Amherst College and was a specialist in the areas of English linguistics and Middle English poetry.

23. Thomas Wentworth Higginson, *The New World and the New Book* (Boston, 1891), p. i; Andrew Lang, "A Patriotic Critic," *The Illustrated London News*, C (2 Ja 1892), 14-15.

24. William Belmont Parker in *DAB*, s.v. "Aldrich, Thomas Bailey."

25. *Unguarded Gates and Other Poems* (Boston, 1895), p. 72; *The Poems of Thomas Bailey Aldrich*, Household Edition (Boston, 1887), p. 222.

26. Thomas Bailey Aldrich, "*In Re* Emily Dickinson," *AM*, LXIX (Ja 1892), 143-44.

27. This promptly yielded him a female protest. In a Boston woman's rights journal, to which Higginson had contributed articles for many years, Ellen Battelle Dietrick objected: "It is very much to be hoped, in the interests of good taste and of justice, that a generation of writers will some day arise, a larger proportion of whom can review the intellectual products of a woman without constant reference to her sex. Such an allusion as that in the last *Atlantic* 'Contributor's Club' is offensive to the last degree" ("One-Sided Criticism," *The Woman's Journal*, XXIII [16 Ja 1892], 18).

28. Molly Elliot Seawell, "On the Absence of the Creative Faculty in Women," *C*, XIX (28 No 1891), 292-94; C.M.E., "To the Editors of the Critic," *C*, XX (13 Fe 1892), 105; Molly Elliot Seawell, " 'The Lilliputian Theory of Woman,' " *C*, XXI (16 Jl 1892), 35-36; Andrew Lang in *The London Daily News*, quoted in *C*, XXI (27 Au 1892), 112. Higginson's objection to Miss Seawell's ideas had been the fourth chapter ("The Lilliputian Theory of Woman") of his collection of essays *Concerning All of Us* (New York, 1892).

29. Genevieve B. Earle, "'Some Watcher of the Skies,'" *The Book Collector's Packet*, III (Mr 1939), 11. "Landon" seems to refer to the New York humorist Melville de Lancey Landon (1839-1910).

30. Daniel Dulany Addison, *Lucy Larcom: Life, Letters, and Diary* (Boston, 1894), p. 285.

31. "A Melancholy Fidelity" (*Commercial Advertiser*, 23 Au 1893), by Grace Herbert Smith, a childhood acquaintance of the poet living in Chicago, identified George Howland (1824-92), who had been superintendent of public schools in Chicago until 1891, as Emily Dickinson's lover. He had studied at Amherst College and had subsequently been tutor there from 1852 to 1855.

CHAPTER IV

1. "The Third of the Gray Sisters," *Chicago Journal*, 26 Se 1896.

2. Florence S. Hoyt, "Intelligent Sociability," *The Congregationalist*, LXXVIII (2 Mr 1893), 337-38; James Warwick Price, "The Poetry of Emily Dickinson," *The Yale Literary Magazine*, LIX (Oc 1893), 25-27; G., "A Connecticut Valley Poet," *Homestead*, XVI (6 Oc 1894), 11; Ellen E. Dickinson, "Emily Dickinson," *BTr*, 28 Se 1894.

3. The sale was slower than in the case of the poems. The first edition of 1000 copies was followed in December 1894 by a second of 1500 of which 1200 were still unsold in 1898. From 1906 to 1924, Little, Brown published several one-volume reprints. Cf. *AB*, pp. 414-15.

4. "Emily Dickinson's Letters," *NYTr*, 20 Ja 1895; [Mary Abbott], "Emily Dickinson's Poems [*sic*]," *The Chicago Times-Herald*, 8 De 1894; "Along the Literary Wayside," *SRep*, 2 De 1894.

5. W. F. Wetcho, "Letters of Emily Dickinson," *Boston Daily Advertiser*, 23 No 1894.

6. Caroline Healy Dall, "Emily Dickinson's Letters," *BTr*, 22 De 1894.

7. "Books and Authors," *O*, LI (23 Mr 1895), 481.

8. "A Thought of God," *Boston Home Journal*, VIII (24 No 1894), 5; "A New England Nun," *The Telegraph* (Philadelphia), 7 De 1894.

9. [Mary Augusta Jordan], "Emily Dickinson's Letters," *N*, LIX (13 De 1894), 446-47.

10. "New Books," *The Spy*, 2 De 1894.

11. "Letters of Emily Dickinson," *LW*, xxv (15 De 1894), 445-46.

12. "A New England Recluse," *SFChr*, 30 De 1894.

13. Jordan in *N;* "Letters of Emily Dickinson," *Evening Bulletin* (Philadelphia), 15 De 1894.

14. "Letters of Emily Dickinson," *C,* xxvi (16 Fe 1895), 119; "Letters of Emily Dickinson," *CR,* lxxiv (12 Ap 1895), 234; Mary J. Reid, "Julia C. Dorr and Some of Her Poet Contemporaries," *The Midland Monthly,* iii (Je 1895), 505-6; "Letters of Emily Dickinson," *BHer,* 26 No 1894; "Letters of Emily Dickinson," *The Evangelist,* lxv (29 No 1894), 16.

15. "Emily Dickinson's Letters," *The Congregationalist,* lxxxi (27 No 1894), 973-74.

16. Louis J. Block, "A New England Nun," *The Dial,* xviii (1 Mr 1895), 146-47.

17. Chelifer [= Rupert Hughes], "Sappho, and Other Princesses of Poetry," *Godey's Magazine,* cxxxii (Ja 1896), 94.

18. "Six Books of Verse," *AM,* lxxvii (Fe 1896), 271, and "Recent Poetry," *N,* lxi (24 Oc 1895), 296.

19. Tabb's poem, like Emily Dickinson's in eight lines, read:

THE HUMMING-BIRD

A flash of harmless lightning,
    A mist of rainbow dyes,
The burnished sunbeams brightening
    From flower to flower he flies;
While wakes the nodding blossom
    But just too late to see
What lip has touched her bosom
    And drained her rosary.

20. "Recent American Poetry," *N,* lx (23 May 1895), 402.

21. "Chronicle and Comment," *B,* iii (Au 1896), 498. Roberts Brothers had had their Dickinson volumes printed by Harvard University Press.

22. *Letters—Grave and Gay and Other Prose of John Banister Tabb,* ed. Francis E. Litz (Washington, 1950), pp. 94, 140.

23. The first printing of 1000 copies was followed on September 21, 1896, by a second. From 1898 to 1923 Little, Brown issued several small reprints. The entire edition can be estimated at 3500 copies.

24. Of the following numbers, the first refers to the page in *Poems* (1896), the second to the number in *Poems* (1955), the third to the line(s): 181 (947); 101 (342); 199 (445). The other examples are: 76 (756) 14; 79 (31) 6; 60 (1203) 3; 179 (272) 1; 133 (290) 8-9.

25. [Thomas Wentworth Higginson], "Recent Poetry," *N,* lxiii (8 Oc 1896), 275.

26. "Literary Notes," *NYTr*, 23 Au 1896.

27. "Aftermath of Emily Dickinson's Verse," *The Telegraph*, 19 Se 1896; Clarence Griffin Child, "Poems by Emily Dickinson," *The Citizen* (Philadelphia), III (May 1897), 61-62; Mary Abbott, "Emily Dickinson's Poems," *The Chicago Times-Herald*, 26 Se 1896; "The Third Series of Emily Dickinson's Poems," *LW*, XXVIII (31 Oc 1896), 361.

28. "Recent Verse," *The Overland Monthly*, XXX (Au 1897), 190; E.R.C., "Emily Dickinson," *Sun*, n.d. (clipping in the Jones Library, Amherst); Lilian Whiting, "Life in Boston," *Inter Ocean*, 26 Se 1896.

29. The use of native themes was a serious matter to Higginson. When Louise Chandler Moulton had a poem published (in *The Century Magazine* in September, 1894) in which the nightingale and lark appeared, he regarded it as a throwback into "the colonial attitude, as to the out-door setting of her poems. The colonial attitude in America was . . . to treat birds and flowers as things not existing in themselves, but only in literature; so that it was the duty of every person of English descent to carry the nightingale and the skylark with him in all works of imagination. Lowell struggled 50 years to get the bobolink and the oriole established in literature; Emerson, the chikadee, Whittier the veery. At a later period, Emily Dickinson added the blue jay." Thomas Wentworth Higginson, "A Step Backward," *The Chap-Book*, I (15 Oc 1894), 332.

30. Bliss Carman, "A Note on Emily Dickinson," *BTr*, 21 No 1896.

31. Harry Lyman Koopman, "Emily Dickinson," *Brown Magazine*, VIII (De 1896), 81-86. Koopman (1860-1937), who hailed from Freeport, Me., studied at Harvard, worked from 1893 to 1930 as librarian at Brown University, and published three volumes of poems.

32. Chelifer [= Rupert Hughes], "The Ideas of Miss Dickinson," *Godey's Magazine*, CXXXIII (No 1896), 541-43. Hughes (1872-1956) became a well-known novelist and playwright.

CHAPTER V

1. *An American Anthology, 1787-1900*, ed. Edmund Clarence Stedman (Boston, 1900), p. xxxii.

2. M.S. McKinney, "In the Twilight of Poetry," *The Saturday Evening Post*, CLXXI (31 De 1898), 426; Jessie B. Rittenhouse, *The Younger American Poets* (Boston, 1904), p. 34; Frederic G. Melcher, "A Boston Bookstore at the Turn of the Century," *Proceedings of the American Antiquarian Society*, LXVI, part 1 (1956), 46-47; O.S., "The Slump in Poets," *Punch*, CXXVIII (25 Ja 1905), 56.

3. Gertrude Atherton, "Why Is American Literature Bourgeois?" *The North American Review,* CLXXVIII (1904), 722.

4. In 1898 Stedman and Aldrich were the leading poets. Cf. "Our Two Most Honored Poets," *AM,* LXXXI (Ja 1898), 136-39. None the less, a few years later this generation to which Higginson (and Emily Dickinson) also belonged was as good as forgotten.

5. Jack London, *The Sea-Wolf* (New York, 1904), pp. 197-98; Frank Norris, *The Octopus: A Story of California* (Garden City, 1901), pp. 61, 9.

6. "Drei Seiten lassen sich aus allen Handbüchern zusammenstellen." —Hans-Joachim Lang, *Studien zur Entstehung der neueren amerikanischen Literaturkritik* (Hamburg, 1961), p. 51.

7. Edmund Clarence Stedman, *Poets of America* (Boston, 1885), p. 448.

8. Julian W. Abernethy, *American Literature* (New York, 1902), p. 206; "this group" refers to the Transcendentalists.

9. Alphonso G. Newcomer, *American Literature* (Chicago, 1901), pp. 288-89.

10. Katharine Lee Bates, *American Literature* (New York, 1897), pp. 178-79.

11. Walter C. Bronson, *A Short History of American Literature* (Boston, 1900), p. 285.

12. Thomas Wentworth Higginson and Henry Walcott Boynton, *A Reader's History of American Literature* (Boston, 1903), pp. 130-31.

13. William J. Long, *American Literature* (Boston, 1913), p. 456; Reuben Post Halleck, *History of American Literature* (New York, 1911), p. 404; William B. Cairns, *A History of American Literature* (New York, 1912), p. 466.

14. Fred Lewis Pattee, *A History of American Literature since 1870* (New York, 1915), pp. 340-41.

15. Barrett Wendell, *A Literary History of America* (New York, 1900), p. 462.

16. Percy H. Boynton, *Literature and American Life* (Boston, 1936), p. 690.

17. "Es soll in der Literaturgeschichte immer alles so nett und sauber etikettirt sein, wie in einer Apotheke. . . .
    "Emily Dickinson musste so schreiben, wie sie schrieb—um das zu werden, was sie ist: die einzigartigste Dichterin, die Amerika bis jetzt hervorgebracht hat." A.E., "Emily Dickinson," *Der Westen* (Chicago,), 12 and 19 Je 1898.

18. *"In Re* Emily Dickinson" appeared as "Un Poète manqué" in *The Writings of Thomas Bailey Aldrich* (Boston, 1903), IX, 83-86.

19. "Recent Verse" (*The Athenaeum*, no. 4036 [4 Mr 1905], 269-70) is the only (polite, but cool) review of this reprint which I have been able to find.

20. James Fullarton Muirhead, *The Land of Contrasts: A Briton's View of His American Kin* (Boston, 1898), pp. 186, 184; John Churton Collins, *Studies in Poetry and Criticism* (London, 1905), p. 75.

21. W. J. Dawson, "American Books That Have Moved Me," *The Congregationalist and Christian World*, CXI (4 De 1909), 779-80. He had already mentioned the poet with praise in his *The Makers of English Poetry*, new and rev. ed. (New York, 1906), p. 404.

22. Frederick J. Pohl, Jr., "The Poetry of Emily Dickinson," *The Amherst Monthly*, XXV (May 1910), 47-50, 48.

23. James Warwick Price, "Three Forgotten Poetesses," *The Forum*, XLII (Mr 1912), 361-66; Martha Hale Shackford, "The Poetry of Emily Dickinson," *AM*, CXI (Ja 1913), 93-97. The author was a professor at Wellesley and a specialist in Middle English, Renaissance, and nineteenth-century literature.

CHAPTER VI

1. Edna St. Vincent Millay's poem "Renascence," which appeared for the first time in *The Lyric Year: One Hundred Poems*, ed. Ferdinand Earle (New York, 1912), pp. 180-88, gave the literary movement after 1910 its name "little renaissance." Horace Gregory and Marya Zaturenska (*A History of American Poetry, 1900-1940* [New York, 1942], pp. 141, 147) use the term "poetic renaissance," which they apply to the decade following 1912.

2. Ethel M. Colson, "The Single Hound," *The Chicago Herald*, 10 Oc 1914.

3. *The Single Hound: Poems of a Lifetime*, ed. Martha Dickinson Bianchi (Boston, 1914), pp. v-vi.

4. Elizabeth Shepley Sergeant, "An Early Imagist," *NR*, IV (14 Au 1914), 52-54.

5. H. M. [Harriet Monroe], "The Single Hound," *Poetry*, V (De 1914), 138-40.

6. F. W. Burrows, "The Single Hound," *The New England Magazine*, LII (De 1914), 165-66.

7. The third quotation is from J.J.D., "The Single Hound," *America*, XII (2 Ja 1915), 299-300.

8. "Both geographical and grammatical peculiarities are lost sight of in consideration of such lines as these . . . ." (Elia W. Peattie, "Muse Not Drowned Out by War Sounds," *The Chicago Tribune*, 10 Oc 1914).—"The poems are thoroughly spontaneous, true fragments of personality. Form seems to have been a wholly secondary consideration—sometimes the verses rhyme, sometimes not; even grammar is not too slavishly regarded." ("Poets Who Must or Who May Write," *NYTBR*, xx [19 Se 1915], 333).— W.S.B. [William Stanley Braithwaite], "Poems of a Life-Time," *BTr*, 30 Se 1914.

9. Stanley J. Kunitz and Howard Haycraft, *Twentieth Century Authors* (New York, 1942), p. 1049.

10. Robert Hillyer, "Emily Dickinson," *The Freeman*, vi (18 Oc 1922), 129-31.

11. Cf. Zoltan Haraszti, "An Emily Dickinson Collection," *BTr*, 8 De 1923.

12. Robert Hillyer, *A Letter to Robert Frost and Others* (New York, 1937), p. 4. The "friend in Sevenels" is, of course, Amy Lowell.

13. Martha Dickinson Bianchi, "Selections from the Unpublished Letters of Emily Dickinson to Her Brother's Family: Chosen and Arranged by Her Niece," *AM*, cxv (Ja 1915), 35-42, 36.

14. Jenkins had written in his reminiscence of October 24, 1891: "As I passed the corner of the house, Miss Emily called me. She was standing on a rug spread for her on the grass, busy with the potted plants which were all about her."—Gamaliel Bradford, "Emily Dickinson," *AM*, cxxiv (Au 1919), 216-26. Bradford (1863-1932) used Taine's term "psychograph" for his biographical sketches which are "condensed, essentially artistic presentations of character. . . . Out of the perpetual flux of actions and circumstances that constitute a man's whole life, it seeks to extract what is essential." Quoted in Kunitz and Haycraft, *op. cit.*, pp. 175-76.

15. Marsden Hartley, "Emily Dickinson," *The Dial*, lxv (Au 1918), 95-97. The parenthetical figures in the text here refer to the pages of this article.

16. Marsden Hartley, *Adventures in the Arts*, ed. Waldo Frank (New York, 1921), p. xvi.

16a. Robert Hillyer, "Emily Dickinson," *The Freeman*, vi (18 Oc 1922), 129-31.

17. Herbert Gorman, *The Procession of Masks* (Boston, 1923), pp. 43-54.

18. Concerning the tripartition of writers into an "Elder" (More, Babbitt), "Middle" (Spingarn, Brooks, Mencken, Dreiser, O'Neill,

Sandburg, Amy Lowell, Masters) and "Younger Generation" (Hemingway, Cummings, Tate and others) see Gorham B. Munson, *Destinations: A Canvas of American Literature since 1900* (New York, 1928), pp. 2-3.

19. Cf. Gorman's autobiographical chapter "My Education," *op. cit.*, pp. 255-70.

19a. Gorman, *op. cit.*, p. 51.

20. Kenneth Slade Alling, "Declaration," *The Measure*, no. 22 (De 1922), 15-16.

21. Amy Lowell, *Tendencies in Modern American Poetry* (New York, 1917); Louis Untermeyer, *The New Era in American Poetry* (New York, 1919); Conrad Aiken, *Skepticisms: Notes on Contemporary Poetry* (New York, 1919).

22. Cf. Aiken's chapter of the same title. Aiken was the first to admit flatly the existence of the *pro domo* standpoint in criticism: "If you examine carefully the writings of any poet-critic you will find, a trace here and a trace there, the gradual emergence of a self-portrait; and one which is only too apt to be heroic size." *Op. cit.*, pp. 19 and 23.

23. Untermeyer, *op. cit.*, pp. 6, 9, 10.

24. Untermeyer, *op. cit.*, pp. 5, 7. In the first chapter (" 'Highbrow' and 'Lowbrow' ") of his study, which did not remain inconsequential for Dickinson criticism, Brooks advanced the thesis that the American character, still "compact in one type" in the seventeenth century, had split in the eighteenth. The irreconcilable poles, which are marked by antitheses like Edwards–Franklin, "piety"–"advertisement," "theory"–"practice," "professor"–"businessman," have since not made possible a "genial middle ground." The axiom propounded at the beginning of the second chapter (" 'Our Poets' ")—"that a society whose end is impersonal and antisocial cannot produce an ideal reflex in literature which is personal and social, and conversely, that the ideal reflex produced in literature by such a society will be unable to educate its own personal and social instincts"—is demonstrated in the cases of Lowell, Bryant, Poe, Hawthorne, Emerson, and Lowell. The new fusion described in the third chapter ("The Precipitant") was attained for the first time by Whitman and the tradition which proceeded from him. Quoted according to the Doubleday Anchor Books edition, pp. 3, 5, 24.

25. S. Foster Damon, *Amy Lowell: A Chronicle* (Boston, 1935), pp. 295-96.

26. Damon, *op. cit.*, pp. 331-32.

27. Damon, *op. cit.*, p. 92. Amy Lowell could never stand Higginson. "Mild, sweet-tempered, sympathetic, and stupid Mr. Higginson!" she exclaimed in her lecture *(ibid.)*. On August 9, 1922, she wrote to Mrs. Todd: "There is not, to my mind, a sadder story in history than the picture of good, well-meaning Mr. Higginson trying to guide Emily Dickinson's marvelous genius" *(ibid.,* p. 611).

28. "3. To allow absolute freedom in the choice of subject. . . . 4. To present an image . . . . We are not a school of painters, but we believe that poetry should render particulars exactly, and not deal in vague generalities, however magnificent and sonorous." Quoted according to the expanded version in the introduction to *Some Imagist Poets* (1915), which was written by Richard Aldington with the help of other Imagists.

29. Amy Lowell, *Poetry and Poets* (Boston, 1930), pp. 102-3.

30. Lowell, *op. cit.,* p. 107.

31. The imitations of John Gould Fletcher (in Amy Lowell's *Tendencies,* p. 340), D.H. Lawrence (*B*, LVIII [Ja 1924], 569), and Amy Lowell herself (*B*, LIX [May 1924], 277) prove what a strong impression this poem made on the Imagists.

32. *A Critical Fable* by a Poker of Fun (Boston, 1922), p. 7.

33. Amy Lowell, *What's o'Clock* (Boston, 1925), p. 136. The poem was first published in *The North American Review*, CCXV (Je 1922), 785-89.

34. Emily's relationships with the other members of the family was to have been the main theme. Amy Lowell had already established contact with Mrs. Todd and begun to collect material. Cf. *AB*, p. 111, and Damon, *op. cit.,* pp. 611-12.

35. *Modern American Poets*, ed. Conrad Aiken (London, 1922), p. viii.

36. *The New Poetry: An Anthology of Twentieth-Century Verse in English*, ed. Harriet Monroe and Alice Corbin Henderson, rev. and enlarged ed. (New York, 1923), p. xlvi.

37. *Century Readings for a Course in American Literature*, ed. Fred Lewis Pattee (New York, 1920), p. 586.

38. *The Cambridge History of American Literature*, ed. William Peterfield Trent *et al.* (New York, 1921), III, 31-32, 34.

39. J.J.D., in *America*, 2 Ja 1915.

40. Willard Wattles, "The Bench *(In Memory of Emily Dickinson)*," *AGQ*, VI (May 1917), 185; "Letters to Dead Imagists," *Chicago Poems* (New York, 1916), p. 176.

CHAPTER VII

1. Genevieve Taggard, "Emily Dickinson," *N*, cxix (8 Oc 1924), 378.

2. Quoted in Burton Rascoe, *A Bookman's Daybook*, ed. C. Hartley Grattan (New York, 1929), pp. 5, 299.

3. Malcolm Cowley, *Exile's Return: A Literary Odyssey of the 1920's* (New York, 1934), p. 176.

4. The second printing was published in May 1924, the third in October 1924, the fourth in August 1925, the fifth in July 1929, the sixth in November 1929, the seventh in July 1930. After the sixth printing the sales had reached 6270 copies.

5. The first edition of *The Complete Poems* (2000 copies) appeared on July 2, 1924, the second (1000 copies) on September 8, 1924, the third (2000 copies) on November 3, 1924. The total printing before mid-1930 can be estimated at 12,500 copies. A pocketbook edition (2000 copies) was published on October 11, 1926. The London edition was distributed at the end of March 1925 by Secker; a pocketbook edition followed in 1928.

6. Martin Armstrong, "The Poetry of Emily Dickinson," *The Spectator*, cxxx (6 Ja 1923), 22-23, and Herbert S. Gorman, *The Procession of Masks* (Boston, 1923), p. 47.

7. Conrad Aiken, "The Dickinson Scandal," *NR*, cxiii (2 Jl 1945), 25.

8. Stephen Vincent Benét, "Emily Dickinson's Biography," *B*, lix (Au 1924), 732.

9. Rolfe Humphries, "A Retouched Portrait," *The Measure*, no. 39 (May 1924), 13.

10. Katharine Lee Bates, "The House of Rose," *YR*, xiv (Ja 1925), 399.

11. Arthur W. Colton, "The Enchanting Emily," *New York Evening Post Literary Review*, iv (31 May 1924), 788; Newton Arvin, "Books," *The Commonweal*, i (25 Mr 1925), 552-53.

12. Herbert S. Gorman, "Life and Letters of a Gentle New England Poet," *NYTBR*, xxix (13 Ap 1924), 7.

13. Kathérine Brégy, "Emily Dickinson," *CW*, cxx (De 1924), 346.

14. Martha Dickinson Bianchi, "Emily Dickinson," *SRL*, i (2 Au 1924), 20.

15. F.M., "Emily Dickinson's Poems," *CSM*, xvi (21 Jl 1924), 11.

16. Edmund Lester Pearson, "Two Poets," *O*, cxxxvii (23 Jl 1924), 479; E. Merrill Root, "Clothes vs. Girl," *The Measure*, no. 39 (May 1924), 15-18; G.F.W[hicher], "The Book Table," *AGQ*, xiv (May 1925), 206-7.

17. "She may one day be a recovered glory of America as we see Blake figuring in Britain. But her claims to rank and merit are still disputed." "Our Poetical New England Nun," *The Literary Digest*, LXXXII (2 Au 1924), 34. Colton wrote: "She was not lyrical enough to be a great lyric poet, but it is rather more than probable that she will be talked of more hereafter than heretofore."

18. Allen Nevins, quoted in *The Literary Digest* (cf. note 17).

19. Edward Sapir, "Emily Dickinson, a Primitive," *Poetry*, XXVI (May 1925), 98-99, 100.

20. Whicher, *op. cit.*, p. 207. Cf. Howard Mumford Jones's similar opinion in "Great American Poetess," *The New Student*, VII (4 Ja 1928), 12: "She is the last expression of the classic New England spirit, and her verse is already big with prophecy of the modern world."

21. Ethel Parton, "Emily Dickinson," *O*, CXXXVI (23 Ap 1924), 701-2.

22. J.M.T., "Selected Poems of Emily Dickinson," *The Vote* (London), 28 No 1924, 382.

23. Harold Monro, "Selected Poems of Emily Dickinson," *The Criterion*, III (Ja 1925), 322-23.

24. "An American Poetess," *TLS*, XXIII (30 Oc 1924), 673-74.

25. Susan Miles, "The Irregularities of Emily Dickinson," *LM*, XIII (De 1925), 145-58. The identity of the author writing under the pseudonym Susan Miles has remained a mystery—even to J. C. Squire, the editor of the journal.

26. Cf. especially the following statements: "Even in 1847 we had our dissident minority, our individualist protesting against the pressure of the group. This condition, too, has persisted, and recent dissenters—if it were their wont to look for precedent—might well claim spiritual kinship with Emily Dickinson. For she was to show herself absolute individualist." Lois Leighton Comings, "Emily Dickinson," *MHAQ*, VIII (Oc 1924), 133.
    "Three quarters of a century later it is still possible to see the hazard of her undertaking. America, after all, is in very much the same state of mind now that it was in then. It is easier than not—just as it was then—to participate in the opinion of the majority. . . . Today the Puritans happen to be the 'outs'; the majority is fixed in its belief that nothing Puritan was ever important. In Emily Dickinson's day the Puritans happened to be the 'ins'; the majority was just as fixed in its belief that everything Puritan had always been important." Rollo Walter Brown, *Lonely Americans* (New York, 1929), pp. 236-37.

27. According to Tate, the solution to her personal riddle lay in her

rejection of the world: "Her seclusion was the fulfillment of her life. All pity for Miss Dickinson's 'starved life' is misdirected. Her life was one of the deepest, one of the richest ever lived out on this continent. She is one of the few Americans who have realized themselves." Her love affair was only a pretext. "She would have found another. . . . It was probably not an accident that her lover was a married man." Tate's essay ("Emily Dickinson," O, CXLIX [15 Au 1928], 621-23) was "one in a series of papers on American literary figures in the light of contemporary criticism." Other writers discussed in the series were Poe, Longfellow, and Hawthorne.

28. Lucy Humphrey Smith, "The Mystery of Emily Dickinson's Life," *The Literary Digest International Book Review*, II (Jl 1924), 587-88; Clara Bellinger Green, "A Reminiscence of Emily Dickinson," *B*, LX (No 1924), 291-93; Lawrence F. Abbott, "Emily Dickinson," *O*, CXL (Je 1925), 211-13.

29. Percival Hunt, H. W. Schornberger, and Frederick P. Mayer, *A Series of Radio Talks on Some Writers of Older New England*, Radio Publication, no. 36 (Pittsburgh, 1928), pp. 48-56; R. Ellis Roberts, *Reading for Pleasure and Other Essays* (London, 1928), pp. 185-90.

30. "Recent Books in Brief Review," *B*, LVIII (Fe 1924), 669.

31. (New York, 1924.)

32. "*À bas* the New Englanders! is his cry; they have been praised too much, so he will refuse them even bare justice." "Poets of America," *O*, CXL (15 Jl 1925), 506.

33. (New York, 1925.)

34. "That fumigation of the vocabulary, which eradicates all poetic left-overs of dead speech, is hers in high degree. An occasional inversion or retreat into the solemn style is found; but she was far too faithful to reality to parrot moribund twitter compound of *athwart, welkin, yestreen, amaranth, asphodel* . . . . So distrustful was she of stock poeticisms, that she fled even from the tinkle of accurate rhyme." *Ibid.*, p. 93.

35. (New York, 1929). The critical voices were scathing. See Eda Lou Walton in *N*, CXXX (29 Ja 1930), 132; Theodore Baird in *SRL*, VI (15 Fe 1930), 731; Allen Tate in *NR*, LXII (26 Fe 1930), 51-52. Kreymborg himself had warned his readers in a "Preliminary Confession": "I cannot surmount a stubborn conviction that the subconscious temper of the beholder colors the thing beheld. Nor can I resist the commentary: this is as it should be" (*op. cit.*, p. 2).

36. (New York, 1925.)

37. To explain the literature after 1860, Ernest Erwin Leisy, *American Literature: An Introduction* (New York, 1929), makes use of the

pair of terms developed by John Livingston Lowes in *Conven-tion and Revolt in Poetry* (Boston, 1919). Emily Dickinson, who is seen by Leisy through the eyes of the older literary historians, is a conventional poet, but at the same time initiated a revolt. She is both "one 'last pale Indian-summer flower of Puritanism'" (p. 218) and a precursor of the Imagists (pp. 219, 224).

38. Fred Lewis Pattee, *The New American Literature* (New York, 1930).

39. Rollo Walter Brown, "A Sublimated Puritan," *SRL*, v (6 Oc 1928), 186-87; reprinted in *Lonely Americans*, pp. 233-57. Matthew Josephson, *Portrait of the Artist as American* (New York, 1930).

40. The thesis that the *malheur d'être poète* was a specifically American exigency caused dissent among the critics. Allen W. Potterfield (*O*, CLV [21 May 1930], 103-4) accused Josephson of unfairness toward his country; Henry Hazlitt (*N*, CXXX [28 May 1930], 627-28) found the thesis credible; Harold Loeb (*SRL*, VI [17 May 1930], 1041-43) declared that the author was suffering from a persecution complex.

CHAPTER VIII

1. Rolfe Humphries, "Too Difficult a Grace," *NR*, LIX (22 May 1929), 40.

2. "150 Poems by Emily Dickinson Discovered: Sister Had Suppressed Them 40 Years Ago," *NYTimes*, 25 Ja 1929.

3. Examples are *Further Poems*, p. 64 (*Poems*, no. 591), line 1; 105 (610) 1; 130 (262) 7; 66 (703) 11.

4. Conrad Aiken, "Emily Dickinson and Her Editors," *YR*, XVIII (Summer 1929), 797.

5. Clara Bellinger Green, "Emily Dickinson," *BTr*, 13 Jl 1929; Anna Mary Wells, "Further Poems of Emily Dickinson," *MHAQ*, XIII (Jl 1929), 78-81; Jessica Nelson North, "Building a Legend," *Poetry*, XXXV (De 1929), 165.

6. Louis Untermeyer, "Colossal Substance," *SRL*, v (16 Mr 1929), 769-70.

7. The letter was later published in *AB*, pp. 87-88.

8. Theodore Spencer, "Book Reviews," *NEQ*, II (Jl 1929), 498-501; Robert Hillyer, "Further Poems of Emily Dickinson," *AM*, CXLIII (Ap 1929), 16, 18. Madame Bianchi compelled the editors of *The Outlook and Independent* to retract a deprecatory review written by Clara Bellinger Green (*O*, CLI, 669, 680). When the same critic once again massively attacked *Further Poems* in the *Boston Transcript* on July 13, 1929, she induced her coeditor to make a public protest (*BTr*, 3 Au 1929).

9. Alfred Kreymborg, "Emily Dickinson: A New Book by the Immortal Tippler," *Sun*, 16 Mr 1929; Percy Hutchison, "Further Poems of That Shy Recluse, Emily Dickinson," *NYTBR*, xxxiv (17 Mr 1929), 3; Helen Cary Chadwick, "Emily Dickinson: A Study," *The Personalist*, x (Oc 1929), 267; Babette Deutsch, "A Sojourn in Infinity," *B*, lxix (May 1929), 305.

10. Mark Van Doren, "Nerves Like Tombs," *N*, cxxviii (20 Mr 1929), 348-49.

11. Lewis Mumford, "Pan's Sister," *NYHTB*, v (17 Mr 1929), 16.

12. A.R.H., "Poet, Mystic, Martyr," *CR*, cviii (2 May 1929), 370.

13. [Elizabeth McCausland], "A Poet's Qualities," *SRep*, 24 Mr 1929.

14. Catherine Tolles, "The Fire and Dew of Emily Dickinson," *The Mount Holyoke Monthly*, xxxvii (Ap 1930), 209-22.

15. "*Mercy Philbrick's Choice* could scarcely have been written by a Helen unaware of Emily's love story. The book was the work of one stirred partly by an impulse to strike at Emily, though it showed a largeness of nature and a generous comprehension" (141, cf. 273-86). The names are distributed accordingly: Penfield = Amherst, Mercy = Emily, Stephen White = Edward Hunt, Parson Dorrance = Wadsworth.

16. In 1930 critics presumed that Mrs. Todd was behind "Mrs. X." This suggestion was obvious but incorrect. The information was supplied by Mary Lee Hall, an Amherst citizen. Cf. Jay Leyda, *The Years and Hours of Emily Dickinson* (New Haven, 1960), I, 177.

17. (Boston, 1930.)

18. Jenkins was in Madame Bianchi's good graces and he, for his part, paid unrestricted tribute to her biographical sketch of 1924: "Already her niece has given us a detailed, authoritative and altogether delightful biography, written with unerring taste and discrimination . . ." (142-43).

19. "It is indeed the object of this slender volume to dispel, if possible, some of this cloud of fable and make Miss Emily a more human and more understandable person" (90). This is exactly what Jenkins did not, and could not, achieve. He had only a few short letters by the poet.

20. George F. Whicher, "Emily's Lover," *NYHTB*, vi (2 Mr 1930), 2; Conrad Aiken, "The Dickinson Scandal," *YR*, xx (Winter 1930), 393-96; Granville Hicks, "Mystery and Mystification," *N*, cxxx (25 Je 1930), 735-36.

21. R. N. Linscott, "Emily Dickinson," *B*, lxxi (Ap-May 1930), 228; Louis Untermeyer, "Emily Dickinson," *SRL*, vi (5 Jl 1930), 1170.

22. Frances Lamont Robbins, "The Week's Reading," *O*, CLV (25 Je 1930), 307.

23. Mabel Loomis Todd, "Miss Taggard's Emily," *SRL*, VII (6 Se 1930), 99.

24. *AL*, I (No 1929), 243-59.

25. *HM*, CLX (Mr 1930), 463-71.

26. Alfred Leete Hampson, *Emily Dickinson: A Bibliography* (Northampton, Mass., 1930), p. 31; *Emily Dickinson: A Bibliography*, with a foreword by George F. Whicher (Amherst, 1930).

27. "Of the authors who are likely to be considered in such an election there immediately come to mind the names of Walt Whitman, whose omission has been widely commented on, Herman Melville, Henry David Thoreau, Bret Harte, Emily Dickinson and John Hay." "New names for the Hall of Fame," *PW*, CXVII (8 Mr 1930), 1136. Only Whitman was elected. By 1965 only Lanier (1945) and Thoreau (1955) had been added.

28. W.T. [Worth Tuttle] wrote his sketch for the fourteenth edition of the *Encyclopaedia Britannica* (New York, 1929) essentially with the help of *Life and Letters* which is why it is one-sided and contains incorrect dates and misinformation. Whicher's summary in *DAB* is critical.

29. Genevieve Taggard, "A Little 'Scholar' of 1848," *Journal of Adult Education*, II (Ja 1930), 75-76.

29a. Hicks, *op. cit.*, p. 736.

30. Babette Deutsch, "Emily Dickinson Again," *NR*, LXIII (9 Jl 1930), 211-12.

31. J. C. Squire, "Editorial Notes," *LM*, XIX (Fe 1929), 337; "Emily Dickinson," *John o'London's Weekly*, XXIII (30 Au 1930), 724.

32. V. R. Friedlaender, "Emily Dickinson," *Country Life*, LXVI (26 Oc 1929), 565.

33. J. C. Squire, "Emily Dickinson," *The Observer*, CXXXVIII (13 Oc 1929), 6.

34. Quoted in *SRL*, VI (10 May 1930), 1030.

CHAPTER IX

1. Genevieve Taggard, "Emily Dickinson," *NR*, LXXXVI (26 Fe 1936), 82.

2. George F. Whicher, "The Deliverance of Emily Dickinson," *NYHTB*, XXVI (13 Au 1950), 2, 12; Jay Leyda, "Late Thaw of a Frozen Image," *NR*, CXXXII (21 Fe 1955), 22-24.

3. *Emily Dickinson Face to Face,* ed. Martha Dickinson Bianchi (Boston, 1932). All editions of Madame Bianchi are preceded by a résumé "of present-day response to her spell," which is usually signed by Hampson, i.e., a parade of "enthusiasts" and the "initiated," the "faithful" and the "pilgrims to Amherst." For Bianchi-Hampson nothing other than "critical consensus" had ever existed, which is why these prefaces, embellished with scraps from flattering reviews, are anything but representative of critical opinion.

4. Louis Untermeyer, "A More Intimate Emily," *SRL,* VII (20 Je 1931), 363; Morris U. Schappes, "Book Reviews," *AL,* v (Mr 1933), 82-85.

5. *Unpublished Poems of Emily Dickinson,* ed. Martha Dickinson Bianchi and Alfred Leete Hampson (Boston, 1935), n.p.

6. *Letters of Emily Dickinson,* ed. Mabel Loomis Todd, new and enlarged ed. (New York, 1931).

7. Millicent Todd Bingham, "Poems of Emily Dickinson: Hitherto Published Only in Part," *NEQ,* xx (Mr 1947), 3-50.

8. Melville Cane, "Dickinsons and Todds," *SRL,* xxviii (9 Je 1945), 48.

9. *Emily Dickinson's Home: Letters of Edward Dickinson and His Family,* ed. Millicent Todd Bingham (New York, 1955), p. xi.

10. *NEQ,* xxviii (Se 1955), 291-318.

11. *Emily Dickinson: A Revelation* (New York, 1954), pp. 3, 8.

12. Thomas H. Johnson, "Emily Dickinson: The Prisms of a Poet," *SRL,* xxxiii (3 Je 1950), 16-17; "Emily Dickinson Papers Given to Harvard," *PW,* clvii (3 Je 1950), 2456.

13. "According to legend, the fast was on Christmas Day, announced dictatorially the day before, and shame attached to the one rebel's refusal to keep it. Really, the fast was on Christmas Eve, plans for it were made public several days ahead, and participation in its observance was voluntary. The dramatic defiance is legend." Sidney R. McLean, "Emily Dickinson at Mount Holyoke," *NEQ,* VII (Mr 1934), 34, 41.

14. Jay Leyda, "Miss Emily's Maggie," *New World Writing,* III (New York, 1953), 255.

15. Jay Leyda, *The Years and Hours of Emily Dickinson* (New Haven, 1960), I, xix.

16. George Frisbie Whicher, *This Was a Poet: A Critical Biography of Emily Dickinson* (New York, 1938), p. 84.

17. George F. Whicher, "Pursuit of the Overtakeless," *N,* clxix (2 Jl 1949), 15.

18. Thomas H. Johnson, *Emily Dickinson: An Interpretive Biography* (Cambridge, Mass., 1955), p. viii.

19. Rebecca Patterson, *The Riddle of Emily Dickinson* (Boston, 1951).

20. George F. Whicher, in *NYHTB*, 4 No 1951.

21. David J.M. Higgins, "Portrait of Emily Dickinson: The Poet and Her Prose," unpubl. diss. (Columbia University, 1960); Winfield T. Scott, "The Errand from My Heart—" *Horizon*, III (Jl 1961), 100-105.

22. Clark Griffith, "Emily and Him: A Modern Approach to Emily Dickinson's Love Poetry," *Iowa English Yearbook*, no. 6 (Autumn 1961), 15-22; Anna Mary Wells, "Was Emily Dickinson Psychotic?" *The American Imago*, XIX (Winter 1962), 309-21.

23. Bernard DeVoto, "The Easy Chair," *HM*, CXC (Je 1945), 602-5.

24. Cf. *AB*, p. 61: "Sue would have annihilated her if she could. They hated each other black and blue. She was scared to death of Sue, though she talked awfully about her." Cf. also pp. 372-74.

25. *Op. cit.*, pp. 603-4. Which is why he reinterprets the love poems: "They and love are altogether incommensurable. They are light without heat, they are flame without fire, they are splendor without substance . . . . There is not a word in them that any woman in love would write" (p. 605).

26. George F. Whicher, "Book Reviews," *NEQ*, XVIII (Je 1945), 262; *idem*, "In Emily Dickinson's Garden," *AM*, CLXXVII (Fe 1946), 65.

27. Desmond Powell, *Emily Dickinson*, College Colorado Publication, General Series, no. 200, Studies Series, no. 19 (May 1934), 6; William Van Wyck, "Emily Dickinson's Songs out of Sorrow," *The Personalist*, XVIII (Spring 1937), 188-89; Donald F. Connors, "The Significance of Emily Dickinson," *College English*, III (April 1942), 633.

28. Howard Mumford Jones, *Guide to American Literature and Its Backgrounds since 1890* (Cambridge, Mass., 1959), p. 169.

29. Richard Chase, *Emily Dickinson* (New York, 1951), p. 5.

30. Herbert Read, "The Poems of Emily Dickinson," *The Spectator*, CLI (20 De 1933), 971.

31. Fred Lewis Pattee, "Gentian, Not Rose: The Real Emily Dickinson," *SR*, XLV (Spring 1937), 180.

32. G. W. Stonier, "Innocence without Experience," *The New Statesman and Nation*, XIV (23 Oc 1937), 655-56.

33. Edward Sackville West, "Keepsake," *The New Statesman and Nation*, xxxiv (29 No 1947), 435-36.

34. "She had a gift, but a small one, and it is only confusing when claims are made on her behalf which there is little to justify." W. Somerset Maugham, *Books and You* (New York, 1940), p. 103.

35. John Farrelly, "Emily Dickinson," *Scrutiny*, xix (Oc 1952,) 76.

36. "Her vowels are overwhelmingly front—vowels of intensity rather than of relaxation; her consonants are strongly infused with liquids, nasals, and sibilants. These sounds in the smaller forms bolster the intensity of her emotion. After much reading of her poems one hungers for the pentameter or longer lines, for heavier vowels, and retarding consonants. One yearns for a more comfortable, earthy talk of men pitched an octave lower, and wants less of the fervour of a person too conscious and too worried by the frugality of time to live." James G. Southworth, *Some Modern American Poets* (Oxford, 1950), pp. 18, 22.

37. Thornton Wilder, "Emily Dickinson," *AM*, cxc (Oc 1952), 44.

38. Thornton Wilder, "The American Loneliness," *AM*, cxc (Au 1952), 65.

39. Mario Maurin, "Book Reviews," *NEQ*, xxxii (Mr 1959), 99.

40. John Nist, "Two American Poets and a Spider," *The Walt Whitman Birthplace Bulletin*, iv (Ja 1961), 11, 9.

41. R. P. Blackmur, *The Southern Review*, iii (Autumn 1937), 326, 332, 334.

42. John Crowe Ransom, *The New Criticism* (Norfolk, Conn., 1941), pp. viii-x. Ransom comments on Blackmur's interpretation: "In depth and precision at once it is beyond all earlier criticism in our language" (p. x).

43. Yvor Winters, *Maule's Curse: Seven Studies in the History of American Obscurantism* (Norfolk, Conn., 1938), p. 149.

44. Mary Elizabeth Barbot, "Emily Dickinson Parallels," *NEQ*, xiv (De 1941), 695; Herbert E. Childs, "Emily Dickinson and Sir Thomas Browne," *AL*, xxii (Ja 1951), 465; James Davidson, "Emily Dickinson and Isaac Watts," *The Boston Public Library Quarterly*, vi (Jl 1954), 147.

45. Morton Dauwen Zabel, "Christina Rossetti and Emily Dickinson," *Poetry*, xxxvii (Ja 1931), 216.

46. Cleanth Brooks, *Modern Poetry and the Tradition* (New York, 1939), pp. viii, 51, 234.

47. Eunice Glenn, "Emily Dickinson: A Revaluation," *SR*, li (Autumn 1943), 574-88.

48. Joseph E. Duncan, *The Revival of Metaphysical Poetry: The History of a Style, 1800 to the Present* (Minneapolis, 1959), p. 77.

49. Sister Mary James Power, *In the Name of the Bee: The Significance of Emily Dickinson* (New York, 1943), pp. 12-13.

50. Sister Mary Humiliata, "Emily Dickinson—Mystic Poet?" *College English*, XII (De 1950), 144-49.

51. Whicher, *This Was a Poet*, p. 153.

52. Henry W. Wells, *Introduction to Emily Dickinson* (Chicago, 1947), p. 119.

52a. Chase, *Emily Dickinson*, pp. 121-22.

53. George F. Whicher, "Emily Dickinson: Centennial Afterthoughts," *AGQ*, xx (Fe 1931), 94.

54. Philip Rahv, "Paleface and Redskin," *KR*, 1 (Summer 1939), 251-56. James, Melville, and Emily Dickinson are "palefaces," Whitman, Twain, and Sandburg rank high among the "redskins." "At one pole there is the literature of the lowlife world of the frontier and of the big cities; at the other the thin, solemn, semiclerical culture of Boston and Concord. The fact is that the creative mind in America is fragmented and one-sided. For the process of polarization has produced a dichotomy between experience and consciousness—a dissociation between energy and sensibility, between conduct and theories of conduct, between life conceived as an opportunity and life conceived as a discipline" (p. 251).

55. "Poe and Longfellow accepted the desiccation, contributing a personal music which perhaps redeemed but never transfigured their talents. Whitman and Emily Dickinson, with more genius, or as we have been saying with more favorable cultural situations, were unable to accept the desiccation and drove forward on the élan of their natural aptitudes for language, resorting regardless to whatever props, scaffolds, obsessive symbols, or intellectual mechanisms came to hand, but neither of them ever finding satisfactory form—and neither, apparently, ever consciously missing it." Blackmur, *The Southern Review*, III, 251.

56. Henry W. Wells, *The American Way of Poetry* (New York, 1943), pp. 4-5.

57. Austin Warren, "Emily Dickinson," *SR*, LXV (Autumn 1957), 576.

58. Charles R. Anderson, *Emily Dickinson's Poetry: Stairway of Surprise* (New York, 1960), p. 10.

CHAPTER X

1. Van Wyck Brooks, *America's Coming-of-Age*, quoted according to the Doubleday Anchor Books edition, p. 20.

2. (Los Angeles, 1933.)

3. In his review of the book (*AL*, v [May 1934], 379-80), Pattee was flustered by the omission of the traditional constellation of New England greats and suggested "American Literary Rebels" as a more fitting title: "It seems to be the fashion now to exclude from the roll of American authors of major importance all who were not condemners of the conventional, damners of Puritanism, shockers of *hoi polloi* readers who are oldfashioned in taste and morals."

4. (New York, 1932.)

5. Granville Hicks, *The Great Tradition: An Interpretation of American Literature since the Civil War* (New York, 1933).

6. (New York, 1932.)

7. (New York, 1940.)

8. (New York, 1931.) R. Smith (*AL*, IV [No 1932], 78-82) praised the work as "the fullest and best of the recent revaluations of American literature": "It forsakes beaten paths, ignores former landmarks" (p. 78). In particular, he welcomed the dethronement of Puritanism and the genteel tradition: "This is deflation indeed. Such deflation has been foreshadowed in many non-academic quarters, but Professor Blankenship's is the first textbook actually to embody these sweeping changes from the verdicts of the older traditions" (p. 80).

9. (New York, 1932.)

10. Dickinson, *The Making of American Literature*. About the New Englander: "New England did indeed have one great poet who was almost totally unknown to her neighbors. Emily Dickinson is now known as one of the greatest poets in American literature. But it was many years after her death before her verse was appreciated at its value or even known" (p. 519). About the poet: "The period did indeed produce the outstanding geniuses of Walt Whitman and Emily Dickinson, but the first came to recognition slowly and the second never was known as a poet until long after her death" (p. 603).

11. (London, 1932.)

12. (Boston, 1936.) Characteristically, Howard Mumford Jones discussed the general problems involved in writing literary history and considered Boynton's work "a valuable illustration of the perplexities in the field" (*AL*, IX [No 1937], 97-98) when he reviewed the book. Perry Miller also confessed that the task had grown to a "Gargantuan undertaking" and evaluated *Literature and American Life* as "a digest of recent scholarship, a synthesis of new criticisms, a codification of fresh evaluations" (*NEQ*, x [Mr 1937], 186).

13. Ed. Arthur Hobson Quinn (New York, 1951).

14. Ed. Robert E. Spiller *et al.* (New York, 1948).

15. Robert E. Spiller, *The Cycle of American Literature: An Essay in Historical Criticism* (New York, 1955), a by-product of the larger work coedited by him; Spiller abandoned the grouping: Lanier has disappeared from the table of contents, and Emily Dickinson is treated with Henry James in chapter VIII ("Art and the Inner Life").

RETROSPECT

1. William Dean Howells, *Criticism and Fiction* (New York, 1892), p. 46.

2. Frederic Thomas Blanchard, in *Dictionary of World Literary Terms*, ed. Joseph T. Shipley (London, 1955), p. 155.

3. A letter from Alabama of December 11, 1891, to Higginson is quoted as a typical example: "Sir, Why not publish the remaining poems of Emily Dickinson for a Christmas present to the sorrowing? Her fingers touch the chords that soothe the aching heart, then why withhold anything of hers from suffering souls?" (MS-D57/To 301). Further expressions of gratitude and requests are printed in *AB*, pp. 73, 76-77, 123, 184-85, 194.

4. G. E. Meredith, "The Poems of Emily Dickinson," *LW*, XXII (11 Ap 1891), 128.

5. *Personae: Collected Shorter Poems of Ezra Pound* (London, 1952), p. 195.

6. Louis Untermeyer, *The New Era in American Poetry* (New York, 1919), p. 11.

7. See s.v. "Research in Progress" in *AL*, IV (May 1932), 211, and *AL*, VIII (Mr 1936), 73; s.v. "Dissertations Dropped" in *AL*, XI (Ja 1940), 461, and *AL*, XV (Mr 1943), 71.

8. Lewis Leary, "Doctoral Dissertations in American Literature, 1933-1948," *AL*, XX (Mr 1948), 169-230.

9. Ed. Floyd Stovall (New York, 1956).

10. The appreciative notices in this small, ambitious paper were probably written by its literary editor Charles E. Hurd. Cf. Joseph Edgar Chamberlain, *The Boston Transcript: A History of Its First Hundred Years* (Boston, 1930), pp. 209-12.

11. The editor himself, Horace Scudder, probably wrote this review. Cf. Martha E. Passe, "Criticism of Poetry in America during the Nineties," unpubl. diss. (Ohio State University, 1957), p. 102.

12. Frank Luther Mott, *A History of American Magazines* (Cambridge, Mass., 1957), III, 541.

13. *Mark Twain-Howells Letters: The Correspondence of Samuel L. Clemens and William D. Howells*, ed. Henry Nash Smith and William M. Gibson (Cambridge, Mass., 1960), II, 681.

14. Leonard Lutwack, "William Dean Howells and the 'Editor's Study,' " *AL*, xxiv (May 1952), 198.

15. John White Chadwick (1840-1904), from Massachusetts, was a radical Unitarian minister and well-known preacher in Brooklyn. He wrote poetry (his *Book of Poems* [1876] was reprinted nine times), book reviews (especially for *The Nation*), and biographies. Cf. Theodore D. Bacon in *DAB*.

16. Nathan Haskell Dole (1852-1935), from Chelsea, Massachusetts, was a versatile writer. "He took everything contemporary in his stride" (Harriet Monroe in *Poetry*, xlvi [Jl 1935], 2). He was among the first American translators of contemporary Russian realists. In his three essays and his letters to the editors of the poems (cf. *AB*, pp. 68, 72, 90 n. 18, 313) he took an active interest in Emily Dickinson's reception. Cf. Harris E. Starr in *DAB*, suppl.

17. Lilian Whiting (1859-1942), a journalist from Niagara Falls, was literary editor of the *Boston Traveller* from 1880 to 1890 and editor of the *Boston Budget* from 1890 to 1893. As late as 1901 she quoted four Dickinson poems on pp. 85, 185, 189, and 227 of her collection of essays *The World Beautiful in Books*.

18. Mary Perkins Abbott (1857-1904) from Salem, Massachusetts, was a novelist and a reviewer for Chicago's *Evening Post* and *Times-Herald*.

19. Robert Hillyer, *A Letter to Robert Frost and Others* (New York, 1937), p. 4.

20. [Kinsley Twining], "Poems by Emily Dickinson," *I*, xlii (11 De 1890), 1759.

21. "Whitman's reputation among the literary groups progressed from a period of doubt and indecision (1892-1906) through a stage of initial biographies and critiques establishing him as a permanent figure in our literature (1906-1914); then followed a period of intense scholarly research (1914-1930)." Charles B. Willard, *Whitman's American Fame: The Growth of His Reputation in America after 1892* (Providence, R.I., 1952), p. 88.

22. Cf. Randall Stewart, "The Growth of Thoreau's Reputation," *College English*, vii (Ja 1946), 208-14.

23. Cf. O.W. Riegel, "The Anatomy of Melville's Fame," *AL*, iii (May 1931), 195-213; Bernard Michael Wolpert, "The Melville Revival: A Study of Twentieth Century Criticism Through Its Treatment of Melville," unpubl. diss. (Ohio State University, 1951).

24. The studies by Thomas Beer (*Stephen Crane* [New York, 1923]) and Vincent Starrett (in his *Buried Caesars* [Chicago, 1923]) contributed decisively to the growth of his reputation, although his collected poems did not appear before 1930. Like Emily Dickinson, Crane the poet had been rediscovered first by the poet-critics of the little renaissance and had been dubbed a precursor of the Imagists. Cf. "The Revival of Interest in Stephen Crane," *Current Opinion*, LXXVI (Ja 1924), 39-41.

25. Cf. "England's Glory in Blake," *The Literary Digest*, LXXXII (2 Au 1924), 31-32.

26. *Circumference: Varieties of Metaphysical Verse, 1456-1928*, ed. Genevieve Taggard (New York, 1929). Donne and Emily Dickinson, who is represented by seven poems, assume the key positions: "I must state at the outset that I find only two genuinely metaphysical poets of the first order of clarity in the entire span of our poetry. . . . I find this kind of mind perfectly exampled only in John Donne and Emily Dickinson" (p. 4). The loose application of "metaphysical" (the anthology contains poems by Gray, Burns, Wordsworth, Shelley, Whitman, and Eliot among others) was commented upon by such reviewers as Morton Dauwen Zabel (in *NR*, LXII [2 Ap 1930], 199) and Austin Warren (in *B*, LXXI [Je 1930], 337-38).

27. Charles R. Anderson, *Emily Dickinson's Poetry: Stairway of Surprise* (New York, 1960), p. xiv.

28. John Paul Pritchard, *Criticism in America* (Norman, Okla., 1956), p. 148.

29. *The Nature and Elements of Poetry* (Boston, 1892), p. 44.

30. *Poets of America* (Boston, 1885), p. 465.

31. George E. DeMille ("Stedman, Arbiter of the Eighties," *PMLA*, XLI [Se 1926], 756-66) criticizes this metaphorical language as verbose without making the obvious inferences about Stedman's aesthetics.

32. Stedman was probably unaware of the discrepancy between his organic theory of art and his purely mechanically based critical practice. The critic in him paid homage to craftsmanship while the theoretician deprecated the practice of poetry as a kind of artistic finesse.

33. "A New Volume by Arlo Bates," *Boston Traveller*, 28 No 1891; "The Poet and His Self," *LW*, XXII (19 De 1891), 486; "Poetry," *The Congregationalist*, LXXV (31 De 1891), 459.

34. Cf. *The Christian Union* (XLV [18 Je 1892], 1212) regarding the poetic interregnum proclaimed by Stedman: "If the critic still be denied that subtle delight in crying 'Hats off, gentlemen: a genius!'

it remains true that the general standard of excellence is preparing the way for the Poet who is to come. That time will bring him is not to be gainsaid."

35. Grant C. Knight (*The Critical Period in American Literature* [Chapel Hill, 1951]), who treats the decade 1890-1900, passes over Emily Dickinson on the grounds that her work had almost no influence on the conflicts in literary criticism (p. viii), regards the first selection of her poems as "part of the romantic output in 1890" (p. 21), and later declares that "hers was the expiring voice of nineteenth-century romanticism" (p. 109).

36. Frank E. Hill, "Emily Dickinson," *Sun*, 26 Jl 1924.

37. *Skepticisms: Notes on Contemporary Poetry* (New York, 1919), pp. 32-33.

38. Cf. *Skepticisms*, pp. 7-8: "It has become habitual to accept, unpleasant to criticize. When we criticize at all, we condemn utterly; when we praise, we sing panegyrics. There has been no middle ground of balanced and impartial analysis, no serene perspective, —above all, no taste."

39. Stuart P. Sherman (*Points of View* [New York, 1924], p. v) complained about the "brotherhood of amateurs"; Herbert S. Gorman ("Poetic Standards," *B*, LVIII [Fe 1924], 666) clearly recognized that the difficulty of assessing contemporary poetry was to be traced to the existence of outmoded norms which had not been superseded by new, and then added that "every little critic has a heaven of his own, into which he puts the gods of his idolatry"; in a review of Gosse and Symons, Robert C. Holliday wrote about the oppressive situation at greater length (*B*, LVIII [Se 1923], 79).

40. (New York, 1929), p. 147.

41. (Boston, 1885.)

42. Max Eastman, *Enjoyment of Poetry* (New York, 1913), p. 180; John Livingston Lowes, *Convention and Revolt in Poetry* (Boston, 1919), p. 250.

43. (New York, 1919), pp. 28-29, 32.

44. (New York, 1929), pp. ix, 199.

45. *A Scientific Study of the Principles of Poetic Composition* (New York, 1901).

46. H.M., "What Next?" *Poetry*, xv (Oc 1919), 33-34.

47. T. Walter Herbert, "Near-Rimes and Paraphones," *SR*, XLV (Autumn 1937), 436.

48. Cf. chapter xv ("Events in a Vacuum") of her *The Life and Mind of Emily Dickinson*.

49. Lewis Leary, "The Poems of Emily Dickinson," *Thought,* xxxi (Summer 1956), 285-86.

49a. John A. Christie, "A New Chapter in American Literature," *Vassar Alumnae Magazine,* xlii (Oc 1956), 2.

50. [Henry Seidel Canby], "On Reading Biographies," *SRL,* vi (2 No 1929), 637.

51. Louise Maunsell Fields, "Biography Boom," *The North American Review,* ccxxx (Oc 1930), 433-40.

52. George W. Douglas, "Life of a Notable New England Poet," *Public Ledger,* 8 Ap 1924.

53. Walter Rollo Brown, "A Sublimated Puritan," *SRL,* v (6 Oc 1928), 186.

54. Richard B. Sewall in *ED,* p. 8.

APPENDIX

1. (New York, 1937), p. 4.

2. *Emily Dickinson: Stairway of Surprise* (New York, 1960), pp. xiii-xiv.

3. Emily E.F. Ford, "Eheu! Emily Dickinson!" *SRep,* 11 Ja 1891.

4. Wallace Gould, "To Emily," *The New American Caravan,* ed. Alfred Kreymborg *et al.* (New York, 1929), pp. 325, 327.

5. Mary Bowen, "To Emily Dickinson," *Under the Scarlet and Black: Poems Selected from the Undergraduate Publications of Iowa College,* ed. Hervey S. McCowan and Frank F. Everest (Grinnell, Ia., 1893), p. 27.

6. (Buffalo, N.Y., 1895), p. 31.

7. "Emily Dickinson," *The Piper* (Mr 1924), 2.

8. n.p.

9. (New York, 1949), p. v.

10. *Classic Comics,* no. 14 (New York, n.d. [1946]).

11. Grace E. Perkinson, "Emily Dickinson and Children," *The Horn Book Magazine,* xxxiii (Fe 1957), 19-27, 26; Caroline C. Allen, "The Homestead in Amherst," *The Horn Book Magazine,* xxxiii (Fe 1957), 30-34.

SOURCES

The list is divided as follows:

(c) *Poems* (Boston, 1891)
(d) *Poems* (Boston, 1896)
(e) *The Single Hound* (Boston, 1914)
(f) *Complete Poems* (Boston, 1924)
(g) *Selected Poems* (London, 1924)
(h) *Further Poems* (Boston, 1929)
(i) *Further Poems* (London, 1929)
(j) *Poems* (Boston, 1930)
(k) *Poems for Youth* (Boston, 1934)
(l) *Unpublished Poems* (Boston, 1935)
(m) *Poems* (Boston, 1937)
(n) *Poems* (London, 1937)
(o) *Bolts of Melody* (New York, London, 1945)
(p) *Poems* (Cambridge, Mass., 1955)
(q) *Selected Poems* (New York, 1959)
(r) *Complete Poems* (Boston, 1960)

2. Editions of Letters

(a) *Letters* (Boston, 1894)
(b) *Life and Letters* (Boston, 1924)
(c) *Life and Letters* (London, 1924)
(d) *Letters* (New York, London, 1931)
(e) *Emily Dickinson Face to Face* (Boston, 1932)
(f) *Letters to . . . Holland* (Cambridge, Mass., 1951)
(g) *Emily Dickinson: A Revelation* (New York, 1954)
(h) *Emily Dickinson's Home* (New York, 1955)
(i) *Letters* (Cambridge, Mass., 1958)

3. Monographs on Emily Dickinson

(a) *Emily Dickinson: The Human Background of Her Poetry*
(b) *The Life and Mind of Emily Dickinson*
(c) *Emily Dickinson: Friend and Neighbor*

XII. Miscellanea

1. Additional Brief Commentaries
2. Early Mention
   (a) In books
   (b) In letters and diaries
3. Glosses on the Sale of Volumes of Poems and Letters in the 1890's
4. Notes on Mrs. Todd's Lectures
5. Notes on Higginson's *Atlantic* Essay

6. Commemorations
    (a) Founder's Day Celebration, Mount Holyoke, 1929
    (b) Emily Dickinson Centenary Celebration, 1930
7. Radio Programs
8. Martha Graham's Dance "Letter to the World"

The material is not arranged as a bibliographical compilation but as a supplementary list of sources. It has been tailored to the requirements of this study and contains only the writings treated here. Reviews of the monographs on Emily Dickinson which have appeared since 1931 and notices of novels and plays about the life of the poet are not included.

Since this study is concerned with the critical reception of Emily Dickinson, most of the material was collected in the area of critical literature. The gaps here are probably smaller than, for example, in the related fields covered under section XII. Completeness (even where it is not achieved) is aspired to in the case of editions of poems and letters, scattered first printings, anthologies (until 1930), poems set to music, dedicatory poems, novels and plays, critical monographs and book chapters, essays appearing in periodicals, doctoral dissertations, literary histories, reference works (until 1930), bibliographies and catalogues, and, in addition, in the case of newspaper reviews and essays from the years 1892-93, 1895, 1897-1923, 1925-28.

Under each heading the arrangement is chronological. Reprints of critical literature, indicated under the date of the first publication, serve to facilitate easier location of the items. In the case of anonymous and pseudonymous essays and reviews, the names of the authors are added in square brackets whenever they could be ascertained.

Periodicals are quoted as follows: title or symbol, respectively, in accordance with the list of abbreviations (pp. 227-29); volume number in Roman numerals; date of publication; page numbers in Arabic numerals. In the case of *The Colophon* and *The Explicator*, which are not paginated, the Arabic numeral refers to the number of the part or contribution, respectively.

I. EDITIONS

1. POEMS

Poems by Emily Dickinson, edited by two of her friends, Mabel Loomis Todd and T. W. Higginson (Boston: Roberts Brothers, 1890).

Poems by Emily Dickinson, edited by two of her friends, Mabel Loomis Todd and T. W. Higginson (London: Osgood, McIlvaine, 1891).

Poems by Emily Dickinson, edited by two of her friends, T. W. Higginson and Mabel Loomis Todd, second series (Boston: Roberts Brothers, 1891).

Poems by Emily Dickinson, edited by Mabel Loomis Todd, third series (Boston: Roberts Brothers, 1896).

The Single Hound: Poems of a Lifetime by Emily Dickinson, with an introduction by her niece, Martha Dickinson Bianchi (Boston: Little, Brown, 1914).

The Complete Poems of Emily Dickinson, with an introduction by her niece, Martha Dickinson Bianchi (Boston: Little, Brown, 1924).

The Complete Poems of Emily Dickinson, with an introduction by Martha Dickinson Bianchi (London: Secker, 1924).

Selected Poems of Emily Dickinson, edited by Conrad Aiken (London: Cape, 1924).

Emily Dickinson, The Pamphlet Poets (New York: Simon & Schuster, 1927).

Further Poems of Emily Dickinson: Withheld from Publication by Her Sister Lavinia, edited by her niece Martha Dickinson Bianchi and Alfred Leete Hampson (Boston: Little, Brown, 1929).

Further Poems of Emily Dickinson, edited by her niece Martha Dickinson Bianchi and Alfred Leete Hampson (London: Secker, 1929).

The Poems of Emily Dickinson, edited by Martha Dickinson Bianchi and Alfred Leete Hampson, centenary edition (Boston: Little, Brown, 1930).

Emily Dickinson: Poems for Youth, edited by Alfred Leete Hampson, foreword by May Lamberton Becker, illustrations by George and Doris Hauman (Boston: Little, Brown, 1934).

Unpublished Poems of Emily Dickinson, edited by her niece Martha Dickinson Bianchi and Alfred Leete Hampson (Boston: Little, Brown, 1935).

The Poems of Emily Dickinson, edited by Martha Dickinson Bianchi and Alfred Leete Hampson, introduction by Alfred Leete Hampson (Boston: Little, Brown, 1937).

The Poems of Emily Dickinson, edited by Martha Dickinson Bianchi and Alfred Leete Hampson, with an introduction by Alfred Leete Hampson (London: Cape, 1937).

Bolts of Melody: New Poems of Emily Dickinson, edited by Mabel Loomis Todd and Millicent Todd Bingham (New York and London: Harper, 1945).

Sources

Emily Dickinson: Poems First & Second Series, edited by two of her friends, Mabel Loomis Todd and T. W. Higginson, illustrations by Leon Jacobson, introduction by Carl Van Doren (Cleveland and New York: World Publishing Co., 1948).

Selected Poems of Emily Dickinson, with an introduction by Conrad Aiken (New York: Modern Library, 1948).

Emily Dickinson: Love Poems and Others (Mount Vernon, N.Y.: Peter Pauper Press, n.d.).

Poems of Emily Dickinson, selected and edited with a commentary by Louis Untermeyer and illustrated with drawings by Helen Sewell (New York: Heritage Press, 1952).

The Poems of Emily Dickinson: Including Variant Readings Critically Compared with All Known Manuscripts, edited by Thomas H. Johnson, 3 vols. (Cambridge, Mass.: Harvard University Press, 1955).

Riddle Poems: Emily Dickinson (Northampton, Mass.: Gehenna Press, 1957).

Selected Poems of Emily Dickinson, edited with an introduction and notes by James Reeves (New York: Macmillan, 1959).

Selected Poems and Letters of Emily Dickinson: Together with Thomas Higginson's Account of His Correspondence with the Poet, and His Visit to Her in Amherst, edited, with an introduction, by Robert N. Linscott (Garden City, N.Y.: Doubleday Anchor Books, 1959).

Love Poems: Emily Dickinson (Mount Vernon, N.Y.: Peter Pauper Press, n.d.).

The Complete Poems of Emily Dickinson, edited by Thomas H. Johnson (Boston: Little, Brown, 1960).

Emily Dickinson, selected, with an introduction and notes, by John Malcolm Brinnin, The Laurel Poetry Series (New York: Dell Publishing Co., 1960).

Final Harvest: Emily Dickinson's Poems, selection and introduction by Thomas H. Johnson (Boston: Little, Brown, 1961).

2. LETTERS

Letters of Emily Dickinson, edited by Mabel Loomis Todd in two volumes (Boston: Roberts Brothers, 1894).

The Life and Letters of Emily Dickinson by her niece, Martha Dickinson Bianchi, with illustrations (Boston: Houghton Mifflin, 1924).

The Life and Letters of Emily Dickinson by her niece, Martha Dickinson Bianchi (London: Cape, 1924).

Letters of Emily Dickinson, edited by Mabel Loomis Todd, new and enlarged edition (New York and London: Harper, 1931).

Emily Dickinson Face to Face: Unpublished Letters with Notes and Reminiscences by her niece, Martha Dickinson Bianchi, with a foreword by Alfred Leete Hampson (Boston: Houghton Mifflin, 1932).

Letters of Emily Dickinson, edited by Mabel Loomis Todd, with an introduction by Mark Van Doren (London: Gollancz, 1951).

Emily Dickinson's Letters to Dr. and Mrs. Josiah Gilbert Holland, edited by their granddaughter, Theodora Van Wagenen Ward (Cambridge, Mass.: Harvard University Press, 1951).

Emily Dickinson: A Revelation by Millicent Todd Bingham (New York: Harper, 1954).

Emily Dickinson's Home: Letters of Edward Dickinson and His Family, with documentation and comment by Millicent Todd Bingham (New York: Harper, 1955).

The Letters of Emily Dickinson, edited by Thomas H. Johnson, associate editor Theodora Ward, 3 vols. (Cambridge, Mass.: Harvard University Press, 1958).

II. VARIOUS FIRST PRINTINGS

1. POEMS

"A Valentine," *SRep,* 20 Fe 1852. ["Sic transit gloria mundi"].

"The May-Wine," *SRep,* 4 May 1861. ["I taste a liquor never brewed"].

"The Sleeping," *SRep,* 1 Mr 1862. ["Safe in their alabaster chambers"].

"My Sabbath," *The Round Table,* 1 (12 Mr 1864), 195. ["Some keep the Sabbath going to church"].

"Sunset," *SRep,* 30 Mr 1864. ["Blazing in gold and quenching in purple"].

"The Snake," *SRep,* 14 Fe 1866. ["A narrow fellow in the grass"].

"Success," *A Masque of Poets* (Boston, 1878), p. 174. ["Success is counted sweetest"].

Emily Dickinson, "Renunciation," *SM,* VIII (Au 1890), 240. ["There came a day at summer's full"].

"Poems by the Late Emily Dickinson," *I,* XLIII (5 Fe 1891), 1. ["Went up a year this evening," "I held a jewel in my fingers," "God made a little gentian"].

"Nobody," *Life,* XVII (5 Mr 1891), 146. ["I'm nobody! who are you"].

"Two Lyrics by the Late Emily Dickinson," *I*, XLIII (12 Mr 1891), 1. ["Just lost, when I was saved," "Through the strait pass of suffering"].

"A Poem," *CR*, LXX (2 Ap 1891), 212. ["God is a distant, stately lover"].

Emily Dickinson, "Morning," *St. Nicholas*, XVIII (May 1891), 491. ["Will there really be a 'Morning' "].

Emily Dickinson, "The Sleeping Flowers," *St. Nicholas*, XVIII (Je 1891), 616. ["Whose are the little beds, I asked"].

Emily Dickinson, "A Nameless Rose," *YC*, LXIV (24 De 1891), 672. ["Nobody knows this little rose"].

Emily Dickinson, "Vanished," *YC*, LXV (25 Au 1892), 420. ["She died —this was the way she died"].

Emily Dickinson, "Autumn," *YC*, LXV (8 Se 1892), 448. ["The name of it is 'Autumn' "].

Emily Dickinson, "Saturday," *YC*, LXV (22 Se 1892), 468. ["From all the jails the boys and girls"].

Emily Dickinson, "In September," *YC*, LXV (29 Se 1892), 484. ["September's baccalaureate"].

Emily Dickinson, "My Little King" [and] "Heart's Ease," *YC*, LXVI (18 May 1893), 256. ["I met a king this afternoon," "I'm the little 'Heart's Ease' "].

"Three Poems by Emily Dickinson," *O*, LIII (25 Ja 1896), 140. ["This world is not conclusion," " 'Tis little I could care for pearls," "We learn in the retreating"].

Emily Dickinson, "Time's Healing," *I*, XLVIII (21 May 1896), 1. ["They say that 'Time assuages' "].

Emily Dickinson, "Parting," *SM*, XIX (Je 1896), 780. ["My life closed twice before its close"].

"Verses by Emily Dickinson," *I*, XLVIII (2 Jl 1896), 1. [4 poems].

Emily Dickinson, "Nature's Way," *YC*, LXXII (20 Ja 1898), 36. ["Were nature mortal lady"].

Emily Dickinson, "Fame," *I*, L (3 Fe 1898), 1. ["Fame is a bee"].

Emily Dickinson, "Spring's Orchestra," *I*, L (2 Je 1898), 1. ["The saddest noise, the sweetest noise"].

"Unpublished Poems by Emily Dickinson," *AM*, CXLIII (Fe 1929), 180-86. [10 poems].

"Twenty New Poems by Emily Dickinson," *LM*, XIX (Fe 1929), 350-59.

"Unpublished Poems by Emily Dickinson," *AM*, cxliii (Mr 1929), 326-32. [10 poems].

"New Poems by Emily Dickinson," *SRL*, v (9 Mr 1929), 751. [8 poems].

"New Poems by Emily Dickinson," *NYHTB*, v (10 Mr 1929), 1, 4. [9 poems].

"Four Poems by Emily Dickinson," *N*, cxxviii (13 Mr 1929), 315.

Margaret Higginson Barney and Frederick Ives Carpenter, "Unpublished Poems of Emily Dickinson," *NEQ*, v (Ap 1932), 217-20 [6 poems].

Emily Dickinson, "Glory," *AM*, clv (Je 1935), 703. ["My triumph lasted till the drums"].

"Two Unpublished Poems by Emily Dickinson," *YR*, xxv (Se 1935), 76. ["More life went out when he went," "Somehow myself survived the night"].

Emily Dickinson, "If I Should Be a Queen," *AM*, clvi (No 1935), 560. ["I'm saying every day"].

"Two Poems by Emily Dickinson," *SRL*, xiii (9 No 1935), 12. ["A tooth upon our peace," "She staked her feathers, gained an arc"].

"An Unpublished Poem by Emily Dickinson," *The Commonweal*, xxiii (29 No 1935), 124. ["We grow accustomed to the dark"].

Millicent Todd Bingham, "Poems of Emily Dickinson: Hitherto Published Only in Part," *NEQ*, xx (Mr 1947), 3-50. [56 poems].

2. LETTERS

Martha Dickinson Bianchi, "Selections from the Unpublished Letters of Emily Dickinson to Her Brother's Family: Chosen and Arranged by Her Niece," *AM*, cxv (Ja 1915), 35-42.

Margaret Higginson Barney, "Fragments from Emily Dickinson," *AM*, cxxxix (Je 1927), 799-801.

"Two Unpublished Autograph Letters of Emily Dickinson," *The Yale University Library Gazette*, vi (Oc 1931), 42-43.

John Howard Birss, "A Letter of Emily Dickinson," *N&Q*, clxiii (17 De 1932), 441.

"Excerpts from a Letter Dated Jan. 13, 1854, to Edward Everett Hale," *The Autograph Album*, i (De 1933), 50.

"Letter from Emily Dickinson to Professor Richard H. Mather," *SM*, xcv (Ap 1934), 290.

Helen H. Arnold, " 'From the Garden We Have Not Seen': New Letters of Emily Dickinson," *NEQ*, xvi (Se 1943), 363-75.

Frank Davidson, "Some Emily Dickinson Letters," *The Indiana Quarterly for Bookmen*, I (Oc 1945), 113-18.

Annie L. Crowell, "Emily Dickinson—an Heritage of Friendship," *MHAQ*, XXIX (Fe 1946), 129-30.

C. J. Weber, " 'Two Notes from Emily Dickinson,' " *Colby Library Quarterly*, I (Je 1946), 239-40.

Millicent Todd Bingham, "Prose Fragments of Emily Dickinson," *NEQ*, XXVIII (Se 1955), 291-318.

III. ANTHOLOGIES

The Lover's Year-Book of Poetry: A Collection of Love Poems for Every Day in the Year, ed. Horace Parker Chandler (Boston, 1891), I, 99. ["To know just how he suffered would be dear"].

The Lovers' Treasury of Verse, ed. John White Chadwick and Annie Hathaway Chadwick (Boston, 1891), pp. 51-52, 69-70, 99, 114, 180. Simultaneously published under the title *Out of the Heart: Poems for Lovers Young and Old.* [5 poems].

Book-Song: An Anthology of Poems of Books and Bookmen from Modern Authors, ed. Gleeson White (New York, 1893), p. 32. ["A precious mouldering pleasure 'tis"].

Stray Violets, gathered and pictured by Mary E. Hart (New York, 1893), p. 23. ["I hide myself within my flower"].

Sun Prints in Sky Tints, ed. Irene E. Jerome (Boston, 1893), p. 15. ["Whose are the little beds, I asked"].

K.D.S. [Kate Dickinson Sweetser], "Emily Dickinson," *The Magazine of Poetry* (Buffalo, N.Y.), VI (Fe 1894), 108-11. [6 poems].

Nature in Verse: A Poetry Reader for Children, ed. Mary I. Lovejoy (Boston, 1896), p. 120. ["A drop fell on the apple tree"].

The Treasury of American Sacred Song, ed. W. Garrett Horder (London, 1896), pp. 179-83, 354. [13 poems].

Later American Poems, ed. J. E. Wetherell (Toronto, 1896), pp. 185-86. ["Success is counted sweetest," "For each ecstatic instant"].

Library of the World's Best Literature: Ancient and Modern, ed. Charles Dudley Warner (New York, 1896), XXVIII, 16532. ["Some keep the Sabbath going to church"].

Voices of Doubt and Trust, ed. Volney Streamer (New York, 1897), pp. 41-42. ["I measure every grief I meet," "Our share of night to bear," "Let down the bars, oh death"].

The Golden Treasury of American Songs and Lyrics, ed. Frederic Lawrence Knowles (Boston, 1898), pp. 251-52, 264-65. [4 poems].

Book Lovers' Verse: Being Songs of Books and Bookmen Compiled from English and American Authors, ed. Howard S. Ruddy (Indianapolis, 1899), pp. 18, 69. ["There is no frigate like a book," "A precious mouldering pleasure 'tis"].

Nature Pictures by American Poets, ed. Annie Russell Marble (New York, 1899), pp. 46, 89, 139, 153. [4 poems].

An American Anthology, 1787-1900, ed. Edmund Clarence Stedman (Boston, 1900), pp. 320-22, 587. [20 poems].

Thoughts, selected and compiled by Ladies of Fabiola Hospital Association (Oakland, Calif., 1901), p. 100. ["If I can stop one heart from breaking"].

A Book of American Humorous Verse (Chicago: Stone, 1904), pp. 86, 234. ["Forbidden fruit a flavor has," "The pedigree of honey"].

The Lover's Mother Goose, ed. John Cecil Clay (Indianapolis, 1905), pp. 78, 88. ["If you were coming in the fall," "Have you got a brook in your little heart"].

One Hundred Best American Poems, ed. John R. Howard (New York, 1905), pp. 284-85. ["I never saw a moor," "These are the days when birds come back"].

Cheery Thoughts, ed. Montrose L. Barnet (Chicago, 1911), p. 9. ["They might not need me, yet they might"].

Happy Thoughts, ed. Everett Thornton Brown (Chicago, 1912), p. 9. ["They might not need me, yet they might"].

Silver Linings, ed. Everett Thornton Brown (Chicago, 1912), p. 40. ["If I can stop one heart from breaking"].

American Poems (1625-1892), ed. Walter C. Bronson (Chicago, 1912), pp. 533-36, 643. [7 poems].

The Spirit of Friendship, ed. Everett T. Brown (Chicago, 1913), p. 63. ["If I can stop one heart from breaking"].

The Little Book of American Poets, 1787-1900, ed. Jessie B. Rittenhouse (Boston, 1915), pp. 146-48. [5 poems].

Modern American Poetry: An Introduction, ed. Louis Untermeyer (New York, 1919), pp. 3-4. ["I never saw a moor," "The sky is low, the clouds are mean," "There is no frigate like a book"].

Century Readings for a Course in American Literature, ed. Fred Lewis Pattee (New York, 1920), pp. 586-88. [11 poems].

Golden Thoughts in Poetry and Prose, ed. J[ames] C. Temple (Columbus, O., 1922), p. 42. ["They might not need me, yet they might"].

Sources

Modern American Poets, ed. Conrad Aiken (London, 1922), pp. 3-16. [23 poems].

American Poets: An Anthology of Contemporary Verse, ed. Leonora Speyer (Munich, 1923), pp. 33-35. [6 poems].

Poems for Youth: An American Anthology, ed. William Rose Benét (New York, 1925), pp. 120-23. [4 poems].

American Poetry and Prose: A Book of Readings, 1607-1916, ed. Norman Foerster (Boston, 1925), pp. 764-68. [29 poems].

The Le Gallienne Book of American Verse, ed. Richard Le Gallienne (New York, 1925), pp. 172-75. [7 poems].

Types of Poetry: Exclusive of the Drama, ed. Howard Judson Hall (Boston, 1927), pp. 161, 190, 429, 430. [6 poems].

The College Book of Verse, 1250-1925, ed. Robert M. Gay (Boston, 1927), pp. 528-29. ["The soul selects her own society," "The murmur of a bee," "This quiet dust was gentlemen and ladies"].

The Oxford Book of American Verse, ed. Bliss Carman (New York, 1927), pp. 282-92. [21 poems].

American Poetry, 1671-1928: A Comprehensive Anthology, ed. Conrad Aiken (New York, 1929), pp. 168-80. [24 poems].

The Best Poems of 1929, ed. Thomas Moult (New York, n.d.), p. 93. ["I reckon when I count it all"].

Circumference: Varieties of Metaphysical Verse, 1456-1928, ed. Genevieve Taggard (New York, 1929).

Three Centuries of American Poetry and Prose, ed. Alphonso Gerald Newcomer *et al.*, rev. ed. (Chicago, 1929), pp. 717-21. [28 poems].

One Hundred Best Poems for Boys and Girls, ed. Marjorie Barrows (Racine, Wis., 1930), p. 119. ["I never saw a moor"].

An Anthology of American Poetry: Lyric America, 1630-1930, ed. Alfred Kreymborg (New York, 1930), pp. 181-86. [8 poems].

IV. POEMS SET TO MUSIC

Have You Got a Brook in Your Little Heart? Music by Etta Parker (Boston: Miles & Thompson, 1896).

Six Songs. Music by Clarence Dickinson (Chicago: Merwin, 1897).

Little Pilgrim (A Child's Fancy). Music by Charles Willeby (Cincinnati: Church, 1907). ["Will there really be a 'Morning'"].

Songs. Music by James G. MacDermid (Chicago: MacDermid, 1908). ["If I can stop one heart from breaking"].

Charity. Music by Oley Speaks (New York: Schirmer, 1911). ["If I can stop one heart from breaking"].

A Day. Music by Adeline Raymond-Ward (Boston: Homeyer, 1913). ["I'll tell you how the sun rose"].

The Sea of Sunset. Music by Arthur Farwell, opus 26 (New York: Schirmer, 1917). ["This is the land the sunset washes"].

Charity. Music by Richard Hageman (New York: Schirmer, 1921). ["If I can stop one heart from breaking"].

Two Poems by Emily Dickinson. Music by Arthur Farwell, opus 66 (New York: Schirmer, 1926). ["I shall know why, when time is over," "At last to be identified"].

Three Dickinson Poems. Music by Arthur Farwell, opus 73 (New York: Schirmer, 1928). ["Mine by the right of the white election," "A drop fell on the apple tree"].

"If I can stop one heart from breaking." Music by Peter C. Lutkin, with optional stanza by Earl Marlatt, *The New Hymnal for American Youth,* ed. H. Augustine Smith (New York, 1930), p. 204.

Songs from Emily Dickinson. Music by Ernst Bacon (San Francisco: Bacon, 1932). [9 poems].

Selected Songs. Music by Floy Little Bartlett (Boston: Schmidt, 1932). ["I shall not live in vain"].

Heart Not So Heavy as Mine. Music by Elliott Carter (New York: Arrow Music Press, 1938).

"The Banks of the Yellow Sea." Music by Ernst Bacon, *New Music,* xv (Ja 1942), 2-3. ["This is the land the sunset washes"].

The Grass. Music by Ernst Bacon (New York: Associated Music Publ., 1944). ["The grass so little has to do"].

Is There Such a Thing as Day? Music by Ernst Bacon (New York: Associated Music Publ., 1944). ["Will there really be a 'Morning' "].

Five Poems by Emily Dickinson. Music by Ernst Bacon (New York: Schirmer, 1944).

Not in Vain: Song. Music by Janie Alexander Patterson (Philadelphia: Presser, 1944). ["If I can stop one heart from breaking"].

Chartless. Music by Isadore Freed (New York: Fischer, 1946). ["I never saw a moor"].

O Friend. Music by Ernst Bacon (New York: Associated Music Publ., 1946). ["Alter! When the hills do"].

The Little Rose. Music by William Roy (New York: Schirmer, 1947). ["Nobody knows this little rose"].

From Emily's Diary: Secular Cantata: For Four-Part Chorus of Women's Voices and Small Orchestra with Incidental Soprano and Contralto Soli. Music by Ernst Bacon (New York: Schirmer, 1947).

Velvet People. Music by Ernst Bacon (New York: Fischer, 1948). ["Pigmy seraphs gone astray"].

Twelve Poems of Emily Dickinson. Music by Aaron Copland (New York: Boosey & Hawkes, 1951).

V. DEDICATORY POEMS

(Mary G. Cutler, "Fulfillment," Unity [Chicago], xxvi [22 Ja 1891], 171).

Emily E. F. Ford, "Eheu! Emily Dickinson!" *SRep*, 11 Ja 1891. Repr. in *SRep*, 16 Ja 1891.

G. E. Meredith, "The Poems of Emily Dickinson," *LW*, xxii (11 Ap 1891), 128.

Mary Elwell Storrs, "Emily Dickinson, 1830-1886," *SRep*, 22 May 1891.

Le Roy Phillips, "The Poems of Emily Dickinson," *The Amherst Literary Monthly*, vi (Je 1891), 90-91. Repr. in *The New England Magazine*, N.S., v (No 1891), 311.

Mary Bowen, "To Emily Dickinson," *Under the Scarlet and Black: Poems Selected from the Undergraduate Publications of Iowa College*, ed. Hervey S. McCowan and Frank F. Everest (Grinnell, Ia., 1893), p. 27. Repr. in *The Dial*, xv (16 Jl 1893), 43.

J. William Lloyd, "Emily Dickinson," *Wind-Harp Songs* (Buffalo, N.Y., 1895), p. 31.

Martha Gilbert Dickinson, "Beneath the Hills," *Within the Hedge* (New York, 1899), pp. 119-27.

Robert Loveman, "Proclamation," *A Book of Verses* (Philadelphia, 1900), p. 32.

Nellie Seelye Evans, "Emily Dickinson," *Poems* (Englewood, N.J., 1906), p. 71.

Fred Raphael Allen, "Emily Dickinson—Her Poems," *In Sonnet Wise* (Boston, 1911), p. 35.

Carl Sandburg, "Letters to Dead Imagists," *Chicago Poems* (New York, 1916), p. 176. Repr. in *Collected Poems* (New York, 1950), p. 73.

Katherine I. H. Porter, "The Poet's Gown," *SRep*, 30 Jl 1916.

Willard Wattles, "The Bench," *AGQ*, vi (May 1917), 185.

Carl Sandburg, "Accomplished Facts," *Poetry*, xv (Fe 1920), 243. Repr. in *Smoke and Steel* (New York, 1922), p. 169; in *Collected Poems* (New York, 1950), p. 226.

Amy Lowell, "The Sisters," *What's o'Clock?* (Boston, 1925), pp. 127-37. Repr. in *Selected Poems*, ed. John L. Lowes (Boston, 1927), pp. 50-56.

Frederick Herbert Adler, "Thoughts while Reading Emily Dickinson," *The Rectangle* (Minneapolis), ii (May 1926), 14.

Leonora Speyer, "Emily Dickinson," *B*, lxv (Ap 1927), 149.

Hart Crane, "To Emily Dickinson," *N*, cxxiv (29 Je 1927), 718. Repr. in *Collected Poems*, ed. Waldo Frank (New York, 1933), p. 128.

Mary Emmeline Bigwood, "For Emily Dickinson," *Wings*, iv (Summer 1927), 10.

Isabel Fiske Conant, "For Emily Dickinson," *Scrapped Silver* (Portland, Me., 1928), n.p.

Grace Warren Landrum, "To Emily Dickinson," *SR*, xxxvi (Ja 1928), 20.

Wallace Gould, "To Emily," *The New American Caravan*, ed. Alfred Kreymborg *et al.* (New York, 1929), pp. 323-27.

Joseph Auslander, "Letter to Emily Dickinson," *Palms* (Guadalajara, Mexico), vi (Fe-Mr 1929), i-viii. Repr. in *Letters to Women* (New York, 1929), pp. 37-48; in *Prize Poems: 1913-1929*, ed. Charles A. Wagner (New York, 1930), pp. 226-35.

William Griffith, "Emily Dickinson," *The Commonweal*, ix (6 Fe 1929), 396. Repr. in *The Garden Book of Verse*, ed. William Griffith and Mrs. John Walton Paris (New York, 1932), i, 15-16.

Jean Starr Untermeyer, "Hidden Meteors," *NYHTB*, v (11 Au 1929), 6. Repr. in *Voices*, no. 86 (Summer 1936), 49.

Anne Kelledy Gilbert, "Postscript to Emily Dickinson," *Contemporary Verse*, xxv (Se 1929), 4.

Edith Richmond Blanchard, "Love Poems of Emily Dickinson," *The Providence Journal*, 30 Oc 1929.

Alice Bidwell Wesenberg, "Emily," *MHAQ*, xiii (Ja 1930), 192.

John I. Smith, "To Emily Dickinson," *The Scholastic*, xv (4 Ja 1930), 8.

Pauline Leader, "Poem to Emily Dickinson," *Poetry*, xxxvi (Au 1930), 85.

Dorothy Aldis, "Emily Dickinson," *Poetry*, xxxvi (Au 1930), 238.

Caroline Giltinan, "Emily Dickinson," *CW*, cxxxii (No 1930), 150.

Yvor Winters, "To Emily Dickinson," *"BHer,* 6 De 1930. Repr. in *The Proof* (New York, 1930), p. 47.

E[lizabeth] McC[ausland], "For a New England Nun: Emily Dickinson, Poet," *SRep,* 7 De 1930. Repr. as "Emily Dickinson: 1830-1930" in *Hot Nights and Other Poems* (Springfield, Mass., 1934), n.p.

Isabel Fiske Conant, "Philadelphia Sunday," *NYHTB,* LXXI (21 De 1930), 13.

M. J. Wise, Jr., "To Emily Dickinson," *Amherst Graduate Verse 1931,* ed. David Morton (Amherst, 1931), p. 71.

Roberta Swartz Chalmers, "Emily Dickinson (One Hundred Years Old)," *MHAQ,* XIV (Ja 1931), 244-45.

Melville Cane, "Emily Dickinson (1830-1930)," *The Literary Digest,* CVIII (3 Ja 1931), 18. Repr. in *Poems New and Selected* (New York, 1938), p. 10.

Isabel Fiske Conant, "Directions for Saddling Pegasus for Emily Dickinson," *SRL,* VII (10 Ja 1931), 528.

Isabel Fiske Conant, "Emily Dickinson" [and] "Ordeal of Genius," *SRL,* VII (14 Mr 1931), 670.

Ruth M. Parks, "Emily Dickinson," *HCour,* 14 Je 1931.

Edward Peale, "Four Poems Not Yet Released (or Even Dreamed of) by Any Branch of the Family of Emily Dickinson," *B,* LXXIII (Au 1931), 584-85.

Louis Ginsberg, "Emily Dickinson," *NYHTr,* 30 Au 1931.

W. W. Christman, "The Hidden Heart," *Bozart and Contemporary Verse* (Oglethorpe University), V (Se-Oc 1931), 16.

Paul Revere [Russell St. Clair Smith], "To Emily Dickinson," *Tampa Morning Tribune,* 12 Ja 1932.

Catharine Bergqvist, "To Emily Dickinson," *Poetry World and Contemporary Vision,* III (Mr 1932), 6.

Myriam Page, "Emily Dickinson," *SRep,* 3 Ap 1932.

Leo Kennedy, "With a Volume of Emily Dickinson," *Canadian Forum,* XIII (De 1932), 96.

Charles H. Forster, "To Emily Dickinson," *The American Spectator,* I (De 1932), 11.

Dorothy Aldis, "For Emily Dickinson," *Any Spring* (New York, 1933), p. 6.

John Richard Moreland, "To Emily Dickinson," *The Moon Mender* (Dallas, 1933), p. 68.

Le Baron Cooke, "Emily Dickinson," *Rutland Herald* (Rutland, Vt.), 2 Mr 1933.

G. A. Taylor, "Emily Dickinson's Garden," *Daily Hampshire Gazette*, 1 Ap 1933. Repr. in *Cincinnati Fine Arts Journal*, v (Je 1933), 10; in *ARec*, 2 Ja 1935.

Robert Alan Green, "To Emily Dickinson (On Viewing Her Home)," *SUnion*, 6 Ap 1933.

Isabel Harriss Barr, "Wreath for Emily Dickinson," *NYHTr*, 20 Au 1933. Repr. in *Sword against the Breast* (London, 1935), p. 27.

E. L. Osgood, "The Range, along a Road Well Known to Emily Dickinson," *NYHTr*, 20 No 1933.

William Rose Benét, "Firefly Serenade," *NYHTr*, 20 No 1933.

Joseph Adelman, "Emily Dickinson," *Poetic Portraits* (Los Angeles, 1934), p. 65.

J. Horace Losh, "To Emily Dickinson," *Driftwind* (Montpelier, Vt.), VIII (Fe 1934), 252.

Paul C. Phillips, "Emily Dickinson," *SRep*, 25 Fe 1934.

Margaret Vauclain, "Emily Dickinson Dies," *The Griffin*, XIII (Ap 1934), 21.

Hortense Pandres Landauer, "For Emily Dickinson," *SRL*, x (5 May 1934), 674.

R.T., "The Grave of E.D., Amherst," *NYHTr*, 15 May 1934.

Ethel Austin, "Emily Dickinson," *HCour*, 28 Ap 1935.

Eunice Brady, "Emily Dickinson," *The Forum*, XCIV (Au 1935), 125.

Samuel French Morse, "Emily Dickinson," *NR*, LXXXVI (15 Ap 1936), 282.

Sydney King Russell, "Emily Dickinson," *Sun*, 9 Oc 1937.

Doris Asquith, "Emily Dickinson's Grave," *ARec*, 10 No 1937.

Isabel Fiske Conant, "Emily Dickinson in the Kitchen," *NYHTr*, 19 De 1937. Repr. in *Orange Feather: Lyrics, Sonnets, Quartrains* (Boston, 1939), p. 39.

Ralph Marcellino, "Letter to Emily Dickinson," *Sun*, 21 De 1937.

Genevieve Taggard, "Two Poems to Emily Dickinson (In Her Own Language)," *Collected Poems, 1918-1938* (New York, 1938), pp. 87-88.

Grover I. Jacoby, Jr., "To Emily Dickinson," *The Human Patina and Other Poems* (Hollywood, 1938), p. 60.

Isabel Fiske Conant, "Quartrains for Emily" [and] "New-Englanders," *Remembered Journey: Lyrics, Quartrains, Sonnets* (Dallas, 1938), pp. 48-49.

Sources

Annie L. Crowell, "Emily Dickinson's Garden," *The Triad Anthology of New England Verse*, ed. Louise Hall Littlefield (Portland, Me., 1938), p. 48.

Isabel Fiske Conant, "Two New Englanders," *Orange Feather* (Boston, 1939), p. 26.

Robert P. Tristam Coffin, "A Summer Christmas Tree," *NYHTr*, 29 Ja 1939.

Isabel Fiske Conant, "Two New England Girls," *Window-Shopping* (Dallas, 1940), p. 36.

John Malcolm Brinnin, "A Visiting Card for Emily," *New Michigan Verse*, ed. Carl Edwin Burklund (Ann Arbor, 1940), p. 98. Repr. in *Accent*, I (Winter 1941), 96-97.

Virginia Scott Miner, "Amherst Town," *SRL*, xxii (6 Jl 1940), 24.

Leo Coglan, "Emily Dickinson," *The Spectator* (Portland, Ore.), lxv (Au 1940), 28.

Elinor Lennen, "Emily Dickinson," *The Ave Maria*, liv (30 Au 1941), 266.

Paul Engle, "Emily Dickinson," *Poetry*, lviii (Se 1941), 298-99. Repr. in *Anthology of American Magazine Verse of 1938-1942 and Yearbook of American Poetry*, ed. Alan F. Pater (New York, 1942), p. 145.

Helen Barton Tuttle, "Emily Dickinson," *American Voice* (New York, 1942), pp. 34-35.

W. F. Jenkins, "To Emily Dickinson," *Nature Magazine*, xxxvi (Oc 1944), 394.

Dorothy Brown Thompson, "Emily Dickinson among Her Biographers," *SRL*, xxviii (31 Mr 1945), 16.

Mae Winkler Goodman, "Emily Dickinson," *The Evening Star* (Washington), 4 May 1945. Repr. in *The Poetry Society of America Anthology*, ed. Amy Bonner *et al.* (New York, 1946), pp. 72-73.

Winfield Townley Scott, "Emily Dickinson," *AM*, clxxv (Je 1945), 61.

Melville Cane, "Dickinsons and Todds," *SRL*, xxviii (9 Je 1945), 48.

Demetrios Capetanakas, "Emily Dickinson," *Portfolio*, I (Summer 1945), leaf 12.

Virginia Dickinson Reynolds, "Round Emily's Name," *SRL*, xxviii (28 Jl 1945), 21.

Louis Ginsberg, "Emily Dickinson," *NYHTr*, 6 Mr 1946. Repr. in *Guests in Eden: Emily Dickinson, Martha Dickinson Bianchi* (New York, 1946), p. 44.

Dorothy Ulrich Troubetzkoy, "From Emily Dickinson's Hill (Amherst, Mass.)," *NYHTr*, 22 Ap 1946. Repr. in *Guests in Eden* (New York, 1946), p. 38.

Frances E. Vernon, "Emily Dickinson," *Guests in Eden* (New York, 1946), p. 42.

Carl Sandburg, "Public Letter to Emily Dickinson," *AM*, CLXXIX (Mr. 1947), 44.

Mark Van Doren, "Emily Dickinson," *KR*, IX (Winter 1947), 71.

Peggy Thompson, "For E.B.B. and E.D.," *The American Scholar*, XVIII (Winter 1948), 67.

Bernice Slote, "To Emily," in Ruth Flanders McNaughton, *The Imagery of Emily Dickinson*, University of Nebraska Studies, N.S., no. 4 (Lincoln, Nebr., 1949), p. iii.

Agnes MacCarthy Hickey, "The Home of Emily Dickinson, Amherst," *Out of Every Day: Book III* (Cedar Rapids, Ia., 1953), pp. 28-29.

Werner Heider, "Emily Dickinson," *NYTBR*, LXI (30 De 1956), 2.

Flora Schneider, " 'I'm Nobody,' " *Collected Poems* (Canton, O., 1959), p. 22; cf. pp. 37, 38, 39.

VI. NOVELS AND DRAMAS

(Saxe Holm [Helen Hunt Jackson], "Esther Wynn's Love-Letters," *Scribner's Monthly*, III [De 1871], 164-76. Repr. in *Saxe Holm's Stories*, first series [New York, 1873], pp. 313-50.)

([Helen Hunt Jackson], *Mercy Philbrick's Choice* [Boston, 1876].)

MacGregor Jenkins, *Emily* (Indianapolis, 1930).

Susan Glaspell, *Alison's House: A Play in Three Acts* (New York, 1930).

Elva E. Knight, "Bulletins from Immortality: Based on the Life and Legends of Emily Dickinson," produced by the Elmira College Workshop, 1932.

Vincent York and Frederick Pohl, *Brittle Heaven: A Drama in Three Acts* (New York, 1935).

Laura Benét, *Come Slowly, Eden: A Novel about Emily Dickinson* (New York, 1942).

Jean Gould, *Miss Emily* (Boston, 1946).

Dorothy Gardner, *Eastward in Eden: The Love Story of Emily Dickinson* (New York, 1949).

Sources

VII. BIOGRAPHY, CRITICISM, INTERPRETATION

1. MONOGRAPHS

Josephine Pollitt, *Emily Dickinson: The Human Background of Her Poetry* (New York, 1930).

Genevieve Taggard, *The Life and Mind of Emily Dickinson* (New York, 1930).

MacGregor Jenkins, *Emily Dickinson: Friend and Neighbor* (Boston, 1930).

Desmond Powell, *Emily Dickinson*, Colorado College Publication, General Series, no. 200, Studies Series, no. 19 (May 1934).

George F. Whicher, *This Was a Poet: A Critical Biography of Emily Dickinson* (New York, 1938).

Sister Mary James Power, S.S.N.D., *In the Name of the Bee: The Significance of Emily Dickinson* (New York, 1943).

Millicent Todd Bingham, *Ancestors' Brocades: The Literary Debut of Emily Dickinson* (New York, 1945).

Henry W. Wells, *Introduction to Emily Dickinson* (Chicago, 1947).

Ruth Flanders McNaughton, *The Imagery of Emily Dickinson*, University of Nebraska Studies, N.S., no. 4 (Lincoln, Nebr., 1949).

Rebecca Patterson, *The Riddle of Emily Dickinson* (Boston, 1951).

Richard Chase, *Emily Dickinson* (New York, 1951).

Donald E. Thackrey, *Emily Dickinson's Approach to Poetry*, University of Nebraska Studies, N.S., no. 13 (Lincoln, Nebr., 1954).

Thomas H. Johnson, *Emily Dickinson: An Interpretive Biography* (Cambridge, Mass., 1955).

Jay Leyda, *The Years and Hours of Emily Dickinson*, 2 vols. (New Haven, 1960).

Charles R. Anderson, *Emily Dickinson's Poetry: Stairway of Surprise* (New York, 1960).

Archibald MacLeish, Louis Bogan, Richard Wilbur, *Emily Dickinson: Three Views* (Amherst, 1960).

Theodora Ward, *The Capsule of the Mind: Chapters in the Life of Emily Dickinson* (Cambridge, Mass., 1961).

2. BOOK CHAPTERS

James Fullarton Muirhead, "Some Literary Straws," *The Land of Contrasts: A Briton's View of His American Kin* (Boston, 1891), pp. 178-86.

William Valentine Kelley, "Emily Dickinson: The Hermit Thrush of Amherst," *Down the Road and Other Essays of Nature, Life, Literature, and Religion* (New York, 1911), pp. 214-83.

Herbert S. Gorman, "Emily Dickinson," *The Procession of Masks* (Boston, 1923), pp. 43-54.

R. Ellis Roberts, "Uncut Stones," *Reading for Pleasure and Other Essays* (London, 1928), pp. 185-90.

Amy Lowell, "Emily Dickinson," *Poetry and Poets* (Boston, 1930), pp. 88-108.

Constance Rourke, "Round Up," *American Humor: A Study of the National Character* (New York, 1931), pp. 266-70.

Rica Brenner, "Emily Dickinson," *Twelve American Poets before 1900* (New York, 1933), pp. 267-95.

Virginia Moore, "Emily Dickinson," *Distinguished Women Writers* (New York, 1934), pp. 147-60.

Gay Wilson Allen, "Emily Dickinson," *American Prosody* (New York, 1935), pp. 307-19. Repr. in *RED*, pp. 176-86.

Yvor Winters, "Emily Dickinson and the Limits of Judgment," *Maule's Curse: Seven Studies in the History of American Obscurantism* (Norfolk, Conn., 1938), pp. 149-68. Repr. in *Defense of Reason* (Denver, 1947), pp. 283-99; in *RED*, pp. 187-200; in *ED*, pp. 28-40.

Cleanth Brooks and Robert Penn Warren, "'After Great Pain a Formal Feeling Comes,'" *Understanding Poetry: An Anthology for College Students* (New York, 1938), pp. 468-71.

W. Somerset Maugham, *Books and You* (New York, 1940), pp. 102-4.

Willard Connely, "Emily Dickinson in Her Life, Letters and Poetry," *Essays by Divers Hands: Being the Transactions of the Royal Society of Literature of the United Kingdom*, ed. Harold Nicolson, N.S., XXIII (London, 1947), 1-19.

James G. Southworth, "Emily Dickinson," *Some Modern American Poets* (Oxford, 1950), pp. 14-27.

Mark Van Doren, "A Commentary on 'I Had Not Minded Walls,'" *Introduction to Poetry* (New York, 1951), pp. 12-16.

M.A. deWolfe Howe, "Emily Dickinson: Enigma," *Who Lived Here? A Baker's Dozen of Historic New England Houses and Their Occupants* (Boston, 1952), pp. 57-68.

Jay Leyda, "Miss Emily's Maggie," *New World Writing*, III (New York, 1953), 255-67.

George F. Whicher, "Emily Dickinson among the Puritans," *Poetry and Civilization: Essays by George Frisbie Whicher*, ed. Harriet

Fox Whicher (Ithaca, N.Y., 1955), pp. 41-62. Repr. in *RED*, pp. 235-50.

Joseph E. Duncan, "Emily Dickinson," *The Revival of Metaphysical Poetry: The History of a Style, 1800 to the Present* (Minneapolis, 1959), pp. 77-88.

W. J. Frohock, "Emily Dickinson: God's Little Girl," *Strangers to This Ground: Cultural Diversity in Contemporary American Writing* (Dallas, 1961), pp. 98-110.

Dennis S. R. Welland, "Emily Dickinson and Her 'Letter to the World,'" *The Great Experiment in American Literature: Six Lectures*, ed. Carl Bode (New York, 1961), pp. 53-78.

3. PERIODICALS AND NEWSPAPERS

Thomas Wentworth Higginson, "An Open Portfolio," *The Christian Union*, XLII (25 Se 1890), 392-93. Repr. in *RED*, pp. 3-10.

"Literary Notes," *NYTr*, 4 Ja 1891.

Henry Park Schauffler, "Suggestions from the Poems of Emily Dickinson," *The Amherst Literary Monthly*, VI (Je 1891), 87-90.

"The Significance of Emily Dickinson," *HCour*, 24 Se 1891.

Thomas Wentworth Higginson, "Emily Dickinson's Letters," *AM*, LXVIII (Oc 1891), 444-56. Repr. in *Carlyle's Laugh and Other Surprises* (Boston, 1909), pp. 249-83.

MacGregor Jenkins, "A Child's Recollections of Emily Dickinson," *The Christian Union*, XLIV (24 Oc 1891), 776-77.

"Emily Dickinson," *Light*, IV (12 De 1891), 349.

[Thomas Bailey Aldrich], *"In Re* Emily Dickinson," *AM*, LXIX (Ja 1892), 143-44. Repr. in *RED*, pp. 54-56; repr. with alterations in *The Writings of Thomas Bailey Aldrich*, IX, *Ponkapog Papers, A Sea Turn and Other Papers* (Boston, 1903), pp. 83-86.

Francis H. Stoddard, "Technique in Emily Dickinson's Poems," *C*, XX (9 Ja 1892), 24-25. Repr. in *RED*, pp. 51-53.

W.M., "Emily Dickinson's Poems," *Housekeeper's Weekly*, III (9 Ap 1892), 4.

"A Melancholy Fidelity," *Commercial Advertiser*, 23 Au 1893.

James Warwick Price, "The Poetry of Emily Dickinson," *The Yale Literary Magazine*, LIX (Oc 1893), 25-27.

Ellen E. Dickinson, "Emily Dickinson," *BTr*, 28 Se 1894.

G., "A Connecticut Valley Poet," *Homestead* (Springfield, Mass.), XVI (6 Oc 1894), 11.

"The Literary Wayside," *SRep*, 2 De 1894.

Mabel Loomis Todd, "Emily Dickinson's Letters," *The Bachelor of Arts*, I (May 1895), 39-66.

Mary J. Reid, "Julia C. Dorr and Some of Her Poet Contemporaries," *The Midland Monthly*, III (Je 1895), 505-6.

W.S.K., "A Fresh Reading of Emily Dickinson," *BTr*, 11 Jl 1895.

Ellen E. Dickinson, "Emily Dickinson: Her Personality and Surroundings in Her Home," *BTr*, 12 Oc 1895.

Chelifer [Rupert Hughes], "Sappho, and Other Princesses of Poetry," *Godey's Magazine*, CXXXII (Ja 1896), 94.

[Thomas Wentworth Higginson], "Recent Poetry," *N*, LXIII (8 Oc 1896), 275.

Chelifer [Rupert Hughes], "The Ideas of Emily Dickinson," *Godey's Magazine*, CXXXIII (No 1896), 541-43.

Bliss Carman, "A Note on Emily Dickinson," *BTr*, 21 No 1896. Repr. in *RED*, pp. 61-68.

Harry Lyman Koopman, "Emily Dickinson," *Brown Magazine*, VIII (De 1896), 82-92.

A.E., "Emily Dickinson," *Der Westen* (Chicago), 12 and 19 Je 1898.

[Mrs. Thomas L. Eliot], "Why Was She a Recluse?" *The Sunday Oregonian* (Portland, Ore.), 19 Mr 1899.

Ella Gilbert Ives, "Emily Dickinson: Her Poetry, Prose and Personality—Their Distinction and Growing Fame," *BTr*, 5 Oc 1907. Repr. in *RED*, pp. 71-78.

W. J. Dawson, D.D., "American Books That Have Moved Me: An Englishman's Praise of Emerson, Hawthorne, Poe and Emily Dickinson," *The Congregationalist and Christian World*, CXI (4 De 1909), 779-80.

Frederick J. Pohl, Jr., "The Poetry of Emily Dickinson," *The Amherst Monthly*, XXV (May 1910), 47-50.

James Warwick Price, "Three Forgotten Poetesses," *The Forum*, XLII (Mr 1912), 361-66.

Martha Hale Shackford, "The Poetry of Emily Dickinson," *AM*, CXI (Ja 1913), 93-97. Repr. in *RED*, pp. 79-88.

Marsden Hartley, "Emily Dickinson," *The Dial*, LXV (Au 1918), 95-97. Repr. with slight changes in *Adventures in the Arts: Informal Chapters on Painters, Vaudeville, and Poets* (New York, 1921), pp. 198-206.

Gamaliel Bradford, "Emily Dickinson," *AM*, CXXIV (Au 1919), 216-26. Repr. in *Portraits of American Women* (Boston, 1919), pp. 229-57; in *Portraits and Personalities*, ed. Mabel A. Bessey (Boston, 1933), pp. 189-212.

Robert Hillyer, "Emily Dickinson," *The Freeman*, vi (18 Oc 1922), 129-31. Repr. in *Essays of Our Time*, ed. Sharon Brown (Chicago, 1928), pp. 203-11; in *RED*, pp. 98-104.

Kenneth Slade Alling, "Declaration," *The Measure*, no. 22 (De 1922), 15-16.

Martin Armstrong, "The Poetry of Emily Dickinson," *The Spectator* (London), cxxx (6 Ja 1923), 22-23. Repr. in *RED*, pp. 105-9.

Conrad Aiken, "Emily Dickinson," *The Dial*, lxxvi (Ap 1924), 301-8. Repr. with slight changes in *Selected Poems of Emily Dickinson* (London, 1924), pp. 5-22; in *B* (London), lxvii (Oc 1924), 8-12; in *A Reviewer's ABC: Collected Criticism of Conrad Aiken from 1916 to the Present*, ed. Rufus A. Blanshard (New York, 1958), pp. 156-63; in *RED*, pp. 110-17; in *ED*, pp. 9-15.

E. Merrill Root, "Clothes vs. Girl," *The Measure*, no. 39 (May 1924), 15-18.

Lucy Humphrey Smith, "The Mystery of Emily Dickinson's Life," *The Literary Digest International Book Review*, ii (Jl 1924), 587-88.

Nixon Waterman, "Our 'Feminine Walt Whitman,'" *BGl*, 1 Jl 1924.

Lois Leighton Comings, "Emily Dickinson," *MHAQ*, viii (Oc 1924), 133-39.

Clara Bellinger Green, "A Reminiscence of Emily Dickinson," *B*, lx (No 1924), 291-93.

Kathérine Brégy, "Emily Dickinson: A New England Anchoress," *CW*, cxx (De 1924), 344-54.

"New England's Poets First," *BGl*, 12 Ap 1925.

Lawrence F. Abbott, "Emily Dickinson," *O*, cxl (10 Je 1925), 211-13.

Mildred Wasson, "Victory Comes Late to Emily Dickinson," *The Literary Digest International Book Review*, iii (No 1925), 780-81.

Susan Miles, "The Irregularities of Emily Dickinson," *LM*, xiii (De 1925), 145-58. Repr. with omissions in *RED*, pp. 123-29.

Charles K. Trueblood, "Emily Dickinson," *The Dial*, lxxx (Ap 1926), 301-11.

"Emily Dickinson," *HCour*, 24 Fe 1927.

Edna Bangs Hinshaw, "Some Early Recollections of Emily Dickinson," *BHer*, 18 De 1927.

Allen Tate, "Emily Dickinson," *O*, cxlix (Au 1928), 621-23. Repr. with changes in *The Symposium*, iii (Ap 1932), 206-26; in *Reactionary Essays on Poetry and Ideas* (New York, 1936), pp. 3-25; in *On the Limits of Poetry: Selected Essays, 1928-1948* (New York, 1948), pp. 197-213; in *RED*, pp. 153-67; in *ED*, pp. 16-27.

Rollo Walter Brown, "A Sublimated Puritan," *SRL*, v (6 Oc 1928), 186-87. Repr. in *Lonely Americans* (New York, 1929), pp. 233-57.

Ernestine C. Perry, "Anecdotes of Noted Amherst Women Related: Incidents of Life of Emily Dickinson and Others Furnish Colorful Club Meeting," *SUnion*, 23 Mr 1929.

Helen Cary Chadwick, "Emily Dickinson: A Study," *The Personalist*, x (Oc 1929), 256-69.

Anna Mary Wells, "Early Criticism of Emily Dickinson," *AL*, I (No 1929), 243-59.

Paula Kurth, "Emily Dickinson in Her Letters," *Thought*, IV (De 1929), 430-39.

Genevieve Taggard, "A Little 'Scholar' of 1848," *Journal of Adult Education*, II (Ja 1930), 75-76.

Gertrude Montague Graves, "A Cousin's Memories of Emily Dickinson," *BGl*, 12 Ja 1930.

Mabel Loomis Todd, "Emily Dickinson's Literary Début," *HM*, CLX (Mr 1930), 463-71.

Edmund Blunden, "Emily Dickinson," *N&A*, XLVI (22 Mr 1930), 863. Repr. in *RED*, pp. 134-37.

Catherine Tolles, "The Fire and Dew of Emily Dickinson," *The Mount Holyoke Monthly*, XXXVII (Ap 1930), 209-22.

Louis Untermeyer, "Emily Dickinson," *SRL*, VI (5 Jl 1930), 1169-71.

W. F. Hardy, "As I View the Thing," *Decatur Herald*, 13 Jl 1930.

"Emily Dickinson and Some Early Critics: Conservative Editors Shocked and a Little Frightened by the Poet's Sentiments," *SRep*, 3 Au 1930.

"Emily Dickinson Seems to Have Won Fame to Spite the Critics: Early Comments on Her Poetry Read Dismally when Contrasted with the Present Laudations," *SFChr*, 10 Au 1930.

Emily R. Sugden, "Emily Dickinson," *SRL*, VII (13 Se 1930), 128.

James H. Powers, "World Acclaims Emily Dickinson, but She's Still 'The Queer Poet' to Amherst," *BGl*, 23 No 1930.

Harry Hansen, "The First Reader," *World*, 10 De 1930.

Rosamond Mills, "Emily Dickinson," *Interludes* (Baltimore), VII (Winter 1930), 80-84.

Morton Dauwen Zabel, "Christina Rossetti and Emily Dickinson," *Poetry*, XXXVII (Ja 1931), 213-16.

George F. Whicher, "Emily Dickinson: Centennial Afterthoughts," *AGQ*, XX (Fe 1931), 94-99. Repr. in *American Writers on American Literature*, ed. John Macy (New York, 1931), pp. 374-88.

Louis Untermeyer, "Thoughts after a Centenary," *SRL*, VII (20 Je 1931), 905-6.

Theodore Maynard, "The Mystery of Emily Dickinson," *CW*, CXXXIV (Oc 1931), 70-81.

Helen Moran, "Queens, Now," *LM*, XXVI (Je 1932), 138-46.

Julia Keleher, "The Enigma of Emily Dickinson," *The New Mexico Quarterly*, II (No 1932), 326-32.

Margaret Bloom, "Emily Dickinson and Dr. Holland," *University of California Chronicle*, XXXV (Ja 1933), 96-103.

E., Merrill Root, "Emily Dickinson: Symbol and Dynamo," *The Christian Century*, L (14 Je 1933), 784-86.

Frederick J. Pohl, "The Emily Dickinson Controversy," *SR*, XLI (Autumn 1933), 467-82.

C. E. Maguire, "Two Poets: Compared and Contrasted," *Thought*, VIII (De 1933), 396-409.

Sidney R. McLean, "Emily Dickinson at Mount Holyoke," *NEQ*, VII (Mr 1934), 25-42.

George F. Whicher, "Emily Dickinson's Earliest Friend," *AL*, VI (Mr 1934), 3-17; (May 1934), 191-93.

George F. Whicher, "A Chronological Grouping of Some of Emily Dickinson's Poems," *The Colophon*, IV (Mr 1934), 16.

Mary Brent Whiteside, "Poe and Dickinson," *The Personalist*, XV (Autumn 1934), 315-26.

Walter Taylor Field, "Another Glimpse of Emily Dickinson," *AGQ*, XXIV (No 1934), 44-45.

Althea Bass, "A Classmate of Emily Dickinson," *The Colophon*, V (De 1934), 19.

Grace B. Sherrer, "A Study of Unusual Verb Constructions in the Poems of Emily Dickinson," *AL*, VII (Mr 1935), 37-46.

"Emily Dickinson Famous Poetess, Outstanding Amherst Personality," *Massachusetts Collegian*, XLVI (21 No 1935), 2.

William Van Wyck, "Emily Dickinson's Songs out of Sorrow," *The Personalist*, XVIII (Spring 1937), 183-89.

Fred Lewis Pattee, "Gentian, Not Rose: The Real Emily Dickinson," *SR*, XLV (Spring 1937), 180-97.

C.C.R., "Letters from Amherst," *CSM*, XXIX (30 Je 1937), 7.

R. P. Blackmur, "Emily Dickinson: Notes on Prejudice and Fact," *The Southern Review*, III (Autumn 1937), 325-47. Repr. in *The Expense of Greatness* (New York, 1940), pp. 106-38; in *Language as Gesture: Essays in Poetry* (New York, 1952), pp. 25-50; in *RED*, pp. 201-23.

T. Walter Herbert, "Near-Rimes and Paraphones," *SR*, XLV (Autumn 1937), 433-52.

Milton Hindus, "Emily's Prose: A Note," *KR*, II (Winter 1940), 88-91.

Ray B. West, "Emily's Forest," *Rocky Mountain Review*, V (Spring-Summer 1941), 1-3.

Gilbert B. Voigt, "The Inner Life of Emily Dickinson," *College English*, III (No 1941), 192-96.

George Curran, "Emily Dickinson and Religion," *The Smith College Monthly*, II (No 1941), 7-9.

Genevieve Taggard, "Notes on Emily Dickinson and Emerson," *The Smith College Monthly*, II (No 1941), 3-6.

Mary Elizabeth Barbot, "Emily Dickinson Parallels," *NEQ*, XIV (De 1941), 689-96.

Donald F. Connors, "The Significance of Emily Dickinson," *College English*, III (Ap 1942), 624-33.

Eunice Glenn, "Emily Dickinson's Poetry: A Revelation," *SR*, LI (Autumn 1943), 574-88.

Ankey Larrabee, "The Use of Death and Puritan Theology in Emily Dickinson's Poetry," *Accent*, III (Winter 1943), 115-17.

Aurelia G. Scott, "Emily Dickinson's 'Three Gems,'" *NEQ*, XVI (De 1943), 627-28.

George Arms, "Dickinson's 'These Are the Days when Birds Come Back,'" *E*, II (Fe 1944), 29.

J. P. Kirby, "Dickinson's 'A Bird Came Down the Walk,'" *E*, II (Je 1944), 61.

Ada M. Klett, "Doom and Fortitude: A Study of Poetic Metaphor in Annette von Droste Hülshoff (1797-1848) and Emily Dickinson (1830-1886)," *Monatshefte für deutschen Unterricht*, XXXVII (Ja 1945), 37-54.

Henry F. Pommer, "Dickinson's 'The Soul Selects Her Own Society,'" *E*, III (Fe 1945), 32.

Bernard DeVoto, "The Easy Chair," *HM*, CXC (Je 1945), 602-5.

Louise Bogan, "The Summers of Hesperides Are Long," *Tomorrow*, IV (Jl 1945), 61-62. Repr. in *Selected Criticism* (London, 1958), pp. 289-94.

John Erskine, "The Dickinson Saga," *YR*, XXXV (Autumn 1945), 74-83.

Frank Davidson, "A Note on Emily Dickinson's Use of Shakespeare," *NEQ*, XVIII (Se 1945), 407-8.

Ralph Marcellino, "Emily Dickinson," *College English,* VII (No 1945), 102-3.

George F. Whicher, "In Emily Dickinson's Garden," *AM,* CLXXVII (Fe 1946), 64-70.

George F. Whicher, "Emily's Suitors," *Forum,* CVI (Au 1946), 162-66.

Ralph Marcellino, "Simonides and Emily Dickinson," *The Classical Journal,* XLII (De 1946), 140.

Russell St. Clair Smith, "Dickinson's 'I Dreaded That First Robin So,'" *E,* V (Fe 1947), 31.

Richard B. Sewall, "Dickinson's 'To Undertake Is To Achieve,'" *E,* VI (Je 1948), 51.

Richard Forrester, "Emily of Amherst," *Yankee,* XII (Au 1948), 32-33, 41, 64-67.

Wilbur Scott, "Dickinson's 'I'll Tell You How the Sun Rose,'" *E,* VII (No 1948), 14.

Grover Smith, "Dickinson's 'A Route of Evanescence,'" *E,* VII (May 1949), 54.

Millicent Todd Bingham, "Emily Dickinson's Handwriting—A Master Key," *NEQ,* XXII (Je 1949), 229-34.

Ruth Flanders McNaughton, "Emily Dickinson on Death," *Prairie Schooner,* XXIII (Summer 1949), 203-14.

George F. Whicher, "Pursuit of the Overtakeless," *N,* CLXIX (2 Jl 1949), 14-15. Repr. in *Poetry and Civilization: Essays by George Frisbie Whicher,* ed. Harriet Fox Whicher (Ithaca, N.Y., 1955), pp. 63-67.

Edwin Moseley, "The Gambit of Emily Dickinson," *UKCR,* XVI (Au 1949), 11-19.

Herbert Ellsworth Childs, "Emily Dickinson, Spinster," *The Western Humanities Review,* III (Oc 1949), 303-9.

Frederick I. Carpenter, "Dickinson's 'Farther in Summer than the Birds,'" *E,* VIII (Mr 1950), 33.

Harry Modean Campbell, "Dickinson's 'The Last Night That She Lived,'" *E,* VIII (May 1950), 54.

Thomas H. Johnson, "Emily Dickinson: The Prisms of a Poet," *SRL,* XXXIII (3 Je 1950), 16-17. Repr. in *RED,* pp. 261-64.

George F. Whicher, "The Deliverance of Emily Dickinson, One of America's Greatest Poets," *NYHTB,* XXVI (13 Au 1950), 2, 12.

Kenneth MacLean, "The Mail from Tunis," *The University of Toronto Quarterly,* XX (Oc 1950), 27-32.

Sister Mary Humiliata, I.H.M., "Emily Dickinson—Mystic Poet?" *College English*, XII (De 1950), 144-49.

Herbert E. Childs, "Emily Dickinson and Sir Thomas Browne," *AL*, XXII (Ja 1951), 455-65.

Kate Flores, "Dickinson's 'I Started Early, Took My Dog,'" *E*, IX (May 1951), 47.

Wilson O. Clough, "Dickinson's 'When I Hoped I Feared,'" *E*, X (No 1951), 10.

Thomas H. Johnson, "Establishing a Text: The Emily Dickinson Papers," *Studies in Bibliography*, V (1952-53), 21-33.

Laurence Perrine, "Dickinson's 'I Started Early, Took My Dog,'" *E*, X (Fe 1952), 28.

Caroline Hogue, "Dickinson's 'When I Hoped I Feared,'" *E*, X (May 1952), 49.

Robert H. and Helen L. Elias, "Dickinson's 'Farther in Summer than the Birds,'" *E*, XI (Oc 1952), 5.

Thornton Wilder, "Emily Dickinson," *AM*, CXC (No 1952), 43-48.

Myron Ochshorn, "Dickinson's 'I Know Some Lonely Houses off the Road,'" *E*, XI (No 1952), 12.

Caroline Hogue, "Dickinson's 'There Came a Day at Summer's Full,'" *E*, XI (De 1952), 17.

Theodora Van Wagenen Ward, "Emily Dickinson and T.W. Higginson," *The Boston Public Library Quarterly*, V (Ja 1953), 3-18.

Thomas H. Johnson, "Dickinson's 'Immured in Heaven!,'" *E*, XI (Mr 1953), 36.

Myron Ochshorn, "In Search of Emily Dickinson," *The New Mexico Quarterly*, XXIII (Spring 1953), 94-106.

Laurence Perrine, "Dickinson's "There's a Certain Slant of Light,'" *E*, XI (May 1953), 50.

Thomas H. Johnson, "Emily Dickinson: Creating the Poems," *HLB*, VII (Autumn 1953), 257-70.

Rene Rapin, "Dickinson's 'Farther in Summer than the Birds,'" *E*, XII (Fe 1954), 18.

Marshall Van Deusen, "Dickinson's 'These Are the Days when Birds Come Back,'" *E*, XII (Ap 1954), 40.

William Howard, "Dickinson's 'There Came a Day at Summer's Full,'" *E*, XII (Ap 1954), 41.

James Davidson, "Emily Dickinson and Isaac Watts," *The Boston Public Library Quarterly*, VI (Jl 1954), 141-49.

Earl Roy Miner, "Dickinson's 'A Clock Stopped—Not the Mantle's,' " *E*, XIII (De 1954), 18.

Ralph Marcellino, "Horace and Emily Dickinson," *The Classical Journal*, L (De 1954), 126.

Jay Leyda, "Late Thaw of a Frozen Image," *NR*, CXXXII (21 Fe 1955), 22-24.

Marshall Van Deusen, "Dickinson's 'Farther in Summer than the Birds,' " *E*, XIII (Ap 1955), 33.

Gerhard Friedrich, "Dickinson's 'I Heard a Fly Buzz when I Died,' " *E*, XIII (Ap 1955), 35.

Ralph Marcellino, "Dickinson's 'The Snow That Never Drifts,' " *E*, XIII (Ap 1955), 36.

Thomas H. Johnson, "The Great Love in the Life of Emily Dickinson," *American Heritage*, VI (Ap 1955), 52-55.

"Emily Dickinson, the Domestication of Terror," *TLS*, LIV (9 Se 1955), 532.

Theodora Ward, "Ourself behind Ourself: An Interpretation of the Crisis in the Life of Emily Dickinson," *HLB*, x (Winter 1955), 5-39. Repr. with slight changes in *The Capsule of the Mind: Chapters in the Life of Emily Dickinson* (Cambridge, Mass., 1961), pp. 40-70.

John Ciardi, "Dickinson's 'I Heard a Fly Buzz when I Died,' " *E*, XIV (Ja 1956), 22.

Joseph H. Satterwhite, "Robert Penn Warren and Emily Dickinson," *Modern Language Notes*, LXXI (May 1956), 347-49.

Betty Miller, "Elizabeth and Emily Elizabeth," *The Twentieth Century*, CLIX (Je 1956), 574-83.

John A. Christie, "A New Chapter in American Literature," *Vassar Alumnae Magazine*, XLII (Oc 1956), 2-6, 10.

Margaret Willy, "The Poetry of Emily Dickinson," *Essays and Studies*, x (1957), 91-104.

Richard P. Adams, "Pure Poetry: Emily Dickinson," *Tulane Studies in English*, VII (1957), 133-52.

Dorothy Waugh, "Dickinson's 'Those Not Live Yet,' " *E*, xv (Ja 1957), 22.

Nathalia Wright, "Emily Dickinson's Boanerges and Thoreau's Atropos: Locomotives on the Same Line?" *Modern Language Notes*, LXXII (Fe 1957), 101-3.

William Howard, "Emily Dickinson's Poetic Vocabulary," *PMLA*, LXXII (Mr 1957), 225-48.

Theodore C. Hoepfner, "Because I Could Not Stop for Death,'" *AL*, xxix (Mr 1957), 96.

The Poetry Workshop, Columbus, Ga., "Dickinson's 'My Life Had Stood—a Loaded Gun'" *E*, xv (May 1957), 51.

Edd Winfield Parks, "The Public and the Private Poet," *The South Atlantic Quarterly*, lvi (Autumn 1957), 480-85.

Jack Garlington, "Emily Dickinson's Curious Biographers," *Colorado Quarterly*, vi (Autumn 1957), 170-77.

Robert W. Russell, "Dickinson's 'At Half Past Three, a Single Bird,'" *E*, xvi (Oc 1957), 3.

Carl Anthony Niemeyer, "The Gentleman with the Deep Voice," *Union College Review*, xlvii (Ja 1958), 6-8.

Ralph Marcellino, "Emily Dickinson's 'Ablative Estate,'" *The Classical Journal*, liii (Fe 1958), 231-32.

Francis Manley, "An Explication of Emily Dickinson's 'After Great Pain,'" *Modern Language Notes*, lxxiii (Ap 1958), 260-64.

Charles R. Anderson, "From a Window in Amherst: Emily Dickinson Looks at the American Scene," *NEQ*, xxxi (Je 1958), 147-71.

Rebecca Patterson, "Emily Dickinson's Hummingbird," *The Educational Leader*, xxii (1 Jl 1958), 12-19.

Mabel Howard, William Howard, and Emily Harvey, "Dickinson's 'My Wheel Is in the Dark,'" *E*, xvii (No 1958), 12.

William Howard and Mother Angela Carson, O.S.U., "Dickinson's 'Safe in Their Alabaster Chambers,'" *E*, xvii (Ja 1959), 62.

Charles R. Anderson, "The Trap of Time in Emily Dickinson's Poetry," *Journal of English Literary History*, xxvi (Se 1959), 402-24.

Owen P. Thomas, Jr., "Dickinson's 'So Glad We Are,'" *E*, xviii (No 1959), 10.

Charles R. Anderson, "The Conscious Self in Emily Dickinson's Poetry," *AL*, xxxi (No 1959), 290-308.

George Monteiro, "Emily Dickinson's Merchant God," *N&Q*, N.S., vi (De 1959), 455-56.

Theodora Ward, "The Final Secret: Emotional Currents in the Life of Emily Dickinson," *HLB*, xiv (Winter 1959), 82-106. Repr. in *The Capsule of the Mind* (Cambridge, Mass., 1961), pp. 78-112.

Charles R. Anderson, "Dickinson's 'Reverse Cannot Befall,'" *E*, xviii (Ap 1960), 46.

Glauco Cambon, "Violence and Abstraction in Emily Dickinson," *SR*, lxviii (Summer 1960), 450-64.

Mother Mary Anthony, "Emily Dickinson's Scriptural Echoes," *The Massachusetts Review*, II (Autumn 1960), 557-61.

Clark Griffith, "Emily Dickinson's Love Poetry," *UKCR*, XXVII (De 1960), 93-100. Expanded version in *Iowa English Yearbook*, no. 6 (Autumn 1961), 15-22.

George Monteiro, "Traditional Ideas in Dickinson's 'I Felt a Funeral in My Brain,' " *Modern Language Notes*, LXXV (De 1960), 656-63.

Judith Banzer, " 'Compound Manner': Emily Dickinson and the Metaphysical Poets," *AL*, XXXII (Ja 1961), 417-33.

John Nist, "Two American Poets and a Spider," *The Walt Whitman Birthplace Bulletin*, IV (Ja 1961), 8-11.

Martha Fodaski, "Dickinson's 'Twas Like a Malstrom,' " *E*, XIX (Ja 1961), 24.

Stephen Whicher, "Dickinson's 'Elysium Is as Far as To,' " *E*, XIX (Ap 1961), 45.

Kenneth B. Newell, "Dickinson's 'We Should Not Mind So Small a Flower,' " *E*, XIX (Je 1961), 65.

Winfield T. Scott, "The Errand from My Heart—," *Horizon*, III (Jl 1961), 100-105.

Kenneth B. Newell, "Dickinson's 'Aurora Is the Effort,' " *E*, XX (Se 1961), 5.

Caroline Hogue, "Dickinson's 'I Heard a Fly Buzz when I Died,' " *E*, XX (No 1961), 26.

John S. Wheatcroft, "Emily Dickinson's Poetry and Jonathan Edwards on the Will," *Bucknell Review*, X (De 1961), 102-27.

James E. Miller, Jr., "Emily Dickinson: The Thunder's Tongue," *The Minnesota Review*, II (Spring 1962), 289-304.

Mordecai Marcus, "Dickinson's 'Not with a Club the Heart Is Broken,' " *E*, XX (Mr 1962), 54.

Eric W. Carlson, "Dickinson's 'I Started Early—I Took My Dog,' " *E*, XX (Ap 1962), 72.

Elizabeth Jennings, "Emily Dickinson and the Poetry of the Inner Life," *A Review of English Literature*, III (Ap 1962), 78-87.

Thomas W. Ford, "Emily Dickinson and Death," *Midwest Quarterly*, IV (Summer 1962), 33-44.

George Monteiro, "Emily Dickinson and Brazil," *N&Q*, IX (Au 1962), 312-13.

David Hiatt, "Dickinson's 'Of Bronze and Blaze,' " *E*, XXI (Se 1962), 6.

William H. Matchett, "Dickinson's Revisions of 'Two Butterflies Went Out at Noon,' " *PMLA*, LXXVII (Se 1962), 436-41.

Laurence Perrine, "The Nature of Proof in the Interpretation of Poetry," *The English Journal*, LI (Se 1962), 393-98.

Ida Fasel, "Emily Dickinson's Walden," *Iowa English Yearbook*, no. 7 (Autumn 1962), 22-28.

Donald W. Bolin, "Emily Dickinson and the Particular Object," *Forum* (Houston), III (Autumn 1962), 28-31.

William Howard, "Dickinson's 'I Never Saw a Moor,'" *E*, XXI (Oc 1962), 13.

Mordecai Marcus, "Walt Whitman and Emily Dickinson," *The Personalist*, XLIII (Oc 1962), 497-514.

Laurence Perrine, "Dickinson's 'My Life Had Stood a Loaded Gun,'" *E*, XXI (No 1962), 21.

David H. Hirsch, "Emily Dickinson's 'Presentiment,'" *American N&Q*, I (No 1962), 36-37.

Anna Mary Wells, "Was Emily Dickinson Psychotic?" *The American Imago*, XIX (Winter 1962), 309-21.

4. DOCTORAL DISSERTATIONS

Louise Kline Kelly, "A Concordance of Emily Dickinson's Poems" (Pennsylvania State College, 1951).

Lee Biggerstaff Copple, "Three Related Themes of Hunger and Thirst, Homelessness, and Obscurity as Symbols of Privation, Renunciation and Compensation in the Poems of Emily Dickinson" (University of Michigan, 1954).

Martha Edelsberg Passe, "Criticism of Poetry in America during the Nineties" (Ohio State University, 1957).

Thomas Wellborn Ford, "The Theme of Death in the Poetry of Emily Dickinson" (University of Texas, 1959).

Suzanne Marie Wilson, "Structure and Imaginary Patterns in the Poetry of Emily Dickinson" (University of Southern California, 1959).

Rowena Revis Jones, "Emily Dickinson's 'Flood Subject': Immortality" (Northwestern University, 1960).

John Stuart Wheatcroft, "Emily Dickinson and the Orthodox Tradition" (Rutgers University, 1960).

David James Monroe Higgins, "Portrait of Emily Dickinson: The Poet and Her Prose" (Columbia University, 1960).

Thomas Roscoe Arp, "Dramatic Poses in the Poetry of Emily Dickinson" (Stanford University, 1962).

5. M. A. THESES

Paula Violet Cohn, "Emily Dickinson: A Study" (Columbia University, 1918).

Isaranda F. Sanborn, "Emily Dickinson: An Interpretation of Her Mind" (Columbia University, 1922).

Josephine Pollitt, "New Light on Emily Dickinson" (Columbia University, 1925).

Sara Saper, "Emily Dickinson: A Study of the Commonplace in Verse" (University of Missouri, 1925).

Anna Mary Wells, "Emily Dickinson" (Southern Methodist University, 1927).

Annie Laurie Robey, "Emily Dickinson: A Forerunner of Modern American Poetry" (University of Oklahoma, 1928).

Julia Chaine, "The Poetry of Emily Dickinson" (Columbia University, 1928).

Helen R. Adams, "The Prosody of Emily Dickinson" (University of Pennsylvania, 1932).

Mary G. Baker, "Emily Dickinson's Knowledge of the Classical and European Philosophers and Their Influence on Her Prose and Poetry" (Massachusetts State College, 1933).

Jessie Estelle Canan, "The Religion of Emily Dickinson" (University of Pittsburgh, 1933).

Harrison L. Reinke, "Emily Dickinson and T.W. Higginson" (Lincoln University, Pa., 1933).

Julia Frantz Shutts, "The Spirit of Childhood in the Poetry of Emily Dickinson" (University of Pittsburgh, 1933).

Clayton R. Bowen, "Do You Know Emily Dickinson?" (Meadville Theological School, 1934).

Sidney McLean, "Emily Dickinson's Year at Mount Holyoke" (Mount Holyoke College, 1934).

Elizabeth L. Reinke, "Puritan and Transcendentalist Influences on Emily Dickinson's Philosophy" (Columbia University, 1935).

Margery McKay, " 'Amazing Sense': The Application of a New Method to the Poems of Emily Dickinson" (Swarthmore College, 1936).

Iva Louise Handy, "Emily Dickinson: A Study of Her Kinship with Childhood, with Nature, and with God" (Cornell University, 1938).

Thomas Dillon Howells, "Images and Symbols in the Poetry of Emily Dickinson" (University of Chicago, 1938).

Mary Ann Evans, "A History of Emily Dickinson Criticism (1890-1937)" (Vanderbilt University, 1939).

VIII. LITERARY HISTORIES

(Including early histories in which Emily Dickinson is not mentioned; these are designated with an asterisk).

*Henry C. Vedder, *American Writers of To-Day* (New York, 1895).

*Brander Matthews, *An Introduction to the Study of American Literature* (New York, 1896).

*Fred Lewis Pattee, *A History of American Literature: With a View to the Fundamental Principles Underlying Its Development* (New York, 1896).

Katharine Lee Bates, *American Literature* (New York, 1897).

*F. V. N. Painter, *Introduction to American Literature: Including Illustrative Selections with Notes* (Boston, 1897).

*M. A. deWolfe Howe, *American Bookmen: Sketches, Chiefly Biographical, of Certain Writers of the Nineteenth Century* (New York, 1898).

*Mary Fisher, *A General Survey of American Literature* (Chicago, 1899).

*Barrett Wendell, *A Literary History of America* (New York, 1900).

Walter C. Bronson, *A Short History of American Literature* (Boston, 1900).

*George E. Woodberry, *Makers of Literature* (New York, 1900).

Alphonso G. Newcomer, *American Literature* (Chicago, 1901).

*Lorenzo Sears, *American Literature in the Colonial and National Periods* (Boston, 1902).

Julian W. Abernethy, *American Literature* (New York, 1902).

*William P. Trent, *A History of American Literature* (London, 1903).

*George Edward Woodberry, *America in Literature* (New York, 1903).

Thomas Wentworth Higginson and Henry Walcott Boynton, *A Reader's History of American Literature* (Boston, 1903).

*Jessie B. Rittenhouse, *The Younger American Poets* (Boston, 1904).

Sources

*Leon H. Vincent, *American Literary Masters* (Boston, 1906).

A Manual of American Literature, ed. Theodore Stanton (Leipzig, 1909).

Reuben Post Halleck, *History of American Literature* (New York, 1911).

*William P. Trent and John Erskine, *Great Writers of America* (London, n.d.).

*Alphonso C. Smith, *Die amerikanische Literatur* (Berlin, 1912).

William B. Cairns, *A History of American Literature* (New York, 1912).

*John Macy, *The Spirit of American Literature* (New York, 1913).

William J. Long, *American Literature: A Study of the Men and the Books That in the Earlier and Later Times Reflect the American Spirit* (Boston, 1913).

Fred Lewis Pattee, *A History of American Literature since 1870* (New York, 1915).

*Bliss Perry, *The American Spirit in Literature: A Chronicle of Great Interpreters* (New Haven, 1918).

The Cambridge History of American Literature, ed. William P. Trent *et al.*, vol. III (New York, 1921).

John Louis Haney, *The Story of Our Literature: An Interpretation of the American Spirit* (New York, 1923).

William T. Hastings, *Syllabus of American Literature* (Chicago, 1923).

Bruce Weirick, *From Whitman to Sandburg in American Poetry: A Critical Survey* (New York, 1924).

Clement Wood, *Poets of America* (New York, 1925).

Carl Van Doren and Mark Van Doren, *American and British Literature since 1890* (New York, 1925).

Gorham B. Munson, *Destinations: A Canvas of American Literature since 1900* (New York, 1928).

Alfred Kreymborg, *Our Singing Strength* (New York, 1929).

Ernest E. Leisy, *American Literature: An Interpretive Survey* (New York, 1929).

Matthew Josephson, *Portrait of the Artist as American* (New York, 1930).

Fred Lewis Pattee, *The New American Literature* (New York, 1930).

Russell Blankenship, *American Literature as an Expression of the National Mind* (New York, 1931).

Thomas H. Dickinson, *The Making of American Literature* (New York, 1932).

A. C. Ward, *American Literature, 1880-1930* (London 1932).

Ludwig Lewisohn, *Expression in America* (New York, 1932).

Carl Van Doren, *American Literature: An Introduction* (Los Angeles, 1933).

Granville Hicks, *The Great Tradition: An Interpretation of American Literature since the Civil War* (New York, 1933).

Percy H. Boynton, *Literature and American Life* (Boston, 1936).

Walter Fuller Taylor, *A History of American Letters* (Boston, 1936).

Van Wyck Brooks, *New England: Indian Summer, 1865-1915* (New York, 1940).

Henry W. Wells, *The American Way of Poetry* (New York, 1943).

Literary History of the United States, ed. Robert E. Spiller *et al.,* vol. II (New York, 1948).

The Literature of the American People, ed. Arthur Hobson Quinn (New York, 1951).

Robert E. Spiller, *The Cycle of American Literature: An Essay in Historical Criticism* (New York, 1955).

Roy Harvey Pearce, *The Continuity of American Poetry* (Princeton, 1961).

IX. REFERENCE WORKS

Lamb's Biographical Dictionary of the United States, ed. John Howard Brown (Boston, 1900), II, 457.

The Americana: A Universal Reference Library (New York, 1903), V, 45.

Appleton's New Practical Cyclopedia, ed. Marcus Benjamin (New York, 1910), II, 185.

Chamber's Encyclopaedia, new ed. (Philadelphia, 1923), p. 807.

Encyclopaedia Britannica, 14th ed. (New York, 1929), VII, 336.

Dictionary of American Biography, ed. Allen Johnson and Dumas Malone (New York, 1930), V, 297-98.

X. BIBLIOGRAPHIES AND CATALOGUES

Margaret Frances Parmelee, "Emily Dickinson: A Reading List of Books and Periodicals on Her Life and Poetry" (Ann Arbor, 1928).

Alfred Leete Hampson, *Emily Dickinson: A Bibliography* (Northampton, Mass., 1930).

Emily Dickinson: A Bibliography, with a foreword by George F. Whicher (Amherst, 1930).

Emily Dickinson: Catalogue of Centennial Celebration, ed. William H. McCarthy, Jr., Yale University Library (10 De 1930).

Russell St. Clair Smith, "A Dickinson Bibliography," M.A. Thesis (Brown University, 1948).

William H. White, "Homage to Emily Dickinson: Tributes by Creative Artists," *Bulletin of Bibliography and Dramatic Index*, xx (May-Au 1952), 112-15.

Jacob Blanck, *A Bibliography of American Literature* (London, 1957), II, 446-54.

XI. BOOK REVIEWS

1. EDITIONS OF POEMS

(a) *Poems* (Boston, 1890)

"The Literary Wayside," *SRep*, 16 No 1890.

A.T., "An Edition of the Poems of Emily Dickinson," *Boston Traveller*, 22 No 1890.

[Lilian Whiting], "Poems," *The Boston Budget*, 23 No 1890.

Louise Chandler Moulton, "A Very Remarkable Book," *BHer*, 23 No 1890.

Arlo Bates, "Miss Dickinson's Poems," *Boston Courier*, 23 No 1890. Repr. in *RED*, pp. 12-18.

Droch [= Robert Bridges], "The Poems of Emily Dickinson," *Life*, xvi (27 No 1890), 303-4.

"Recent Poetry," *N*, li (27 No 1890), 422-23.

Noah Brooks, "Books of the Christmas Season," *BB*, vii (De 1890), 521.

Nathan Haskell Dole, "Literary Topics in Boston," *BB*, VII (De 1890), 546.

"What the Critics Say about Emily Dickinson's Poems," *ARec*, 3 De 1890.

"Poems," *The Congregationalist*, LXXV (5 De 1890), 426.

"Emily Dickinson's Poems," *LW*, XXI (6 De 1890), 466.

"Recent Publications," *The Providence Journal*, 7 De 1890.

[Kinsley Twining], "Poems by Emily Dickinson," *I*, XLII (11 De 1890), 1759.

"Emily Dickinson's Poems," *The Beacon*, 13 De 1890.

"The Poems of Emily Dickinson," *C*, XVII (13 De 1890), 305-6.

Francis A. Nichols, "Some Powerful Poems by Emily Dickinson," *BGl*, 14 De 1890.

"Strolls by Starlight and Sunshine," *BGl*, 14 De 1890.

"The Poems of Emily Dickinson," *BTr*, 15 De 1890.

J.W.C. [John White Chadwick], "Poems by Emily Dickinson," *CR*, LXIX (18 De 1890), 828.

"Scraps of Verse from the Pen of Emily Dickinson," *BHer*, 29 De 1890.

"Comment on New Books," *AM*, LXVII (Ja 1891), 128-29.

William Dean Howells, "Editor's Study," *HM*, LXXXII (Ja 1891), 318-20. Repr. in *RED*, pp. 18-24.

"Talk about New Books," *CW*, LII (Ja 1891), 600-604.

[Andrew Lang], "The Newest Poet," *The London Daily News*, 2 Ja 1891. Repr. in *RED*, pp. 24-27.

"Poems by Emily Dickinson," *People and Patriot* (Concord, N.H.), 2 Ja 1891.

"Literary Notes," *NYTr*, 4 Ja 1891.

"Grim Slumber Songs," *Commercial Advertiser*, 6 Ja 1891.

Maurice Thompson, "Miss Dickinson's Poems," *America*, V (8 Ja 1891), 425. Repr. in *RED*, pp. 28-33.

John W. Chadwick, "Emily Dickinson," *Unity*, XXVI (22 Ja 1891), 171.

A.L. [Andrew Lang], "A Literary Causerie," *The Speaker* (London), III (31 Ja 1891), 135-36.

Arlo Bates, "Literary Topics in Boston," *BB*, VIII (Fe 1891), 10.

"Emily Dickinson's Poems," *Standard Union* (Brooklyn), 31 Ja 1891.

William Morton Payne, "Recent Books of Poetry," *The Dial*, XI (Fe 1891), 313.

"Emily Dickinson's Poems," *Chicago Figaro*, II (12 Fe 1891), 428.

"Form and Substance," *SM*, IX (Mr 1891), 395-96. Repr. in *RED*, pp. 34-36.

[Andrew Lang], "Some American Poets," *The Illustrated London News*, XCVIII (7 Mr 1891), 307. Repr. in *RED*, pp. 36-38.

"Gossip of Authors and Writers," *Current Literature*, VI (Ap 1891), 498-99.

"Miss Dickinson's Poems," *San José Mercury*, 19 Ap 1891.

[Samuel J. Barrows], "Emily Dickinson's Poems," *CR*, LXX (30 Ap 1891), 274.

"Some Books of Verse," *Overland Monthly*, XVII (May 1891), 549-50.

"Poems by Emily Dickinson," *Bookseller* (London), no. 402 (6 May 1891), 447.

Denis Wortman, "The Reading Room," *Christian Intelligencer*, LXII (27 May 1891), 12.

"Poems by Emily Dickinson," *Packer Alumna*, VII (Je 1891), 139.

"Miss Dickinson's Poems," *The Providence Journal*, 14 Je 1891.

"New Books and Reprints," *The Saturday Review* (London), LXXII (18 Jl 1891), 94.

(b) *Poems* (London, 1891)

"New Books of the Month," *The Review of Reviews* (London), IV (Se 1891), 308.

"A Poet and Some Others," *The Saturday Review* (London), LXXII (5 Se 1891), 279. Repr. in *RED*, pp. 38-41.

"Recent Poetry and Verse," *The Graphic*, 12 Se 1891.

"An American Sappho," *The London Daily News*, 3 Oc 1891.

"Recent Verse," *The Athenaeum*, no. 4036 (4 Mr 1905), 269-70.

(c) *Poems* (Boston, 1891)

"Recent Poetry," *N*, LIII (15 Oc 1891), 297.

Henry Park Schauffler, "Second Edition of Emily Dickinson's Poems," *The Amherst Literary Monthly*, VI (No 1891), 175-82.

"The Literary Wayside," *SRep*, 8 No 1891.

"More of Miss Dickinson's Poems," *The Beacon*, 14 No 1891.

"Emily Dickinson's Poems," *The Boston Budget*, 15 No 1891.

Louise Chandler Moulton, "Emily Dickinson's 'Second Series' of 'Poems,' " *BHer*, 22 No. 1891.

"Miss Dickinson's Poems," *Boston Courier*, 22 No 1891.

"A Second Series of Remarkable Poems," *Boston Traveller*, 28 No 1891.

"Talk about New Books," *CW*, LIV (De 1891), 448.

"Emily Dickinson's Poems, Second Series," *ARec*, 2 De 1891.

"Books and Bookmen," *Light*, IV (5 De 1891), 322.

"Poems Fresh from the Press," *Cleveland Plain Dealer*, 6 De 1891.

"Library and Foyer," *BTr*, 9 De 1891.

"Boston Literary Letter," *SRep*, 10 De 1891.

"Second Series of the Poems of Emily Dickinson," *The Chicago Tribune*, 12 De 1891. Repr. in *RED*, pp. 45-49.

"Poems by Emily Dickinson," *BTr*, 15 De 1891.

"Recent Poetry and Verse," *C*, XIX (19 De 1891), 346. Repr. in *RED*, pp. 50-51.

"Poems by Emily Dickinson," *LW*, XXII (19 De 1891), 486.

Arthur Chamberlain, "The Poems of Emily Dickinson," *Boston Commonwealth*, XXX (26 De 1891), 7.

"Poetry," *The Congregationalist*, LXXV (31 De 1891), 459.

"Poems by Emily Dickinson," *CR*, LXX (31 De 1891), 868-69.

"Volumes of Poems," *BB*, VIII (Ja 1892), 650-51.

"Talk about Books," *The Chautauquan*, XIV (Ja 1892), 509-10.

"Poems by Emily Dickinson," *Christian Intelligencer*, LXIII (13 Ja 1892), 12.

"Recent Verse," *The Overland Monthly*, XIX (Fe 1892), 218-19.

Hamilton Aidé, "Poems by Emily Dickinson," *The Nineteenth Century*, XXXI (Ap 1892), 703-6.

"Recent Books of Verse," *The Christian Union*, XLV (18 Je 1892), 1212.

(d) *Poems* (Boston, 1896)

"Salt Water Pipes," *BTr*, 8 Au 1896.

"Literary Notes," *NYTr*, 23 Au 1896.

"Poems: Emily Dickinson," *Boston Courier*, 6 Se 1896.

"Along the Literary Wayside," *SRep*, 13 Se 1896.

"Verse of Emily Dickinson," *NYTimes*, 19 Se 1896.

"Aftermath of Emily Dickinson's Verse," *The Telegraph* (Philadelphia), 19 Se 1896.

Grace S. Musser, "Emily Dickinson," *The San Francisco Call*, 20 Se 1896.

Mary Abbott, "Emily Dickinson's Poems," *The Chicago Times-Herald*, 26 Se 1896.

"The Third of the Gray Sisters," *Chicago Journal*, 26 Se 1896.

Lilian Whiting, "Life in Boston," *Inter Ocean*, 26 Se 1896.

Talcott Williams, "With the New Books," *Book News*, xv (Oc 1896), 42.

"Emily Dickinson's Poems," *Book News*, xv (Oc 1896), 56.

"Emily Dickinson Again," *The Chicago Tribune*, 3 Oc 1896.

Lilian Whiting, "Exquisite Verse," *Inter Ocean*, 3 Oc 1896.

"Emily Dickinson's Poems," *Commercial Advertiser*, 10 Oc 1896.

"Briefer Notices," *Public Opinion*, xxi (22 Oc 1896), 537.

"Poems by Emily Dickinson," *I*, xlviii (29 Oc 1896), 1463.

"The Third Series of Emily Dickinson's Poems," *LW*, xxviii (31 Oc 1896), 361.

"Poems by Emily Dickinson," *The Church*, ii (No 1896), 44.

"Tatlings," *The Daily Tatler*, I (11 No 1896), 5.

Van der Dater, "Some Recent Publications," *Bradley: His Book* (Springfield, Mass.), ii (De 1896), 66.

William Morton Payne, "Recent Poetry," *The Dial*, xxii (1 Fe 1897), 90.

Clarence Griffin Child, "Poems by Emily Dickinson," *The Citizen* (Philadelphia), iii (May 1897), 61-62.

"Recent Verse," *The Overland Monthly*, xxx (Au 1897), 190.

"Emily Dickinson," *Newport News*, 16 May 1899.

E.R.C., "Emily Dickinson: Notes on Her Personality and Her Latest Poems," *Sun*, n.d. (clipping in the Jones Library, Amherst).

(e) *The Single Hound* (Boston, 1914)

"Poems by Emily Dickinson: About to Be Published for the First Time," *SRep*, 22 Se 1914.

W.S.B. [William Stanley Braithwaite], "Poems of a Life-Time: A New Collection of Emily Dickinson's Verse," *BTr*, 30 Se 1914.

Elia W. Peattie, "Muses Not Drowned Out by War Sounds," *The Chicago Tribune*, 10 Oc 1914.

Ethel M. Colson, "The Single Hound," *The Chicago Herald*, 10 Oc 1914.

"Poems by Emily Dickinson," *SRep*, 18 Oc 1914.

"Three Poets and As Many Moods," *BHer*, 24 Oc 1914.

F. W. Burrows, "The Single Hound," *New England Magazine*, LII (De 1914), 165-66.

H.M. [Harriet Monroe], "The Single Hound," *Poetry*, V (De 1914), 138-40.

"The Single Hound," *Chicago Evening Post*, 4 De 1914.

J.J.D., "The Single Hound," *America*, XII (2 Ja 1915), 299-300.

Elizabeth Shepley Sergeant, "An Early Imagist," *NR*, IV (Au 1915), 52-54. Repr. in *RED*, pp. 88-93.

"Poets Who Must or Who May Write," *NYTBR*, XX (19 Se 1915), 333.

(f) *Complete Poems* (Boston, 1924)
(Titles designated with an asterisk also review *Life and Letters*.)

*Sidney Williams, "The Singular Life and Striking Poetry of Emily Dickinson," *The North American* (Philadelphia), 19 Jl 1924.

F.M., "Emily Dickinson's Poems," *CSM*, XVI (21 Jl 1924), 11.

Edmund Lester Pearson, "Two Poets," *O*, CXXXVII (23 Jl 1924), 479.

Frank E. Hill, "Emily Dickinson," *Sun*, 26 Jl 1924.

"Our Poetical New England Nun," *The Literary Digest*, LXXXII (2 Au 1924), 34.

Walter Yust, "A Poet Who Stands Alone," *New York Evening Post Literary Review*, IV (9 Au 1924), 949.

*John Gould Fletcher, "Woman and Poet," *SRL*, I (30 Au 1924), 77-78.

*Genevieve Taggard, "Emily Dickinson," *N*, CXIX (Oc 1924), 376-78.

"Mystical Poet Whose Ideas Were Heretical," *SRep*, 26 Oc 1924.

*Katharine Lee Bates, "A House of Rose," *YR*, XIV (Ja 1925), 396-99.

*G.F.W. [George F. Whicher], "The Book Table," *AGQ*, XIV (May 1925), 206-7.

Edward Sapir, "Emily Dickinson, a Primitive," *Poetry*, xxvi (May 1925), 97-105.

*H. L. Mencken, "Poetry," *The American Mercury*, vi (Oc 1925), 254.

Howard Mumford Jones, "Great American Poetess," *The New Student*, vii (4 Ja 1928), 12.

(g) *Selected Poems* (London, 1924)
(Titles designated with an asterisk also review the London edition of *Life and Letters*.)

*Percy Lubbock, "Determined Little Anchoress," *N&A*, xxxvi (18 Oc 1924), 114. Repr. in *RED*, pp. 118-20.

*Alan Porter, "Emily Dickinson," *The Spectator*, cxxxiii (18 Oc 1924), 549-50.

*"An American Poetess," *TLS*, xxiii (30 Oc 1924), 673-74.

J.M.T., "Selected Poems of Emily Dickinson," *The Vote* (London), 28 No 1924.

Harold Monro, "Selected Poems of Emily Dickinson," *The Criterion*, iii (Ja 1925), 322-24. Repr. in *RED*, pp. 121-22.

"Emily Dickinson: Volume of Selected Poems Published in England," *SRep*, 1 Fe 1925.

(h) *Further Poems* (Boston, 1929)

"Discovery of Poems of Emily Dickinson Valued as Milestone in Literary History," *CSM*, xxi (25 Ja 1929), 1.

Louis Untermeyer and Robert Hillyer, "Associated Press Account of Discovery of Further Poems of Emily Dickinson," *NYTimes*, 25 Ja 1929.

"Suppressed Verse of Amherst Poet Located by Niece," *SRep*, 25 Ja 1929.

"150 Poems by Emily Dickinson Discovered: Sister Had Suppressed Them 40 Years Ago," *NYTimes*, 25 Ja 1929.

"Amherst Poet Puts Best Work in Hidden Gems," *SUnion*, 26 Ja 1929.

William Whitman, "New Poems by Emily Dickinson," *BGl*, 3 Fe 1929.

Alfred Kreymborg, "Emily Dickinson," *Sun*, 16 Mr 1929.

Robert Hillyer, "Beauty out of the Past," *BHer*, 16 Mr 1929.

Louis Untermeyer, "Colossal Substance," *SRL*, v (16 Mr 1929), 769-70.

" 'Lost' Poems of Emily Dickinson Given to World," *BHer*, 17 Mr 1929.

"Emily Dickinson as Revealed in Poems Withheld by Sister," *SRep*, 17 Mr 1929.

Lewis Mumford, "Pan's Sister," *NYHTB*, v (17 Mr 1929), 1, 6.

Percy Hutchison, "Further Poems of That Shy Recluse, Emily Dickinson," *NYTBR*, xxxiv (17 Mr 1929), 3.

Mark Van Doren, "Nerves like Tombs," *N*, cxxviii (20 Mr 1929), 348-49.

Elspeth O'Halloran, "A Gallant Woman," *SUnion*, 22 Mr 1929.

[Elizabeth McCausland], "A Poet's Qualities: As Gleaned in New Emily Dickinson Volume," *SRep*, 24 Mr 1929.

J.S.C. [=Clara Bellinger Green], "Further Poems of Emily Dickinson," *O*, cli (27 Mr 1929), 504-5.

William Stanley Braithwaite, "Further Poems of Emily Dickinson," *BTr*, 30 Mr 1929.

"Newly Found Poems by Emily Dickinson Are Intimate Lyrics," *Richmond Times-Dispatch*, 31 Mr 1929.

Robert Hillyer, "Further Poems of Emily Dickinson," *AM*, cxliii (Ap 1929), 16, 18.

"Witness for the Crown," *CSM*, xxi (3 Ap 1929), 10.

"Impregnable of Eye," *Time*, xiii (8 Ap 1929), 46.

"Emily Dickinson's Poems," *SRep*, 12 Ap 1929.

Babette Deutsch, "A Sojourn in Infinity," *B*, lxix (May 1929), 303-6.

A.R.H., "Poet, Mystic, Martyr," *CR*, cviii (2 May 1929), 370-71.

Rolfe Humphries, "Too Difficult a Grace," *NR*, lix (22 May 1929), 38-40.

Conrad Aiken, "Emily Dickinson and Her Editors," *YR*, xviii (Summer 1929), 796-98.

J. Dana Tasker, "Intangible," *The Commonweal*, x (26 Je 1929), 234.

Theodore Spencer, "Book Reviews," *NEQ*, ii (Jl 1929), 498-501.

Anna Mary Wells, "Further Poems of Emily Dickinson," *MHAQ*, xiii (Jl 1929), 78-81.

Robert Hillyer, "The Later Emily Dickinson," *The Hound and Horn*, ii (Summer 1929), 423-25.

Clara Bellinger Green, "Emily Dickinson," *BTr*, 13 Jl 1929.

Alfred Leete Hampson, "Evidence of the Authenticity of Her 'Further Poems,' " *BTr*, 3 Au 1929.

Sources

B.M.K., "The Further Poems of Emily Dickinson," *CW*, cxxx (Oc 1929), 115-16.

Frederick Clarke Prescott, "Book Reviews," *AL*, I (No 1929), 306-7.

Jessica Nelson North, "Building a Legend," *Poetry*, xxxv (De 1929), 164-67.

G. R. Elliott, "Book Reviews," *AL*, I (Ja 1930), 439-42.

(i) *Further Poems* (London, 1929)

J. C. Squire, "Emily Dickinson," *The Observer*, cxxxviii (13 Oc 1929), . 6.

V. R. Friedlaender, "Emily Dickinson," *Country Life*, lxvi (26 Oc 1929), 565.

"Emily Dickinson," *TLS*, xxviii (31 Oc 1929), 869.

E. G. Twitchett, "Further Poems of Emily Dickinson," *LM*, xxi (No 1929), 76-77.

V. Sackville-West, "New Poetry," *N&A*, xlvi (2 No 1929), 178.

(j) *Poems* (Boston, 1930)

"Emily Dickinson's Poems," *SRep*, 18 May 1930.

"The Poems of Emily Dickinson," *SRL*, vii (6 De 1930), 443.

Greenville Vernon, "The Single Hound," *The Commonweal*, xiii (7 Ja 1931), 275.

Herbert Read, "The Poems of Emily Dickinson," *The Spectator*, cli (29 De 1933), 971, Repr. in *RED*, pp. 173-75.

(k) *Poems for Youth* (Boston, 1934)

Edna L. Skinner, "A Review," *ARec*, 21 No 1934.

"Emily Dickinson," *SRep*, 9 De 1934.

May Lamberton Becker, "Poems for Youth," *NYHTB*, xi (6 Ja 1935), 7.

(l) *Unpublished Poems* (Boston, 1935)

"More Emily Dickinson Poems," *SRep*, 1 Oc 1935.

"New Dickinson Poems Found," *PW*, cxxviii (5 Oc 1935), 1269.

"Review of New Emily Dickinson Volume," *ARec*, 27 No 1935.

Mark Van Doren, "The Untired Genius," *N*, cxli (15 De 1935), 746.

P. E. G. Quercus, "Trade Winds," *SRL*, xiii (28 De 1935), 24.

F. O. Matthiessen, " 'Midsummer in the Mind,' " *SRL*, xiii (18 Ja 1936) 12.

Sidney R. McLean, "Emily Dickinson," *MHAQ*, xix (Fe 1936), 221-23.

Genevieve Taggard, "Emily Dickinson," *NR*, lxxxvi (26 Fe 1936), 82.

Ernest E. Leisy, "Book Reviews," *AL*, viii (Mr 1936), 102-3.

W. E. Sedgwick, "Book Reviews," *NEQ*, ix (Mr 1936), 143-45.

William H. McCarthy, Jr., " 'We Temples Build,' " *YR*, xxiv (Spring 1936), 615-16.

May Lamberton Becker, "More from Emily Dickinson," *NYHTB*, xii (26 Ap 1936), 4.

Louise Bogan, "The Poet Dickinson," *Poetry*, xlviii (Je 1936), 162-66.

Kimball Flaccus, "Lyric Telegrams," *Voices*, no. 86 (Summer 1936), 49-50.

(m) *Poems* (Boston, 1937)

"Emily Dickinson Poems to Be in New Edition," *SRep*, 26 Ja 1937.

Lilian Whiting, "Life and Imagination of Emily Dickinson," *SRep*, 16 May 1937.

Kenneth B. Murdock, "Book Reviews," *NEQ*, x (Se 1937), 613.

(n) *Poems* (London, 1937)

G. W. Stonier, "Innocence without Experience," *The New Statesman and Nation*, iv (23 Oc 1937), 655-56.

Evelyn Underhill, "Emily Dickinson," *LM*, xxxvii (No 1937), 72-73.

Edward Sackville West, "Keepsake," *The New Statesman and Nation*, xxxiv (29 No 1947), 435-36.

"The Wounded Poet," *TLS*, xlvi (6 De 1947), 628.

Waldemar Hansen, "Land Ho! Infinity!" *Horizon*, xvii (Ja 1948), 71-76.

(o) *Bolts of Melody* (New York, London, 1945)

(Titles designated with an asterisk also review *Ancestors' Brocades*.)

"Our Emily," *BGl*, 5 Ap 1945.

Francis Hackett, "Books of the Times," *NYTimes*, 5 Ap 1945.

Lewis Gannett, "Books and Things," *NYHTr*, 5 Ap 1945.

Jerry Rand and C.H., "The Book of the Day," *Sun*, 5 Ap 1945.

*George F. Whicher, "Emily Dickinson Fifty-Nine Years After," *NYHTB*, xxi (8 Ap 1945), 1-2.

W. T. Scott, "More of Emily's Letters to the World," *The Providence Journal*, 8 Ap 1945.

*Adelbert M. Jakeman, "Emily Dickinson Books Give New Poems, Insights," *SRep*, 8 Ap 1945.

*Robert Hillyer, "Emily Dickinson's Unpublished Poems—and Their Genesis," *NYTBR*, XLIX (15 Ap 1945), 3, 20, 22, 24.

*"Memories of Emily," *Time*, XLV (16 Ap 1945), 100-104.

Louise Bogan, "Verse," *The New Yorker*, XXI (21 Ap 1945), 84-86.

*R. N. Linscott, "Literary Footnote and Literary Event," *SRL*, XXVIII (21 Ap 1945), 10.

G.F.W. [George F. Whicher], "Emily Dickinson's Poetry," *ARec*, 26 Ap 1945.

*Theodore Maynard, "More Books of the Week," *The Commonweal*, XLII (4 May 1945), 75-76.

*Genevieve Taggard, "Emily Dickinson and Her Editor," *Quarterly Review of Literature*, II (Summer 1945), 350-53.

*James Southall Wilson, "The Second Debut of Emily Dickinson," *The Virginia Quarterly Review*, XXI (Summer 1945), 447-52.

Henry W. Wells, "Bolts of Melody," *AM*, CLXXVI (Jl 1945), 129-30.

*Conrad Aiken, "The Dickinson Scandal," *NR*, CXIII (2 Jl 1945), 25-26.

*Babette Deutsch, "Miracle and Mystery," *Poetry*, LXVI (Au 1945), 274-80.

Arthur N. Stunz, " 'Bolts of Melody,' " *SRL*, XXVIII (18 Au 1945), 19.

Richard B. Sewall, "Book Reviews," *NEQ*, XVIII (Se 1945), 409-11.

*F. O. Matthiessen, "The Problem of the Private Poet," *KR*, VII (Autumn 1945), 584-97.

*Coleman Rosenberger, "The Rediscovery of Emily Dickinson," *Queen's Quarterly*, LII (Autumn 1945), 352-55.

*John Gould Fletcher, "The Ablative Estate," *SR*, LIII (Autumn 1945), 661-70.

*Sidney R. McLean, "Book Reviews," *AL*, XVII (Ja 1946), 363-65.

(p) *Poems* (Cambridge, Mass., 1955)

(Titles designated with an asterisk also review *Emily Dickinson: An Interpretive Biography*.)

Louis Untermeyer, "The Compleat Spinster Poet," *SRL*, XXXVIII (10 Se 1955), 37-39.

Robert Hillyer, "What Emily Really Wrote," *NYTBR*, LIX (11 Se 1955), 7.

Louise Bogan, "The Poet Comes to Life," *The New Yorker*, XXXI (8 Oc 1955), 190-91.

John Ciardi, "Out of the Top Drawer," *N*, CLXXXI (5 No 1955), 397-98.

*"Emily Dickinson: The Making of an American Poet," *TLS*, LV (13 Ja 1956), 13-15.

John Crowe Ransom, "Emily Dickinson: A Poet Restored," *Perspectives USA*, no. 15 (Spring 1956), 5-20. Repr. in *ED*, pp. 88-100.

R. P. Blackmur, "Emily Dickinson's Notation," *KR*, XVIII (Spring 1956), 224-37. Repr. in *ED*, pp. 78-87.

Newton Arvin, "Book Reviews," *AL*, XXVIII (May 1956), 232-36.

Jay Leyda, "Book Reviews," *NEQ*, XXIX (Je 1956), 239-45.

John L. Spicer, "The Poems of Emily Dickinson," *The Boston Public Library Quarterly*, VIII (Jl 1956), 135-43.

Arlin Turner, "Emily Dickinson Complete," *The South Atlantic Quarterly*, LV (Oc 1956), 501-4.

*James Southall Wilson, "Emily Dickinson and Her Poems," *The Virginia Quarterly Review*, XXXII (Winter 1956), 154-57.

*Austin Warren, "Emily Dickinson," *SR*, LXV (Autumn 1957), 565-86. Repr. in *RED*, pp. 268-86; in *ED*, pp. 101-16.

(q) *Selected Poems* (New York, 1959)

"Poetry Bookshelf," *TLS*, LVIII (20 Mr 1959), 162.

Dudley Fitts, "New Verse for Midsummer Night Dreamers," *SRL*, XLII (25 Jl 1959), 14.

N. Ray Adams, "Book Reviews," *NEQ*, XXXII (De 1959), 555-58.

(r) *Complete Poems* (Boston, 1960)

(Titles designated with an asterisk also review *The Years and Hours of Emily Dickinson*.)

*Robert Hillyer, "All of Her Poems and Most of Her Life," *NYHTB*, XXXVII (27 No 1960), 26.

*M. M. duPont, "The Endless Study," *NR*, CXLIII (28 No 1960), 30-32.

*Odell Shepard, "Bringing Emily Dickinson Downstairs," *N*, CXCI (17 De 1960), 479.

Sources

2. EDITIONS OF LETTERS

(a) *Letters* (Boston, 1894)

"Emily Dickinson's Letters," *BB*, xi (No 1894), 485-86.

[W. F. Wetcho], "Letters of Emily Dickinson," *Boston Daily Advertiser*, 23 No 1894.

"A Thought of God," *Boston Home Journal*, viii (24 No 1894), 5.

"Emily Dickinson's Letters," *NYTimes*, 25 No 1894.

"Letters of Emily Dickinson," *BHer*, 27 No 1894.

"Letters of Emily Dickinson," *The Evangelist*, lxv (29 No 1894), 16.

Lilian Whiting, "Life in Boston," *Inter Ocean*, 1 De 1894.

"Emily Dickinson's Letters," *The Chicago Tribune*, 1 De 1894.

"The Literary Wayside," *SRep*, 2 De 1894.

[Lilian Whiting], "Boston Days," *Times-Democrat* (New Orleans), 2 De 1894.

"New Books," *The Spy* (Worcester, Mass.), 2 De 1894.

"Emily Dickinson's Letters," *Denver Times*, 7 De 1894.

"Emily Dickinson's Letters," *Public Ledger* (Philadelphia), 7 De 1894.

[Mary Abbott], "Emily Dickinson's Poems," *The Chicago Times-Herald*, 8 De 1894.

"A New England Nun," *The Telegraph* (Philadelphia), 8 De 1894.

[Mary Augusta Jordan], "Emily Dickinson's Letters," *N*, lix (13 De 1894), 446-47. Repr. in *RED*, pp. 57-61.

"Letters of Emily Dickinson," *LW*, xxv (15 De 1894), 445-46.

"Letters of Emily Dickinson," *Evening Bulletin* (Philadelphia), 15 De 1894.

"Emily Dickinson's Letters," *The New York Evening Post*, 18 De 1894.

"Emily Dickinson's Letters," *ARec*, 19 De 1894.

Caroline Healy Dall, "Emily Dickinson's Letters," *BTr*, 22 De 1894.

Mary D. Cutting, "Letters of Emily Dickinson," *The Christian Inquirer*, vii (27 De 1894), 7.

"Emily Dickinson's Letters," *The Congregationalist*, lxxxi (27 De 1894), 973-74.

D.W. [Denis Wortman], "Emily Dickinson's Letters," *Public Opinion*, xvii (27 De 1894), 952.

"The Emily Dickinson Letters," *HCour*, 28 De 1894.

"A New England Recluse," *SFChr*, 30 De 1894.

"Letters of Emily Dickinson," *The Review of Reviews*, xi (Ja 1895), 110-11.

"Emily Dickinson's Letters," *The Beacon*, 19 Ja 1895.

"Emily Dickinson's Letters," *NYTr*, 20 Ja 1895.

"Emily Dickinson's Letters," *People and Patriot* (Concord, N.H.), 21 Ja 1895.

"Emily Dickinson's Letters," *Book News*, xiii (Fe 1895), 267-68. Repr. from *NYTimes*.

"Letters of Emily Dickinson," *C*, xxvi (16 Fe 1895), 119.

"Letters of Emily Dickinson," *I*, xlvii (21 Fe 1895), 245.

Louis J. Block, "A New England Nun," *The Dial*, xviii (1 Mr 1895), 146-47.

Richard Henry Stoddard, "World of Letters," *The Mail and Express* (New York), 2 Mr 1895.

"Books and Authors," *O*, li (23 Mr 1895), 481.

"Letters of Emily Dickinson," *CR*, lxxiv (12 Ap 1895), 234.

(b) *Life and Letters* (Boston, 1924)
(Cf. xi, 1, f).

"Life of Emily Dickinson," *SRep*, 27 Mr 1924.

Clifford Orr, "Life and Letters of Emily Dickinson," *BTr*, 29 Mr 1924.

"Lifts Veil of Myths from Emily Dickinson," *SRep*, 30 Mr 1924.

F. Vinci-Roman, "Emily Dickinson," *World*, 30 Mr 1924.

George W. Douglas, "Life of a Notable New England Poet," *Public Ledger* (Philadelphia), 8 Ap 1924.

Kenneth Rede, "Emily Dickinson, Poetic Rebel," *CSM*, xvi (9 Ap 1924), 10.

Herbert S. Gorman, "Life and Letters of a Gentle New England Poet," *NYTBR*, xxix (13 Ap 1924), 7.

Esther Murphy, "The Curious History of Emily Dickinson," *NYHTB*, 1 (20 Ap 1924), 25, 30.

Ethel Parton, "Emily Dickinson," *O*, cxxxvi (23 Ap 1924), 701-2.

"The New Books," *The American Review of Reviews*, lxix (May 1924), 558.

Rolfe Humphries, "A Retouched Portrait," *The Measure*, no. 39 (May 1924), 13-15.

Sources

"Book Reviews," *Amherst Writing*, XXXVIII (May 1924), 28-30.

Gamaliel Bradford, "The Atlantic Bookshelf," *AM*, CXXXIII (May 1924), 10.

"Good Books," *Time*, III (12 May 1924), 14.

Arthur W. Colton, "The Enchanting Emily," *New York Evening Post Literary Review*, IV (31 May 1924), 788.

"'Alabaster Filled with Flame,'" *Current Opinion*, LXXVI (Je 1924), 780.

F. V. Keys, "The Poet in Time and Space," *The North American Review*, CCXIX (Je 1924), 911-12.

H.B., "Books on Our Table," *The New York Evening Post*, 11 Je 1924.

"Emily Dickinson the White Moth of American Literature," *SFChr*, 15 Je 1924.

Percy H. Boynton, "A New England Nun," *NR*, XXXIX (25 Je 1924), 130-31.

Stephen Vincent Benét, "Emily Dickinson's Biography," *B*, LIX (Au 1924), 732-35.

Newton Arvin, "Books," *The Commonweal*, I (25 Mr 1925), 552-53.

J.F.F., "The Bookshelf," *The Woman's Journal*, XV (Au 1930), 24.

Morris U. Schappes, "Errors in Mrs. Bianchi's Edition of Emily Dickinson's 'Letters,'" *AL*, IV (Ja 1933), 369-84.

(c) *Life and Letters* (London, 1924)
(s.v. XI, 1, g).

(d) *Letters* (New York, London, 1931)

"Letters of Emily Dickinson Revised," *SRep*, 1 No 1931.

Lewis Gannett, "Books and Things," *NYHTr*, 4 No 1931.

Hervey Allen, "Emily Dickinson's Editors," *Sun*, 7 No 1931.

Louis Untermeyer, "At the Source," *SRL*, VIII (21 No 1931), 307-8.

"'The Letters of Emily Dickinson,'" *ARec*, 25 No 1931.

"New Edition of Emily Dickinson's Letters Sheds Further Light on Her Personality," *SRep*, 6 De 1931.

Genevieve Taggard, "Poet as Letter Writer," *NYHTB*, VIII (13 De 1931), 1-2.

S.C.C., "Emily's House," *CSM*, XXIV (16 Ja 1932), 5.

Granville Hicks, "'The Mystic and Bizarre Emily,'" *N*, CXXXIV (27 Ja 1932), 119.

M. A. Jordan, "A Valuable Record," *YR*, xxi (Spring 1932), 625-26.

Morris U. Schappes, "Book Reviews," *The Symposium*, iii (Ap 1932), 260-69.

Constance Rourke, "Emily Dickinson's Own Story," *NR*, lxx (20 Ap 1932), 279-80.

George F. Whicher, "Book Reviews," *AL*, iv (No 1932), 318-22.

Marianne Moore, "Emily Dickinson," *Poetry*, xli (Ja 1933), 219-26.

Yvonne French, "Chronicles: Poetry," *LM*, xxix (De 1933), 161-63.

(e) *Emily Dickinson Face to Face* (Boston, 1932)

Lewis Gannett, "Books and Things," *NYHTr*, 5 De 1932.

Genevieve Taggard, "Tantalizing New Facts about Emily Dickinson," *NYHTB*, ix (11 De 1932), 3.

P.H., "New Letters and Memories of Emily Dickinson," *NYTBR*, xxxvi (11 De 1932), 4, 21.

"A Review," *ARec*, 21 De 1932.

R.R.S., "Emily Dickinson No Thwarted Recluse," *SRep*, 25 De 1932.

"Biography," *NR*, lxxiii (4 Ja 1933), 223.

Louis Untermeyer, "A More Intimate Emily," *SRL*, ix (7 Ja 1933), 363.

Frances Bartlett, "Emily Dickinson Face to Face," *BTr*, 14 Ja 1933.

"Through a Niece's Eyes," *CSM*, xxv (14 Ja 1933), 6.

"Emily Dickinson in Everyday Life," *SRep*, 15 Ja 1933.

Ruth Huntington Sessions, "Letter to the Editors," *N*, cxxxvi (18 Ja 1933), 65-66.

"Shorter Notices," *N*, cxxxvi (18 Ja 1933), 71.

Morris U. Schappes, "Book Reviews," *AL*, v (Mr 1933), 82-85.

R.H., "Short Notices," *NEQ*, vi (Je 1933), 417.

(f) *Letters to . . . Holland* (Cambridge, Mass., 1951)

Richard Chase, "Letters to the World," *N*, clxxii (21 Ap 1951), 380.

George F. Whicher, "More Light on Emily Dickinson," *NYHTB*, xxvii (29 Ap 1951), 6.

Elizabeth Bishop, "Love from Emily," *NR*, cxxv (27 Au 1951), 20-21.

Henry W. Wells, "Contradictions of Life and Art," *SRL*, xxxiv (29 Se 1951), 17-18.

Josephine Young Case, "Book Reviews," *NEQ*, xxiv (De 1951), 546-48.

(g) *Emily Dickinson: A Revelation* (New York, 1954)

Jay Leyda, "Book Reviews," *AL*, xxvii (Ja 1955), 436-37.

Nicholas Joost, "Brief Notices," *Poetry*, lxxxvi (May 1955), 119-20

Walter McIntosh Merrill, "Book Reviews," *NEQ*, xxviii (Je 1955), 283-84.

(h) *Emily Dickinson's Home* (New York, 1955)

Henry W. Wells, "A Lyricist's Milieu," *SRL*, xxxviii (11 Je 1955), 17.

Grace B. Sherrer, "Book Reviews," *AL*, xxvii (Ja 1956), 598-600.

William Meredith, "Book Reviews," *NEQ*, xxix (Je 1956), 252-54.

(i) *Letters* (Cambridge, Mass., 1958)

Robert Hillyer, "On the Letter Writer Was the Indelible Mark of the Poet," *NYTBR*, lxii (16 Mr 1958), 3.

Richard B. Sewall, "A Poet All the Time," *SRL*, xli (22 Mr 1958), 21.

Dilys Laing, "The Non-Corporeal Friend," *N*, clxxxvi (26 Ap 1958), 368-69.

Perry Miller, "Emily Dickinson: The Shunning of Joy," *The Reporter*, xviii (29 May 1958), 34-36.

[James Reeves], "The Primitive Vision," *TLS*, lvii (30 May 1958), 296.

Horace Gregory, "The Real Emily Dickinson," *The Commonweal*, lxviii (1 Au 1958), 449-50.

Mario Maurin, "Book Reviews," *NEQ*, xxxii (Mr 1959), 99-102.

3. MONOGRAPHS ON EMILY DICKINSON

(a) *Emily Dickinson: The Human Background of Her Poetry*

(Titles designated with an asterisk also review *The Life and Mind of Emily Dickinson;* titles with two asterisks review this and, in addition, *Emily Dickinson: Friend and Neighbor.*)

"The Week's Reading," *O*, cliv (19 Fe 1930), 309-11.

Isabel Paterson, "Emily Dickinson's Mysterious Love Affair," *NYHTr*, 21 Fe 1930.

Percy Hutchison, "The Mystery of Emily Dickinson," *NYTBR*, xxxiv (23 Fe 1930), 5.

George F. Whicher, "Emily's Lover," *NYHTB*, vi (2 Mr 1930), 2.

Granville Hicks, "The Mind of Emily Dickinson," *N*, cxxx (19 Mr 1930), 329.

Frances Bartlett, "The Human Aspect of Emily Dickinson," *BTr*, 29 Mr 1930.

R. N. Linscott, "Emily Dickinson," *B*, LXXI (Ap-May 1930), 228.

E. Merrill Root, "Sunlight at Last," *The Christian Century*, XLVII (2 Ap 1930), 436-37.

"A Life of Emily Dickinson," *TLS*, XXIX (3 Ap 1930), 293.

"Emily Dickinson," *The Indianapolis News*, 5 Ap 1930.

Helen Welshimer, "Emily Dickinson's Real Lover Revealed," *BTr*, 4 May 1930.

Babette Deutsch, "A Beam of Sunlight," *NR*, LXII (7 May 1930), 332.

George H. Shuster, "Emily Dickinson," *The Commonweal*, XII (7 May 1930), 23-24.

**"Emily Dickinson's Life: Fact and Conjecture," *The Chicago Evening Post*, 27 Je 1930.

**Clyde Beck, "New Light on the Life of a Peculiar Genius," *The Detroit News*, 29 Je 1930.

*Walter Yust, "Of Making Many Books," *Public Ledger* (Philadelphia), 2 Je 1930.

J. Walter Fairbank, "Mysterious Emily Dickinson," *BHer*, 6 Jl 1930.

*Mark Van Doren, "The Mystery of Emily Dickinson," *Theatre Guild Magazine*, VII (Au 1930), 40-41.

**C. Hartley Grattan, "Emily Dickinson: Her Life, Mind, Poems and Lovers," *World*, 10 Au 1930.

*"Emily Dickinson," *John o' London's Weekly*, XXIII (30 Au 1930), 724.

*Richard Church, "The Life-Story of Emily Dickinson," *The Spectator*, CXLV (6 Se 1930), 316.

**C.E.S., "Emily Dickinson," *SM*, LXXXVIII (Oc 1930), 32, 34.

**Frederick I. Carpenter, "Book Reviews," *NEQ*, III (Oc 1930), 753-57.

Morris U. Schappes, "An Obvious Error," *SRL*, VII (18 Oc 1930), 256.

Mary A. Bennett, "A Note on Josephine Pollitt's 'Emily Dickinson: The Human Background of Her Poetry,'" *AL*, II (No 1930), 283-86.

**Anna Mary Wells, "Book Reviews," *AL*, II (Ja 1931), 455-58.

Sources

(b) *The Life and Mind of Emily Dickinson*
(Cf. XI, 3, a. Titles designated with an asterisk also review *Emily Dickinson: Friend and Neighbor.*)

"Man Emily Dickinson Loved," *SUnion*, 11 Je 1930.

Floyd Van Vuren, "In Printing House Square," *The Milwaukee Journal*, 14 Je 1930.

Isabel Paterson, "The New England Sappho," *NYHTr*, 20 Je 1930.

Harry Hansen, "The First Reader," *World*, 20 Je 1930.

*James Price, "Genevieve Taggard Reveals Mysterious Love Affair of Emily Dickinson," *The Philadelphia Record*, 21 Je 1930.

George F. Whicher, "Emily at Last," *NYHTB*, VI (22 Je 1930), 1-2.

Percy Hutchison, "That Unsolved Enigma in the Life of Emily Dickinson," *NYTBR*, XXXIV (22 Je 1930), 3.

Granville Hicks, "Mystery and Mystification," *N*, CXXX (25 Je 1930), 735-36.

Frances Lamont Robbins, "The Week's Reading," *O*, CLV (25 Je 1930), 307.

Theodore Spencer, "A Search for a Lover," *BHer*, 28 Je 1930.

"Amherst, Brave Amherst," *Time*, XV (30 Je 1930), 56.

Rockwell Lawrence, "Biography," *B*, LXXI (Jl 1930), 445-56.

Josephine Pollitt, "Emily and Major Hunt," *SRL*, VI (5 Jl 1930), 1180.

*Babette Deutsch, "Emily Dickinson Again," *NR*, LXIII (9 Jl 1930), 211-12.

C.V.D. [Carl Van Doren], "The Life and Mind of Emily Dickinson," *Wings*, IV (Au 1930), 16.

Gilbert Thomas, "Emily Dickinson," *B* (London), LXXVIII (Se 1930), 326-27.

Mabel Loomis Todd, "Miss Taggard's Emily," *SRL*, VII (6 Se 1930), 99.

Shane Leslie, "A New England Poetess," *The Saturday Review* (London), CL (20 Se 1930), 346-47.

Anna Mary Wells, "A Poet's Biography of a Poet," *MHAQ*, XIV (Oc 1930), 161-63.

Morris U. Schappes, "The Life and Mind of Emily Dickinson," *The Symposium*, I (Oc 1930), 545-50.

*James Southall Wilson, "Emily Dickinson and the 'Ghosts,'" *The Virginia Quarterly Review*, VI (Oc 1930), 624-30.

Louise Maunsell Field, "Biography Boom," *The North American Review*, CCXXX (30 Oc 1930), 438-39.

Horace Gregory, "The Real Emily Dickinson," *The New Freeman*, II (12 No 1930), 212-13.

(c) *Emily Dickinson: Friend and Neighbor*

(Cf. XI, 3, a and XI, 3, b).

Frances Lamont Robbins, "The Week's Reading," *O*, CLV (7 May 1930), 22.

"Friendship of a Lunar Moth," *CSM*, XXII (10 May 1930), 15.

"An Intimate View of the Mystic Emily Dickinson," *NYTBR*, XXXIV (18 May 1930), 2.

"Biography," *B*, LXXI (Je 1930), 336.

Genevieve Taggard, "Memories of Emily," *NYHTB*, VI (1 Je 1930), 2.

Clara Bellinger Green, "The Lover of Emily," *BHer*, 27 Se 1930.

Ben Lapidus, "A Made-to-Measure Emily," *The New Freeman*, II (29 Oc 1930), 164.

XII. MISCELLANEA

1. ADDITIONAL BRIEF COMMENTARIES

"Literary Chat," *NYTr*, 15 Mr 1891.

F. B. Sanborn, "The Breakfast Table," *Boston Daily Advertiser*, 27 Oc 1891.

Arlo Bates, "Literary Topics in Boston," *BB*, VIII (May 1891), 153.

[Thomas Wentworth Higginson], "Recent American Poetry," *N*, LX (23 May 1895), 402-3.

"Notes," *The Chap-Book*, III (15 Oc 1895), 446.

"Chronicle and Comment," *B*, III (Au 1896), 498.

A. Williams-Ellis, "Modern American Poets," *The Spectator*, CXXIX (18 No 1922), 732-33.

Martha Dickinson Bianchi, "Emily Dickinson," *SRL*, I (2 Au 1924), 20.

J. C. Squire, "Emily Dickinson," *LM*, XIX (Fe 1929), 337.

2. EARLY MENTION

(a) In books

Anna C. Brackett, *The Technique of Rest* (New York, 1893), p. 25.

Lilian Whiting, *The World Beautiful in Books* (Boston, 1901), pp. 85, 185, 189, 227.

Rufus Rockwell Wilson, *New England in Letters* (New York, 1904), pp. 304-5.

John Churton Collins, *Studies in Poetry and Criticism* (London, 1905), p. 75.

W. J. Dawson, *The Makers of English Literature*, new and rev. ed. (New York, 1906), pp. 403-4.

Elizabeth Atkins, *The Poet's Poet* (Boston, 1922), pp. 205, 284, 285.

(b) In letters and diaries

1892 Edwin Markham	Genevieve B. Earle, "'Some Watcher of the Skies,'" *The Book Collector's Packet*, III (Mr 1939), 11-12.
6 Ja 1892 Alice James	*Alice James, Her Brothers, Her Journal*, ed. Anna Robeson Burr (New York, 1934), pp. 248-49.
14 Mr 1893 Lucy Larcom	Daniel Dulany Addison, *Lucy Larcom: Life, Letters, and Diary* (Boston, 1894), p. 285.
27 De 1894 John B. Tabb	*John Bannister Tabb on Emily Dickinson* (New York, 1950). *Letters—Grave and Gay and Other Prose of John Banister* [sic] *Tabb*, ed. Francis E. Litz (Washington, 1950), pp. 61-63, 140.
23 Oc 1898 W. D. Howells	*Mark Twain-Howells Letters: The Correspondence of Samuel L. Clemens and William D. Howells*, ed. Henry Nash Smith and William M. Gibson (Cambridge, Mass., 1960), II, 681.
2 Fe 1902 Hamlin Garland	Hamlin Garland, *Companions on the Trail: A Literary Chronicle* (New York, 1931), p. 121.

3. GLOSSES ON THE SALE OF VOLUMES OF POEMS AND LETTERS IN THE 1890'S

Alexander Young, "Boston Letter," *C*, XVII (6 De 1890), 297.

Alexander Young, "Boston Letter," *C*, XVII (27 De 1890), 340.

Arlo Bates, "Literary Topics in Boston," *BB*, VIII (Fe 1891), 10.

"Literary Notes," *I*, XLIII (5 Fe 1891), 202.

"Notes," *N*, LIII (16 Jl 1891), 48.

"Literary Notes," *I*, XLIII (3 Se 1891), 1321.

Charles E. L. Wingate, "Boston Letters," *C*, XIX (5 De 1891), 320.

M. A. deWolfe Howe, Jr., "Literary Affairs in Boston," *BB*, XI (Oc 1894), 425.

"Notes," *N*, LIX (1 No 1894), 325-26.

4. NOTES ON MRS. TODD'S LECTURES

W. [Charles E. L. Wingate], "Boston Letter," *C*, XVIII (18 Ap 1891), 212.

Charles E. L. Wingate, "Boston Letter," *C*, XVIII (9 May 1891), 253.

Arthur Chamberlain, "Emily Dickinson—Poet and Woman," *Boston Commonwealth*, XXXI (20 Fe 1892), 6-7.

Nathan Haskell Dole, "Notes from Boston," *Book News*, X (Mr 1892), 307-8.

"Notes," *C*, XX (11 Je 1892), 334.

5. NOTES ON HIGGINSON'S *Atlantic* ESSAY

"Literary Notes," *I*, XLIII (10 Se 1891), 19.

Charles E. L. Wingate, "Boston Letter," *C*, XIX (19 Se 1891), 141.

"Literary Notes," *I*, XLIII (24 Se 1891), 21.

Lilian Whiting, "The Strangely Isolated Life of Emily Dickinson," *The Standard Union* (Brooklyn), 26 Se 1891.

"The Literary Wayside," *SRep*, 27 Se 1891.

Mary Abbott, "Emily Dickinson's Rare Genius," *The Chicago Evening Post*, 6 Oc 1891.

"Emily Dickinson," *The Review of Reviews*, IV (No 1891), 459.

Arlo Bates, "Literary Affairs in Boston," *BB*, VIII (No 1891), 417.

Louise B. Edwards, "Emily Dickinson," *Housekeeper's Weekly*, III (9 Ap 1892), 2-3.

6. COMMEMORATIONS

(a) Founder's Day Celebration, Mount Holyoke, 1929

"Emily Dickinson Poetry Conference," *MHAQ*, XIII (Oc 1929), 173.

" 'Play and Poetry Talk Shop' Opens at Mt. Holyoke Friday," *SRep*, 3 No 1929.
"Founder's Day Is Observed at Mount Holyoke," *SRep*, 9 No 1929.

"Mount Holyoke Honors Founder and Emily Dickinson," *NYHTr*, 10 No 1929.

"Emily Dickinson under Discussion at Mount Holyoke," *SRep*, 10 No 1929.

"Alumnae Conference Impressions," *MHAQ*, XIII (Ja 1930), 182-92.

(b) Emily Dickinson Centenary Celebration, 1930

Elizabeth McCausland, "They Will Gather in Homage to Emily Dickinson," *SRep*, 4 May 1930.

May Lamberton Becker, "The Reader's Guide," *SRL*, VI (10 May 1930), 1030.

"The Emily Dickinson Centenary," *SRep*, 10 May 1930.

"Emily Dickinson, Poet, Is Honored at Northampton," *SRep*, 11 May 1930.

"Homage to Memory of Emily Dickinson," *BGl*, 12 May 1930.

"Homage Paid to Memory of Emily Dickinson," *Daily Hampshire Gazette*, 12 May 1930.

"Pilgrimage," *Daily Hampshire Gazette*, 12 May 1930.

"Emily Dickinson: One Hundred Years Old," *MHAQ*, XVII (Ja 1931), 244-45.

7. RADIO PROGRAMS

Percival Hunt, H. W. Schornberger and Frederick P. Mayer, *A Series of Radio Talks on Some Writers of Older New England*, Radio Publication, no. 36 (Pittsburgh, 1928), pp. 48-56.

"National Network Will Come to 'Evergreens' Sunday for Broadcast," *ARec*, 15 May 1940.

8. MARTHA GRAHAM'S DANCE "LETTER TO THE WORLD"

"Martha Graham Dances the Life of a Poet," *Harper's Bazaar*, LXXIV (Ap 1941), 80-81.

"Letter to the World," *The Smith College Monthly*, II (No 1941), 13-16.

"Letter to the World," *Life*, XXII (17 Mr 1947), 103.

Margaret Lloyd, "Jubilee Fortnight of a Dance: Premières and Revivals Presented on Broadway," *CSM*, XLV (18 Ap 1953), 6.

INDEX

Tate, Allen, 132-33, 139, 173-74, 287
Taylor, Bayard, 4, 89, 116
Taylor, G. A., 280
Taylor, Walter Fuller, 300
Teasdale, Sarah, 119
Telegraph, The (Philadelphia), 65, 73, 200, 305, 313
Temple, James C., 274
Thackrey, Donald E., 283
Thaxter, Celia, 19, 89, 95
Thayer, William Roscoe, 32
Thomas, Gilbert, 319
Thomas, Owen P., Jr., 294
Thompson, Dorothy B., 281
Thompson, Maurice, 14, 24-27, 32, 34, 76, 204, 302
Thompson, Peggy, 282
Thoreau, Henry David, 32, 78, 87, 177, 187, 193, 205, 293
Time, 308, 311, 315, 319
Times-Democrat (New Orleans), 313
Times Literary Supplement, 130, 293, 307, 309-10, 312, 317-18
Todd, David P., 20, 94
Todd, Mabel Loomis, 4, 10-12, 14-18, 21-22, 30-31, 35, 43, 46-49, 54, 60-61, 63, 68, 70-72, 83-84, 119, 121, 123, 141, 153-54, 163-65, 168, 198, 202, 208, 220, 233, 267-70, 286, 288, 319
Tolles, Catherine, 148, 205, 288
Trent, William Peterfield, 88, 298-99
Troubetzkoy, Dorothy U., 282
Trueblood, Charles K., 133, 287
Turner, Arlin, 312
Turner, Catharine Scott, 4-5, 167
Tuttle, Helen B., 281
Twain, Mark, 87, 191-93
Twining, Kinsley, 30, 34, 302
Twitchett, E. G., 309
Tyler, Moses Coit, 53

Underhill, Evelyn, 310
Untermeyer, Jean Starr, 278
Untermeyer, Louis, 110-11, 114, 127, 136, 140, 144-45, 152-53, 155, 162, 203, 213, 217, 269, 274, 288-89, 307, 311, 315-16

Van Deusen, Marshall, 292-93
Van Doren, Carl, 134, 136-37, 184-86, 195, 203, 213, 269, 299-300, 319
Van Doren, Mark, 110, 134, 136-37, 146, 184, 203, 213, 221, 270, 282, 284, 299, 308-9, 318
Van Loon, Hendrik Willem, 226
Van Vuren, Floyd, 319
Van Wyck, William, 169, 289
Vauclain, Margaret, 280
Vaughan, Henry, 108, 147, 206
Vedder, Henry C., 298
Vernon, Frances E., 282
Vernon, Greenville, 309
Very, Jones, 67
Vincent, Leon H., 299
Vinci-Roman, F., 314
Voigt, Gilbert B., 290
Vote, The, 129, 307

Wadsworth, Charles, 143, 150, 166-68, 177, 224
Wagner, Richard, 47, 53, 96
Ward, A. C., 191, 300
Ward, Samuel G., 33, 132
Ward, Theodora Van Wagenen, 165, 167, 270, 283, 292-94
Ward, William Hayes, 26
Warner, Charles Dudley, 200, 273
Warren, Austin, 106, 312
Warren, Robert Penn, 176, 284, 293
Wasson, David A., 4
Wasson, Mildred, 287
Waterman, Nixon, 287
Wattles, Willard, 117, 278
Watts-Dunton, Theodore, 210
Waugh, Dorothy, 293
Weber, J. C., 273
Weirick, Bruce, 134-35, 138, 184, 204, 213, 299
Welland, Dennis S. R., 285
Wellek, René, viii
Wells, Anna Mary, 144, 147, 153, 168, 288, 296-97, 308, 318-19